RUARK

REMEMBERED –
By the Man Who Knew Him Best

RUARK

By
*Alan
Ritchie*

**Edited by
Jim Casada**

**Published by
SPORTING
CLASSICS**

REMEMBERED –
*By the Man Who Knew
Him Best*

RUARK REMEMBERED – By The Man Who Knew Him Best
is published by *Sporting Classics*.

Copyright © 2006 by George Saffo and Judith Bliss.

Editor: **JIM CASADA**
Publisher: **CHUCK WECHSLER**
Art Director: **RYAN STALVEY**

All rights reserved. No part of this book may be reproduced, stored or introduced into a retrieval system, or transmitted in any form by any means without written permission of the publisher, except by a reviewer who may quote brief passages in a review.

Printed in the United States.

First Edition
Library of Congress Catalog Card Number 2007931046
ISBN 0-9778551-3-9
978-0-9778551-3-1

ACKNOWLEDGMENTS

Any undertaking of this sort – with a fifty-year-old biography written in Spain, manuscript owners who are dedicated to perpetuating the legacy of Robert Ruark but tyros in the world of outdoor book publishing, a staff at *Sporting Classics* burdened with an incredible work load yet dedicated to producing enduring books on hunting and fishing, a major contributor in distant Africa, and an editor with a penchant for piling his work plate too high – is of necessity a team effort.

My first debt of gratitude goes to the folks who found and purchased the biography of Ruark and then did me the singular honor of asking me not only to edit it for publication but to assist them in deciding on the most appropriate publisher to bring this work to the legions of fans still drawn to the life of the "Old Man's Boy."

Judy Bliss, Steve Bliss and George Saffo have been inspirational in their enthusiasm, doggedly determined in their efforts to leave no stone unturned when it came to getting things done right, and ever willing to assist in any way possible. In addition, George, who had the distinct pleasure of spending a bit of time as Ruark's guest at Palamos when he was a young man, has written the Epilogue. I am deeply indebted to each of them.

I have never met Harry Selby, but as someone who has long been interested in the history of safari and sport in Africa, his name was almost as familiar to me as that of Robert Ruark. A living legend in his own right and perhaps our most tangible link to Ruark, Selby has been an important part of this book in many ways.

Through the miracles of e-mail (with occasionally burps along the way as something went awry in cyberspace), he has not only evinced a keen interest in the project and answered important questions connected with it, Harry has graciously provided a Foreword that adds immeasurably to the book. I am grateful, as should be everyone who wants to know more about the complex, fascinating man who was Robert Ruark.

The folks at *Sporting Classics* have shared my enthusiasm for this project from the outset. I've known and worked with Chuck Wechsler since he first came to the magazine, have watched him ease slowly but surely into the transition required to adapt and adopt the Southern way of life, and have always admired his superb work ethic. We worked together on a previous Ruark book, *The Lost Classics of Robert Ruark*, as well as others, and as both of us mellow with years and as our friendship deepens, joint enterprises give us mutual pleasure. This undertaking has been truly special in that regard.

Thanks must also be tendered to others at *Sporting Classics* who tolerated my endless phone calls, conveyed my messages, and in general put up with me. Kudos go to Ryan Stalvey, the magazine's creative director who is just what his title says – creative. He worked his usual magic with photos, layout, design and all the aesthetic considerations vital to this book.

Most of the photographs in the book come from the Ruark Collection at the University of North Carolina at Chapel Hill, Ruark's alma mater. All of Ruark's papers have been fully organized and are housed under Call Number 4001. Interested parties can get an overview of the holdings by visiting www.lib.unc.edu/mss/inv/htm/04001.html. As someone who labored in the vineyards of academe for better than a quarter of a century, I think I have a pretty shrewd appreciation of what it takes to make a genial and effective archival staff. The folks who handle the Southern Historical Collection where Ruark's papers are housed are polite, professional and admirably prompt. My thanks to Manuscripts Reference Librarian Matthew Turi and his staff, and most especially to Nathaniel King, the individual with whom I had most of my dealings.

Identifying the many photographs presented on these pages was possible thanks to several key individuals, notably Harry Selby and another former African professional hunter, Joe Coogan, now of Benelli USA. Joe also deserves credit for providing important research information regarding Ruark's numerous African safaris.

Some mention, however inadequate, needs to be made of those with whom I have discussed Ruark over the years. He has been a frequent topic of discussion in one of my time-wasting weaknesses – participation in the Outdoor Writers Forum. Likewise, his name comes up time and again when I talk about the craft of outdoor writing with fellow scribblers. Almost without exception, they name *The Old Man and the Boy* as their favorite book. Then too, I must not forget those folks who share my keen interest in Ruark the man and the untold hundreds of thousands of words he wrote. This book is for them – my fellow travelers in the literary footsteps of America's greatest sporting scribe.

Finally, as is ever the case, I would be woefully remiss if I did not thank my companion of 40 years, Ann. She endured my exasperation, rescued me when my technological ineptitude produced yet another in an endless string of computer glitches, and listened patiently as I bored her to abstraction with more Ruark talk than she could possibly have wanted to hear. She is my sounding board, proofreader, friend and love. Words fail when I endeavor to express my feelings to and for her, but I hope she understands they are there. – *Jim Casada*

CONTENTS

INTRODUCTION 1

HARRY SELBY LOOKS BACK 5

AUTHOR'S NOTE 17

Chapter 1 **THE BOY ALONE** 19

Chapter 2 **CHAPEL HILL DAYS** 25

Chapter 3 **THE BOY TAKES ON THE WORLD** 27

Chapter 4 **NEW HORIZONS** 31

Chapter 5 **BELT-LEVEL JOURNALIST** 35

Chapter 6 **FIRST FOOTSTEPS IN AFRICA** 45

Chapter 7 **RITCHIE JOINS RUARK** 53

Chapter 8 **PUTTING DOWN ROOTS IN SPAIN** 57

Chapter 9 **THE EARLY BOOKS** 73

Chapter 10 **A LOVE AFFAIR WITH AFRICA BEGINS** 81

CHAPTER 11	**EXPANDING LITERARY HORIZONS**	85
CHAPTER 12	**RUARK IN HIS PRIME**	99
CHAPTER 13	**NEW PROBLEMS & POOR NO MORE**	113
CHAPTER 14	**AFRICA AGAIN**	123
CHAPTER 15	**THE LAST BOOKS**	133
CHAPTER 16	**RUARK AS A COLUMNIST**	145
CHAPTER 17	**THE MAN WHO WAS ROBERT RUARK**	155
CHAPTER 18	**PROBLEMS WITH PARENTS**	169
CHAPTER 19	**MONEY MATTERS**	175
CHAPTER 20	**A LOVE AFFAIR WITH AFRICA CONTINUES**	179
CHAPTER 21	**RUARK ON SAFARI**	185
CHAPTER 22	**ATTACKED BY A LEOPARD**	195
CHAPTER 23	**NEW VISTAS IN AFRICA**	199
CHAPTER 24	**PERSONAL INSIGHTS**	205
CHAPTER 25	**DEMON RUM & HEALTH PROBLEMS**	215
CHAPTER 26	**PLAYBOY BOB**	225

CHAPTER 27	**'I KNOW HE'S A BASTARD'**	231
CHAPTER 28	**LIFE'S COMPASS LOST**	243
CHAPTER 29	**LAST TRIP TO PALAMOS**	247
CHAPTER 30	**THE HONEY BADGERS AT WORK**	251
CHAPTER 31	**THE END OF A GRAND RUN**	263
	EPILOGUE	267

INTRODUCTION
By Jim Casada

Unearthing this strikingly candid biography of Robert Ruark has to be reckoned as one of the greatest discoveries in the annals of American sporting literature.

Without doubt, Robert Ruark belongs in the top rank of our country's outdoor writers. His real life was every bit as colorful as those wonderful tales of his boyhood, blending fact with a seasoning of fiction, which he gave us in *The Old Man and the Boy* and *The Old Man's Boy Grows Older*. Absolutely no one was better qualified to share the details of that life than Alan Ritchie, who served as Ruark's private secretary for a span of 12 years – from when he was hired, somewhat impulsively, in 1953 until Ruark's death in 1965.

Clearly consumed by a deep sense of loss and driven by equally strong feelings of devotion, Ritchie filled the years immediately following his friend's passing with work on this biography. As readers will learn, Ritchie was much more than just a secretary who handled daily office details, who typed up correspondence and manuscripts, filed clippings and sorted the daily mail. He was a confidant, sometime chauffeur, constant sounding board, patient listener, safari companion and loyal jack-of-all-trades. Despite its overtones of hagiography, Ritchie's biography is surprisingly fair and balanced for an author so close to his subject. He presents Ruark, warts and wonder alike, as he really was.

Internal evidence and the author's notes indicate this manuscript was completed in 1969 with some minor revisions made afterwards. From that point it would languish in obscurity for almost four decades. Its discovery is an intriguing saga in itself.

George Saffo and Steve and Judy Bliss, who reside in the Wilmington/Southport area of North Carolina, had devoted considerable time and effort to establishing a Robert Ruark Museum. Their goal was to create a collection that would remember the man and memorialize his literary legacy.

While pursuing that initiative they established contact with Alice Prescott, who had been a close friend of both Ruark and Ritchie. She donated several items to the museum and it was through correspondence on these gifts that existence of this manuscript came to light.

Once they had read the material they realized its potential, and it was at this juncture that I entered the picture. Pleased with my earlier work on Ruark, which had resulted in publication of *The Lost Classics of Robert Ruark*, they asked me to edit this book.

They sought my advice on a potential publisher, and I unhesitatingly recommended *Sporting Classics*. One of the first features I wrote for the magazine was a profile of Ruark, and I have served as the Books columnist for the past 15 years.

INTRODUCTION

We still know relatively little about Alan Ritchie. Born in 1919, he was an Englishman whose first career was as a sergeant in the British Army. Ritchie and Ruark met in 1953 in Spain, where both men were seeking to escape the hurly burly of city life and become permanent residents. Ritchie had already been there a few years, having joined the staff of a cork manufacturing company in 1950. He was bored with the position and was searching for a new job when, by sheer serendipity, he was introduced to Ruark.

This occurred in August, 1953, and in typically impulsive Ruark fashion, he hired Ritchie on the spot as his personal secretary. Thus began, on a sunny Sunday afternoon, what Ritchie characterized as "twelve years of fascinating association with the most wonderful employer and friend." From a work standpoint, they proved to be a perfectly matched pair. Ritchie was quite capable of keeping pace during Ruark's frenetic spells of writing. He provided a sense of balance in the Ruark household and displayed talents that extended well beyond the traditional realms of being a secretary.

In some senses this is unusual, because the differences between Ruark and Ritchie were striking. Ritchie was a taciturn individual who willingly remained in the background, perhaps basking in a bit of his employer's glory but otherwise being as consistently unassuming in his demeanor as he was devoted to his duties. That was critical to the working relationship because Ruark's very nature demanded that he be constantly in the limelight and the center of attention.

Another striking difference lay in their attitude toward women. Ruark was a womanizer of the first order while Ritchie never married or apparently even showed serious interest in the fair sex. There was also a marked contrast in their views of hunting. Obviously Ruark loved it, but Ritchie had no interest whatsoever in pursuing wild game. He was an avid skier whereas Ruark, after one decidedly tentative venture, avoided the slopes like the plague.

The two did share a love of travel, and Ritchie accompanied Ruark to Africa and elsewhere on combination business/pleasure trips. Ritchie was an accomplished photographer and some of the images in this book reflect his skills in that regard.

Ritchie eventually built his own home quite close to the Ruark estate in Palamos, and he remained there following Ruark's death. Ritchie would live another 17 years, dying in 1982. Fittingly, given the closeness of the two men, he was buried next to Ruark. A simple cross, inscribed with his name and the dates of his birth and death, marks the site.

Much of Ritchie's time during the post-Ruark years was consumed with writing this biography, dealing with the endless problems associated with the Ruark estate, and doing his modest best to retain at least a remnant of the Ruark legacy in Palamos.

It seems fair, in the short term, to say his endeavors were an exercise in futility. Taking the longer view though, this biography serves as his ultimate tribute to Robert Ruark, the man he characterizes as "the most incredibly wonderful, generous, humorous, and likeable sonofabitch who ever lived."

Editing Ritchie's manuscript posed an appreciable challenge. The biography is incredibly long, running to almost 800 typed, double-spaced pages and more than 220,000 words. Then there was the necessity of changing British spelling conventions into the American form, and Ritchie had a distinct propensity

INTRODUCTION

for starting sentences with archaic words such as "whilst." The original work contains a great deal of the "scissors-and-paste" approach; that is to say, lengthy quotations from Ruark's writings and correspondence as well as published material from others are inserted throughout Ritchie's text. Where it seemed appropriate, especially in the case of material such as book reviews or excerpts from Ruark's best-known works, portions of this quoted material have been removed. Elsewhere, when these quotations were left intact and came from printed materials, the source is identified whenever possible. Likewise, I exercised an editor's discretion in deleting overly long treatments of comparatively trivial matters such as the family dogs and Ginny's decorative efforts in the house at Palamos.

Another problem with the original manuscript focused on its organization (or lack thereof). While it was for the most part written in fairly straightforward, chronological fashion, Ritchie did not include chapter breaks or divisions of any kind. I have taken editorial prerogative to do so. Finally, when it comes to stylistic problems, Ritchie evidently belonged to what might be described as the Teutonic school of sentence structure. Some interminable sentences, running to three or even four conjunctions, have been changed with an eye to coherence and clarity.

I have striven valiantly to resist adding appreciable amounts of material or do extensive rewriting. After all, the editor's job is just what the word implies – to edit. Where I did find it necessary to do some rewriting or to add material, I can only hope it meshes smoothly and unobtrusively with Ritchie's style. Here and there in the book the reader will find an Editor's Note inserted in the text. Beyond that, what you have is the whole cloth of Ritchie's biography.

Some of Ritchie's coverage in the concluding chapters grates on the reader's nerves like fingernails on a chalk board, but I left it intact for the simple reason that it is essential for a full appreciation of Ruark's sexual and marital peccadilloes. In this portion of the biography, much more than anywhere else, Ritchie's biases show through. He clearly had great affection for Ginny and found some of Ruark's post-divorce female acquaintances despicable. His attitude is understandable, given the chaotic situation that enveloped the house at Palamos after Ruark's death.

From my perspective, and it is one shaped by a lifetime of keen interest in Robert Ruark, there are a number of points about this biography that stand out with considerable prominence. It is the product of personal knowledge of the man, something neither of Ruark's previous biographers, Hugh Foster and Terry Wieland, enjoyed. Ritchie had access to research materials that have either disappeared or, if present in the Ruark collection at the University of North Carolina at Chapel Hill, have eluded others. He maintained detailed files of news clippings, tear sheets, book reviews and correspondence, and these sources are used to good effect in this look at Ruark's life.

Even more significant than the firsthand information Ritchie brings to his task is the manner in which he fleshes out his portrait of Ruark. The details of Ruark's public life are fairly well known, and in particular, Terry Wieland did a fine job of capturing his passionate love affair with Africa in *A View from a Tall Hill*. In these pages though, we gain meaningful insight into how Ruark worked as a writer, his

INTRODUCTION

personality with all its undoubted quirks, the role Ginny played in his life, and a general measure of the man. The fact that Ritchie knew Ruark when he was at the height of his powers and prominence adds to the biography's impact.

Ritchie was not, by any stretch, a masterful literary craftsman. Still, his prose is consistently readable, and his subject, a truly fascinating personage, amply compensates for any shortcomings in his writing ability.

There have been four previous book-length works, two biographies and two anthologies, which delved into Ruark's life and attempted to capture the essence of this captivating man. They are Wieland's work; *Someone of Value*, what I consider a decidedly indifferent biography by Hugh Foster; *Robert Ruark's Africa* by Michael McIntosh, which includes an incisive introductory assessment of Ruark; and my own *The Lost Classics of Robert Ruark* with its biographical introduction and bibliographical essay.

Quite simply, this work easily transcends all earlier efforts, and I feel confident that when you turn the last page you will agree that Ritchie triumphantly achieves his modest goal of writing "an honest biography of a much-loved personage."

At this point I must salute the meaningful contributions of two individuals who were privileged to know Ruark personally: Harry Selby and George Saffo.

One of Africa's most revered professional hunters, Harry Selby was the "matchmaker" who orchestrated Ruark's love affair with the continent. Together for hours, days and even weeks at a time, the two men shared the excitement of pursuing Africa's dangerous game and the quiet relaxation of the evening campfire. In Africa, Ruark was as close to being at peace with himself and the world as he ever came. In his foreword, Selby provides a fascinating account of their safari days.

Saffo's acquaintance with Ruark was of much shorter duration, but as a fellow Tar Heel and resident of the Carolina coast, he speaks for all Ruark fans. In his epilogue, Saffo relives an experience most of us can only dream about, and his impressions of those fleeting, halcyon days in Palamos are a delight.

Season the entire mix with a striking selection of photographs from the collection at the University of North Carolina and a variety of other sources, and the end product is as close as we are ever likely to come to a definitive biography of Robert Ruark.

HARRY SELBY LOOKS BACK

By Harry Selby

As I write this foreword to Alan Ritchie's book, which is based on the time he spent as Robert Ruark's secretary cum right-hand man, my mind is drawn back over the span of 55 years . . . back to a day when Bob, Virginia and I eased our way out of the Nairobi traffic, climbed laboriously up the Kikuyu escarpment, and then plunged down a couple of thousand feet to the floor of the Great Rift Valley. We were in a short wheelbase Land Rover, with Virginia straddling the gear lever between Bob and me, and with our two gunbearers in the back. A five-ton baggage truck heavily laden with all the camp gear, food, fuel and last but not least, a goodly supply of gin and beer, followed behind. Perched on top of the loaded truck, clinging precariously to ropes that secured the tarpaulin cover, were about a dozen camp staff who were trying to make themselves as comfortable as possible for the long, hard ride.

Leaving the main highway, which runs roughly north-south along the Rift Valley floor, and following a rough track between two extinct volcanoes, we cut across the great gash in the earth's surface. After many hours and many miles of slow traveling we started seeing goodly numbers of common game – zebra, wildebeest, kongoni, Grant's and Thomson's gazelle. We also passed large herds of Masai cattle guarded by slim morani (young warriors), each standing on one leg in typical Nilotic stance. They leaned on their long stabbing spears wearing nothing but their ochre-colored chukkas draped across one shoulder.

We talked continuously as we traveled . . . mostly Bob asking questions about the country and all we were seeing, while I tried to answer them as best I could. Bob was soaking up information like a sponge, and only later would I realize that he never took notes, other than the names of people or places, and that he never forgot anything he was told.

I knew he was a journalist. It had been impressed on me by Ker & Downey Safaris that a successful Ruark safari would bring good publicity to the country and all concerned. However, I don't think any of us in Kenya realized just how widely read he was through his syndicated column and contributions to magazines. Surely no one, perhaps not even Bob himself, could have predicted the book, *Horn of the Hunter*, which resulted from the safari.

I found Bob Ruark to be really outgoing, witty and humorous, ever ready to laugh, and to take the rough with the smooth. He looked upon himself as very much the "Bwana" and he was acutely aware of how he would be perceived as such, especially by the Africans, after all his reading about hunting safaris.

We discussed all aspects of the forthcoming safari and Bob's attitude toward it. He was most enthusiastic and hoped to collect some excellent trophies. Still, he insisted he was not hunting in Africa just to see his name in the record book, and he made it quite clear that if he wounded a dangerous animal, I was welcome to help finish it off, whether coming or going. Most of all, he hoped it would be an experience he could cherish for the rest of his life.

Virginia was very pleasant and possessed a tremendously wicked sense of humor. I have no doubt she would much rather have been in New York, but once on safari in Africa, dressed in hastily tailored slacks and bush jacket topped off with a safari hat on her blond head, she was doing a fine job of "making the best of it." Starting out with these attitudes, it looked as though we would have a good safari.

Toward dusk I shot a Thomson's gazelle, dinner for ourselves and the crew, and after a couple more hours traveling, swerved off the track and bivouacked the safari for the night. I could not have chosen a livelier spot had I tried. Everything – lions, hyenas, baboons, jackals and a leopard – serenaded the Ruarks with roars, grunts, barks, shrieks, and chuckles non-stop on that first night. Then, just as dawn was breaking a pair of Hadada ibis in a mocking "grand finale" swept low over our makeshift camp uttering their raucous haa-haa-haa-haaaa cries on their way to distant feeding grounds.

The next morning, over a hasty breakfast, I was interested to observe how the night's concert had gone down with my charges. Bob was a little awed, I think, finding himself in Africa after dreaming of it since boyhood. He now had the chance to fill the boots of Bwana wa Safari (leader of the safari) from the Africa of his literary hero, Ernest Hemingway. He wondered how well he might do but was ecstatic and rearing to go. Virginia was merely resigned to her fate. She now knew her husband was crazy for getting them into this situation and that she would have another month of riding with her knees straddling the Rover's gear lever, provided she wasn't eaten before then.

We crossed into Tanganyika and paid a visit to the Loliondo Government offices where we applied for Bob's hunting licenses. While they were being made out we visited the owner of the local duka and my friend, Mr. Dillon, to refuel. As usual he insisted on us partaking of several cups of very sweet and milky cinnamon tea, and he took great pride in showing off his mature buffalo bull, which grazed alongside his cattle.

It was incidents such as the tea drinking with the Indian shopkeeper that made me realize Bob was enjoying every aspect of what was happening. Many clients would have been impatient and would be thinking valuable time was being wasted, but not Bob. It was all part of the safari experience to him.

Formalities taken care of, we drove on to the famous Serengeti plain, which had been a game reserve since 1934. In those days it was still very wild, with no tourists and few roads. In fact, it was a game reserve in name only.

Leaving the east-west track we drove cross-country southwards to Banagi, the reserve exit point. En route we passed through huge herds of wild animals and also saw some lions that allowed our vehicle to approach quite close. This was quite an experience for Bob and Virginia, freshly out of New York, and both agreed they would never forget that day on the Serengeti, ever!!

Finally, after many hours of traveling, we arrived at our hunting camp site along the Grummetti River in the Ikoma area. It was well after dark when we pitched camp, but our crew, skilled campers as they were, made it "home away from home" within a couple of hours.

Bob claimed that we had been lost getting there, but in fact we knew very well where we were. It was just necessary to feel our way in the dark through 20 miles of bush where all tracks from the previous season had been obliterated by the recent long rains. I thought we did a pretty good job because we had saved an entire day by not camping out a second night. Regardless, Bob never let me forget about getting the safari lost in the "wilds of Africa."

From camp on the Grummetti we hunted with considerable success and collected many fine trophies. Game of many species was everywhere, and the nights were a bedlam of animal noises.

I found Bob to be an ethical hunter. He was a fair marksman and a true sportsman who only killed for a good trophy or food. He seemed to be rather unsure of himself when we were about to tackle the big ones, and after shooting one of them, he would be quite pale and so shaky that I would have to light his cigarette for him. I think much of the problem was due to his "Bwana" fixation. He believe that everything he did was being closely watched and that he had to be seen as performing like a "Bwana." He often asked me, after killing a significant trophy, if the gunbearers thought he had excelled. I have to admit that whenever we were after buffalo, possibly in very thick brush or wading through a swamp, while Bob may not have liked it, he was always right there in the thick of it.

At that time Bob was still a Scripps Howard syndicated columnist, and periodically he mentioned that he needed to get some columns written in order to mail them from Musoma, a port of Lake Victoria some 90 miles from our camp where I would send the truck to replenish fuel and provisions. He was enjoying the safari so much that he was loath to take time off to get his writing done. He repeatedly postponed it, but finally one morning I said we were about to run out of fuel and the truck would have to leave on the morrow. Bob decided that he would hunt that morning and then write in the afternoon while Virginia and I went photographing.

After we returned to camp following the morning hunt, we had lunch preceded by several martinis. When Virginia and I left that afternoon, Bob was at his typewriter in the dining tent, and I remember wondering what he would produce in the way of columns. Arriving back at dusk we were surprised to find him sitting at the campfire, drink in hand. I was even more surprised to discover that he had, during our absence of perhaps four hours, completed ten columns . . . and they were extremely good columns with only minor corrections required before they were sent off to Musoma the next day for mailing to New York.

When I expressed surprise and admiration at what he had done, Bob said that he had written the columns in his head while we were hunting. They merely needed to be put on paper. He was greatly relieved to get this chore behind him so he could continue enjoying the safari. We had quite a few more martinis that night.

The safari moved on to other areas, hunting with varying success but basically getting most of the game we were after. An unfortunate incident occurred while we were moving one of our camps, and to this day I do not know how it happened. A leather bag containing the cameras – three belonging to the Ruarks along with my Leica – disappeared. We never discovered whether it was stolen from the Land Rover at one of the small settlements we passed through or jolted out of the vehicle while traveling.

On most safaris this incident would be a disaster, but I was both surprised and relieved at Bob's reaction. He said he hated cameras anyway, and now we could concentrate on the hunting without bothering about picture-taking. The staff couldn't believe it. They had envisioned all sorts of recriminations and were quite amazed at Bob's philosophical reaction.

This was typical of Bob Ruark. His approach was "if there is nothing that can be done about a problem, accept the situation and make the best of it." This attitude was often demonstrated when we would get hopelessly bogged down in either sand or mud. Bob would find somewhere to sit and laughingly say: "OK, Haraka (Swahili word meaning 'hurry' or 'quick'), let's see you get out of this one." In a similar situation other clients would be looking at their watch and counting how much the delay was costing them.

On one occasion, while trying to reach some inaccessible country, we came to a river where at the only passable ford the water was too deep. I had the camp pitched a little way back from the riverbank, and with the aid of some friendly locals and a long, thick rope, we hauled the Land Rover, almost submerged, across to the opposite side. We allowed it to drain overnight, filled it up with fuel and oil in the morning, and used it each day to hunt on the other side of the river. We either waded or used a dugout canoe to ferry ourselves back and forth. To Bob, that episode meant more than collecting a trophy.

Looking back, I have to say that was one of the happiest safaris of my hunting career. The three of us became fast friends; gone was the client-hunter divide. There had been no trophy-itis, a virulent affliction that grips some hunters when a desired trophy is pursued long and hard yet proves to be elusive. No angry word had been spoken by any of us. We had worked hard and laughed a lot . . . we had rejoiced in our triumphs and accepted our failures.

It was a sad day for all of us when we rolled back into Nairobi. The safari was over, but my long association with Robert Ruark was just beginning.

Bob's next safari developed into a somewhat different exercise. First, the Mau Mau insurrection had recently erupted and the old happy-go-lucky Kenya attitude was being replaced by uncertainty and foreboding. Certainly that was the case in the areas where the Kikuyu tribe predominated. Some hunters, including myself and some game wardens, had been drafted into the Kenya Police Reserve to assist the regular force in tracking terrorist gangs in the forests. In fact, I had returned from such duty only days before Bob's arrival.

Talk of Mau Mau was the main topic of conversation as nothing like it had happened before, and many people carried sidearms. A further complication arose due to Bob arriving in company with a photographer. He had made a deal with a film company to shoot a commercial movie depicting all aspects of the safari, from hunting right through to the bread-making.

I pointed out to him that it was quite impossible to do both the hunting and photography using only one professional hunter and one vehicle and expect good results in both areas. Either he lowered his sights in regard to the trophies –

elephant, rhino and other desert game – and concentrated on photography, or we would have to bring another professional hunter and vehicle to take care of the photographer while we were doing the actual shooting.

This would leave Bob and I free to maneuver into position for the shot while relying on the other hunter to safeguard the cameraman who had to follow close behind, so he would be in the right place at the right time. They would also need to do a lot of filming by themselves, gathering scenes of game and the nomadic tribal people going about their daily lives.

Bob saw the logic of my argument and agreed that we should do as I suggested. Considering the very small monetary outlay involved, a surprisingly good film resulted. We covered the Northern Frontier Province and Masailand in Kenya, and then traveled to the Great Lakes region of Uganda.

Bob designated himself Bwana Director, and apart from not seeing eye to eye with the camera crew occasionally, all went off pretty well. Alcohol consumption was moderate throughout the safari, and once out in the bush Bob soon lost his rather bloated, pasty look. The film, entitled *Africa Adventure*, was ultimately shown around the world. In fact it still is aired on late-night programs.

I will not attempt to recount all our adventures while making the film and collecting Bob's trophies. However, one amusing, frustrating and finally most fortunate episode does merit sharing. On New Year's Day, our first morning in the field, we were driving along a rarely used track when we spotted three elephants some distance off in the bush. Only their backs were visible, but judging by their size they were obviously bulls. They were a strange reddish color and one appeared to carry sizable ivory. Bob was convinced he was seeing "pink elephants," attributing it to our celebrations the previous evening. Actually, the explanation was simple enough. The soil in that area was quite red, and as it had been raining, the elephants had taken on a reddish color after spraying themselves with muddy water.

One of our main objectives was to get some spectacular footage of shooting of a really fine tusker. We left the vehicles and carefully approached the larger animal through the thick bush to get a better view of his tusks. We got pretty close to him but still had not seen his tusk clearly when he suddenly became aware of us. He swung 'round without warning and came straight for us with his head held high, his massive tusks now clearly visible above the bush, and his great ears spread wide like the sails of an Arab dhow.

We had to shoot him whether we intended to or not. He was too close to allow any other option. Bob fired twice with the .470 as he came on, and then as the bull slewed around, I sent a .416 bullet into his shoulder as insurance. He staggered, ran a short distance and collapsed.

Fortunately for us, he was carrying very fine tusks, and we were elated not only with the trophy – the tusk were evenly matched and weighed well over 100 pounds each – but also for the great sequence it provided for the movie. Imagine our dismay when we learned that the shooting had not been filmed. When our camera crew saw the monster bearing down, they obviously decided to try "filming from a different angle."

We had anticipated spending weeks hunting for a really good elephant. It is generally reckoned in hunting circles that one hundred miles is walked, on average, for every good elephant trophy taken. And here we were with a hundred-pounder on the first day.

FOREWORD

Time-wise, taking the great bull completely altered our plans. Because we now had some time to spare, Bob asked if we could leave the safari for a few days and visit the district where we had been conducting anti-terrorist operations. The idea was for him to gather material for his column and magazine pieces. I agreed, believing that through Bob's extensive readership, the outside world would get to know something of what was happening in Kenya.

Later, after we had filmed many of the required sequences and collected most of Bob's trophies, we left the safari and traveled to the camp in the forest from which I had recently been operating. Bob was able to see for himself what was going on and even met some of the captured terrorists. Since I had become friendly with a lot of the local farmers, I was able to arrange interviews with prominent people in the community. Some of these interviews took place in the victim's homes where they had been attacked.

These interviews along with others he had in Nairobi and what he picked up here and there from hunters, policemen, game wardens and local people, formed the basis for *Something of Value*. Most of the Kikuyu folklore he used was gleaned from Louis Leakey's writings, and there was also a liberal infusion of Elspeth Huxley's *Red Strangers* thrown in. Much later, when the book appeared, I was disappointed to read the way he had portrayed some of the very accommodating people with whom I had arranged interviews. That was especially true of the two courageous ladies who had turned the tables on a gang that had attacked them in their home, bent on murder.

During the ensuing years my own situation changed. I got married, but in order to make a living I continued to hunt professionally. In due course my wife, Miki, became pregnant. Bob happened to be in Nairobi when she went into the hospital to give birth. He was due to fly home within a day or two, but as he had all along insisted, if the baby was a boy he would be the godfather, he wanted to be on hand for the birth. When he would order a drink he would say: "We need it, we're having a baby."

The baby was slow in coming, however, and though Bob delayed his departure several days, finally he could wait no longer. His parting farewell was: "Well, I'm leaving, but it's going to be a big, fat, ugly girl anyway."

Mark Arthur Robert Selby came into the world a couple of hours after Bob's departure. Sometime later when passing through London, Bob came across two rifles originally owned by Karamojo Bell. The great elephant hunter had recently died and his rifles were for sale. Bob bought them both and had a plate affixed to the stock of each, inscribed "To Mark Robert Selby from Uncle Bob Ruark."

From then on Bob made numerous visits to Kenya for safaris or in connection with the film rights to *Something of Value*. Scripps Howard also assigned him to cover the political "winds of change" that were sweeping Africa, and together we visit Uganda, Tanganyika, Ethiopia, Somalia, Rhodesia and South Africa. In those countries we collected information for his column, with Bob being particularly interested in those countries approaching independence from various colonial powers.

An amusing incident took place in Ethiopia. We were granted an interview with Emperor Haille Salassie, and upon our arrival at the palace we were met by the "Minister for the Palace." He put us in the picture regarding formalities and etiquette. We would be allowed 20 minutes, and the minister would act as interpreter. We were duly ushered into His presence and the usual pleasantries were exchanged, with nothing of much importance being said.

When the interview came to an end, we rose, shook hands and proceeded in reverse, as one must never turn his back on the Emperor, in direction of the door. We eventually reached it in some confusion, and in the passageway were confronted by an enormous, fully maned lion dragging a chain. It had obviously been put there to test the "great hunters" reaction.

Bob's reacted by saying: "Damn it Haraka!! Where's the .470?" So ended our interview with "The Conquering Lion of Judah."

After the success of *Something of Value* and sale of film rights, Bob flaunted his fame and wealth shamelessly while spending lavishly on entertainment. I remember meeting him at the Nairobi airport, and while we were still separated by the customs barrier, he called out: "Haraka, man are we rich!!" It has only been since several biographies have appeared, most notably this one with Ritchie's incomparable insight, that we have learned that in reality, Bob was always pressed financially.

Throughout this period Bob was drinking as usual but able to cope. It was when he started on the "Winds of Change" assignment that he began drinking more heavily. Few people realized just how momentous this rush for independence by people totally unprepared for it would become. I think the assignment was just too big for one man. Also, it became clear to Bob that his beloved East Africa, the East Africa he felt was his, with all it held for him, was about to slip away and change beyond recognition. This combination of factors precipitated a total collapse.

Fortunately, my friend Dr. Roy Thomson and a few of Bob's dedicated friends supported him through the crisis and eventually got him on a plane bound for Europe. He was subdued but on the wagon, a state that lasted all of nine months.

When Bob returned to Nairobi to research and collect material for a book he had in mind (it would be entitled *Uhuru*), he was drinking again. He had obviously decided he could not live without alcohol and was contemptuous of anyone, especially the doctors (he referred to them as quacks), who warned him of the consequences of continued drinking.

Although I had noticed a gradual change in Bob's general attitude over the years, it was now much more marked. He assumed an arrogant "I know it all" attitude to all things concerning African hunting and politics. We remained close friends nonetheless and made a couple of short safaris, one with Walker Stone and one with Alan Ritchie, Bob's very diplomatic and capable right-hand man.

I might add here that there never was a "falling" out between Bob and myself as was speculated in one Ruark biography. I declined to talk about him with several "would be" biographers simply because I felt that Bob was already a highly controversial character and that adding what I knew about him would only add fuel to that controversy.

While Bob was researching Kenya's changing, volatile political scene, one of the main topics of conversation was the looming "Uhuru" – the Swahili word for freedom (political independence) and the end of British rule. There was speculation as to whether it might become another Congo debacle. Looking to the future, Bob had already made a safari in Mozambique. There the Portuguese gave him the red carpet treatment in hopes that the resulting publicity would benefit its newly established safari industry.

As for myself and my family, Ker, Downey & Selby Safaris was planning to expand south to Bechuanaland, a British protectorate bordering South Africa, reputedly teeming with many varieties of game. I was offered the job of setting up and running the operation. It was a bit of a gamble, as we were not sure whether the local people would agree to the establishment of a full-blown safari organization or if the game population could support it. Only time would tell, but it was a challenge I was happy to take up.

Bob and I decided that one last safari in Kenya would be a fitting farewell to our years of hunting together. Coincidentally, a large section of country lying east of the Mathews Range in the Northern Frontier was about to be opened to hunters using horses and camels instead of vehicles. It had been a game reserve since the turn of the century and was renowned for elephants carrying big ivory.

The Northern Frontier had always been my favorite hunting ground anyway, so it seemed the ideal location for our last safari together. We would be in an area never hunted before, and since we would be using horses instead of a vehicle, it would be a unique experience. An elephant with tusks each weighing one hundred pounds or more would be the object of the safari. I reserved the area for a month.

We arrived at the designated campsite where the vehicles would remain for the duration of the safari. There, we found the horses and camels hired from the local tribal authority, along with their attendants. Henceforth, all hunting would be on foot or from horseback, and the gear would be carried by camels when we moved camp. Our camping equipment was not as sophisticated as that found on the typical safari, but it was amazing how comfortable a camp transported by camels can be when only the essentials are carried and loaded by experienced packers.

We assembled a light but reasonably comfortable "fly camp," which we loaded onto the camels. We then said "goodbye" to base camp and proceeded to wander northward, skirting the foothills of the Mathews Range. We hunted from one waterhole to another, camped at places where promising sign was discovered, and kept the whole safari enclosed by a strong thornbrush boma to deter the numerous lions and other predators from attacking our animals during the night.

With us were some of the old hands from Bob's previous safaris, for whom he had formed lasting bonds. They included the incomparable Juma, our head man extraordinaire, flashing the gold tooth he had insisted be added in the dentures Bob had arranged for him; ancient Ali, the best safari cook in East Africa; Matheke, an outstanding and fearless hunter and tracker; and old Katunga, an artist with a skinning knife, camp entertainer, medicine man and philosopher. We were free as air.

Game animals and birds were plentiful and varied. They were extremely tame, being used to and unafraid of horses and camels. As a result we had no difficulty feeding ourselves and our retinue, including the horse and camel handlers. However, we had to be careful to avoid disturbing the numerous rhino lying up in the thick suaki bush, which grew along the banks of the luggers. The last thing we needed was a rhino charging about among our strung-out caravan.

There had been heavy rains before we arrived, and the bush was lush and green, which limited our visibility. But there were a number of fairly high rocky hills, from which we were able to locate game with our binoculars. Literally hundreds of elephants were on view, all of a pronounced reddish color, which made them stand out amongst the green bush where they were feeding.

This was the first time Bob and I had been on safari together without others along, and his old witty, cheerful and happy self reemerged. Since there was just the two of us, he no longer needed to portray the "Bwana" image. We sat up late each evening 'round our small campfire and had a great time reminiscing about our past safaris. We talked about the old-time ivory hunters such as Karamojo Bell, Jim Sutherland and others, along with more recent greats like Phil Percival and Pat Ayer who had shown me the way. We conversed about the Kenya of yesteryear and wondered what the future held in store for this magical land.

Hemingway's name cropped up from time to time. Although Bob admired him and seemed to model his own life on that of Papa's, he could not resist the occasional "put down." I was reminded of the time I passed on to Bob the news of Hemingway's death. The love-hate relationship that had always lurked in Bob's subconscious surfaced. He became as excited as I had ever seen him, exclaiming "Haraka, I'm now the herd bull. Do you realize that? I'm the herd bull."

From the outset we had seen some fair tuskers, but not what we were seeking. Having already collected an elephant with tusks in excess of a hundred pounds, Bob was unwilling to take a bull unless it was in that class. I admired his sportsmanship.

One day we were riding along in light bush beside a lugga at the head of our lengthy caravan. Suddenly, with a piercing scream, a young bull elephant came charging across the sand, straight at our line of animals. This caused instant panic. Bob and I tried to urge our reluctant mounts into action, but his horse just lay down. Fortunately, the bank was quite high, and the enraged elephant, unable to climb it, turned aside. Bob joked later that he should have just picked up his horse and followed the general stampede.

We walked and rode many miles, and we sat on hillsides for hours in the hot sun trying to spot a large bull. Diana did not appear to be riding along with us on this hunt, or if she was, she felt that we needed to work even harder for our game. The distinct possibility began to dawn on us that the hundred-pounder we had set our hearts on might elude us even in this country where there had never been any hunting. But then elephant hunting is always unpredictable.

Then one morning a young Samburu moran, head and shoulders glistening with red ochre mixed with sheep's fat and carrying two long, razor-sharp stabbing spears, came into camp. He casually mentioned that an old elephant with big tusks frequented a watering place named Illaut some 20 miles to the north. He claimed the old bull had lived there for years and he was the only elephant drinking there. All the others had migrated south to feed on the green bush we had recently passed through, but he was apparently too old to follow.

FOREWORD

Quite often, information gleaned from local natives can be very misleading. They tend to tell you what they think you would like to hear, or they think that if they can persuade you to follow them to some out of-the-way place, an elephant might be encountered and possibly collected. Should this happen the informant will gladly claim full credit and the reward.

But this young fellow seemed different. He was totally unsophisticated and had never heard of a reward for information about elephants. Since we were getting pretty desperate anyway, we decided to give it a try. We packed up camp, loaded the camels and set off for Illaut.

We arrived at the Illaut wells after a long march under broiling sun and late in the evening set up our small camp. Some people living close by confirmed the young moran's story; an old elephant with large tusks did drink regularly at the wells, though we would have to wait until morning to see whether he would return. We went to bed with high hopes for the morrow.

Early next morning we discovered that the bull had visited the wells during the night. We decided to have a quick breakfast, then take up the spoor. While we were eating, Sala, the head camel handler, brought us a young Samburu girl who claimed she had seen the bull not very far away while escorting her flock to water. This was great news. We quickly saddled up and rode off in the direction she indicated.

We had not ridden more than a couple of miles when, on cresting a low ridge, we saw him. He literally filled the eye! Every inch of him, from his toenails to the top of his head, was visible. He stood absolutely motionless, as if carved out of stone, his long symmetrical tusks nearly touching the ground. What a sight! I know of nothing as thrilling as one's first glimpse of a really fine tusker. No doubt, here was the trophy we sought.

We dismounted and walked to within 30 or 40 yards of him. There was no reaction – he was probably partially blind and possibly deaf. Small wonder he had remained behind when all the others had moved to greener pastures. No need to relate the actual shooting in detail. It was in fact an anticlimax in comparison to the hunt. Suffice it to say, Bob did a good clean job of it.

After rewarding the young girl for having brought us the news, we removed the tusks, which we estimated would easily exceed one hundred pounds each. We had collected our "hundred-pounder" and the safari was over.

Next morning it was time to show our appreciation with a generous gratuity to the cheerful, helpful horse and camel handlers and to say goodbye. They had been indispensable throughout the safari. We had become quite fond of our little troop of horses and camels, though it takes quite a lot of togetherness to become fond of a hissing, spitting, quarreling camel. Still, we were sorry to leave them.

With camp once more packed, we took Bob to a prearranged landing strip in the bush, where he was picked up by charter plane and flown to Nairobi. There, he was to meet up with some friends who would join us on the second leg of our hunt, this one in Masailand. I elected to remain with the safari.

FOREWORD

In the last evening before we reached base camp we were sitting by our little campfire, chatting about our experiences with this unfamiliar method of hunting, as new to me as it was to Bob, and the unspoiled area we had explored. We were both aware that this would be the last campfire we would share in the beloved NFD. We congratulated each other on the extremely satisfactory outcome of the hunt, realizing we were very lucky to have collected such a beautiful pair of tusks. However, our enthusiasm was somewhat muted by the thought of the lonely old patriarch who had been left alone at Illaut and who for years had so majestically carried those tusks.

As we were about to turn in, Bob said to me: "Haraka, you might not realize it, but for years I have fed off your carcass like a hyena."

When Bob and I shook hands and said goodbye just before he climbed aboard the charter plane, I had no idea that our many years of association were about to come to an end – right there. That would be the last time I would see him.

When Bob arrived at his hotel in Nairobi, he found a summons awaiting him. Someone he had mentioned in his writings about the prevailing political situation in Kenya had been aggrieved and had instituted legal proceedings. Bob decided that he could not risk the possibility of having to surrender his travel documents and so he decided to fly out of Nairobi that same evening.

Imagine my surprise when I arrived in Nairobi with the safari two days later to find that Bob was no longer in the country. Together with his friends, I would continue on safari to Masailand without him. As the result of this incident and the publication of *Uhuru*, he was banned from returning to Kenya and pronounced persona non grata by the authorities.

Bob returned to hunt in Mozambique during the next couple of years, but his health was failing and he died in London in 1965. Meanwhile, we moved our family south to Bechuanaland at the end of 1962, and for a few years I was totally occupied in reconnoitering the Okavango Delta and Kalahari Desert regions. Then, once convinced of their potential, I was busy in establishing Ker, Downey & Selby Safaris in that sparsely populated, unspoiled, game-rich county. It was a veritable wildlife paradise, a quiet backwater that time and the rush of the twentieth century appeared to have passed by. Bob Ruark would have loved it.

AUTHOR'S NOTE
By Alan Ritchie

This book is not intended to be an exposé or a scandal sheet, but by the same token I have made no effort to fluff lightly over possibly controversial or offensive subjects. My intention, quite simply, is to provide an honest, forthright biography of a widely loved individual. I want to give a definite impression of Robert Ruark as he really was – the most incredibly wonderful, generous, humorous and likeable sonofabitch who ever lived.

For the first two years following Ruark's death I entertained no thoughts whatsoever of writing a biography of my cherished friend and employer. In fact, I repeatedly resisted suggestions from people who said I should do so, since I was the person who knew him best. My reluctance came in part from knowing that the undertaking would involve a great deal of internal stress, not to mention complications from others, because there were bound to be things that some people would feel should not be exposed. Also, I fully realized that there were controversial incidents that would be difficult to include and even more difficult to ignore.

When I finally decided to go ahead, it was with the thought in mind that I would simply write about the way things had been. In my view, that could not be wrong.

On the pages that follow you will meet Robert Ruark as I knew him. – *Alan Ritchie*, 1969

Chapter 1
THE BOY ALONE

"All he left me was the world." This thought pounded through the head of the 15-year-old boy as he slipped out of the house to escape the crowd gathered to pay their respects to his grandfather, the Old Man. They had come to see the Old Man off, to offer a final "goodbye" to the Cap'n. The boy didn't need to say goodbye. He had already done so in private.

"I ain't got to tell you that I am going to die," the Old Man said. "You would know it. You've had the best of me, and you're on your own from now on. You'll go to college next year and you'll be a man, with all a man's problems, and there won't be no Old Man around to steer you. I raised you as best I could and now you're the Old Man, because I'm tired, and I think I'll leave."

Tears had filled the boy's eyes as he said all those things the young say in the face of death. "Leave it, leave it," the Old Man had said. "Like I always told you, if there was a way to beat it, I would have heard about it. It'll even happen to you, unlikely as it seems."

"But how? When? Why?" the boy had questioned, lacking anything better to say.

That last conversation raced though his mind as the lad, small for his age, grabbed the oars from beneath the house and raced for the boat. He rowed hard for a nearby island and as he rowed, trying not to think of the Old Man being dead, he thought of their last conversation. "I ain't going to leave you much," the Old Man had said. "This sickness cost an awful lot of money. The house is mortgaged, and there's a note in the bank, and the Depression is still on. There won't be much left but some shotguns and a cast net and a boat. And, maybe, a memory."

Suddenly the sun appeared and with it a warm thought. "What did the Old Man mean, he wasn't going to leave me much? I've had 15 years of the Old Man, and nearly everything I know he's taught me." With that comforting thought, the boy began checking his assets.

He'd been raised as a man among men, without condescension, without patronizing. He'd been allowed companionship on an equal basis with the Old Man and his cronies. He had been given pride and equality. He had been taught compassion and tolerance, especially toward the less fortunate. He had been given the vast gift of reading, and it opened up a treasure house of knowledge. The Old Man had taught him good manners, sometimes painfully impressed, and he said "Sir," "M'am," "Please" and "Thank you" as a matter of course.

He'd been shown how to throw a cast net, shoot a gun, row a boat, build a duck blind, tong an oyster, train a puppy, stand a deer, bait a turkey blind (illegal), call turkeys to the blind, cast in the surf, pitch a tent, make a bed of pine boughs, follow a coonhound, skin anything that had to be skinned, scale and fillet a fish, dig clams, build a cave, draw pictures, isolate edible mushrooms from poisonous toadstools, pole a boat, identify all the trees and most of the plants, cook a meal, get along with colored folks, practice a rude but practical kind of game conservation, and much more.

As gentle waves rocked his boat, that seemed to sum it up. When it came to hard assets, there were two shotguns, a cast net, a boat and a house that wouldn't be their much longer. College lay just around the corner, if only he could figure out how to pay his way. Then the boy suddenly realized that he was educated without ever darkening the doors of academia. The Old Man, a wise and winsome mentor, had left him the world.

The heartbroken boy was Robert Ruark, standing on the threshold of his life. The Old Man was his maternal grandfather, Captain E. H. Adkins, a retired sea captain. The two had enjoyed a timeless partnership, and from it Ruark would fashion a remarkable career.

Robert Chester Ruark was born on December 29, 1915, in Wilmington, North Carolina and was the only child of Robert Chester and Charlotte Adkins Ruark. Robert Ruark, Junior was born prematurely, and according to his later explanation, he only lived because he at least reached seven months at birth. All his mother's previous children were stillborn. Later there was an adopted son, David, who would become more the responsibility of his older brother than his parents.

The name Ruark could have originated from the Irish O'Rourke, or more likely, O'Ruark. According to one description of the O'Ruark's of Breffni coat of arms, the family belonged to a royal line. One branch can be traced back to the seventh century, when in the early annals of Ireland there appears a Fergal O'Ruark, King of Cannaght. Thereafter the O'Ruarks appear periodically in accounts of battles, and there are scattered records of the name up to the 17th century.

The Ruark family lived in the Wilmington area, where young Robert got his schooling at New Hanover High School. But much of his youth was spent in and around Southport, a fishing hamlet at the mouth of the Cape Fear River some 30 miles away. Interestingly, Southport was almost an exact duplicate of his eventual home in Palamos, Spain. Some aspects of Ruark's early youth and education are described in the first pages of his semi-autobiographical novel, *Poor No More*, through the character of Craig Price.

Although Ruark had plenty of friends as a youngster, most were adults and many were colored. He took no interest in team sports but relished hunting and fishing. A book was his constant companion. While he had not been taught to read, Ruark was able, by age four, to photograph a book's page mentally. He lived inside his books and was fiercely protective of both his independence and his love of literature. One day during play period, Robert was reading *Ivanhoe* while sitting atop the flat roof of a garage.

A big, athletic boy looked up at him and shouted: "Come on down off that roof and play football."

Wedging one finger into the book to keep his place, Ruark replied: "I don't want to. I'm reading."

"You're yellow. Old sissy Ruark. That's why he's so fat," the bully said to a swarm of sadistic children who always flock to a bear-baiting.

"I am not yellow. I'm reading and don't want to play," was Ruark's response.

"Cowardy cat, cowardy cat. Fatty Ruark is a sissy," the young mob began to chant.

"I'll bet you're afraid to jump off that roof," the chief tormentor said. "I dare you. I double dog dare you to jump."

Robert calmly closed his book and dog-eared the page to mark it.

"All right," he said, "I'll jump."

Placing the book under his arm, he jumped ten feet straight down, landing with both feet in the upturned face of his enemy, breaking the bully's nose and knocking out several of his teeth. This happened when Ruark was only six years of age. By general consensus he was immediately withdrawn from kindergarten. His mother put him to bed for a week as punishment. But this enabled him to complete *Ivanhoe* and *Robin Hood*, and he was just finishing *Treasure Island* when granted his return to freedom.

As a youngster Ruark lived almost completely inside himself and thanks to his early accumulation of knowledge, he soon became bored with standard school instruction. Fortunately, a perceptive teacher decided to let him skip from the first to third grade, where he made straight As. He promptly lost interest again until he was moved to the sixth grade, where for three consecutive years he was known as the brightest child in the area.

Schoolboy Ruark had a remarkable imagination, formed mainly as the result of extensive reading. When he ventured off into the woods with his dogs or went fishing, he was not Robert Ruark at all. He became someone straight out of his adventure stories and gave his imagination free rein.

Alone in his woods and fields Mysterious Robert Ruark, aged ten and already in the seventh grade, thought of himself as The Chief, The Chief of what he wasn't quite sure. But certainly Mysterious Robert Ruark, The Chief, who needed tremendous secrecy for his treasure of bullion and stolen gems, so he began to dig caves. He had an interlocking series of them covering acres, with secret passages so that not even Injun Joe could trap him.

When he took his fishing gear and unshipped oars to head for Money Key where the pirate gold was supposedly buried, he was Columbus standing stoutly out to sea, or Balboa prowling the Pacific. Astride his pitching quarterdeck, staring sternly toward vast unknown lands, he knew that scanty rations, weevily biscuits, and salt horse would not move his rascally crew of gutter sweepings to mutiny. Not so long as The Captain strode his bridge, a belaying pin close to hand, a cutlass by his side, and two pistols stuck into his belt. He'd shoot them down like dogs and carve his way to the ringleaders, whom he would keelhaul, make to walk the plank, flog through the fleet, and hang from the yardarm. He was too old a hand to be betrayed, and had not he himself been a pirate off Barbados?

At this point Ruark was everyone from Captain Ahab in search of Moby Dick to Captain Blood sailing the Spanish Main. He pictured himself as having sunk the Spanish Armada single handed, sailing the dark rivers of Malaya while standing off pirate junks with grapeshot, and being involved in the South Pacific slave trade. Then, momentarily returning to reality, Robert shipped his oars and anchored near a sand bar.

First he would gather some clams, which he did by wading barefoot in the mud and feeling for them with his toes. If possible he would locate some soft-shell crabs and tong up a few bushels of somebody else's oysters. This came under the head of free-booting on the high seas. Then, after laying in a supply of fiddler crabs for bait, he would make for a barnacle-laden old wreck he knew, where sheepshead and stone crabs were sure to lurk. He would need shrimp, and possibly, some small mullet for bait as well, so he wet his cast net, shook it free of water, spread it out between hand and teeth until it swirled like a dancer's skirt, and cast it so it hovered over a school of skipping shrimp like a huge butterfly. They were just right for bait, small and yellow-gray, as they kicked and bucked on the deck when he opened the net. Another caste provided a double dozen tiny mullet, and the master of the good ship *Arabella* was ready for business.

As his writings about his youth indicate, Ruark spent a great deal of his boyhood on his own, apparently by choice, and the following scenario would have been similar to countless other leisure-filled days. However, this particular outing ended with some drama. Robert reached the old wreck and lunched sumptuously on a smorgasbord from his catch of trout, perch, croakers, Virginia mullet, skipjacks and Moorish crabs. He lazed away the afternoon with *Huckleberry Finn* and finally fell asleep.

When Robert woke a feeling of tremendous calm and well-being possessed him. He set about washing up and stowing his gear properly, and as he moved about, barefoot, he experienced a sudden, searing pain just behind his right big toe. He took the foot in his hand and saw a blurred blue object deep under the opaque skin of the ball of his foot. He sat down hurriedly to discover he had stepped on a rusty nail embedded in an old piece of planking. It had broken off as it entered his foot, and half of the nail was firmly wedged under the callus. He bit his lips against the pain and resolved that a man had to do what he had to do. Surgery at sea was part of a sailor's pay, painful but terribly necessary.

There were still some coals left in the fire. Robert got out his knife and whetted it against the oilstone he carried in his tackle box. Then he placed the blade in the coals and left it until it was searing hot. He wished for a bullet to bite but made do with a four-ounce pyramid sinker. Using the tip of his knife, he dug in and around the nail and prized it out. Blood flowed and he was slightly sick with pain, but he cut a strip from his shirttail and bound the wound tightly. He would sneak some iodine when he got home and not mention a word of his heroism to his grandmother. He limped to his boat, with blood spreading under the rough bandage, and prepared to shove off.

The wounded Captain-Admiral sent imaginary hands aloft to set the sails, while Robert Ruark bent to the reality of oars with a right goodwill. He owned a feeling of accomplishment that Balboa must have felt when he first sighted the Pacific. He had made his landfall, victualed his ship, and quelled a budding mutiny. It mattered little that he was the entire rowing crew of a slave galley, for the *Sea Hawk* would be along at any moment to rescue him.

The wind has risen, and saucy little droplets from brash wavelets bounced off his sunburned nose. He smelled of fish scales and grease and marsh mud, but it was a blithesome craft with a jaunty skipper who arrived half-dead from fatigue-cum-sore foot in an unknown port in the Far Caribees. He dragged the *Santa*

Maria up on the beach, turned her over, and shouldered his oars, fishing rod, sack of fish, hoard of oysters and clams, then limped home, salty, sun-burned, dirty, and happy.

As the young dreamer entered the house via the back porch his grandmother met him on the stoop with a disapproving stare.

"Where have you been all day?" she asked.

"Fishin'," he replied. "I got a mess of fish and some crabs and clams and oysters and..."

"Clean the fish and wash up," his grandmother interrupted. "You're late for supper." Then, glaring suspiciously, she added: "What's the matter with your foot?"

"I cut it on a piece of glass," lied the Captain-Admiral of the *Ocean Sea.* What could a mere woman know of far places and a man with the look of eagles in his eyes, a man who could, if necessary, cut off his own leg with scarcely a whimper? But tomorrow he would tell the Old Man, and his grandfather wouldn't say: "Wash up, you're late for supper," to a man who had just discovered a new trade route to the Indies and who had bitten a bullet as he sawed at his own flesh."

Before Robert Ruark developed a sound and definite confidence from his grandfather, he went through a disturbing time when his desire for solitude and the opportunity to let his imagination run wild were repeatedly disrupted by bullying from other boys. Young Robert was fat and had no interest in their activities, so he was singled out as a "softie" and persecuted accordingly. He was often known as Bobby, which he didn't like, and the fact that his family called him Rosebud did little to help his self-confidence. Also his middle name, Chester, evoked hilarity. Almost daily Robert found himself the object of some form of boy-baiting and would run home to escape his tormentors. One day as he made the safety of his garden gate and clanked it shut, his mother met him with a stick and beat him unmercifully.

"Every time you run from that boy," she said, "I intend to wear you out so bad you'll be glad to run back to him." His grandmother witnessed the beating and protested vociferously, but to no avail. "Now Robert," his mother said to the sobbing child, "you go back out there and fight that little bastard." The tormentor, who was at the time leaning over the fence, seemed delighted in what appeared to be a double triumph.

"I'm scared, I'm scared," Ruark sobbed. "I try to hold his arms and he keeps hitting me in the face! I don't want to fight him!"

"Robert's mother again whacked him viciously across the behind. "You fight him or I'll keep this up all day!" she said. "Will you fight him or will I beat you again?"

"Ruark looked at his two enemies, one jeering, the other coldly implacable. "I'll fight him," he sobbed. "Just don't hit me any more!"

He raced for the gate, flung it open, and hurled himself on the jeering bully. His small, fat fists were flails, and he sobbed as he hit, kicked and even bit his adversary. Surprised, the bully lost his balance and fell with Robert on top. When they finally managed to pry him off the fallen enemy, Ruark had him by the ears and was pounding his head up and down on the sidewalk. Robert was still weeping, but now it was his tormentor who ran away, bawling at the top of his voice.

Ruark's mother broke the stick across her knee and went into the house without a word. After that Robert regarded his mother with guarded hostility, but he never again backed down from a fight.

During the Depression years of the late 1920s, Robert Ruark's developing character was probably influenced by the decline of family fortunes. He saw their cars dwindle to a single ramshackle Ford, the sale of the family home, and then one day, returning from high school, the hunting dogs did not race to meet him. He whistled and no dogs answered or came running to leap against him and administer the daily wet slap of eager tongues across his face. He went to look for his gun and it was missing from the rack. Desperately he walked the fields and searched the woods. When his father arrived home that night, young Robert was panic stricken.

"Somebody's stolen the dogs and my gun!" he cried. "I've looked everywhere."

His father's face was gray and deeply bitten by lines around his mouth. "You may as well know," he said. "I had to sell the dogs. I got a good offer and I had to make a turn. The man who wanted the dogs needed a gun too. He'll sell everything back to me if I can raise the money when the bird season's finished."

"You won't raise the money," Robert said. "You always say you will but you won't. What right have you got to sell my dogs and my gun?"

"I'm your father," was the gentle reply. "And I sold my own gun some time back."

Father and son looked at each other, and both turned away. There was very little to say after that, but the occasion was a watershed in Ruark's life. From this point on he would become increasingly independent and self-sufficient, and for much of what remained of his life, supporting his parents would weigh on his shoulders, often quite heavily.

Chapter 2
CHAPEL HILL DAYS

In September of 1931 Robert Ruark, dressed in brown knickerbockers and white tennis shoes, presented himself for enrollment at the University of North Carolina at Chapel Hill. He stood before the University's historic buildings with a wonderful sense of relief as his mother departed in the family's Model-A Ford. With an invigorating sense of freedom he walked across campus carrying a single suitcase containing one suit, a few shirts, a spare pair of shoes and a speller his grandfather had given him. Though Ruark's family had once been comparatively well off, they were now decidedly short of funds. He was to have a thin time during his college years. His tuition was paid for the first quarter and he had about $50 in his pocket. But with his father unemployed and the family having lost their house, the future was uncertain.

His first college experience was unusual and unnerving. He was assigned an older boy, a divinity student who claimed to be a basketball player, as a roommate. That saintly cager immediately locked the door and tried to kill Ruark. The 20-year-old roommate decided he was Abraham and Ruark a 15-year-old Isaac ready for sacrifice. Just before the slaughter, thanks to Ruark's yelling for help, the locked door was broken down and he was rescued by some other athletes residing in the same dormitory.

This inauspicious beginning had no lasting impact on Ruark's freshman year. He did his best to remain on his own, though he couldn't avoid having another new boy sharing his room. This time the roommate was inoffensive but Ruark soon realized he was a rich, somewhat pansified youth. They quarreled, despite the roommate's generous offer to lend Ruark any clothes he wished to use.

When Ruark began his studies, he had no clear intention of pursuing a writing career. In fact, he was engaged, among other things, in a course of art studies. It seems that a pretty journalism coed was entirely responsible for this change of direction. By taking the same course as the girl, he could walk her to class in the morning without doubling back across campus to another course he didn't like, and he could accompany her to breakfast during the period set aside for chapel. With the lovely lass as a catalyst, he switched his major to journalism. When he sold his first article to the *Raleigh News & Observer,* he was convinced he had made the right choice.

Ruark's years at Chapel Hill were satisfactory from an academic point of view, but it wasn't a happy time for him socially. He never had enough money or clothes to participate in extracurricular activities. He augmented his meager means in various ways. Periodically there were sketches for the campus newspaper; he served as editor of the college magazine, *The Carolina Buccaneer,* until it was banned for off-color material; and he was a first-rate boarding house hustler. One semester he even assumed the role of campus bootlegger, making and selling "bathtub gin" to richer classmates. Later he would claim he did a good job inasmuch as no one died or lost their eyesight.

Ruark's experience with bootlegging would lead to a brush with authorities immediately after his graduation. In company with three of his best friends, George Rowe, Nick Powell and Jim Queen, he had made arrangements to beat the anticipated boredom of the long graduation ceremony. They had supplied themselves with a crock of home brew, consisting of medical alcohol mixed with grapefruit juice, and rubber tubes through which they could suck up the libation, which was secreted beneath their academic regalia.

The speaker for commencement was Eleanor Roosevelt, who told the graduates at considerable length that the weight of the world now rested on their stout young shoulders. By the time Ruark and his fellow imbibers were called to step forward for their diplomas, they were all well advanced toward drunkenness. With the graduation over, the drinking continued apace as the four scholars made their way toward Wilmington by car. En route they ran out of gasoline, and since nobody had any money, the decided to put the rubber tubes to further use in siphoning gasoline from some cars parked nearby.

Unfortunately, they had no way of knowing that there had been a rash of gasoline stealing in the area, and so they walked right into a police trap with half the town's force waiting to pounce on thieves. As the foursome made off through a cornfield with a container of stolen gasoline, the police opened fire. Graduate Ruark immediately surrendered and was taken to jail in handcuffs. He spent an unpleasant night in a cell, where he had time to sober up and reflect on his folly. Following processing and proper identification by family members the next morning, he was released.

It was hardly an auspicious start to his post-college career, but fortunately the police showed sufficient compassion to erase any record from their blotter. According to Ruark, this saved him from a life of crime, though later, when bitterly disillusioned while working his first newspaper job, he expressed regret that he hadn't stuck to gasoline stealing as a career.

Still a teenager and staring straight into the jaws of the Depression, Robert Ruark had graduated with a degree in journalism. He was offered, thanks to intercession from a professor, the first job that became available to the 1935 graduates. This professor said he gave Ruark the opportunity primarily because "He was the only person he knew who was ornery enough to make a go of it."

The job was in Hamlet, North Carolina, where for a salary of $10 a week Ruark was editor, reporter, advertising manager, subscription seller, make-up man, circulation manager and janitor (his duties included sweeping out the office every day). This was for the *Hamlet News Messenger*, a small weekly. The job lasted three months, with Ruark quitting because he felt the walls were moving in on him. It was a tiny town with no nightlife. Also, Ruark complained, if he got drunk on Saturday the preacher would tell about it in church the next day, though he was never in church to hear the denunciation of his sins.

At this juncture Ruark left North Carolina, with no qualifications other than a stint of bootlegging at Chapel Hill, a bit of newspaper work, a rich heritage of seagoing ancestors and a fiddle foot. He struck off to see the world with his thumb in the air.

CHAPTER 3
THE BOY TAKES ON THE WORLD

First stop was Washington, D. C., where he got a job with the Works Progress Administration as a statistician and accountant. The position paid $1,440 a year, a decent salary at the time, but it lasted only three months. His employers discovered that he was neither a statistician nor an accountant, and his later life would prove he was a failure as a money manager in general.

Jobless once again, Ruark set off hitchhiking in the general direction of Florida and eventually to Jacksonville. Sitting on the sun-warmed, tar-smelling dock, watching ships come in and down to his final four dollars, Ruark wondered what his next move should be. Suddenly there was a commotion aboard a nearby freighter, the *S. S. Sundance* out of Savannah. The ship had just berthed, and a crew member was unceremoniously heaved over the side by the mate. As the man landed heavily on the dock's iron sheathing, the mate shouted: "Show your face on this ship again, you son-of-a-bitch, and I'll kill you."

From this Ruark assumed that a vacancy now existed, and he shouted up to the ship: "Mister Mate, I bet you can't do that to me."

"Come on up and we'll see about that. Come aboard, friend." yelled the mate.

"Well, if you can't throw me off, can I have his job?" Ruark replied.

They fought for half an hour, with the result being a bloody standstill. Ruark may have been willowy at this point in his life, but he stood a muscular, lean six feet tall. The mate was older and heavier as well as being deceptively agile. He roared with laughter as he slung his punches, most of which missed. One didn't. It caught Ruark on the bridge of his nose and he could hear the cartilage crunch. He fell backward onto the anchor winch, but as the mate came after him Ruark kicked out and caught him in the testicles. The man clapped a hand to his groin, groaned and abruptly sat down. Ruark went over and held out a hand. The mate grasped it and was yanked to his feet.

"Of all the goddamn crazy kids!" the mate bellowed. "You got yourself a job, sonny."

Then he suddenly swung his right fist and caught Ruark squarely in the jaw with a knockout blow. When Ruark returned to consciousness the mate reached out a hand and yanked him to his feet. "You got yourself a job," he said, "if you still want it. That last punch was just to tell you I'm still the boss on this bucket. You think I'm the boss?"

"Yessir," Ruark mumbled, "you're the boss."

"Can I throw you over the side?"

"You could of."

"Okay," the mate said, and shoved out a friendly paw. "Shake. It pays ten bucks a week and you're the number two ordinary, and there ain't nothing lower than a number two ordinary, unless it's the cadet."

Once at sea, Ruark settled into his new job, but at the same time he continued to develop his mind. While standing watch, he would pick out one particular subject and then would try to take it to pieces from every conceivable angle. In this way he trained his powers of concentration. Ruark later said: "I had myself some real fine thoughts through the night, and also passed the dog watch in double-quick time."

Ruark soon found that food aboard the ship was not particularly good, and the night luncheon was almost non-existent, since the able seamen disposed of whatever was put out before he could get to it. On one exceptionally cold night, Ruark worked up a considerable appetite thanks to having spent his watch thinking of delectable fare. Arriving in the mess hall, he found nothing left and impulsively decided to scout around in the officers' galley to see what he could find. Opening the captain's icebox he started feeding on the officers' night lunch and helped himself to cups of freshly boiled coffee.

Before he could finish his repast, he heard determined steps approaching, as either hunger or intuition had roused the skipper. Ruark escaped in the nick of time, and once on deck with the captain in close pursuit, he found himself still holding the silver coffee pot. As they raced around the ship, Ruark found time to dispose of the evidence by flinging the coffee pot overboard. The enraged captain rounded up the crew in his efforts to identify the night thief, but ordinary seaman Ruark was lost in the crowd.

Ruark experienced one particularly bad storm when a cargo of logs broke loose and threatened to wreck the ship. Ruark was given the job of helmsman and was required to hold the ship into the rough seas whilst other crew members tackled the job of lashing down the shifting cargo. It was at this time Ruark encountered his first death at sea. During the crew's struggle to secure the logs, a sea surge threw one man against a bulkhead and killed him. Ruark was troubled that others might think he was somehow responsible for the man's death because he did an inadequate job of holding the ship fully into the weather, but later the mate told him: "You did a good job, son. We'll use your steady wheel watch from now on."

Ruark made three transatlantic trips and missed none of the shoreside attractions of the rougher North Atlantic ports such as Bremen, Hamburg, Antwerp and Liverpool. As the only college boy aboard he had to fight just about every man on the ship in order to prove his right to be a crew member, since jobs were in such short supply during the Depression. He started out being disparagingly called "the Duke," but six months later, when he signed off, he had affectionately become "the Iron Duke."

While Ruark enjoyed the rough, rugged life of a sailor, he knew that it was not a likely livelihood. So when the *S.S. Sundance* arrived in Norfolk, Virginia, he reluctantly signed off. Once ashore, he won a bus ticket in a crap game and ended up in Washington, D. C. There, for many months he unsuccessfully plagued all the newspapers in town for a reporting job. He was forced to gloss over his editorship of the *Hamlet News Messenger* and settled for trying to be hired as copy boy. But jobs were scarce and he was turned down by all four dailies in Washington. Finally, he was offered a position as classified advertising clerk, at $14 a week, in the front office of the *Washington Post*. Two months later, in the autumn of 1936, a copy boy job became available at the *Washington Star* and Ruark took it at a reduced salary of $12 a week.

During this impoverished period in Ruark's life, he supplemented his wages by writing publicity for a small hotel and a nightclub. Even so, he barely made enough to feed himself properly. So when his best friend asked him to look after his girlfriend when he left Washington to return to law school, Ruark was really in no position to oblige. But he did oblige, dating her twice a week on his meager $12 salary. Still, there were compensations, such as meals provided by the woman in question. "I had two dates a week when I was courting Virginia, Wednesday and Sunday. On Wednesday nights, I ate enough to do me until Sunday and on Sunday nights I ate enough to do me until Wednesday. She fed me when I was just a $12 a week copy boy . . . and she's a lovely girl besides."

The girl was Virginia Webb, who at the time was an interior decorator in a Washington department store. Soon enough Ruark decided that he would not return her to his lawyer friend but would instead marry her. They were wed in August 1938 and started off together on the upward climb of Ruark's career.

Although Ruark's weekly wage had dropped when he took the copy boy position, he knew it was a step in the right direction. Sure enough, at the end of the year he was offered a similar position with the *Washington Daily News* at $15 a week, and with it came a promise that he would fill the first reporting staff vacancy that occurred.

That vacancy happened to be in sports, a subject about which Ruark knew virtually nothing, and he wrote most of his copy by the seat of his pants. Still, his brashness soon achieved notoriety because of a number of exclusive stories. Most of these came about through his lack of knowledge – he asked stupid questions and people gave him answers that turned out to be newsworthy. Within a short time he was given his own sports column.

Among his early targets was the millionaire owner of the Washington Redskins football team. His unflattering coverage resulted in a libel suit, but it was later dropped. During the same period Ruark wrote some powerful copy concerning a fastball pitcher named Louis Norman Newsom, otherwise known as Bobo Newsom, a brawny star for the Detroit Tigers. Ruark referred to him as "a big, loud-mouthed, sloppy-jowled, South Carolina pitcher," among other less-than-flattering descriptions.

When Ruark got to the ball park the day after the piece appeared, he heard that Newsom was gunning for him. Rather than avoiding confrontation, he decided to visit the team's locker room. As soon as Ruark entered, Newsom began cursing him. Ruark decided that warranted action on his part, so he gave him what he considered his best punch right in the jaw. According to Ruark's account, Newsom didn't even drop the coke he had in his hand. A merry scramble ensued, but thanks to intercession from a fellow columnist, Ruark managed to escape serious harm.

Newsom pitched superbly in that day's game and helped the Tigers to a win. Subsequently, a disgruntled Washington fan stopped in front of the press box and snarled to Ruark: "Why don't you take a punch at some of our bums once in a while?" He then picked up the young reporter's portable typewriter and hit him over the head with it.

In later life Ruark would look back on the incident with some fondness. He would relate the episode and then add, "It seems to me I have been hit over the head with a typewriter ever since."

Nobody really got hurt in these dustups, but the resulting publicity was priceless. It put the brash young reporter in the sports headlines of every newspaper in the country. While he was working in a state of profound ignorance when it came to the subjects he covered, and while he cared little for team sports, Ruark did become an assiduous student of the great sportswriters of the day. He admired Westbrook Pegler enormously and was also a big fan of the work of Damon Runyon.

CHAPTER 4
NEW HORIZONS

On Sunday, December 7, 1941, the day the Japanese attacked Pearl Harbor, Robert Ruark was in the press box covering a football game between the Washington Redskins and the Philadelphia Eagles. His office signaled him over the wire and gave him the job of gathering up all the editors, reporters and linotype men who were in the grandstands. He rounded up a crew, returned to the office to get out an extra, and went to bed 72 hours later knowing he had been promoted from the sports department into the far more serious job of reporting the news of the world. Over the next few months he would have a short fling as a top feature writer and would serve as local general assignment reporter, Capitol Hill man and assistant city editor for the *Daily News*.

In short order Ruark honed some remarkable skills. A man who went out on a story assignment for the *News* not only had to be able to gather facts and find a telephone, he also had to dictate a complete, accurate and grammatically correct story to the typist he called. Ruark got so he could dictate several thousand words a day under high pressure and make them sound as if they had been carved out by a painstaking wordsmith with all the time in the world. He also garnered an amazing number of scoops. Among them was the "discovery" of General George Patton, and the article he wrote on him was widely acclaimed.

Ruark was brash, ambitious, cocky, fast and good, and he soon felt with considerable justification that he could do anything a newspaper required, and do most of it with his left hand. His salary rose to a maximum of $80 a week.

Ruark volunteered for the Navy as soon as the United States entered the war, but his acceptance was delayed until late 1942 pending the outcome of a leg operation required to qualify him physically for duty. Ruark remembered his entrance into the Navy as a signal shock and once described its impact.

The last story I did before putting on my uniform to go to Dartmouth was an interview with Greer Garson who was temporarily hospitalized in Washington from exhaustion after a bond tour. The hospital room was small and there wasn't any chair and Miss Garson who was wearing a very pretty blue nightgown asked me to sit on the edge of the bed while we talked. I went back to the office and wrote the story, and the next day when I boarded the train for New York, lo and behold, there was Miss Garson on the same train surrounded by a flock of incipient ensigns and j.gs. She spied me and I was invited to her compartment, while she explained brightly to the flabbergasted fledgling officers . . . "Mr. Ruark and I spent all yesterday afternoon in bed together.

Thereafter, Ruark boasted that no freshman officer ever entered training with such an aura of importance.

Robert Ruark underwent the standard training course, was commissioned as ensign, and then shipped out as a gunnery officer on an ammunition ship bound for Europe. He was soon promoted to lieutenant and made a good officer, though on his first trip he had his authority severely tested. There was a difficult, recalcitrant member of his gun crew who always managed to display some form of dumb insolence. This soon became painfully obvious to everyone on board the ship. After a particularly obnoxious demonstration of disrespect by the man, Ruark lost patience and decided to take the matter into his own hands. He challenged the troublemaker to a bout of boxing. While he proclaimed it was to be for recreational purposes, he also whispered to the man that he intended to beat the hell out of him.

The boxing match was announced, and with the ship's entire crew in attendance, the men commenced the first two-minute round on top of the forward hatch. Within the first ten seconds it was obvious that the rough sailor was an old hand at boxing, and it turned out most of the crew knew he had been a semi-professional in the middleweight ranks. The prevailing opinion of the seamen was that Ruark should have asked one of them to deal with the renegade, as he was obviously mismatched.

After the third round, with blood pouring from Ruark's face, he called a temporary halt, saying he wished to retire to his quarters briefly to repair a few cuts and then he would be right back. He even told his adversary to take a breather. Once in his stateroom Ruark quickly attended to the cuts on his face, and then searched out a wrapped roll of dimes. He inserted this roll into his right glove, flexed his fingers comfortably around the weight, then laced his glove up tightly. Sliding back down the ladder to the deck, he jumped on the hatch and said: "Okay, let's go."

Since it had been a comparatively one-sided affair, the seaman had decided to toy with his commanding officer, acting up for the rest of the crew and allowing the odd punch to get through. He seemed quite content to continue this cat-and-mouse affair and left himself open to receive what he assumed would be another futile punch from Ruark. However, the next punch that came through was different. Ruark swung from the heels and smashed his weighted fist against the man's jaw. The resulting crack could be heard clearly by everyone present. It knocked the man out cold and broke his jaw in a number of places.

Staring coldly at the crew, Lieutenant Ruark pushed his way through the gaping crowd, went to his room and restored the roll of dimes to his safe. Thereafter, he had no more personnel trouble aboard ship.

Gradually Lt. Ruark settled down to the serious business of war. He would make a number of dangerous North Atlantic crossings and his ship would have a number of narrow escapes. These included being rammed by a submarine on one trip, attacked by another submarine, strafed from the air and even struck by lightning. The worst run of all came when his ship was selected by the naval port director at a convoy conference as "Commodore" ship. Ruark was given the honorary title of "Commodore" and was responsible for receiving all signals from the escorting destroyers for relay to other liberty ships in station. On this particular crossing, his ship was part of a 120-ship convoy bound for Murmansk, a trip known as the Death Run.

He had made the Murmansk run before and knew what it represented. So on arrival off northern Scotland, having already lost over 30 ships and with the prospect that the Luftwaffe would be waiting in strength to finish off survivors from the U-boat attacks, he was not disappointed when the convoy was diverted to London.

The convoy had been under near constant attack by a wolf pack of submarines for seven days. During this period Ruark had gotten little sleep and had worn the same clothes, so on the eighth day he decided that he had to bathe, no matter what the circumstances. He was enjoying a hot, steaming shower when he heard the hoarse scream of the ship's general alarm. This fetched Ruark from the shower at the double. He hit the deck naked except for a pistol and helmet and clambered topside to his gun station on the flying bridge. As he took command of his gun crew, a ship in the center of the convoy that had been hit began drifting back and sinking.

Perilous duty at sea wasn't the only action Ruark saw. While he was in London, where his convoy had been redirected, the city was singled out for a series of heavy air raids that concentrated on the dockyard area and damaged his ship. Also, a recently acquired girlfriend was killed while waiting for Ruark to arrive for a date. When he arrived at her flat, a half-hour late because of the air raid, the entire building where she lived had been gutted.

A few months later, in 1943, Ruark was engaged in the Mediterranean theater. His ship led the first American convoy up the Adriatic and into the mine-infested Ionian Sea. While berthed in Bari, Italy, he continued to have a lively time from aerial attacks, though in one incident it came in the form of misdirected friendly fire.

Over time, Ruark experienced so many narrow escapes that when his ship eventually was struck by a torpedo, he was almost fatalistic, showing more surprise than fright. The attack came off Oran in the Mediterranean while on a trip to Malta. His convoy came under attack from Heinkel bombers carrying torpedoes. The action was winding down when Ruark's ship was struck. Amazingly, considering that the vessel carried a full load of ammunition and aviation gasoline, it did not blow up, though its deck plates popped and there were some fires. No one understood why the ship didn't explode, as other ammo ships in the convoy had gone up in spectacular fashion.

As the crippled and listing ship continued her voyage to Malta, Ruark felt more indignation than anything else. This was a trip he should not have been making. He had already far exceeded his quota of ammunition convoy duty and should have been relieved when last in Baltimore.

After the Malta adventure, Ruark was reassigned to the Pacific theatre as a gunnery officer on a troop transport ship. After landing in the Solomons, having successfully survived all sorts of enemy action, he was involved in a jeep crash. The accident threw him clear of the vehicle, and he smashed his left arm when he struck a tree. He was extremely lucky not to lose his arm, thanks to one of America's top orthopedic surgeons who was on the island and had a set of newly designed, screw-in splints. Although Ruark was left with one arm an inch shorter than the other, the reconstruction job was so successful that he was able to return to full duty nine months later.

During Ruark's lengthy convalescence, the Navy discovered that Gunnery Officer Ruark was the same man who had been writing magazine articles about the war. This led to his reassignment to press censorship on the staff of Admiral Chester W. Nimitz. Following a short stay in Hawaii, Ruark was first transferred to the forward area command of Admiral John Hoover on a seaplane tender at Saipan, then lend-leased to the marine command on Guam, sub-leased to the B-29s that were making their first strikes on Japan. He eventually wound up as liaison press censor in the Royal Navy under Admiral Sir Bruce Fraser in Australia.

Later, Ruark would jokingly boast that he was the only two-striper who ever outranked a fleet admiral, and he could and did tell the British admiral "no" on a daily basis. Ruark enjoyed this unusual situation because the British were admitted into the final months of the Pacific theatre under American supervision and because he was technically chief of joint security for the combined British-American effort there.

Towards the war's end, Ruark was stationed in Australia, and he forever talked about the wonderful time he had there. "I spent the last six months of the war delightfully surrounded by lovely Australian women, lovely Australian beer, and lovely Australian race horses," he wrote.

Although he enjoyed himself immensely while in Australia, when hostilities ceased with Japan, Ruark decided to get out of the service as quickly as possible. He wanted to get back into harness as a newspaperman and realized there would be some vacant holes in the newspapers, as the Scripps-Howard-United Feature axis had lost a whole constellation of top writers – Heywood Broun dead, Ray Clapped killed at Kwajalein, General Hugh Johnson dead, Ernie Pyle killed at Ie Shim in the final days of the war, Westbrook Pegler gone across the street to Hearst, and Mrs. Roosevelt, a not-so-hot a commodity since the President's death.

Figuring that going through normal channels would take far too long, on VJ Day Lieutenant (junior grade) Robert C. Ruark wrote himself a set of rigged orders authorizing his return to the United States. Orders automatically became effective unless rejected within 48 hours, an obvious impossibility in the hectic, disorganized situation following the war's end. Ruark obtained almost immediate air transport back to the States by wrangling the removal of a full general from the flight he wished to take. He was back in Washington within a week, where the Navy decided to take the easiest way out. They gave him a discharge instead of a court-martial.

CHAPTER 5
BELT-LEVEL JOURNALIST

During his Navy service, Ruark had written a number of magazine articles for *Collier's, Saturday Evening Post* and *Liberty*. These articles were about the war and no doubt kept him in practice, but his real thinking on the journalistic front had revolved around what strategy to employ once peace came and he was again a free agent. He figured there would be about 12 million ex-GIs as an audience, along with their wives, children and parents. Ruark decided he would speak for this broad spread of humanity, but not in Walter Lippman's lofty fashion, not in Walter Winchell's gossip vein, and not with Westbrook Pegler's anger. He would instead be a cosmic columnist, a belt-level journalist, and anything that made him mad, glad or sad was bound to appeal to a vast, belt-level audience.

So Ruark returned home from the war having decided to look for the biggest stone to throw at the biggest glass house. He soon found what he was looking for and decided his target was to be American women. As staff writer from the Scripps-Howard *Washington Daily News*, he wrote a column describing what he and other military men had returned home to find. It was entitled "Now He Wants to Go Back to the Wars."

Since I have been, from Boy Scout days, an ardent admirer of American female beauty, I am pained, as a returned serviceman, to discover I have been dead wrong. American women today are very curious looking critters – they seem to have sabotaged themselves.

During the tough months in Funa Futi of Peleiu, one of the things which made fox holes, K rations, and dysentery bearable was the thought that some day we would come home and there would be wonderful American women. So every day batches of us return. So what do we find? What we find shouldn't happen to a war criminal. Our girls, who kept our souls a-light when we were sleeping in mud or being ill on destroyers, look like something Salvador Dali might muster up after a midnight snack of Welsh rarebit with garlic.

That lovely hair we remembered curling sweetly about our ladies' shoulders; it has been tortured into two patterns, both repulsive. Either it has been snatched up in one pink fist, hauled taut with a windlass, and screwed into a silly topknot; or else it is clubbed into a nauseous bundle and hangs down the neck like a sackful of mud, or maybe a beaver's tail.

Now this is all wrong, girls. You are providing no change for us men who've been in the Pacific. The native girls in the Admiralties arrange their locks likewise. They pin their crests with shells, feathers, and grandpa's shinbone. They manage to look just like Miss Fire House No. 3, who strangles her tresses with a

rubber band and crams the overflow full of flowers, beads, and bric-a-brac. As for this business of dumping the hair into a crocus sack and letting it flap soggily down the nape, our dolls are missing a couple of tricks. As any Melanesian belle can tell you, a similar but more enduring hair-do may be achieved by daubing the strands with rancid cocoa butter and mud. Chief difference between this and the stateside cutie's locks, lathered with fixative unguents, is that it is easier to stand downwind from our dames.

Ruark continued in this delightfully disparaging vein for several more paragraphs, concluding on a particularly jarring note. "It won't be surprising if the boys start remembering Australia, England, and even Germany over fondly. Over there, at least the women look like women. Hanged if I know what our girls do look like, but whatever it is, 'tain't what we left behind in '42."

Subsequently, when someone referred to this explosive column as a piece on women's clothes, Ruark would reply: "It was not a column on women's clothes at all, but a piece on naked sex, with a twist, pointing out that women had been dressing for other women for the four years that men had been away at war."

However this column was assessed, Ruark was in business. It goaded nearly 3,000 delighted or infuriated readers, mostly feminine, to write letters to the editor. Many of the correspondents sent photographs to show that they didn't look the way Ruark described. His blast had produced the desired effect. He had been noticed. More important, Roy W. Howard, head of the Scripps-Howard newspaper chain, had telegraphed to Walker Stone, head of the Washington office:

"Please tell Robert Ruark for me that if he can keep to the line and maintain the humorous attitude attained in his story on how our gals look to returning men, he will prove God's greatest 1945 gift to Scripps-Howard circulation managers."

With this encouragement, Ruark continued to write along similar lines, and a month later Howard signed him to a contract as a syndicated columnist for the Scripps-Howard Newspaper Alliance at $15,000 a year, plus a percentage of the syndication returns. From this fine post-war start, bigger things were soon to come. In August, 1946 a deal was negotiated with United Feature Syndicate to relay Ruark's column to the open newspaper market.

Ruark always maintained that the jump from junior reporter to columnist was not a long one and that he had benefited by following an old-fashioned tenet advanced by Somerset Maugham – to write pieces that had a beginning, a middle and an end. Ruark said that a columnist is not much more than a reporter with a point of view, and to that attitude one adds a touch of special flavor, and if possible, one's own flavor.

Ruark definitely added his own flavor. A good proportion of his columns exuded a delightfully humorous and sarcastically funny trend as he surveyed the news and foibles of modern civilization, and one would come to the conclusion shared by millions of readers – the whole operation was too rich for a country boy's blood. This helped make Ruark's readership an extensive one, since so many people felt this way about their own lives and personal problems.

Ruark's column, like all good prose, appeared as if it gave him little trouble to produce. This really wasn't true, as his whole career as a columnist had been as carefully contrived as the grand strategy of a great diplomat, with its trial balloons, calculated risks and gestures toward public opinion. Ruark explained his tactical approach to his column: "I don't intend to give you any 30,000-feet-in-the-air punditing. Maybe I'll give you some labor talk on a day when they're picketing the little restaurant across the street from me, or I'll give you sports when I know something about them and a Joe DiMaggio or a World Series is in the news. But mostly I'll give you boys, girls, men, women, dogs, alligators and strip-teasers. After all, you got to remember what business you're in – and I figure my primary purpose is to sell some newspapers."

Ruark always gave the impression that writing a column was the world's easiest way to make a living, and he would frequently be approached by old acquaintances or even complete strangers who would, in the form of a salutation, say: "Hi, you old bastard. I wish I had a racket like yours!" This was said out of envy more than anything else, but Ruark's racket, while a good one, had its drawbacks.

As a columnist he soon began to realize that five columns a week consumed an incredible number of subjects, angles and approaches, similes and metaphors, and jokes. A daily output of 600-700 words per column represents a yearly count of over 160,000 words, with maybe another 100,000 expended in false starts or columns rejected by editors. This is a demanding regimen, and Ruark found it necessary to be constantly on the lookout for column ideas. In fact, much of his time was taken up by reading newspapers for ideas, running down news tips, interviewing his subjects, racking his brain, discarding bad ideas while embellishing good ones, and finally, sitting down at the typewriter.

Sometimes he would say ruefully: "The finished column never shows what has gone into it, and the business of writing one in half an hour sounds good, but it's like saying you can have a baby after half an hour on the delivery table – it's the gestation period that makes your teeth fall out."

Continuing along the same line of thought, he added: "Don't forget that all those words have got to be pleasing the Methodists, Baptists, Catholics, Negroes, Jews, Republicans, Democrats, Communists, old people, young people, Westerners, Easterners, Southerners, Texans, males, and females. They've got to be inspirational, educational, sarcastic, funny, serious, and full of zip. And they've got to get past editors who might have mortgages, ulcers, wives, labor trouble, sick children, parking tickets, and an overdraft at the bank."

Ruark would also point out that when on the road, he would work a 60-hour week just attending to such chores as catching planes, sending out laundry, riding taxis, packing and unpacking, finding hotel rooms, dining with his editors, getting passports, passing through customs, and exchanging his money on the black market . . . before he could ever get around to the business of researching and writing his column. Ruark would then complain that a terrific burden was placed on the columnist's digestive system. That was because his interviews nearly always took place in a barroom, since he insisted there was nowhere else to go.

The strain of finding timely topics and writing them up in the Ruark style, through the years, took its toll on his health. It is a great tribute to his energy and imagination that he could be so consistently amusing to so many people day after day. Ruark fully realized that there were days when a column just didn't come off, and he would rapidly disarm any critic by saying: "Naturally, there are days when the piece is no damn good and you know it, but it's the best no-good piece you could write that day. If you're a columnist who wants to be entertaining, what are you supposed to do in a week when the news is nothing but coal strikes, a steel strike, and a Senate hearing on the excess profits tax?

"Or, what do you do on a day when you've got a terrible hangover, no ideas for a three-hour editorial conference, a bad cold, mislaid notes, three of the leads you're following blow up, it's raining outside, you can't get a cab, the dog has to be taken to the veterinarian, the mortgage is due, the baby's crying and your wife breaks a leg?" Ruark loved to reel off lists of woes of this sort, never mind the fact that he had neither a mortgage nor a baby, his wife had not broken a leg, and he had never taken a dog to the vet.

Some years after these comments, in another attempt to explain the difficulties he faced as a writer, Ruark addressed the matter in a column. "To the average non-writer a writin' man is a curiosity, like a two-headed calf. Ordinary thought processes and habits are supposed to differ from those of normal people. The innermost crannies of his life are peeked at and he is supposed to have a lot of wild and colorful habits such as beard-growing, whisky-drinking, girl-chasing, and opium-eating.

"People are especially interested in how long it takes a man to do a certain chore like a column or a book or a magazine article, and they seem slightly hurt when you explain that you haven't gone without sleep or food for days. I write easy and I write fast and I don't write at all until I know beforehand what I am going to put on paper.

"Why anybody would want to be a writer I cannot say because it is the lonesomest business in the world, shut off in some bleak room with a lot of old papers and nobody to talk to. People ask you how you got into the business and I say frankly I don't know. In my case, I fell in love and went to sea and in order not to starve got a job mixing paste and running errands on the *Washington Daily News* after doing a lot of menial things in menial places. I had a wonderful teacher for three years on the *News* and I taught myself – by writing and not being able to sell anything – the trade of magazine writing, which is nearly as standardized as building a house.

"There are compensations, of course. The hours are short because a man will drain more juice out of himself in two hours at a typewriter than a ditch digger will exhaust in a day."

When he wished, Ruark was also a fine reporter, as when he filed an exclusive on the loss of the U. S. cruiser *Indianapolis* in Philippine waters. He revealed that the crew struggled helplessly for five days after the ship was sunk before rescue vessels were dispatched. He reported that there was to be a court-martial of the cruiser's skipper to fix guilt on the persons responsible for the slip-up, which needlessly cost the lives of most of the 880 men lost out of her complement of 1196. He stated that the cruiser, carrying atomic bomb material, had departed the Marianas for Leyte en route to Guam. It was torpedoed by a Japanese submarine but according to Ruark the Navy conveniently failed to mention this loss. The

The Early Years

NORTH CAROLINA SOUTHERN HISTORICAL COLLECTION, UNC – CHAPEL HILL

Young Robert Ruark, who resented the nickname Bobby, had a consuming curiosity for the out-of-doors and a passion for hunting and fishing. Interestingly, Ruark was a loner as a youngster, but as an adult he greatly enjoyed being around people. Circa 1922.

SOUTHPORT ART MUSEUM

NORTH CAROLINA SOUTHERN HISTORICAL COLLECTION, UNC – CHAPEL HILL

Ruark's grandparent's home in Southport, North Carolina, was of similar vintage to his parent's house in nearby Wilmington. Right: Ruark's grandfather, Capt. Ned Adkins, was the "Old Man" who introduced young Robert to hunting and fishing. Circa late 1920s. Adkins captained a fishing boat in the small seaport town on the banks of the Cape Fear River.

NORTH CAROLINA SOUTHERN HISTORICAL COLLECTION, UNC – CHAPEL HILL

Robert Ruark was a handsome young lieutenant in the U.S. Navy in 1944. His ships made a number of dangerous North Atlantic crossings as well as venturing into the Mediterranean. He and his shipmates survived several attacks from enemy submarines and aircraft.

NORTH CAROLINA SOUTHERN HISTORICAL COLLECTION, UNC – CHAPEL HILL

A nationally syndicated columnist, Ruark was a proud member of Pan-American's "Million Mile Club." During that era it was fashionable for airlines to photograph their more prominent travelers as they boarded overseas flights. Circa 1960.

NORTH CAROLINA SOUTHERN HISTORICAL COLLECTION, UNC – CHAPEL HILL

Ruark posed with his trusty Remington typewriter for this publicity shot in the 1950s when he was one of America's most popular – and controversial – newspaper columnists.

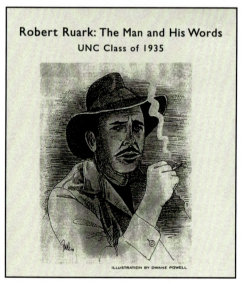

BOTH NORTH CAROLINA SOUTHERN HISTORICAL COLLECTION, UNC – CHAPEL HILL

In 1957 Robert Ruark shipped his Rolls Royce all the way from Spain for his University of North Carolina class reunion at Chapel Hill. Top: He hugs Sue Campbell Dawson, an old friend, and above, chats with an unidentified UNC fraternity brother.

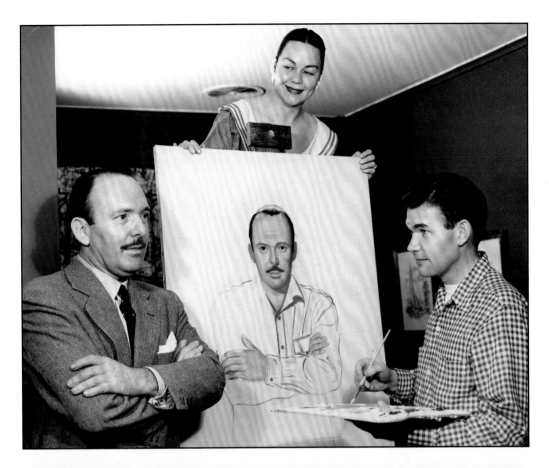

BOTH NORTH CAROLINA SOUTHERN HISTORICAL COLLECTION, UNC – CHAPEL HILL

Ruark and Ginny (next to the setter) with friends on a preserve pheasant shoot sometime in the 1950s. Top: Ruark poses for Texan Tom Lea, a prominent portraitist and author.

NORTH CAROLINA SOUTHERN HISTORICAL COLLECTION, UNC – CHAPEL HILL

Ruark frolics with a friend's gundog during a pheasant hunt in the '50s. He preferred double guns for bird hunting, whether stateside or in distant Africa.

Navy denied any attempt at a cover-up and insisted that Naval Public Relations had been attempting to release the sad story of the *Indianapolis* for a week before the Japanese surrendered in August, 1945. The Navy said the only reason the matter had been kept quiet was their inability to amass sufficient information for a press release.

Ruark insisted that he had acquired this story largely by accident, and he was called to attend the court marital and explain exactly what happened. The Japanese submarine commander responsible for the sinking of the *Indianapolis* was also called to give evidence. Ruark considered all of this highly unusual for a court martial, and of course, this made for powerful copy.

His next journalistic coup centered on the gangster Charles "Lucky" Luciano's connection with the narcotics and prostitution rackets. This came about when he ran into a summit meeting of the mob while in Havana. Luciano, who earned his nickname because of his ability to stay alive in an extremely dangerous vocation, had recently been released after serving 10 years of a 30- to 50-year jail sentence. He supposedly had been deported to his native Italy.

Ruark's story brought his presence in Havana to light and thereby upset any future plans the mobster might have had for operating from Cuba. As a result of this exposé, the Cuban government deported Luciano to Italy. This came about as the result of pressure from the U.S. Bureau of Narcotics, which notified Cuban authorities that as long as Lucky Luciano was on the loose, there would be no shipment of narcotics for medical use to Cuba.

The story caused a considerable amount of embarrassment to Thomas E. Dewey, who was then the governor of New York. He had been involved in Luciano's release, and the shortening of his jail sentence was never satisfactorily explained. One theory bandied about in the press suggested that Luciano, while being held in Sing Sing Prison during the war, had been helpful to military authorities through his knowledge of the Sicilian and Italian coasts. Supposedly his information had been of considerable assistance in planning invasion landings, and there was even some discussion of considering him for a medal. Ruark dug around and found this information to be completely without foundation. He considered it a clever public relations ploy meant to improve Luciano's image so that he could re-enter the United States.

An additional fillet to his Luciano story was that Ruark reported the presence of singer Frank Sinatra in Cuba. He found that Sinatra had had social contact with Luciano and his friends and made the point that a popular public figure should be more careful in choosing associates. Outraged by Ruark's story, Sinatra said: "I was brought up to shake a man's hand when I am introduced to him without first investigating his past. Any report that I fraternized with goons and racketeers is a vicious lie."

For a long time thereafter Ruark wouldn't leave Sinatra alone. He wrote a number of heavily critical columns focusing on him. This caused considerable uproar, and matters even went so far that some 300 ladies who were fans of Sinatra wrote to Ruark from the home for the elderly where they lived.

"Dear Mr. Ruark:

"Our only real pleasure for the past five years has been listening to the songs of Frank Sinatra. You, in your mean, lying way, have decided to destroy his career. Many of our friends have powerful connections and while we have no column to answer your infamous lies, we have our religion.

"Each night in chapel we have evening prayers and we now pray, 300 of us, that God will bring sorrow, destruction, and eternal torture to you and others like you. Each week for the next five years we will write to you and keep you informed on our continued prayers for your destruction.

"We know it (your attack on Sinatra) is a Republican campaign, but God ignores campaigns. Expect to hear from us weekly and remember, when sorrow strikes, it is the answer to our prayers. The 300."

In response, Ruark initially treated the message from the harpies as a joke. He wrote that while he had noticed a change for the worse in his general affairs, he was having headaches and the flu regularly, and Mrs. Ruark had fallen into the fireplace. Somehow he was managing to get by. When he was next scheduled to take a plane trip, Ruark took a different tack. He penned an open letter to the old ladies, asking for a truce. He pointed out that he didn't think their voodoo exercises were fair to his fellow passengers. Ruark promised to make amends in the future and offered to help them all get jobs in road companies producing "Arsenic and Old Lace," a play that was popular at the time. Later, he would joke that his peace offer must have been accepted as he had flown on a number of foreign airlines, traveled on Arab trains, and eaten Arab food without anything bad happening to him.

Once he discovered Lucky Luciano, it seemed for a time that Ruark could not get away from the topic. He clearly played the key role in the gangster's deportation from Cuba in the spring of 1947, and it was something of a shock, six months later, to find himself sharing a hotel in Capri with Luciano and his entourage. This happened when Ruark was taking some time off from a reporting trip through Europe, and during a visit to Naples he decided to cross to the Mediterranean island. Ruark would later comment that they were practically cell mates in the Hotel Quisisana. They bumped into one another on the beach, and Ruark kept finding the gangster and his armed bodyguards seated at the table next to him in the hotel's restaurant. He admitted that while he was curious to know more about Lucky's doings, he lacked sufficient courage to approach him for any further information. "I didn't wish to spoil the gangster's fun in Capri, and I didn't want to spoil mine either."

This somewhat nerve-wracking encounter notwithstanding, Ruark stayed on the warpath and displayed an uncanny knack for unearthing high-powered stories. He had taken on a reporting mission that involved following the trail blazed by GIs in North Africa, Italy and the rest of Europe during the latter stages of World War II. His itinerary included Gibraltar, Casablanca, Marrakech, Rabat, Algiers, Tunis, Bizerte, Sfax, Bari, Trieste, Rome, Naples, Madrid, Marseilles, Paris and London. His plan was to report on the feel and atmosphere of those places now that American soldiers had departed. He did some fine early reporting and was rambling around looking for additional pieces when he uncovered the sorry state of the GIs still stationed in Italy under the command of Lt. General John C. H. Lee.

Ruark alleged that officers were enjoying excessive luxuries while enlisted men in the U. S. Army received unfair, intolerable treatment. He reported that some GIs were being treated almost like slaves and recounted outrageous violations of personal integrity, brutality and general misuse of the privileges of rank. He charged that living conditions were shocking, with enlisted men being ill-housed and poorly fed while being used as flunkeys, servants and helpless targets of officer conceit. Ruark further charged that there were abuses in rank and that Lee's command was so salute crazy that GIs were required to salute officers at distances of 100 yards.

He reported that there had been and continued to be waste of taxpayer money, saying that General Lee operated a sumptuously equipped private train with lounge, sleeper and dining cars, not to mention one to carry his Cadillac. Also at the General's disposal was a $14,000 trailer, and he maintained permanent suites in Rome, Florence and Viareggio. In one of his many critical reports, Ruark wrote: "I don't know whether General Lee or his gabbling flock of tame colonels write the rules, but as Emperor of the area he has to hold still for the rap. It may be an army that General Lee is running, but to me it looks more like a combination of junket, political shakedown, misuse of government material, maltreatment of subordinates and a happy hunting ground for desk-bound brass which spent most of its war at home and is now trying to embalm its rank abroad."

Ruark's scathing columns were accompanied by equally telling headlines on the front pages of national newspapers. Among them were "Ruark Exposes GI Slavery Under Army Brass in Italy," "Ruark Reveals Salute-Crazy Brass Uses GIs in Italy as Nursemaids," "General Lee's Whims Expensive" and "Inquiry Promised on Gen. Lee."

Various aspects of the story kept Ruark on front pages for weeks, and he became a news topic in his own right. In order to enable opposition press and news services to cover Ruark, the Army laid on special aircraft and transport. He was the ultimate authority on the unfolding story and maintained he had more unpaid spies than the CIA.

Ruark always claimed that the Lee story was the best one he ever covered, and he kept it going with a battery of blistering reports. "In those days," he said, "I could use gin as a substitute for slumber, and on the second phase of the Lee story I actually wrote 16 long columns at a sitting, as I had a lot I wanted to say."

Ruark's incessant criticism of Lee and his Mediterranean Theater Command eventually produced significant action. General Dwight Eisenhower ordered a full investigation and dispatched the U. S. Army Inspector General, Major General Ira T. Wyche, to conduct the inquiry.

General Lee, who came to be widely known by the derisive nickname of "Courthouse" Lee, retired shortly after completion of the investigation. It was widely assumed he did so because of Ruark's accusations, though in reality, Lee had requested permission to retire six months before Ruark began reporting on his activities. Some also suggested that Ruark had gone too far in his criticism and that his aim had not been truth and just for the common soldier but cheap sensationalism. In fact, General Lee himself branded the stories as slanted and demanded an investigation of Ruark's reporting.

When the investigation of Lee finally got underway, Ruark claimed it was apparent that changes and improvements had already been made. The investigators, however, found that he had given a wholly erroneous picture of conditions in Italy. They completely exonerated General Lee and, in a 12,000-word report, Major General Wyche dismissed Ruark's charges as "Half facts, rumors, and untruths." Scripps-Howard newspapers defended their star reporter and branded Wyche's findings "a masterpiece of double-talk and an obvious fulfillment of the urge to whitewash."

In reality, the evidence for the authenticity of Ruark's charges was overwhelming. Letters from serving GIs confirming the truth of what had been printed poured into Scripps-Howard newspapers, and there were even letters from veteran officers and former GIs listing old criticisms of Gen. Lee.

Ruark went to considerable lengths in responding to the Army report of Major General Wyche. He pointed out that far from breezing into Italy and right out again, he spent a total of six weeks, on two separate visits, investigating and confirming his information. He pointed out that his initial three-week visit produced a total of 17 columns, then added he didn't believe that even a genius could haul that much copy out of thin air. Ruark also disclosed that three weeks before publication of his findings, he cross-checked his information with some of General Lee's officers who were aware of what he intended to do. They were unable to find any factual fault with his material.

In response to the formal Army report, Ruark wrote: "Possibly I was naïve to expect anything other than an attempted whitewash of the inquiry into Lt. Gen. Courthouse Lee's Mediterranean theater. No mouse, to my knowledge, ever successfully investigated a cat." That was pretty much where the matter rested, except that by complete coincidence, the same newspaper page that carried this piece contained a story headlined "Mouse Traps Cat!" It was a story of a cat that had chased a mouse behind a kitchen sink and got stuck, necessitating removal of some wood in order to free the feline.

Two months after having stirred up the hoorah's nest, Ruark offered his final newspaper words on the matter. "Left-handedly, in Gen. Wyche's pitiful effort to sidestep the truth, all the charges have stood up. General Eisenhower's separate report knocks the Wyche report cranksided. Even if that had not occurred, General Wyche's own report unwillingly bore me out. As far as I'm concerned, the case rests."

Thus did matters stand for a few months. Then, in the December, 1947 issue of *True* magazine, Ruark recapped the whole business in "The Bitter Pork of General Lee." Ruark had found it necessary to defend himself against accusations made by officers in Lee's command, who had branded his reporting as that of "a communist, a liar, and a traitor." Ruark sardonically explained that in fact it was the fat, greasy pork he was served in the GI mess hall on a summer day when the temperature was 95 degrees that had sparked his investigation. His final paragraph read: "A plate of fat pork, eaten at a 95-degree temperature, is a powerful thing sometimes. I can cite at least one instance in which it turned an Army upside down."

From this point forward Ruark was a hot commodity, and he kept the literary fires well stoked, coming out against almost everything – motherhood, Southern cooking, Texans, dogs, modern art and psychiatrists. He was acclaimed by *Time* magazine as the country's fastest climbing columnist. Full-page advertisements in the *New York World Telegram* proclaimed that "Rambunctious Robert Rides Again," and his name in large letters, accompanied by his photograph, was carried on the side-boards of the Scripps-Howard newspaper delivery vans.

In various write-ups Ruark was declared to be the "Great American Common Denominator" and the "Real Voice of America." It was suggested that any foreigner seeking to fathom the mysteries and inconsistencies of the American mass mind could learn more from reading Ruark than he could from all the canned propaganda that ever came out of Washington.

Ruark continued to write his daily column in deliberately colloquial language, and he became a master of wild similes and the casual rape of grammar, the colorful verb and the humorous twist on old clichés. Yet his buffoonery was an extremely artful thing. He felt the trick to writing columns was to craft pieces in which you felt the same way countless readers felt. He maintained it was only necessary to take a crack at one little thing to gain millions of followers, provided you had crystallized for them something they had been thinking about but had been unable to express for themselves. You suddenly found that you had both millions of admirers and millions of passionate objectors hanging onto your paragraphs. Admirers plus violent objectors spelled readers for Ruark at one point in his career

The United Feature Syndicate calculated that Ruark had at least 15 million daily readers at one point in his career. Ruark, for his part, called himself lucky in journalism. When giving advice to young hopefuls he would say: "There is no substitute for luck in this business. You can have talent and be a great writer, but if don't have luck you might as well drop dead!"

Ruark was never considered an intellectual columnist or an astute analyst; rather, he was really a terrific everyday humorist. His theory on column writing was that "kidding" is fun not only for the "kidder" but that it sometimes prevents those in high places from taking themselves too seriously. He would then say about himself: "You show me a guy who writes a column or book and ain't a ham and I'll show you a bad writer. Man, I'm ham inside, outside and all around. I'm a dissenter, too, but I'm a pretty ordinary hack, and also a political eunuch, and I don't evaluate myself as a heavy thinker."

After several years of success as a columnist, Ruark asked his readers to submit a letter of 50 words or less concerning what they liked best about him. The winning letter summed up Ruark quite nicely. "I like Ruark's column. Typically unorthodox, Ruark will hunt lions one day and lampoon a deserving senator the next, employing always a clean, candid humor foreign to competing bylines. No salvist is Ruark. Somehow your indignities become his wounds, your thoughts his campaigns. He is you and me, in print."

Periodically Ruark would take off on trips around the country, when he would receive considerable advance publicity from his syndicated newspapers. Although he liked the reporter's life and was happy when on the road, sometimes he returned displeased with what he had done. On one occasion after a three-week reporting jaunt, he remarked: "I guess I'm just not the Ernie Pyle type. I'd rather stay in New York and sneer."

Ruark continued to sneer in every direction, and one morning, after noticing an excessive number of rude and critical fan letters, he was pleased to find a friendly message. This was in answer to a column questioning the sanctity of baseball as an institution. He read the letter, which was in complete agreement with his column and concluded with the remark: "Nobody ever wrote a column better than you."

Ruark started to say that here was a man who would go far, and was about to dictate a letter of thanks when he read the postscript: "The above was written by a mental patient at St. Elizabeth's Hospital, Washington, D. C. He is a great baseball fan and I am glad he took an interest in your column. I am his nurse. As things are, he hasn't been able to find anyone else who agrees with him on any sports question except you. I really appreciate his believing in your column, as it is the first column that any person has ever read to him that he agreed with. Thank you."

Sometimes Ruark attended to fan mail, but as a rule his answers were short and to the point, such as when he replied to a critical letter from an army corporal: "Received your letter and judging by what you have written, I'm betting you never make sergeant."

Ruark's fan mail at this time was a cross-section of every possible reaction, but the trend was that he was generally considered a top columnist. Among many letters-to-editors was the following: "You ought to put Ruark's column on the front page in ten-point, bold-face type with boldest headlines. There is more hard practical common sense in his writing than in most of the editorials and mouthings of the politicians – and withal, Ruark writes so entertainingly."

Then, from a less appreciative reader: "You damned bastard communist son of a bitch. You are pleased with yourself now, but wait!" Ruark received many unfriendly messages and was called, among other things, a race-baiter, a fascist, a warmonger, a draft dodger, a horse hater, a war criminal, a heel, a wife-beater, a moron, a sadist and a throwback to the Dark Ages. Complaining or otherwise, they were all readers.

CHAPTER 6
FIRST FOOTSTEPS IN AFRICA

Along with his newspaper work, Ruark was a prolific contributor to magazines. Throughout most of his career he averaged at least a dozen full-scale magazine articles a year. Amongst this impressive output during the immediate post-war years were two biographical pieces on Margaret Mitchell, the author of *Gone with the Wind*, for *McCall's*; a piece on actor Paul Douglas for *Collier's*; a profile of financial wizard and political figure Bernard Baruch for *Flair*; and an assortment of articles for *Esquire, Look* and *American* attacking women. The latter pieces carried intriguing titles such as "What Hath God Wrought?," "Mystery Unincorporated," "Cupid Has Two Heads," "I'm Tired of Women's Problems" and "My War with the Women."

There were also special studies on things such as leprosy, critical pieces on the average American (entitled "Portrait of Joe" and Portrait of Mabel") for *Esquire*, a lengthy two-piece profile on Baruch entitled "Prophet without Portfolio," and a pair of descriptive pieces on European cities, "Mistress Paris" and "Rome Was Never Like This." He profiled singer Lena Horne in "Lady in a High Key" and wrote about Texas in "Even the Midgets Stand Six Feet Tall." There was his account of a trip to Hawaii, "Report on Paradise," for *True* magazine, and much more.

Gradually Ruark took on more and more work, and by 1952 it is difficult to see how he kept pace with his increased commitments. In that year alone he wrote more than 20 magazine features, was twice in Africa and Europe, and for good measure wrote a 300-page safari novel, *Horn of the Hunter*, which he personally illustrated with two dozen sketches of animal and camp life. All of this was on top of his customary five newspaper columns a week!

Still, the most important development on the magazine front, and arguably one of the two or three most significant in Ruark's career, came in 1951 when he began writing for *Field & Stream* magazine. His early contributions to this major outdoor publication focused on quail hunting and waterfowling in America, along with hunting in Australia, but later features would include experiences in Africa, India, Alaska, Spain and Scotland. These were really only a forerunner of things to come. Once his "Old Man and the Boy" pieces started to appear in *Field & Stream* in 1953, his total number of magazine pieces annually would top the 30 mark. There was always a book in production and a trip to make, and the later books were as much as five times longer than the safari book written in 1952.

During the summer of 1951 Ruark realized a boyhood dream when he arranged his first African safari. He had to take a bank overdraft to do so, but these first footsteps in Africa would be a career-changing experience.

Although he had many offers of company, he decided that on this initial safari he would take nobody except his wife, Virginia, accompanied of course by the white hunter and the African boys. The safari was outfitted by Ker & Downey Safaris and this was when Ruark first met Harry Selby, the white hunter about whom he later wrote extensively.

On Ruark's return to New York he explained that he had spent the two happiest months of his life in the bush of British East Africa. For a man with Ruark's outlook, it was impossible not to write about the experience. So he wrote a batch of magazine articles describing at length the wonderful life in the African bush, and the trip furnished the basis for *Horn of the Hunter*. The book was actually finished the following year while Ruark was on a boat once more en route to Africa.

Ruark's second visit was a carefully organized affair. Apart from a burning desire to get back to Africa, he had decided to make a film about safari life. He took Chester Kronfeld, an experienced photographer, with him, and with the help of his white hunters made a fascinating pictorial record of safari. The footage includes many exciting big game hunting sequences. With Ruark himself as the star, this documentary, called *Africa Adventure,* was later described as being "free of hokum, with no fraud and no heroes, but a movie of what you might see if you were lucky enough to get to Africa."

Ruark had traveled by boat to Genoa and then, applying his instinctive feel for pending events, he stopped in Egypt on his way south. He was in Egypt when King Farouk was thrown out of his country. Ruark spent a week with the new head of state, Mohammed Naguid, all the while expecting to be handed a bomb by mistake. This gave him material for a number of newspaper columns and magazine articles.

Continuing his wondrous time of lucky reporting, that same week Ruark was present for the discovery of a new pyramid and a long lost Egyptian queen. This was in company with Dr. Ahmed Fakhry, Egypt's leading archaeologist, and the findings made an interesting piece for *Collier's,* which was entitled "Date with a Dame – Age 5,000." As it turned out, the Dame was a nude Egyptian dancing girl, a fact that tickled Ruark's fancy. He likened the discovery to "having a date with a lady of easy virtue who practiced her ancient profession 5,000 years ago."

Upon reaching Kenya a couple of weeks later, Ruark found himself surrounded by endless possibilities for his ability as a reporter. The first of the Mau Mau kills were taking place, and he immediately hammered out a rush article for *Life* magazine, which he called "Your Guns Go with You." The title was a literal one, and supporting photography showed a Kenyan farmer taking a bath with his pistol resting atop the soap dish, ready for immediate use. Ruark's presence in Africa at this juncture was probably the luckiest thing that ever happened to him. The Mau Mau emergency would become the basis for his first big best-seller, which was written the following year.

Ruark's success continued unabated. By the early 1950s his popular syndicated column reached nearly 200 newspapers across the country, his articles were appearing in all the slick, general readership magazines, and his hunting stories graced the pages of outdoor publications. He had become a subject of interest to other writers, and there were profiles of him in *Life, Redbook, Pic* and *Cue*. Appearances on radio and television became standard fare; he received regular requests for commercial testimonials and to go on the lecture circuit, he had five novels to his name as well as an unsuccessful musical play; and he was living life at a frenetic pace. This meant a luxuriously appointed penthouse apartment on Fifth Avenue, an attractive and talented wife, two pedigree dogs, a maid and a valet, a whole host of friends and a thousand ideas for new projects. All of this was linked to a yearly income topping the $100,000 mark.

To the average onlooker, these signs of success would have appeared to be more than sufficient for a life of great contentment – but this was not the way Robert Ruark felt. There was a problem – New York. It may well be that the hurly-burly of the city had always presented issues for Ruark, but it is quite clear that his exposure to Africa made a deep, lasting impact on him. This process of self-discovery was outlined in a piece for *Esquire* written immediately after his first safari in Kenya. He entitled it "The First Time I Saw God" and in the article explained quite clearly how he had been affected by his African experience.

From the conclusion of his initial safari onward, Ruark's general discontent with New York gradually increased to the boiling point. He debated the advisability of making a permanent home outside the United States, and initially Nairobi ranked high on his list of preferred places to relocate. With the Mau Mau insurrection in Kenya, though, it became obvious this would not be a wise move. Eventually, Ruark decided that a permanent residence in Italy might be suitable, and he selected Rome as his home base.

While these thoughts ran through Ruark's mind, at the beginning of 1953 he was once again off to East Africa. While there, he came to the irrevocable conclusion that he had to get out of New York City as a place of permanent residence. Once he returned from safari the tie was severed, and in the spring of that year he turned his back on the United States and took off for Europe. He subsequently wrote a piece for *Reader's Digest* explaining fully the reasons for his departure. The title he chose, "Good-bye, New York!," made his point all too painfully clear.

"It was a good job," he wrote, "$65,000 a year for writing five short columns a week about anything that crossed my thoughts. I had nearly 200 newspapers and my contract still had five years to run." But, as he pointedly stated, "there was only one trouble – the job was located in New York."

He frankly acknowledged being "neurotic about New York. Nobody I knew was happy in the city any more. Nobody smiled. Everybody complained – about the heat, the cold, the dirt, the noise; about the parking problem, the rising cost of living, politics. People spent most of their time trying to get away from the city and the rest of the time cursing the necessity of coming back. Every time I went to one of those damned standarounds, as Pa called cocktail parties, I got madder. New York had lost its glamour for a country boy."

Ruark found his average day to be telephones, appointments and invitations he couldn't duck. "As a writin' man I never seemed to have time to write until everybody else was in bed. My face was settling into the same constant frown I saw on people on the streets. I was building a bad disposition that operated the whole time I was in New York." He increasingly found that he was happy only when he got away from the city.

He frankly admitted "the column showed it, too. I was getting less and less patient with humanity, and increasingly less humorous. I looked at the semi-hysteria around me and got scared." Still, Ruark admitted that "New York had been very kind to me. By all the hallmarks of the New Yorker I was a howling success. We lived in a penthouse and Mama had her mink. Billingsley [*Editors Note:* Sherman Billingsley, the founder of the premier gathering spot for New York's rich and famous] sent me free champagne from the Stork Club. I knew everybody from Bernie Baruch to Frank Costello. But I couldn't stand it any longer."

Ruark, in customary fashion, found an ironic twist to his changed perspective on New York. "I blame one man more than any other for sowing the seeds of discontent that led me to what I call freedom and the right to go anywhere, any time, without consulting anybody. That man is a Texan named Tom Lea, a painter and author of two fine books, *The Brave Bulls* and *The Wonderful Country*. Ruark described Lea as "a shortish, slightly bow-legged, typical Texan, except for shyness. He lives on a hillside with his wife, son, and indeterminate dog. He paints hard while the light lasts, in his back-yard studio, and then he writes. Afterward he sits on the porch with friends in the cool of the evening and looks at his mountain. He is serene, enthusiastic, and the happiest man I ever knew.

Tom and I had sat, jabbering. I was talking to him about Africa, and he was telling me about the Southwest and why he loved it. I guess I was waving my hands some when I started to talk about columning and editors and speeches and barnstorming trips. He looked at me a long time and said a short sentence.

"You poor, poor S. O. B.," he said softly. "How I pity you."

It had not occurred to me that I was a poor anything. I had thought I was pretty hot stuff – but sad, I suddenly thought.

"Why don't you quit that rat race before it quits you?" he said. "Money ain't very important. What the government doesn't take you spend trying to live up to the other people. Be a smart boy and kick it before it kicks you."

Later that year I went out to Africa, to Kenya, which I love. There is no place I know so beautiful as East Africa. Its trees and flowers and mountains and animals are lovely, and its peace is sublime. You eat like a starved hyena, and you sleep deeply and without dreams. There is an acute consciousness of God in the African bush, which is largely obscured in the hustle of man-made cities. You cannot see an elephant standing in an acacia grove or an impala leaping high into the bright sunlight against the cool green grass without becoming reverent.

Reverence was a feeling I had never enjoyed in New York. I had not enjoyed it since I was a kid in Carolina, off with a dog or a boat, or as a Navy man at sea, with a chance to think and look and marvel.

Each day the thought of going back to the grinding crush became more unbearable. Each day Tom Lea's quiet accusation came into my head. And each day I asked myself: Dare I give up a job most newspapermen would give an arm for?

This thing hammered me all the way home. On the plane – from Nairobi to Addis to Cairo to Rome to Paris to Shannon to Gander to New York – it beat on my brain. At the airport I crawled into the car and fought the traffic and smelled its stink. By the time I hit my penthouse I had made my decision.

After nearly 20 years in the same firm, I quit. I quit on a little money and some prospects. I had already told Mama that she had better prepare for poverty. Mama said she married me on $25 a week, so poverty wouldn't be anything new.

But there was a sick feeling in my guts, a search in my soul, when I walked out of the office with all my bridges burnt. Twenty years tossed away, against almost everyone's advice. I got home, feeling sicker and scareder. I didn't know where I was going. I decided to point in the general direction of Spain.

It is peculiar what can happen to a man when he fights a decision and then makes it. Larry Rutman of United Feature Syndicate called me the next day and said he would be happy to continue the column on a three-a-week basis, from wherever I wanted to be.

Then people in the magazine and book business started calling up and hurling work at me – enough to keep me busy for the rest of my life.

Then the doctor called. For two years I had been sweating out a disorder, which was supposed to kill me in three years. "You won't believe this," he said, "but by some miracle you are now a candidate to live to be ninety. Congratulations!"

Ruark's story in *Reader's Digest* initiated a general outcry and heavy criticism from all directions, including articles headed "Good-Bye, Mr. Ruark!" But nobody seemed to touch on the real reason for the Ruarks' departure. Despite his large annual income, the accounts just didn't balance in the Ruark household. There was a deficit year after year, and a large degree of his desire to leave the United States stemmed from the tax advantage that would result if foreign residence was established.

In order to become bona fide residents abroad, the Ruarks terminated the lease on their Fifth Avenue penthouse and leased an apartment in a villa just outside Rome. Their furniture was shipped to Genoa, a definite indication of their intention to leave. Ruark explained to everyone that he was not taking advantage of 18 months continuous absence from the United States to enjoy tax breaks the way some movie stars did. Rather, he had left the country to reside abroad permanently.

Ruark joined the local press club in Rome and obtained Italian and international driving licenses. He began to refer to himself as a "pretty well established bona fide fugitive." At the same time he made sure that no one could doubt his intention to live abroad. He wrote to some of his clubs requesting to change his status to that of a permanent, non-resident member. He belonged to many clubs but figured that advice to five key clubs – the National Press Club in Washington and Sigma Delta Chi, Dutch Treat Club, Skeeters and Chuck Wagon Glee Club, all in New York – would be sufficient.

This change of domicile enabled Ruark to exclude his gross income earnings from sources outside the United States, and there were many other tax advantages as well. Even later, when limits on the foreign earned income exclusion were included in the tax code, it was financially advantageous to live abroad. But under his new tax status, Ruark did have to be careful that his visits to the United States were not too long and that he did no actual writing while there. So when he returned for the first time in December, 1954, he arrived with a big backlog of columns. These would cover him for at least a two-month period, and he went off to Cuba for a spell when additional columns were required.

As it developed, Ruark's Italian residence was never really established. He stayed in Rome only long enough to buy a Studebaker Champion automobile, then headed to Spain where he had rented Madeleine Carrol's castle, located just outside the small fishing village of Palamos on the Costa Brava, for the summer. Ruark made the thousand-mile journey in two days and turned up at what he thought was the property he had rented. Arriving at the end of a long driveway he met a gardener and asked to be shown to the Castillo Magdelena. The gardener seemed to explain that the property was farther along the coast and that Ruark had taken the wrong entrance, but Ruark had difficulty understanding him. Possibly in his tired condition, he was not paying too much attention. He just assumed the gardener was speaking Catalan. It turned out that the "gardener" was actually a Scotsman from Glasgow who owned the large property Ruark had entered. When the misunderstanding was cleared up, Ruark was asked in for a much-needed whisky, and the two became good friends.

Soon after arriving in his new country of residence, Ruark reaffirmed his intent to reside abroad by accrediting himself to the Spanish Press Department. He had burnt his bridges, and as he settled down to work he looked around him and liked what he saw. He later explained his impressions in some detail:

Shortly Mama, the dogs, the piano, the books, the furniture, the clothes – everything I owned – landed in Barcelona. I took a house in Spain for the summer. It is lovely here, with the pines growing down to the sea. There are no telephones, no taxis, no television, no dirt, no hustle. Everybody in my little fishing town smiles at me and Mama and smiles at the dogs. It is nice to get up in the morning.

I have been working harder at what I like to do, which is write and read, than ever before in my life. This is because now I have the time – time untainted by the rat race of metropolitan existence. I also have time to sit in the sun and think, especially after lunch at siesta time.

All this makes me a happy man, and a rich man in the Tom Lea sense, because I am fettered by no chains not of my own welding.

Here I can contemplate the folly of the young who make big cities their mecca. There's a glitter about the city all right but it is phosphorescence like that of a dead fish – and there's a bad smell around. There's lots to be done in the small towns and on the farms where there's more fun to be had and more time to live. To trade space and neighbors and real leisure and maybe a fishin' hole and green acres for the ulcer-making goose step of overcrowded cities is from where I sit sheer nonsense.

People keep writing me and asking when am I coming home? Well, here in Spain is home. Southport, N. C. is home. Washington and New York and Sydney and London and Nairobi and Paris and Rome are home. I have a simple answer. To me, today, the whole wide world is home, and I like it!

CHAPTER 7
RITCHIE JOINS RUARK

Just over three years before Ruark arrived in Spain, I made similar decisions and found my way to the same Mediterranean Catalan coastal town of Palamos. I had also escaped from a big city, though in my case it was London. My reasons for departure differed from those of Ruark because my circumstances were quite different. Nevertheless, I was running away from the overall problem of big city life. I had come to Spain in order to join the staff of a cork manufacturing company, and now, thinking back over the 20 years I have lived here, I remember well my arrival and feelings. I had traveled by train from London via Paris and arrived in the Spanish border town of Port Bou. Inquiring why an express train could not continue another hundred miles to reach its destination of Barcelona, I was told that the Spanish rail gauge was different from that in France, the Spanish being over nine inches wider.

This was my first realization of just how different Spain was in the days prior to the tourist invasion. I was soon to have a further awakening. Between misinformation and my own miscalculation, I managed to miss my train stop. I was eating lunch in the dining car when I should have been getting off the train. My destination was a small town called Flassa, and as the train was running late, I was uncertain about the exact arrival time. I made repeated inquiries and the invariable response was: "Don't preoccupy yourself. There is plenty of time."

Despite the many assurances, I became impatient to leave the dining car and return to my compartment and baggage. As I did so a tiny sign appeared – Flassa – and the train slowed down. Settling my bill in a scramble, I rushed along the corridor of the train. I never stood a chance. Within a few minutes the train started moving, and so I had missed my stop. Rather stupid of course, but I hadn't begun to realize that I had come to a country where the people had very little idea of time.

Getting off at the next stop, Gerona, I found an ancient coke-burning taxi and retraced my steps about twenty kilometers to Flassa. There, I boarded a 19th-century miniature steam train with quaint wooden carriages. I hadn't asked how long it took to get to Palamos, a distance of about thirty kilometers, though after three hours or so it didn't seem to matter much. It was a fascinating journey with everybody carrying live chickens and eating oranges, and for the entire trip I was the center of attention as apparently foreigners hadn't come that way before.

Alighting stiffly from this wonderful but extremely uncomfortable train at the crossroads of Palamos, I could see very clearly what I had come to. Here was a primitive, falling down, unpainted, undeveloped, delightful little fishing town with some cork factories in the background. I at once thought this was a peaceful place to be as there was only a little horse-drawn traffic and no motor vehicles at all.

As I looked about me a small boy appeared with a luggage trolley. He seemed to know where I wanted to go, so I followed him down the main street. I soon became increasingly self-conscious as everyone was taking a special look at me, peering out of their doors and peeping out of their windows. I suppose I must have been quite noticeable, as I had come directly from London and was dressed accordingly – black pin-stripe suit, black shoes, white shirt and grey tie, black Anthony Eden homburg, black umbrella and briefcase. I also sported an enormous mustache, which I soon removed as I didn't want to be so conspicuous.

I gradually adjusted to local customs and accepted the *mañana* attitude, fitting comfortably into the slower tempo of daily life. I preferred the more casual approach to one's leisure hours and enjoyed the continental-type cafes with their chairs and tables spilling across the sidewalk. I liked Spanish food and wine, siestas and the long midday break. Then there was the Catalan dance called the *sardana*, which was often performed in the middle of the roadway irrespective of passing traffic. I liked everything that was different from anything I had known in my native country. There were some things that I didn't care for, such as bullfighting, and I found the lack of good communications, primitive public transport, and bad, pot-holed roads to be most irritating. But the few dislikes were fully compensated for by real sunshine and friendly people.

This was the Spain I found in February, 1950, and this was the Spain Robert Ruark found a little later. Both of us liked it and decided to stay and enjoy the country. So I suppose somehow we were destined to meet, which we did by complete chance in the summer of 1953. By this time I had become dissatisfied with my job and was anxious to make a change though I was reluctant to leave the area. I had decided I would face the problem later and in the meantime stay to enjoy the summer. It was at this point I had a chance meeting with this distinguished expatriate from New York.

For the first time in my working years I could stop looking for another job. By sheer chance I had met the well-known American author and columnist, Robert Ruark, and was being offered the position of private secretary. This came about as the result of an introduction by someone with whom I had only just become acquainted, thanks to a chance meeting in the local garage. As a result I was invited to visit a large property on the coast for lunch one Sunday morning in August, 1953. Following the instructions I had been given, I drove down a long private roadway leading to a stately courtyard. As I casually parked my rusty Spanish bicycle alongside highly polished, chauffeur-driven Rolls Royces and Bentleys, little did I realize that my future was about to take an interesting, unusual turn.

There had been a luncheon party of about 20 people, and after lunch we joined a large group of strangers gathered in the square of a nearby village to watch the folkloric Sardana dance. I found myself seated next to Robert Ruark, who turned to me without knowing who I was or what I did and said: "You're English, aren't you? Do you think it would be difficult for me to find an English male secretary? I'm starting this Mau Mau book and will need some help."

I was extremely quick with my reply. "No, not at all difficult," I said. "Will I do?"

There was some discussion, and I was employed more or less on the spot. So started 12 years of a fascinating association with the most wonderful employer and friend.

My association with Robert Ruark was a close one for all the years I was employed by him, but it did dwindle a little towards the end. I lost him to some extent in a confused haze of alcohol and women, and I think a similar thing happened with most of the friends who knew him well.

CHAPTER 8
PUTTING DOWN ROOTS IN SPAIN

On the day I commenced working for the Ruarks, I arrived at the Castillo Magdelena where Bob and his wife, Virginia, were living for the summer of 1953. I proceeded somewhat nervously to enter the large foyer of this magnificent home, nervous because I had already heard the thunderous barking of a dog and then was practically overwhelmed by a large, ugly boxer and a very large, vicious poodle. Or so I thought at the time. These animals quickly became two of my better friends and of course were Schnorkel and Miss Mamselle. Virginia, who soon informed me that everyone else called her Ginny, appeared almost immediately and came to my rescue. She assured me they didn't bite, at least not much, and would I please come in.

Castillo Magdelena was built by Madeleine Carroll, the British movie star, shortly after the war. As I entered its enormous baronial hall, which served as the living room, I thought it a fitting home for these two wild dogs and Bob and Ginny Ruark. They seemed a suitable couple to live in a castle.

Ginny told me that "Bobby" would soon be down and offered me a cup of coffee while I waited. After a short while there was a sliding and slipping sound, then a crash, followed by loud, rude curses about living in a something castle. This was followed by a short silence then another sliding and slipping sound, another loud crash, and further profanity. Bob appeared, apologizing for anything I may have overhead. Later, I would come to realize that this was a regular occurrence. It happened almost every time he came down from his bedroom. He could not safely negotiate the two highly polished circular staircases, and it was really a miracle that he didn't do himself some serious damage.

Bob and I got down to work at once. He hadn't had a secretary since he left New York six months previously, and he was impatient to send out proper letters. He didn't know how he had survived, explaining that he had written magazine articles, the monthly *Field & Stream* column, five pieces a week for the United Feature Syndicate and Scripps-Howard Newspapers, not to mention travels to Rome, Germany and London, along with a month in Tangier (where he wrote articles about the French Foreign Legion). The latter trip had been necessary because the castle had previously been promised to a French couple for a month.

Accordingly, Bob, Ginny, and the two dogs had sailed from Barcelona to Cadiz, and then across from Algeciras to Tangier. There they set up house for a spell in the Minza Hotel. Bob was away most of the time ferreting out information. This left Ginny on her own with the dogs. This didn't please her much, because wherever she went to walk Schnorkel and Mamselle, she could hear the sound of knife-sharpening. According to Ginny, this was in preparation for the next riot before independence.

While in Tangier Bob bought me an Underwood typewriter, since they were almost impossible to obtain in Spain at the time. He smuggled this into Algeciras in the back of the blue Studebaker Champion with Schnorkel and Mamselle sitting on top, making sure to dangle some sausages at the right moment. The dogs would surge forward as customs inspectors approached, and they decided no detailed search was required.

All my previous office jobs had been just that, office jobs, with normal working conditions and one position more or less like the next. I'd had a dozen, but all featured normal, ordinary, regular hours; typing, filing, coffee break, shorthand, lunchtime, etc. I had also been in the Army and worked on a farm for a year, but I soon realized that I had landed no ordinary job with Robert Ruark. We went outside in the sun and sat on steps in front of the castle to do dictation. Thus commenced my 12 years of devotion to Ruark's requirements.

Soon enough I discovered Bob Ruark was very complete in himself. He knew exactly what he wanted and he did not require anyone to correct his work. This suited me admirably as I was not and never had been a literary genius, nor had I ever been a particularly good scholar. But Bob did not require any help whatsoever to do his work and as I quickly realized, my usefulness lay in other directions. He was the author and I did everything else except the writing and most of the research. He was accustomed to digging out his own information. I doubt whether two people could ever have been better adjusted to work together, and it appeared that my temperament and generally quiet character suited him exactly. We never actually had a cross word that mattered.

I saw clearly right from the start what Ruark wanted in a secretary – someone who was honest, had a lot of patience, was normally sober, never repeated anything he saw or heard, whilst being present was remarkably unobtrusive, really did not want to be a writer, and could do the everyday chores quietly and without a fuss. The idea was to make it easier for Bob himself to be the writer. In my own view, I was happy with my good fortune to have finally obtained what I considered the ideal job. I was more than pleased when on a great many occasions Bob indicated to me I was still right for the job.

In America Bob had always had female secretaries, but he figured they either fell in love with him or he felt guilty when Ginny put the hard eye on him because all his secretaries were extremely attractive. Here was a state of affairs that perhaps could work in reverse, with the secretary becoming involved with the wife. At least that is what a number of the Ruarks' friends suggested, much to my embarrassment and annoyance. While I became extremely fond of Ginny, and she of me, we always remembered the old saying – that it is better not to on one's own doorstep. I believe that a great many people at one time assumed we had something going, as Bob was away so much and I was left to look after Ginny, help her buy the furniture, build the house and transplant the trees. Then later, I would help her through her emotional upsets during the pre-divorce period.

In any event, in 1953 a female secretary would have been unsuitable in Spain, though this would not now apply. In those days a girl was only just beginning to be noticed beyond the sewing circle, and it would have been difficult for her to deal with things such as house-building, customs processing of trophies and earth-moving, not to mention driving the Studebaker to Rome once a year in order to legalize the car papers. This was a distance of over one thousand miles and Spain was different in those days.

While Bob didn't necessarily require a "yes" man around him, he didn't want someone who had too many definite ideas and certainly not someone who forced his ideas. Bob liked to talk a lot and admitted it, and I noticed that certain people got dropped out of circulation because they also liked to talk a lot. Really, there was never room for more than one Robert Ruark at a time. One of my great assets in his eyes was that I am a natural-born listener if I am in the company of superior brainpower or a person who likes to speak continuously. Also, I am an introvert and Bob was of course an extrovert. Apparently these two opposites go well together.

I had no wish to write or be anything more than Robert Ruark's private secretary. I had been a sergeant in the British Army during the war years, and I merely wished to act in a similar capacity with Robert Ruark. He was the officer, and I was fully aware of that. Together we made an excellent team, though sometimes in his expansive way Bob depicted me as having been a sergeant major in the British infantry just because it sounded better.

I found my new employer an extremely likeable person, and I was amused with his humorous approach to practically everything. Occasionally he would call me "junior" and eventually I referred to him as "father," which he seemed rather to like.

We had a bit of extra admiration for one another because we had both suffered war wounds to our left arms (Bob in the Philippines and myself in Europe). Both of us had seriously broken humerus bones and suffered from a subsequent shortening of the arm.

One of the first things Bob said to me was "Alan, if you steal, sooner or later I'll know, and you'll get caught . . . and it won't be worth it." Also at the beginning he explained, almost apologetically, that the big problem would be that I wouldn't have much work to do. In the overall picture this was hardly the case, though what he had in mind was that he would be away a good deal. As I soon learned, though, any slack period was well balanced by those times when we got down to the heavy grind of book-writing.

Bob impressed on me from the outset that if I went along with him he would, after a reasonable number of years, make me rich far beyond my dreams and far beyond the normal potential of the abilities at my disposal. He said I couldn't be as well off as he intended to be, but he assured me I would benefit abundantly from his future successes.

On arrival in Spain, the Ruarks immediately started looking for a house to buy. They did find a building lot they liked, but since there were no clear deeds to the land, Bob lost interest. One of the first questions the Ruarks had put to me regarded the whereabouts of any houses for sale in the area. Since I had lived around Palamos, I was able to show them a number. I took them at once to a small chalet on the beach just outside Palamos, which had stood unwanted for a number of years. Pushing through the undergrowth to reach the building,

Bob peered in through a broken shutter and then turned to me. "Alan, let's buy it" was his quick decision.

The property stood completely on its own against the beach and was a peaceful haven for a writer. The chalet lent itself to conversion and additions, and during the first winter in Spain it underwent a transformation from a small, abandoned beach cottage to a large, rambling ranch-style home. It became what Ruark saw as fulfillment of a boyhood dream.

Shortly after purchasing the house, Bob decided it would be wise to acquire some more land out front. While it was not possible to build on, since it was within the marine zone, Bob felt there was a possibility of someone erecting a hot dog stand. We commenced further negotiations, and during the ensuing dealings when the landowner started to argue the price, Ginny excelled herself as a negotiator. She screamed *"cuatro pesetas"* and stormed out of the room thus settling the argument. She was referring to four *pesetas a palmo*, which is the measurement for land purchase in this part of Spain (a *palmo* is a hand span, of which there are 26 to a square meter).

The Ruarks' arrival in Palamos changed a number of things, and to some extent it marked the beginning of the tourist discovery of the Costa Brava. Bob began to put the coast on the map by mentioning it in a number of his columns, and the man responsible for arranging the Ruarks' house-buying deal switched from being a dealer in cork to work he described as "five minutes of bad English speaking." In other words, he became the first real estate agent on the coast.

Bob often said he had never been able to work in real peace until he came to Palamos, as in New York he had too many people wanting to see him and was never free to do any serious writing until after midnight. He told me he actually wrote a complete book working only between midnight and four in the morning. After so many obstacles to book-writing, he found Palamos perfect for his needs.

From the outside, the house in Palamos became a mixed confusion of roof angles because of additions and extensions built at different times, but the interior was ideally arranged for the Ruarks' requirements. Although the end product proved a great success, during the actual construction of the house there were a great many strange happenings. We started off on a very friendly basis with the builder, but this didn't last long. Bob and Ginny had accepted a plan, then departed for Australia for a number of months. They intended for the shell of the building to be done in their absence. Construction started at the end of 1953 with plans calling for Ginny to return in the spring and deal with the final details. She returned a bit earlier than scheduled, and it was at this point that the friendship with the builder suffered a serious setback. The building was not as far advanced as she had expected.

The battle started almost immediately. She pointed out a number of mistakes, and this continued on a daily basis, usually escalating into a screaming and shouting performance. I was required to do the translating, which in any event was difficult for me, and things could really get lost when Ginny required me to translate into Spanish such phrases as "Tell that stupid Catalan son-of-a-bitch to get off his fucking ass and finish the goddamn job because my husband is returning soon and has a book to write." Although I would generally translate along the lines of "the senora is angry, so please hurry along," the builder had already received the message.

One day I was sure Ginny fully intended to kill the builder. In the big office we had gone to considerable trouble and expense to build one whole long wall of exposed stone. To our amazement we discovered that about a third of it had been covered with cement, and the bricklayers were busily preparing to cover the remainder. Ginny exploded and presumably the builder got the drift of what might happen to him. At any rate he didn't come on the site for a week. The cement had not set very hard and was removed, though with great difficulty.

Then there alterations to work already done, such as ripping out window frames that didn't meet Ginny's specifications, alterations to a dozen Catalan arches, and altering the new square front entrance into another arch. All over the house the floors presented an enormous amount of confusion. In the original chalet they were completely changed, first to a slate-type tile Ginny didn't like once it was down, then to a marble tile that has remained. The wooden floors laid in the new wing also presented problems. They began buckling upwards almost immediately, so all this was ripped out and replaced with parquet blocks.

Eventually, when Ginny really thought all the flooring problems had been solved, she encountered her first experience with the plumbing. The sewage, instead of going away from the house, reversed itself and came up through the new kitchen floor. In order to fix the defective pipes, the newly laid floor had to be ripped out. This occurred just as Ginny appeared on the scene. One look was sufficient for her to burst into tears, though later, since similar problems emerged on many occasions, she joked "that to be on the safe side, one really needed a resident plumber."

Later, many other things were built twice, including the front terrace bench. It was knocked down then rebuilt the following day. The bench was constructed of solid brick and ran the full length of the large front window in the living room. Bob had become accustomed to using this and found it comfortable and practical, but one day as he walked out onto the terrace, he discovered it had been removed. The replacement was made of wrought iron. Bob was extremely angry at this alteration, because at the time the brick bench was about the only thing he liked. He told Ginny in graphic terms to put back his bench. It was done at once. There was also a large, expensive barbeque grill with lots of iron work and storage spaces on each side. When Ruark saw the finished article, he didn't want to know how much it cost, but he only used it twice. Once he grilled steaks for about 20 people and the other time he cooked a large fish, which broke into small pieces. It was then he decided to let his paid cook handle all the cooking in the newly completed kitchen. Henceforth the barbeque became a place to store coal.

Another addition was an enormous, hangar-type garage. For years it leaked, and whenever it rained Bob would shout for me to remove the cars because a chemical in the cement mixture left marks on the Rolls Royce. Eventually we managed to seal up all the holes and were pleased with the garage, though Ginny always maintained it was too modern for the Catalan-style house. Still, it was extremely practical as it stretched across the driveway and was left without doors so we could drive in one end and out the other.

The Rolls Royce and Studebaker station wagon suitably impressed the local village people. Indeed, when the Ruarks first arrived in Spain, it was difficult to have any kind of vehicle, since the only car being manufactured in the country was a go-kart type called a Biscooter. It barely held two people a foot off the ground.

After getting rid of an obstructionist gardener who objected every time Ginny wanted to plant something, his assistant was hired and matters progressed nicely. The garden was created from nothing. The whole property was sand, and all the earth had to be brought in by horse and cart. The same method was used to move some 40- to 50-year-old pine trees that were transplanted onto the property. Once finished, the spacious garden included a beautifully kept lawn between the main terrace and beach wall in front, while the area behind the house was arranged so that no matter what the wind direction, it was always possible to find sheltered spots to take the sun or to work in the open.

The orchard on the left side of the driveway, with a somewhat doubtful collection of apricot, peach, pear, plum, cherry and fig trees, was a great favorite for Bob. To be sure, the fruit was invariably of poor quality, presumably because of inferior tree stock, unsuitable soil and our proximity to the sea. This didn't seem to worry Bob. He loved to go out and pick his own fruit. On the other hand, Pascual, the Andaluz gardener, wanted to pull up all the fruit trees. He wasn't happy with anything second rate and said pine trees would be more suitable.

Eventually Pascual, in a conversation with Bob, understood that the trees could be removed. There was some miscommunication, occasioned by the fact the gardener spoke in the Moorish fashion and when excited was extremely difficult to understand. Bob probably appeared to agree in order to terminate the heated conversation. At any rate, all the trees were removed and replaced by pines. Bob returned from a long absence to find his fruit trees gone, but when I pointed out this had been his instruction to the gardener he dropped the subject.

In the conversion and extension of the original small chalet, top consideration was given to making a comfortable work place and to having rooms suitable for displaying trophies. So the old part more or less became the guest wing, with the new addition becoming the work area. It featured a very large, double-vaulted studio office with wooden beams for Bob. My office was built out through a bookcase, thus making a large L-shaped room. The new section also contained the Ruarks' sleeping quarters, and a 20-foot corridor separated the new wing from the rest of the house and front terrace.

This corridor was a sort of no-man's land. The house rules were quite clear – the wing where Bob did his writing was out-of-bounds to everyone, including the dogs, since Schnorkel snored. Guests ventured into the office studio by invitation only. This arrangement worked quite nicely, as the guest wing contained the main living area of the house. This consisted of a large dining room and the main kitchen along with a most excellent living room leading to the front terrace. Bob always said that the living room was the best conversation setting he had ever known. It was not too big, about 15 by 20 feet, with a high, wood-beamed ceiling, two large sofas for adequate seating, and a half-circular staircase coming into the room that provided additional casual seating.

At one end stood an alcoved bar and a small library, and at the other a large Bengal tiger with a fireplace underneath. For further decoration there was a 15-foot philodendron, a large oil painting of three Spanish ballerinas, and two 18th-century Spanish muzzleloaders. The latter were given to Bobby by a local Spanish count shortly after the Ruarks took up residence in 1954. But the dominating feature, of course, was the tiger. It relaxed full length on the wall, with its enormous head hanging over the fireplace and with the car keys hanging from its teeth. A standing house rule required the car keys to be returned to the tiger's teeth when not in use. Failure to do so involved a fine of one pound sterling being enforced. From the outset Bob said he only wanted to host a few carefully selected friends, so there were only two guest bedrooms. Ginny's office and library could be used as a spare room when required.

A great deal of trouble and enormous expense went into decorating and furnishing the house. Apart from some furniture the Ruarks had shipped from their New York penthouse, everything else had to be purchased. Most furnishings came from antique shops in Barcelona and Arenys de Mar on the coast. Ginny had tasteful decorating abilities, and with the help of numerous hunting trophies from Bob's days on shikar and safari, together with lavish use of Japanese grass cloth, she produced a remarkably well-balanced writer's home. Bob's big game trophies did present some challenges, and when a large batch arrived from a taxidermist in Nairobi, she consulted with a decorator friend back in New York on how best to use them. The cabled reply gave pithy advice: "BETTER GET A DIVORCE DEARIE."

Ginny found a giant-sized desk for Bob at a second-hand furniture ship in Barcelona. It was more than seven feet long and some four feet wide. She attached large brass rings as drawer handles. Bob suggested these looked more like coffin handles than anything else, but he was pleased with the size of the desk and found it ideal for spreading out papers when he was working.

Ginny did all the searching for antiques and other bric-a-brac that went into decorating the home, and Bob reckoned that ashtrays and lampshades cost as much as anything. For the most, he left matters to Ginny, though once in a while he would step in with a suggestion that a certain trophy would go well in a specific place. These helpful hints were not always considered acceptable by Ginny, and sometimes there would be heated arguments while three or four carpenters clinging to the ceiling or a wall while supporting a heavy buffalo or greater kudu head.

There was, for example, the occasion when Bob and Ginny had just completed a long, very alcoholic lunch and got into an argument about the exact position of one of the kudu mounts. The situation was made worse because the man in charge of the operation was also very unsteady on his feet. Fortunately, when matters seemed critical, by mutual consent the entire operation was stopped and left until the next day.

Finally the house was finished and the trophies hung, and there was never a person to enter without exclaiming with genuine feeling about the wonderful atmosphere the Ruarks had created. It was this atmosphere that helped Bob to write, and he found his office/study was an ideal writer's workshop. With the addition of my office, he felt we had the best possible writer/secretary arrangement.

He said that to write alone was one of the most difficult things for him to do. He didn't want anyone on top of him, but knowing that someone sympathetic to the project was close at hand meant a great deal. He couldn't see me around the corner, but he could shout or walk around for a cigarette and a chat about a plot or something when his flow of words slackened off a fraction or his shoulder started to ache. As he sat down, he would invariably remark that I had a better office than any big business executive he knew, then he would add that I even had a better office that his literary agent. The thought pleased us both.

When writing about Africa, Bob got considerable support from his surroundings. From his desk he could easily observe on the opposite wall an attractive trio of gazelles – an impala with a very wide spread, a Grant's and a rare Robert's Eye. Then to the left on the stone wall over the massive fireplace there were two Cape buffalo, one being just a tad shy of a world record. Also visible from Bob's writing corner was a beautifully mounted sable with the head turned and the scimitar curve of the black horns silhouetted against the white wall. A little higher on the same wall was a fine example of a greater kudu, but with closely pitched horns, as opposed to the other greater kudu almost over Bob's head, which had widely placed horns.

With all that, along with a glance toward the fireplace providing a view of his enormous elephant tusks, it wasn't difficult for Bob to get the feeling of Africa into his writing. The tusks weighed 109 and 110 pounds, and while not record class, they were bigger than most and certainly bigger than can be obtained today. More than that, they represented to Bob his first elephant, a subject he wrote about many times.

Along with some good antiques, the Ruarks' bedrooms held zebra rugs, and there were also two circular colobus monkey rugs, each containing about 20 skins. Since these monkeys had become a protected animal, the rugs were a real treasure. Even in the bathroom between the bedrooms there was another African trophy, a full mount of a dainty dik-dik antelope. Although it stood no higher than 15 inches, it was a trophy for the species.

Everyone who visited the house once it was completed was enchanted with the effect Ginny obtained. Temple Fielding, in his *Travel Guide to Europe*, expressed admiration for the property and stated there were only two establishments on Costa Brava worthy of consideration: the luxury hotel, Hostal de la Gavina in S'Agaro, and the Ruarks' home in Palamos. This gave some the mistaken impression that the Ruarks' house was also a hotel. For many years Bob received letters and telegrams addressed to Hotel Ruark, Palamos, and telephone calls from all over Europe requested "a double room with a bath." On one occasion Bob answered one of these telephonic enquiries and his rather pithy remarks no doubt left the prospective client with an unusual impression of the hospitality of Spanish hotels.

Ruark had created an ideal place to write, but it wasn't for working arrangements alone that he loved his Palamos home. He derived great satisfaction from what he considered a smooth-working machine. This involved an absolutely first-class Catalan cook, a Catalan maid who certainly qualified as a skilled butler and valet, a good floor-washing woman who never seemed to let go of her bucket, an Andaluz gardener with a green thumb, a second gardener named Pepe, a reliable part-time chauffeur who drove the Rolls Royce carefully and could find his way to Barcelona, and lastly, his English secretary.

Bob always boasted to everyone about his household, and he regularly expressed his gratitude for loyal service and effort. That was easy to give, since Bob had a knack for getting the best out of anyone associated with him. Quite soon one felt you were working with, not for, him. We all extended ourselves when required to do so. For example, Pascual the gardener came in at six in the morning and left at ten in the evening on a fairly regular basis during the summer, and the house staff would have done literally anything for Bob at any time.

Cristina the cook and Carmen often worked up to twelve or one at night, as dinner was always served very late. Then Cristina would be up at six the next morning to go to the market, since in the summer you had to be early to beat the tourists. This was not daily, of course, and Bob would periodically make a point of dining out or order staff to leave a cold dinner so they could have some time off. If we were book-writing with a deadline though, nobody was spared, least of all Bob himself. For my part there were times when I don't think I could have hung on much longer, as working on the typewriter from six or seven in the morning to twelve at night when were racing to finish a book and air freight it to New York was almost more than I could stand.

This devotion on part of the staff was created because Bob encouraged them to feel that it was their book, their new Rolls Royce, their dogs, or within limits, their house. Giving everyone a sense of importance also let everyone know their place. It would have been impossible to have a more efficient, happier home from a staff point of view.

Ruark's feelings along these lines appeared in a specially written article for *Saturday Evening Post*, dated April, 1964 and entitled "Why Spain Is Home." A few excerpts from this piece also help illustrate Ruark's love for his adopted country.

It is difficult to answer a simple question about why I love Spain – why I have chosen to live for the last ten years in what some liberals call a police state. I suppose I love Spain because I love the Spanish people, and among those I love best are Carmen and Cristina. Carmen is the lady who runs my house, and I suppose you could call her a maid of all work. Cristina is Carmen's aunt, and she is the cook. Cristina is vice-president in charge of both her niece and me. They operate on a basis of what the Spanish call *pundonor* – point of honor, or pride of person. So does the local cop on the corner and the smuggler on the beach.

There is still pride of service in Spain, pride of hard work, pride of family, pride of shared ownership, but basically pride of person, the individual. This all comes under the head of *pundonor*, and no Spaniard is so poor or downtrodden

that he is bereft of *pundonor*. The bullfighter has it, and so does even the gypsy beggar with the rented baby. There is no such thing of pandering of mind or soul in Spain. Everybody is as good as you are, and maybe a little bit better.

Nobody has ever written very well of the actual face of Spain, its savagery and kindness, its tenderness and toughness, because the Spaniard is so many things in one package that he positively defies pat description. The Spaniard is a fantastic mixture of Greek and Roman, Carthaginian and Phoenician, invading Moor and Iberian aboriginal. Spain is Africa on one side of the mountains and France on the other. Castilian is spoken with a lisp because one princeling was a sissy; Madrid is the capitol because a king had asthma and did not like the lowlands. El Cid, the classic hero, was an approximation of a hired gunman with a sense of fair play; the late Juan Belmonte invented modern bullfighting because he was a semi-crippled weakling unable to run from the bulls. It is all attributable to *pundonor*.

I will offer an example of *pundonor*. I must confess to a nice house in Spain – a happy, sprawling house, full of African trophies, fresh flowers, books and a functional bar which cost me about forty years and a near-miss cirrhosis to perfect. Fires burn brightly in my house; the grass is green in front, the sea blue beyond. But nobody actually envies me my house.

This house is called by the servants "our house." The books are "our books." It is "our dogs," and "our friends." When unexpected affluence permitted me a really fine car, it became "our Rolls," just as the tiger on the wall is "our tiger." The typewriter from which all blessings flow is called "the peseta tree."

If I had to list what I see most deeply manifest in the Spanish people, it would be that pride. The Spaniards have endured grinding poverty with undiminished pride. They endured possibly the bloodiest civil war ever recorded with undiminished pride and courage. Brother fought brother for principle. Generalissimo Francisco Franco has been in power for a quarter century and is still barely tolerated in Cataluna, Spain's richest sector. The Catalans spoke and wrote Catalan when it was forbidden by Madrid; Jose Pla, the country's foremost writer, writes only in Catalan and persistently thumbs his literary nose at Madrid. And Madrid does not lay a glove on him. There is a certain tolerance underlaid in this pride, a recognition of the other person's strength, and also a tolerance of personal weakness.

Although children are regularly taken to bullfights and accustomed to blood almost before they teethe, there is no juvenile delinquency in Spain that I know of – no Teddy boys, no organized hoodlums. I have never seen a badly mannered child, a disrespectful Spanish child.

There is respect for all authority in Spain, and that authority is founded on the family. Papa is boss, and Mama is boss also, on her side of the family fence. It is not unusual to see a man in his sixties deferring to Papa, who controls the purse strings and bosses the business until he dies. The Spaniard runs a dead heat with the Chinese for being the most respected and possibly the wisest parent in the world. Any Sunday in any town in Spain presents a delightful pageant of parenthood, with the little girls enchanting in their pigtails and starched white dresses, the little boys grave and complete *caballeros* from the cradle, the papas and mamas proud and beaming, the grandpapas and grandmamas happily approving from the sidelines. The family firmness is founded on rigid observance of decorum.

People who have not been to Spain always ask me the same question: "How can you bear to live under a dictatorship, in a police state?"

I have an easy answer for this one. I like living in a police state, if Spain is a police state. Nobody sent for me, any more than anybody sends for the millions of tourists who make the country uncomfortable – even if we are polite about it – for us Spaniards during the summer season. Nobody shoves a machine gun in your back and commands you to live in a police state. I would not know much about the "police state." Apart from the highway patrol – and we never needed them until the foreigners came with their hot rods – the only cops I see are apt to be found in my kitchen, pinching the cook and drinking a bottle of my beer when rain drives the Guardia Civil beach patrol (we smuggle, you know, in Spain) into my house for shelter. The only drawn gun I have ever seen in Spain I saw when the local cops lent me a pistol to put my best-beloved dog out of his ancient misery.

I live in Spain because I like the people better than any other people I ever met. The climate agrees with me. I have been treated kindly by the forces of law and order. I am allowed to own property. I have not changed a servant during my ten years here. Nobody gives a damn about who or what I am as long as I pay my bills and do not allow my guests to get drunk and run down the locals in an imported sports car. I have passed in easy stages from *El Autor Norteamericano* to Senor Ruark to Don Roberto.

I have no political ax to grind. I am not here to tell Franco how to run his country. In return the Caudillo does not tell me how to write. I do not meddle. This is not head-hiding. I simply believe that a guest should not quarrel with his host over the way he runs the house.

Spain is certainly a dictatorship. But Spain to me is also very nearly the last stronghold of individualism. The people of Spain have faces, and the faces are not mass-produced assembly-line replicas of a dictated trend. The people of Spain have style, and style is almost obsolete.

But mostly Spain has pride, and some of it has rubbed off on me. After ten years of happy acceptance, I am proud to be a Spaniard in the mood in which I am accepted – as an American who lives quietly in a foreign country which makes no objection to my passport or my appalling accent. I am, I trust, a good guest, and so I hope to remain until they plant me under the pine trees in the backyard next to the dogs.

While this was generally considered to be an indifferent piece, it demonstrated Robert Ruark's liking for Spain. It was warmly reciprocated by the Spanish people and he was greatly respected. In 1961 the Franco government decorated him with the Order of Civil Merit. This was probably because of his sympathetic attitude to the Spanish way of life in his columns and also his acceptance of the form of government – "a guest should not quarrel with his host over the way he runs the house." By way of sharp contrast, at the time many British and American correspondents were anti-Spanish and continuously criticized the country.

About the same time the Ruarks bought their Palamos property, they found a suitable apartment in Barcelona. It was situated towards Tibidabo Mountain at the back of the city. The apartment was the lower two floors of a four-story, 18th-century mansion that had been modernized. It was absolutely ideal for our purposes. On the first floor there were half a dozen bedrooms, all with adjacent bathrooms; a spacious entrance hall leading onto a sweeping stairway down to an enormous living and dining area; and the most important requirement of all, a big back garden for the dogs. All of this for about a hundred dollars month.

This apartment was much enjoyed. To begin with it was used extensively, mostly in winter. Schnorkel and Mamselle particularly liked the big garden and at cocktail time a game developed whereby someone would shout "cats" whenever one appeared, and the two dogs would leap from the rug and race at breakneck speed into the garden. To my knowledge they never actually caught a cat, though on one occasion when the poodle was a little quicker than usual and was about to overtake a slow cat, she suddenly turned tail and ran back to the protection of the house with the cat chasing her.

One day we all had a grand laugh at the expense of the dogs. We had fetched a tiger's head mount from Palamos, and it had already caused a stir on the highway as Bob had placed it to look out the window of the Studebaker as it if were a passenger. On arrival at the apartment, Bob quietly placed the head in the shrubbery at the bottom of the garden. Later, when we were relaxing and having a pre-lunch drink in the living room, he suddenly shouted "cats." As usual, the two dogs raced into the garden to defend their honor. They charged headlong towards this big cat in the bushes, then suddenly both came to a dead stop a few feet from the tiger's head. This was a bigger cat than they had ever seen before, and instead of attacking, they nervously retired to the house as if they hadn't seen anything unusual.

Since the Barcelona apartment was in a very old building, to start with we had a slight problem with cockroaches and flying ants coming out of the walls. There were also a few mice, and in fact at one time Bob had his own private mouse to which he became quite attached. It was his custom to eat through the night, so he always had some fruit, raisins, nuts and biscuits by his bedside. There would be a nightly visit from this particular mouse, but it didn't seem to bother Bob. Later, when I temporarily used this bedroom, the mouse continued to visit and would actually sit on the night table and complain about the lack of food. He wouldn't even bother to run away when I put on the light. Eventually, I found some holes in the wall and had them cemented up. When Bob returned, he complained bitterly at what I had done to his mouse friend, though maybe he was joking.

At the beginning of our residency in Barcelona, Ginny showed the cook, Cristina, some of her special dishes. Then Bob introduced her to Southern fried chicken, a dish on which he considered himself an expert. He maintained that it was necessary to burn your arms in order to do the job properly. My initiation to fried chicken was on the Ruarks' first Thanksgiving Day in Barcelona. I remember that after Bob had suffered sufficiently, he announced that the chicken was practically ready. At that moment there was an urgent telephone call from the customs agent, which required my immediate presence in town to help recently arrived furniture clear customs. It was decided that the furniture was more important than lunch, which they said would be held for my return. I left the house drooling with expectancy of enjoying something I had never eaten. Just as I boarded a taxi, Bob came running out through a crowd of people with the first finished pieces of his special Southern fried chicken, and I munched on it all the way to customs.

We had been using the Barcelona apartment for about seven years when the owner decided he would like to move back in. He made the first approach to Ginny while Bob was away on safari, and Bob didn't care too much for that tactic. On his return from Africa Bob refused to move, pointing out that it was more his home than that of the actual owner, as the latter had never actually lived in it. He also noted that the owner was in the renting business and that so long as the rent came when due there should be no argument. The real point, however, was that Bob wouldn't be troubled by anyone and could really show resistance when his hackles were up. After discussion of the issue, he threw a statement in French at the Spanish landlord which, in his view, settled everything. *"Je suis le roi et la loi. J'y suis, j'y reste"* (I am the king and the law. I am here and here I stay).

Shortly afterward the rent was refused, and for about 18 troubled months we forcibly paid the rent into a special account arranged with lawyers. The whole situation was somewhat unpleasant, since we had been friendly with the owners. Eventually, when Bob and Ginny were using London more frequently and Barcelona less, they decided it would be more sensible to have an apartment in London. Ginny found a quite suitable place in Park Lane and moving plans were put in place. At that point our Barcelona lawyer extracted from the apartment owner an agreement to pay some $3,000 if we were out by a specified date. Since this date coincided exactly with the planned move to London and the money covered all costs of the move, Bob was understandably quite pleased with himself.

When the house in Palamos was completed and everything was in good shape, Ginny said she was happy with the result. Even so, she didn't ever really settle down in Spain. She seemed a little lost a good deal of the time. This was possibly because of the language difficulty, but mostly the problem was Bob's continuous absence. Spain was not a good country for a woman on her own, and in truth she was really a big city girl.

So Ginny began pleading for an alternative residence outside of Spain. She developed great enthusiasm for building a home in the Isle of Pines (*Editor's Note:* Renamed the Isle of Youth in 1978, this is the largest of the Cuban islands after Cuba itself), because she really wanted to be closer to the United States. She seemed to think we could commute between Spain and Cuba and the States, and that would have meant myself and the dogs. She visited the Isle of Pines and looked around quite a bit. Fortunately she found nothing suitable.

London then became her preference for another residence, and while Bob was on safari in Kenya she searched and found a town house in central London she considered quite suitable. Located in Chester Square, it was priced at about $25,000, but it was in such poor condition at least another $15,000 would be required to fix it up. At the time Ginny must have thought it was a good deal, though as an interior decorator she could be easily carried away with the challenge presented by an old, run-down property. She cabled for and got Bob's full agreement to make the purchase, and then placed a hefty down payment.

A month later, when Bob returned from Africa, he took one look at the town house and said "No!" It was the type of place he couldn't stand, up and down, with endless stairways he considered an unnecessary hazard for everyday living. So even though he lost the down payment, Bob afterwards considered himself lucky he didn't have to reside in that particular house.

Despite this setback, Ginny continued with her search in London. Eventually she located a one-floor apartment in Fountain House, Park Lane. Situated on the seventh floor of the building, it overlooked Hyde Park. This was ideal and Bob agreed at once, since he was beginning to use London more both from a business perspective and socially.

Right from the start of my association with the Ruarks I was encouraged to regard their home as if it were my own. In effect, I became one of the Ruark family. Though I generally lived out and eventually had my own house close by in Palamos, I ate nearly all my meals with the Ruarks. There was one definite house rule in this respect. I automatically stayed for lunch, but for the evening Bob often told me: "You had better figure on going out for dinner so that Ginny and I can feel free to quarrel in peace." This arrangement worked very well and no feelings were hurt, but when we were laboring on a book, I would live in the house for long periods.

I never actually received a high salary. Bob didn't wish to be tied to something that perhaps he couldn't maintain in a bad year. He preferred to operate on a salary bonus system when things went well. My highest salary was based on $5,000 a year, half being paid monthly and half paid in a lump sum, generally after the completion of a particular project. In most years there were extra payments for additional projects successfully finished. Bob often said that I lived at an equivalent of $100,000 a year, on the basis that I was benefiting from 20 years of hard spadework done by him without the worry or necessary talent to make that much money. After all, he noted, I had full use of his luxurious country home and town apartment, his Rolls Royce and Studebaker station wagon, his dogs and his servants, and access to his high-quality friends, not to mention the opportunity to go on expensive African safaris.

Soon after the big house was finished in Palamos, the Ruarks suggested that I look around for a property of my own. They indicated they would supply the necessary financial assistance at the outset. After looking up and down the coast for a long while, I decided that the best possible building site was on the beach within 200 yards of the Ruark property. My house was built in stages, with Bob stressing all the while the importance of renting a portion of it as a source of income should necessity arise. Accordingly, my house was built so that I could rent half and live in the other half. There were two completely separate units, but with the possibility of being one big house. This eventually came out exceptionally well. I did all the plans and worked out the arrangements for the first-floor rooms.

Bob took great interest in the construction of my house, and he would regularly wander over to see how it was progressing. He liked the short walk along the beach and would invariably bring his friends over for a drink. On one occasion he brought an editor friend who instead of using the ladders employed by the construction workers, elected to climb out a window and shinny down a builder's rope. Unfortunately, it was too thin and unsuitable for hand over hand descent, and he burned his hand rather severely in getting down.

Although I paid for my house out of salary, I was fully aware that Bob had made it possible. Indeed, I had willed it to him in the event of my death. This seemed to me only fair.

Bob continuously worried about my future security. He maintained I had been completely spoiled and was virtually unemployable in any other capacity. He realized, and rightly, that I was completely dependent on him. He worried that something could happen to him and insisted that I insure his life against possible accident. I really wanted to insure him on a normal life policy, but as he insisted, I took out an accident policy for $25,000. As it turned out I did the wrong thing. Now, on reflection, I really should have known better. He had told friends he only wanted to live to age 50.

Bob was consistently generous and one of his intentions was to set aside certain sums of money to be placed in special joint accounts in our names. The money was to be escrowed so far as we were concerned and available only to Bob during his lifetime. He also wanted to be sure that if anything happened to him, there would be no problems with taxes or death duties. All this stemmed from the fact that one day on the front terrace we were reading the English newspapers and Bob found out about what had happened to the estate of Marilyn Monroe. Because of poor planning, practically everything was going to taxes. Bob said that under similar circumstances he didn't want this to happen to his hard-earned money. He promised that after his next big success, he would create the special accounts, but he died before he could make the necessary arrangements.

L ife in the Ruark house was always extremely interesting, so of course it was only natural that their dogs were unlike other dogs. Basically, the dogs thought they were people, and certainly they were treated as such. Miss Mamselle and Schnorkel had been brought over from New York to Barcelona by Ginny on an American ship, and they soon became very important members of the Ruark family.

I definitely started off on the right foot with the Ruarks by offering to look after the two dogs for a month before I was formally employed. This offer I am sure registered me as a suitable secretary to the household, as there would have been no room for anyone who did not love dogs.

Even before I met the Ruarks they had been identified by the village people as "los Americanos con los dos perros," as in those days it was a rare thing to have two dogs as pets and even rarer to transport them around in a luxury automobile. Ginny always did this when collecting the mail from the old Hotel Trias in Palamos.

Bob and Ginny were extremely fond of these two fortunate animals, and when the house became properly established, the dogs acquired many more willing slaves. The entire staff became devoted to them, which was fortunate as the idea of having pets was not generally accepted in Spain.

So Mamselle and Schnorkel settled down to their new country of residence and soon began to control my life. It wasn't long before I discovered that while a poodle is generally well-mannered, a boxer is not. Certainly Schnorkel was a cantankerous character, and there were many embarrassing experiences, not to mention the dogfights. Apart from his revolting table manners, the old boxer was a fighter of all other dogs, irrespective of sex, size or numbers. Even when riding in the car he would visually attack all dogs in sight.

Once, after we had settled in Palamos, I was taking Schnorkel down to Barcelona for one of his many veterinarian's visits when I stopped in a village to see some friends and have lunch. It was a busy holiday, and I soon realized that nobody was interested in finding anything for a dog. After considerable trouble I persuaded the restaurant owner to give me some scraps, though they consisted mostly of rice from a paella. I placed them in front of Schnorkel, thinking he was lucky to get anything at all. He looked at it with a fair degree of disinterest, took one sniff, walked slowly around the plate, eyed me, then deliberately raised his leg and urinated all over it. He then walked nonchalantly away in disgust. At this point I well understood what Bob meant when he told me this dog was different.

There always seemed to be some sort of dog problem, and if it wasn't fighting, then it was one of the boxers [Editor's note: The Ruarks eventually added Schnorkel's son, Satchmo, to make a trio of pets.] that had skin trouble or the poodle that had bumps on her back. Whenever Bob and I were away, Ginny kept us advised of the latest canine calamity. On one occasion she wrote: "The dogs are all right, and everything is fine. Well, almost everything, but have you ever tried to get dog shit out of a straw rug?"

Bob loved all the dogs, but I believe he had an extra special regard for the old boxer, Schnorkel. He gave him the status of "elder statesman," and when it was clear the end of the dog's life was approaching, Bob was quite distressed. This is shown in a piece he wrote for the May, 1960, issue of *Field & Stream* entitled "The Saga of Schnorkel." He set a light tone in the piece, but his emotions were clear at the end.

"Schnorkel is gray, and he walks spraddled-legged, and his teeth are worn down so he can't even fight his son any more, and noise bothers him, and his hide is abraded and his eyesight is going and he has forgotten his last girl friend. My old puppy, my dog Schnorkel, is dying, in the midst of all the love he has mustered since he was ten weeks old, and by the time this sees print he will very possibly be dead. But by the Lord Harry, for the dozen years we had him he was all dog."

As the years went by all our dog friends died and went on their way. One by one they were planted out back underneath the pine trees. One day it became Satchmo's turn, and that was the end of a long line of good people.

CHAPTER 9
THE EARLY BOOKS

Quite soon after I began to work with the Ruarks I noticed certain subjects caused domestic disharmony. One of these was any reference to Australia during the war. As a young and very active lieutenant, Ruark had spent considerable time in Australia, primarily in Sydney and Melbourne, where he thoroughly enjoyed himself. So it came as no real surprise when Bob announced his plans to return to Australia toward the end of 1953. It was something he had wanted to do ever since his service days.

Possibly Bob was unwise to have spoken and written so highly of the good times he had in Australia, as periodically for the remainder of his marriage this produced matrimonial distress. Bob had gone ashore often and for long periods, had his own private apartment, and had sufficient money to turn the town upside down. It appears that his main activities were horse racing, whisky and women. There were ample supplies of all three.

When Bob had been around Sydney long enough to become thoroughly accustomed to the lush life available there, his love for Australia underwent a slight setback. Smartly dressed in his Navy officer's uniform, he was setting off for an evening's entertainment when three particularly tough-looking Australian servicemen confronted him. They straddled the sidewalk in his path, and as Bob was about to greet the three comrades-in-arms, one stepped forward with a mumbled "Sorry Yank" and let go a hard, sharp punch to Bob's jaw, knocking him to the ground. Somewhat dazed, Bob started to pick himself up when, to his considerable surprise, the three Australian soldiers began to help him to his feet. They then invited him to have a drink at a nearby pub.

There, over pints of beer, they explained there wasn't any personal bad feeling behind the punch that had landed on Ruark's jaw. But the three Australians had been campaigning in Burma under impossible conditions, and while there, they had repeatedly heard that the Americans were having a great time in their country with their women. They swore many times that when they got back home they would slug the first American they came across. Lieutenant Robert Ruark happened to be that American.

Amongst Bob's many good Australian chums, there was one who regularly moved in with him after being locked out by his wife. He would then proceed to borrow Bob's clothes and wear his shirts, but his primary contribution to Bob's activities was as a drinking companion. They would start out to visit possible girl friends armed with a case of whisky and a case of gin. The procedure usually proved successful.

On one of these escapades, they collected a girl who seemed to be a normal companion, but they subsequently discovered such was not the case. She had been picked up at a boxing match where she left a party of four, and from that point they went on to a respectable nightclub, the Checkers. Well lubricated, they were making considerable noise and annoying all the people around them. Some people nearby persisted in glaring their annoyance at them. After a while and to everyone's surprise, their new female acquaintance suddenly pulled out and flounced a naked breast in the direction of those who were staring. The rather stuffy group sat in shocked silence for a short while, then got up and left hurriedly.

Bob and his friends continued their revelry, and somewhere in the course of the evening he discovered that the girl was staying at the same hotel, The Australia, as he was. Initially he thought this was a grand advantage, but subsequently he changed his mind.

After a few days Bob decided to leave Sydney for a spell. His plans were to make a trip to Melbourne and visit another girlfriend. The present girlfriend threatened to jump out the window if he left. Bob studiously ignored this possibility and continued to pack. When halfway down the corridor to the elevator with his Australian drinking chum, who was helping him with his luggage, he discovered that the girl had one leg out the window and was preparing to jump the six floors to the street. His buddy plaintively asked what he should do. Ruark's last words as he departed were: "Tell her to come back or jump."

During Bob's absence it was discovered that the gifts the girl had given Bob and his friend had been stolen from the jewelry shop in the hotel. On top of that, she hadn't paid her bill for three weeks and had no money to do so. Ruark later learned that in certain circles she was considered to be an accomplished thief and nut case.

Bob was never a gambler on a continuous basis, but whenever horse-racing was available, he could not resist. On these occasions he was an erratic gambler, with the result being times of most remarkable luck. Once he won £14,000 at the Flemington race track in Melbourne, a sum in those days worth about $70,000. Bob proceeded to go on a two-day binge, returning to the track on the third day and promptly losing what money he had left. Afterwards he walked away from the race with the remark, "Well, it's only spending money."

It seemed that whenever he arrived in Australia, some sort of restriction was lifted from Bob, for he immediately had a compulsion to spend money. This applied in particular on his second peacetime visit in 1956, when he announced that he had just been paid some of his *Something of Value* money and that he felt an obligation to spend $120,000.

In between the horse-racing and other activities, Bob got down to some serious reporting. He wrote pieces for his friend Sir Frank Packer, who owned the *Sydney Daily Telegraph*, and the newspaper also picked up some of his syndicated columns written for American publication. Although Bob normally wrote complimentary things about Australia, he never hesitated to speak his mind when there was something of which he disapproved. Such was the case when he wrote a critical article concerning a dock strike and found himself challenged by the Waterside Workers' Federation.

One morning Bob was told there were 13 delegates, including four women, demanding his presence in the hotel lobby. Although he initially refused to see them, they were so persistent he really had no alternative. Bob was quite nervous until he got a drink in his hand, and then he sent word for them to come up to his suite. When they arrived they confronted him with a piece they said was an insult to the Australian people.

Bob had written: "It is not true that the first Australian pastime is cricket, or football, or even racing. The first pastime is striking. There have been so many strikes in Australia, especially among the waterfront people, that it takes a daring shipping company indeed to risk a cargo in what is known as the longest turn-around country in the world."

Warming to his subject, Ruark had gone a good bit further, this time presumably referring to the war years. "I can remember one crucial period of the country's history when the beer-craving Aussie, who prizes his beer above rubies, was unable to work enough hours to keep himself sodden in his favorite beverage."

The wharfies insisted that the Australian worker was not a drunkard and questioned the accuracy of Ruark's report, pointing out that only a few strikes had taken place in the past year. He was told that he was not representative of the American people and then accused of being a stooge for big business.

While the wharfies were not particularly aggressive, they were also not particularly friendly. Still, from the start Bob found himself at a disadvantage as he was suffering from a bad hangover, It didn't help matters when the wharfies noticed that the sitting room was full of booze. Then, even though it was well past noon, his breakfast arrived.

After making a good many more strong points, the delegation formally invited Bob to address an assembly of waterside strikers and was promised a fair hearing if he did so. By this time Bob had pulled himself together sufficiently to make a suitable answer. Without much interruption he said:

"I think it would be absolutely idiotic for me to stand up and try to justify to you all my writing of this particular piece. I am not representing vested interests, and I am not a representative of the working man. I am a commentator on this as they appear to me and I am more or less known for a rather sweeping, light approach to what people talk about in the street.

"I don't hold with striking as a weapon, as I have seen too much grief come of it for too little accomplishment. I see that you are a force diametrically opposed to anything I espouse because you think I am a representative of capitalists, and I think it would be a complete waste of my time and yours for me to address the assembly.

"This article was not intended as an insult to this country. I merely drew a conclusion which could have been erroneous, but I used my right to say as an American what I thought."

Bob saw no point in attempting to talk to a meeting of strikers, and he certainly didn't want to end up in Sydney Harbor if they turned nasty. In any case the fact that the meeting was to be at nine the next morning settled the matter for Bob. "It was just too early to make a speech to which nobody was going to listen."

So the matter seemed to be finished, until a few days later in a newspaper called *The Advertiser,* Bob was referred to as a cheapjack foreign slanderer and his words were reported as being even stronger than had been the case.

Part of the article read: "To describe Australians as a loafing, lazy lot of beer-guzzling gamblers who strike at will, is a downright lying statement – and something that should earn the writer a good smack in the teeth, at least.

"We thought the wharf-siders showed commendable restraint in merely making a verbal protest, and even courteously invited Mr. Ruark to address their mass meeting, and guaranteed him freedom of speech. Mr. Ruark in the true manner of a disciple of the American Yellow Press declined the invitation. In other words readers, we put it in pure unadulterated Australianese. He 'dingoed!' "

Once Robert Ruark had settled down to his column writing, he decided to try his hand at writing books. Towards the end of 1947 his first book was published. He had been pestered by 14 publishers and literary agents to write a burlesque historical novel and finally agreed to do so. This really came about because of a column he wrote parodying historical novels and complaining they all followed the same pattern. So Bob got to work on a different pattern and produced *Grenadine Etching*, key-lined as "A Very Historical Novel." It was a riotous takeoff on *Forever Amber, The Hucksters, Gone With the Wind* and many others. He described it as a historical novel to end all historical novels.

"It is a very adequate historical novel, suitable for Hollywood, book clubs, or for lighting the fire. You want sex? Sex we have. You desire action, intrigue, discussions of food and clothes and philosophy? We have them all. The supernatural, ships and kings and famous characters, historic New Orleans, the slave trade, revenge, torment and travelogue? Of course. Our girl Grenadine is bigger and lustier than anyone you ever met. She gets around more. She has more odd friends than a night-club columnist."

Writing the book was a difficult task for Bob. He had never really been able to work in peace in New York. There were always too many people wanting to see him. He told me that the only time he worked on the book was in the wee hours of the morning, and he freely admitted that there wasn't a sober word in it and that it read that way. When interviewed at the time the book was published, Ruark said: "I armed myself with a large bottle of bourbon and I wrote very well polluted. I would wake up in the morning to find twenty pages of copy I'd never seen before."

Whatever Ruark thought of his product, it was widely acclaimed as a hilariously brilliant burlesque, though it also collected a fair amount of adverse criticism. Some of this came from *Time* magazine: "Merely exaggerating the absurd is no sure way to hilarity; satire must make its own kind of sense and this makes little or none. Readers will admire Ruark's choice of target but deplore his aim." A similarly harsh review appeared in the *Washington Daily News:* "It's all very confusing and gaudy. The idea, as we get it, is a satire on everything. The result has all the selective good taste of a dish composed of jambalaya, Irish stew, poi, wieners and sauerkraut, hush puppies and bouillabaisse."

THE EARLY BOOKS

On the other hand, Bob received some excellent publicity for *Grenadine Etching* thanks to a large picture spread in *Life* magazine, where a good number of explicit illustrations appeared. These were by R. Taylor of Montreal, who sketched and did the cover art for all of Bob's humorous novels.

The following year Bob put together a collection of satirical essays, some of which had been previously published and others that were original. He embellished those developed from his columns with phrases and episodes no newspaper would print. Bob dealt with a great many things, but he was thinking of his typewriter when he chose the book's title, *I Didn't Know It Was Loaded*. The book stuck verbal darts into everyone and everything.

In a column for the *New York World Telegram*, Frederick C. Othman wrote of Ruark and the book: "He is a brave man and the beauty of this author is that he isn't scared of anybody, except possibly his wife, and then not much. For a pen he uses a large instrument, which isn't blunt; he dips this in a mixture of engraving acid and champagne (for the bubbly effect), and he leaves squirming: the Andrews sisters, women in bars, Edna Woolman Chase, Salvador Dali, the ladies who operate the Du Barry Success School, Errol Flynn, Jim Folsom, furniture movers, Samuel Goldwyn, the editors of *Gourmet Magazine*, juke box fanciers, Henry Morgenthau, Clementine Paddleford, soap opera authors, Norman Taurog, and a couple of hundred more of the unlikeliest people ever to populate the pages of any book.

Bob also dealt humorously with southern cooking, phony advertising, the "new look," perfumes, book censors, birds, bees, flowers and psychiatry. He also goaded Linda Darnell, Leo Durocher, Sono Osato, Olivia de Haviland, and dozens of others. He even took on lady wrestlers in a chapter entitled "Occupational Hazard."

Described as a mad mélange of personalities, gripes, anecdotes and satire, *I Didn't Know It Was Loaded* was well received by the critics. Bob was described as the ablest gripe artist in the business and as a clean-fighting humorist who demanded that the reader laugh with him at foolish things. He was referred to as "Misanthropic Mr. Ruark," and certainly his book satirized with a sweeping brush. He came down especially heavy on women, and one reviewer suggested females would want to buy the book, but only to throw it at the author.

Spurred on by the success of *I Didn't Know It Was Loaded*, Bob was in print with another book in less than a year. This was again a collection of essays, many of them based on his columns. This latest effort, entitled *One for the Road*, was more of the same menu he had served up in his previous book. It continued his wide-ranging attack on the American scene and way of life.

He found plenty of new targets, but there was also ample carryover from *I Didn't Know It Was Loaded*. He was particular pointed in his ongoing assault on women, so much so that some reviewers actually suggested he might be in real danger. Small wonder with comments from Ruark such as "their heads are full of soap flakes and rabble rousing, or they have spent all afternoon telling some psychiatrist that they are not understood."

In unabashedly chauvinistic fashion Ruark suggested:

"They just ain't tired enough. They got too much time on their hands, unless they have nine or ten kids pulling and hauling at them. . . . The old man staggers home from a rough session at the ropewalk, or whatever, and this dewy dynamo is just laying for him. She has had all day to think about how women get the dirty end of the stick, and she's spoiling for a row. Unless her ever-loving takes her out and wears her down on a dance floor somewhere, she's a cinch to start chewing on him before sack time."

Nothing was sacred to Ruark. He bashed Mae West, wrote about "The Vanishing G-String," waxed eloquent on alcohol in general and Christmas drinks in particular, covered duck hunting and duck-billed platypuses, not to mention dozens of other topics. One reviewer summed it all up quite succinctly, if with something less than enthusiastic coverage. He suggested it was "some of the most important drivel ever written about the more hilariously deplorable aspects of the American scene that bulgybrows and professional worriers have forgotten to get upset about."

Other critics were kinder. Several suggested Ruark had established himself as a leading American humorist. Perhaps the finest critique came from *True*, a magazine to which Ruark contributed from time to time. Its reviewer wrote: "*One for the Road* by Robert C. Ruark boils down to a loud, lusty, lively and thoroughly uninhibited survey of the current American scene in town and country from every point of the compass, covering every stratum of society from bankers to burlesque and from science to sex."

In his next book Ruark returned to Grenadine Etching, mainly because he wanted to do something about her children. Choosing the title *Grenadine's Spawn*, Bob wrote humorously about the antics of these unusual offspring.

There were five known surviving children. Grenadine thought there had been others, but she couldn't be sure. The book's crazy framework further demonstrated Ruark's delight in satire and his feel for the absurd. In the introduction he wrote: "There aren't but two kinds of novels, really – historical novels and modern novels, so this thing in your hand is a kind of modern novel. By modern I mean full of bared bosoms, jet planes, pirates, treasure, lust in lots of places and blood all over everything. Plus conflict. In novel-writing, conflict is very important."

The reviews were not particularly favorable, with the general feeling being that a sequel was not really a good thing. One reviewer referred to *Grenadine's Spawn* as "about the silliest and emptiest piece of writing I have ever encountered. With newsprint selling for $126 per ton and the price of book paper slightly higher, it is an economic tragedy to waste valuable paper on such a product." Another reviewer suggested that "vulgar, obscene, pornographic are the descriptive terms which may be applied; the book is not only valueless but would be harmful to any class of reader." Others condemned the book in similar tones.

There were scattered favorable receptions as well. For example, Richard Blakesley, writing for the *Chicago Sunday Tribune*, commented: "It's highly refreshing these days to come upon a book which offers nothing but pure entertainment. Such is *Grenadine's Spawn*, a novel of our times by that master of subtle, rowdy satire, Robert C. Ruark. The story is caustically and continually funny."

No matter what reviewers thought, Bob Ruark thoroughly enjoyed himself writing *Grenadine's Spawn* and was obviously in a light mood from the beginning to the end. In his dedication he wrote: "This book is respectfully dedicated to the author's liver, without whose constant encouragement he would feel no choler and would also be dead." Then there are his final words on the dust jacket: "This, then, was Grenadine's spawn. Any similarity between characters living or dead is purely unmentionable."

Chapter 10
A Love Affair with Africa Begins

After four satirical novels, Robert Ruark decided it was time for a change of pace and something more serious. When he went on his first African safari in the summer of 1951, he had in mind writing a book about big game hunting. This was not really surprising, as in his youth the horn of the hunter had sounded early and in a powerful way for him, and it had been calling him to Africa ever since. Quite naturally, his choice of a title for this book was *Horn of the Hunter*.

It was purely a story of a safari in Kenya and Tanganyika, then known as British East Africa. It dealt with a serious subject, but Bob still used his flair for rapid, wise-cracking prose. This made the book a fast, easy read. He illustrated it with excellent black-and-white drawings he did while in Africa. This previously undisclosed talent (*Editor's Note:* He had done some work of this type for the college newspaper while at Chapel Hill) depicted wildlife, Africans and camp scenes. The sketches were extremely good, and there is no reason to doubt that if Bob had wanted, he could have become a successful artist.

The book also included a number of fine photographs. The first of these shows Bob and Ginny about to board a TWA aircraft from New York and carries a caption that is vintage Ruark: "The grin on the author is three parts martinis. The grin on the *memsaab* is a pleased one, owing to having gotten the author to the plane at all." This rather fixed the theme for the entire trip, when an incredibly large amount of gin was consumed. It has been suggested that Africa had probably never seen a safari quite like this one, which was a six-week shooting spree that saw Bob collect some remarkably good trophies for a first safari. Some critics suggest that a statistical analysis would show there were more bottles of liquor killed than heads of game, since the Ruarks drank to their success whenever they got a fine trophy, drank to failure if they didn't and sometimes just drank.

Bob's white hunter friend, Harry Selby, played an important part in the safari, and Bob showed his appreciation in the book's dedication: "This book is for Harry Selby of Nanyuki, Kenya, and for our good friends, Juma, Kidogo, Adam, Chabani, Chalo, Katunga, Ali, Karioki, Chege, Mala, Gitau, Bathiru, Kaluku, and Kibiriti, all good men of assorted tribes." Ruark's enthusiasm for the people he met on this safari can be understood, for all of these characters were used repeatedly in his books and articles on hunting in Africa.

Horn of the Hunter is full of hair-raising episodes and descriptions of wild animals, all presented in an informal, breezy and occasionally hilarious fashion. This was coupled with a degree of philosophy, some excellent narration, and descriptive passages of rare beauty.

On the first day's hunting, Bob shot a lion and was suitably impressed.

Every man has to face a lion at least once in his life, and whether the lion is a woman or a boss or the prospect of death by disease makes no difference. I had met mine and killed him fairly and saved him from the hyenas which would have had him in a year or so if one of his sons didn't assassinate him first. I was suddenly free of a great many inhibitions.

A man and a gun and a star and a beast are still ponderable in a world of imponderables. The essence of the simple ponderable is man's potential ability to slay a lion. It is an opportunity that comes to few, but the urge is always present.

The hunter's horn sounds early for some, later for others. For some unfortunates, prisoned by city sidewalks and sentenced to a cement jungle more horrifying than anything found in Tanganyika, the horn of the hunter never sounds at all. But deep in the guts of most men is buried the involuntary response to the hunter's horn, a prickle of the nape hairs, an acceleration of the pulse, an atavistic memory of his fathers, who killed first with stone, and then with club, and then with spear, and then with bow, and then with gun, and finally with formulas. How meek the man is of no importance; somewhere in the pigeon chest of the clerk is still the vestigial remnant of the hunter's heart; somewhere in his nostrils the half-forgotten smell of blood.

There is no man with such impoverishment of imagination that at some time he has not wondered how he would handle himself if a lion broke loose from a zoo and he were forced to face him without the protection of bars or handy, climbable trees.

This is a simple manifestation of ancient age, almost as simple as the breeding instinct, simpler than the urge for shelter, because man the hunter lives basically in his belly. It is only when progress puts him in the business of killing other men that the bloodlust surges upward to his brain. And even war is still regarded by the individual as sport – the man himself against a larger and more dangerous lion.

Then, in some pure poetry, Bob described his surroundings in Tanganyika:

I stacked the guns against a big tree's butt, set up the mess table, opened the typewriter, pried the top off a bottle of beer, untangled a camp chair, and sat down to look and listen. I would write for a while, maybe after I had finished lunch and a nap. There was nobody around but me, nobody else in the world but me and a million animals and a thousand noises and the bright sun and the cool breeze and the shade from the big trees that made it cathedral-cool but a lot less must and damp and full of century-old fear and trembling. I got to thinking that maybe this was what God had in mind when He invented religion, instead of all the don't and must-nots and sins and confessions of sins. I got to thinking about all the big churches I had been in, including those in Rome, and how none of them could possibly compare with this place, with its brilliant birds and its soothing sounds of intense life all around and the feeling of ineffable peace and good will, so that not even man would be capable of behaving very badly in such a place. I thought that this was maybe the kind of place the Lord would come to sit in and get His strength back after a hard day's work trying to straighten out mankind. Certainly He wouldn't go inside a church. If the Lord was tired He would be uneasy inside a church.

> I was very happy to be here, and very grateful to be here, all by myself with a bottle of cool beer and some peaceful thoughts, and presently I would try to put some of them down on paper. I was awfully grateful to have been allowed to live long enough to have made enough money to allow me to take this trip with a man I liked and admired and the only woman I had ever been married to and a baker's dozen of black men whom I respected and who respected me.

Ruark's descriptions of the landscape evoked the essence of Africa, and one of his greatest talents as a writer was to give the reader a vicarious sense of being a part of the experience. A good example of his lyrical descriptions came on a moonlit night:

"The moon had climbed steeply into the sky, and you could see the little hills plainly under it, like a long caravan of camels suddenly stopped and still waiting beside a well."

Ruark's irreverent humor came through as he described the sounds of wild Africa.

"The sounds become wonderfully important. There is a dove that sounds like a goosed schoolgirl. He says: 'Oooh, oooh! OOOHH!' The bush babies cry. The colobus monkeys snort like lions, except that it does not carry the implied threat. At first it is hard to tell the baboons from the leopards when they curse each other in a series of guttural grunts. A hyena can roar like a lion. A lion mostly mutters with an asthmatic catch in his throat. The bugs are tumultuous. A well-situated jungle camp is not quiet. But the noise makes itself into a pattern which is soothing when with the hyenas start to giggle. A hyena's giggle is date night in the female ward of a madhouse."

While the reception for *Horn of the Hunter* was generally satisfactory, the reviews were not very startling, and the reviewers were mainly non-committal (Editor's note: Today the book is widely considered a classic of its genre). There were, however, suggestions that Bob had copied, and copied badly, Hemingway's style of writing.

"He falls," one reviewer suggested, "into the tempting trap of all emulators of Ernest Hemingway – and Ruark admits he is one – when it interjects the earthy language of a men's bar, apparently under the impression that it denotes fine writing. Hemingway can get away with it. Ruark can't. The result is a series of tasteless interludes, neither appropriate nor enlightening."

This accusation of having "copied" Hemingway, which would become a recurrent nuisance, was toned down a little by one critic: "Ruark is no Hemingway, but he's good, nonetheless." There were many complaints. "Ruark's safari account is disappointing," ran one, while another said "there are too many words for what he has to say, too much dependence for effect on tough talk and grammatical error, too much reference to the medicinal merits of scotch and warm martinis and to New York's Stork-21 Club circuit."

Balancing such criticism were statements full of praise such as: "*Horn of the Hunter*, a wonderfully entertaining book about a safari by one of the ace newspapermen of our time, alive with humor and thrill, excellently illustrated, and probably the best book about its subject since Hemingway did his *Green Hills*."

Horn of the Hunter, a book of 315 pages, stayed on the best-seller lists for only a few weeks and never climbed very high (Editor's Note: At this point, Ritchie left blank spaces for listing the number of copies sold and Ruark's income from the book). Still, Bob considered the sales to be quite acceptable for a book which in actual writing time had taken him exactly one month to complete.

CHAPTER 11
EXPANDING LITERARY HORIZONS

On arrival in Spain in 1953, Bob began working very hard on articles for magazines. During his first six months in his adopted country he produced more than 20 full-length pieces. He was on the staff of *Reader's Digest*, more or less an unofficial staff member for *Collier's, Esquire* and *The Saturday Evening Post;* and he was an associate editor for *Field & Stream* as well.

In the early 1950s Bob wrote a number of pieces for *Reader's Digest*. He had a pleasant association with the magazine, and after each contribution would receive letters of encouragement from the editorial offices. For example, the editor-in-chief wrote him: "Once again, I'll say that 'Goodbye, New York' is a superb *Digest* piece. If you can do as well, again and again, your name will be WONDERFUL." That was followed by Bob's Mau Mau piece digested from *Life* magazine, "Your Guns Go With You," and then his profile of Harry Selby, entitled "The Most Unforgettable Character I've Ever Met." The latter piece earned further editorial praise.

A telegram from *Reader's Digest* read: "I hope you will give us the same lift again, and again – until you are recognized as the *Digest's* ablest reporter!"

Those were heady days, but they didn't last. For a time Ruark had an article in the magazine almost monthly, and he was well paid for his efforts. While he held a masthead position, Ruark initially earned a retainer of $833 a month plus $2,500 per article. This agreement later switched to a flat rate of $4,000 per article. This arrangement with *Reader's Digest* lasted about two years, then suddenly faded to nothing.

Apart from an article about women's problems in 1946, Bob never did much for *Look Magazine,* though there was one piece of interest in a special African issue in 1955 that included contributions by John Gunther and Adlai Stevenson, and a preface by Ernest Hemingway. Bob's piece struck his usual blood-and-guts melodramatic approach to African problems. Entitled "Land of Violence," it made the point that no matter how much the people fought amongst themselves, the only real victor was the hyena, along with the vultures and the ants. Bob said that "the hyena will always win, which is possibly why he laughs so much."

Over the years *Collier's* was a favorite landing place for Bob, and they took a good number of his pieces on Africa. Especially noteworthy was a three-part series dealing with different African animals. The titles made the subject matter abundantly clear – "Ruark Shoots a Lion," "Ruark Shoots a Buffalo" and "Ruark Shoots a Waterbuck." Bob was hoping to do a lot more for *Collier's*, and his hopes soared when he got in touch with an attractive lady editor. Unfortunately for him there was a change in staff, then a little later on, in 1956, the magazine folded altogether (Editor's note: The magazine actually ceased publication in 1957).

As his experiences with *Reader's Digest* and *Collier's* suggest, it seemed that whenever Bob got settled down with a particular magazine, something would always happen. Just as he was being accepted on a regular basis, the editorial staff would change and he would find himself out in the cold again.

Periodically Bob was published in *The Saturday Evening Post*, but he was never able to settle down there for very long. This was not for lack of trying, as he always said the magazine was a good showcase for his work. He did contribute a few African pieces, and there was an article on India entitled "The Tiger Doesn't Stand a Chance." The article caused a spot of bother because of alleged duplication of similar material. Bob had written this tiger piece for *The Saturday Evening Post* and then, a number of months later, he wrote one for *Field & Stream* on the same subject with the title "Flying Tiger." Apparently the circulation department at the *Post* protested that the *Field & Stream* piece, while not an exact duplicate of the *Post* article, nonetheless impaired its appeal to readers. This was because its publication had been delayed and the *Field & Stream* account appeared first.

Naturally Bob was extremely sorry to have blundered in this fashion, if blunder it was, but any suggestion of duplication was completely unintentional. As Bob pointed out in the correspondence that ensued, it was necessary for freelance writers to use by-products growing out of trips to gather story material. Unless he could come back home with at least a dozen separate properties, he would lose money on the deal.

While Bob realized he had laid himself open to criticism, he wasn't really convinced at any time he was completely in the wrong. He expressed his views on the matter to his agent in these terms:

"As you know in the past I have given *Field & Stream* the by-products of all my doings, for which they pay me a comfortable $15,000 a year. I wrote no duplicate slick tiger piece for anybody else but the *Post*, and I wrote the *Field & Stream* [article] several months after the *Post* had already accepted the Tigers.

"I wrote *Field & Stream* two tiger pieces, neither one of which touched very strongly on the *Post* piece, except that it had to do with tigers and India, and were more or less technical outdoor style pieces, and I say again, that these pieces were not written until months after I had delivered the original piece to the *Post*. However, I am not going to spend the rest of the year brooding about it – it happened, and I am sorry, but I still cannot offer complete allegiance on one short article on anything as extensive and expensive as these trips I take. In all I must have pulled two dozen magaziners out of Africa by now. Only one of which the *Post* published."

His agent, Harold Matson, replied to the effect that any defense on the grounds of being a freelance writer or on the grounds of the piece having been delayed so long wouldn't hold up. He noted that the *Post* bought all periodical rights and offered no timeline on when the article would be published.

Spain & Beyond

SOUTHPORT ART MUSEUM

Robert Ruark was a charismatic figure who dazzled men and women alike with his intelligence and seemingly boundless energy. A chain-smoker, he appears with cigarette in hand in many photographs, almost as if it were his signature. Circa 1955.

NORTH CAROLINA SOUTHERN HISTORICAL COLLECTION, UNC – CHAPEL HILL

Sixty-hour work weeks were typical for Ruark at the peak of his newspaper career. He typically wrote five columns a week, each from 600 to 700 words, and also contributed regularly to national magazines. Circa mid-1950s.

ALL NORTH CAROLINA SOUTHERN HISTORICAL COLLECTION, UNC – CHAPEL HILL

The Ruarks transformed a small seaside chalet just outside Palomos into a spacious and elegantly appointed home where they regularly entertained guests from around the world. All circa 1960.

NORTH CAROLINA SOUTHERN HISTORICAL COLLECTION, UNC – CHAPEL HILL

Ruark stands next to his African leopard, one of many trophies displayed at his home in Palamos. The author was badly mauled by a leopard in India and almost died when his wounds became infected.

BOTH NORTH CAROLINA SOUTHERN HISTORICAL COLLECTION, UNC – CHAPEL HILL

Ruark's taste in the bizarre is represented by this odd statue of a monkey and by his unruly dog, Schnorkel. According to Alan Ritchie, the old boxer "was a born fighter, of all other dogs irrespective of sex, size or numbers." Top: Ruark enjoys a night out, possibly while on a magazine assignment in the Phillipines. Circa late 1950s.

BOTH NORTH CAROLINA SOUTHERN HISTORICAL COLLECTION, UNC – CHAPEL HILL

Ruark purchased his Rolls Royce in London in 1956. He came to regard – and show off – his beloved Rolls as a symbol of his success. Top: Ruark staged this photograph while staying at a residence in an area where the Mau Mau were attacking white settlers. The government encouraged gun-owners to keep their firearms close at hand.

SOUTHPORT ART MUSEUM

These candids of Alan Ritchie were probably taken in the mid-1950s. Top: Ritchie and his acclaimed author make corrections to one of Ruark's book manuscripts, probably in the late 1950s.

BOTTOM: NORTH CAROLINA SOUTHERN HISTORICAL COLLECTION, UNC – CHAPEL HILL

Alan Ritchie died 17 years after Ruark's death in December of 1965. Their graves rest side by side at the public cemetery in Palomos. Translated, the inscription on Ruark's headstone reads: "Robert Ruark, Writer. Born in North Carolina the 29 of December 1915. Died in London, the 1 of July of 1965. Great friend of Spain. E.P.D. (May He Rest In Peace)

In a letter to *The Saturday Evening Post*, Bob wrote:

"I would never knowingly write two competing pieces even for different mediums, unless I thought that the principal piece – in this case the tiger piece I did for you – would be honorably authored as exclusive both as to treatment and to prior publication. That is a long way of saying that I thought your tiger piece would be out very far in advance of *Field & Stream,* due to the difference in time of writing."

But I think his true feelings on the whole business were conveyed in a note written to his literary agent:

"I am sorry that we have got two strikes on us with the *Post*, but the *Post* ain't worth nowhere near the solid fifteen grand that *Field & Stream* is going to pay me for the next four and a half years, on which I count. Finally, it would never have occurred to me that the *Post* would get its ass in an uproar about an outdoor magazine."

Possibly Bob's biggest prestige effort with the *Post* was a three-part series about New Guinea that resulted from a 1957 trip to the Far East. The New Guinea pieces were entitled "The Land That Time Forgot," "Stronghold of the Kukukuku" and "Ten Thousand Years to Make Up." At one time they were to be the foundation of a book that Bob had in mind, but he never found the time to write it.

There was then a lapse until 1963 when he got back into *The Saturday Evening Post* with a good piece called "The Last Safari," which was followed by an insignificant effort on sick humor featuring Lenny Bruce. After that Bob began having real trouble writing anything the *Post* editors found satisfactory. That was true of an expense account piece he called "Goodbye to All That" and an Africa-related article that should have been easy for him, "Women on Safari."

In a letter to Harold Matson, Ruark complained bitterly about these rejections. He mentioned what he considered some inferior articles they had recently run, specifically referred to the factors connected with the rejection of "Women on Safari," and lambasted a female editor.

"I will take a look at the peerless Armenian's rewrite blue prints, but if they aren't any classier than the so-called 'research' she sent me, I toss in the towel, because her concept of research would be unusable for a *Field & Stream* version of *Seventeen*. Honest to God what she sent me as accumulated research was an Abercrombie and Fitch catalog, and the astounding news that they don't run safaris any more, but that this business has been taken over by the white hunters. She also included three interviews with three broads on a rough Q & A of bad high school journalism."

Later in 1963, after a trip to Mozambique, Bob produced a pro-Portugal article called "Bum Rap for Portugal." It was rejected as being boring, but in truth it was probably too political. There had also been a piece on Ibiza, which had not been accepted. Then Bob started out to write a piece that he wanted to call "I Hate Paris," but he decided not to do so, feeling he might run out of countries to visit (having already been officially banned from Kenya).

Some of this conflict may have been due to changing editors or bad timing, but more likely was because Bob had lost the knack of writing a first-time article. In April, 1964, *The Saturday Evening Post* published "Why Spain Is Home," but Ruark wasn't very pleased. He felt the photographs did not give the homey personal flavor he had wished to portray. After this, Bob did no more work for the *Post* and turned his efforts to *True* and *Playboy*.

There had been a lull of some five years since his last contribution to *True Magazine*, when in 1954 Douglas Kennedy wrote to Bob and introduced himself as the new editor. He suggested that he would like for Bob to start writing for *True* once more. Ruark liked the idea but nothing was done until Kennedy wrote again in 1958, pointing out that as an old newspaper man, he recalled that Bob "had made the initial splash as a columnist by making an all-out attack on the fair (or should I say unfair) sex."

On this occasion Ruark replied:"I am afraid I have overdrawn my anti-female stuff to a point where anything I could possibly do in this vein would be a rather dreary rehash of a lot of stuff I did for *Esquire*, the columns and God knows how many other magazines quite a long time ago. I am afraid my current boredom with womanhood as a topic wouldn't make for very bright reading."

In 1962 Douglas Kennedy made another attempt to get Bob to write for *True* with the suggestion he do an autobiographical profile. This appealed to Bob and during subsequent personal discussion the title "The Man I Know Best" was created. The first draft of the piece came out at 49 pages, and after cutting and some adjustment, it was published in September, 1963.

At first there was disagreement on payment, as it had been assumed that this profile would warrant the agreed-upon amount of $2,500 per article. But since this autobiographical effort was so long, Bob and his agent put his price at $10,000. There was some discussion and bargaining with Matson, then the editor of *True* wrote: "To say that I was stunned by Bob's $10,000 price would be the understatement of the year. As discussed on the phone, we have never paid more than $2,500 for a manuscript in the magazine's history. Now, in the interest of fairness and because it is an extra-long piece, I am willing to break all precedent and pay $4,000. Personally, I think this is eminently fair."

During the editorial discussion concerning this piece, Bob indicated that one reason he was so keen to do it was that it could prove useful as the basis for an autobiography at some point in the future. The price was later jumped to $6,000 and Bob was quite satisfied. He liked working with Douglas Kennedy. He was always keen to cooperate with the Fawcett Group, because they had always dealt with him quite fairly.

After the autobiographical piece, he wrote a number of further pieces for *True*. One of them was "Game Animals That Fight Back." It gave many anecdotes of Bob's hunting experiences dealing with wounded animals and also recounted some narrow escapes by various white hunters.

Bob was then requested to do a rush piece of not less than 2,500 words on the subject of the mounting fever for passage of new laws restricting the use and sale of firearms. The concept was for him to call for some sober thought before the enactment of any new legislation. Within a few days of the request, Bob sent off 4,000-plus words plus some suitable art, despite the fact that we were in heavy toil with *The Honey Badger*.

By this time Bob had developed a good understanding with *True*, and from this linkage came a grand piece, "The Most Unforgettable Sonovabitch I Ever Knew," which painted a lovely picture of the way Bob remembered his grandfather. Bob also did an original sketch of the old man for this piece. *True's* Douglas Kennedy visited Palamos periodically, and I remember that on his last visit the subject turned to future contributions to the magazine. Bob regrettably was unable to produce a single suggestion when it came to topics for future articles, and this seemed to embarrass him since he had always had so many ideas. This visit came towards the end of 1964, and the two men met up for the last time in May, 1965 when both were in London.

Following his return to New York, Kennedy wrote to Bob:

Dear Roberto,

Absolutely great seeing you in London the other night – and I must say I am completely bowled over by your fabulous living Establishment there. As usual, I am completely bowled over by your broads, too. In fact, I wanted to smuggle her back to New York in my suitcase.

I think your 3-week trip to Italy is just what the doctor ordered. Sorry about the Hemingway-Gritti Palace mention. It was unconscious, but then I equate you two, anyway.

When I say above that it's just what the doctor ordered, let me further presume on an old friendship and add my concerned thought: You look a little beat, buddy boy, and I hope to hell you begin taking care of yourself. I'm not speaking as a selfish editor (even though I expect two pieces from you virtually immediately); I'm speaking as a friend who is concerned for your life, liberty and pursuit of broads.

Take care, Roberto. Fond regards.

Bob didn't take any heed of his friend's advice, and he didn't take care.

"The Most Unforgettable Sonovabitch I Ever Knew" article was printed in the June issue. Later there was a letter of appreciation from a subscriber, and underneath it, in an editor's note, Douglas Kennedy added: "You may have noted that author Ruark died in London recently. In many ways Bob Ruark was the most unforgettable S. O. B. we've ever met. He'd like that as an epitaph."

Initially, Bob's attitude towards *Playboy Magazine* was quite unfriendly, despite the fact that his literary agent saw it as a good possibility as a market for his work. As a postscript to a letter written to Harold Matson in August, 1954, Bob wrote: "I quarrel with your judgment in selling anything we write to such a magazine as *Playboy*. It is a jerk-off sheet and the money we get ain't enough for the company we are in. I mention this because I don't think that the *Digest* or the *Post*, or even *Field & Stream* would like their boy appearing in such subway restroom publications."

Then in August, 1956, when a letter from Hugh Hefner of *Playboy* requested that Bob write an article of 400-500 words on any chosen subject for $250, Bob replied he was too busy working on a couple of books. There was no further contact with *Playboy* until October, 1962, when having changed his opinion of the magazine, Bob wrote "Gentleman's Hunting Arsenal," on the charm a fine gun holds for a sportsman. Then there was a lull until May, 1964, when he wrote "Babes in the Wood" on contract. It dealt mostly with the natural superiority of women on safari. Most of the people in this article were middle-aged and presumed to be long married, and the husbands were presented as red-faced, short-winded, poor-shooting incompetents. Of course, these were not the type of men *Playboy* wished to depict. It was suggested this piece would be more suitable for a lady's magazine.

Bob strove mightily to place pieces with *Playboy*, but he had difficulty in satisfying their requirements. His next effort was made while on safari in 1964. He had been asked to prepare a how-to-do-it safari piece, which he wrote in the bush in Mozambique, thus giving it some added flavor. Since the story included a touch of African witchcraft, Bob first used the title "Kush-Kush Safari," *kush-kush* being the name of the greeting ceremony on arrival at safari camp. Later this was changed to "Far-Out Safari." It was published in March, 1956.

Bob had a great many ideas for suitable *Playboy* pieces but continued to receive rejections. When in the United States during March and April of 1965 (the year he died), he had every intention of going to Chicago in order to talk with the magazine's editors and get a fuller understanding of what they required. Instead he return to Palamos, leaving many things undone.

No doubt one of the reasons he failed to please *Playboy* was that he had too many things going at once. During the second half of 1964 he was working on the screenplay of *Uhuru,* finishing off *The Honey Badger* and still writing columns. He was away on safari during August and did not return to Palamos until the end of September. There were also trips to London before and after the African safari, and then in December a trip to Morocco and a tour of southern Spain in the Rolls Royce.

At this time he wrote a letter to the editor at *Playboy*: "I am very happy with our set-up and hope to get on with the polishing of some short stories later this year, but unfortunately I only have two heads and eight hands." He would have needed these in order to perform the amount of work and travel he had set for himself.

In another attempt to have some short fiction accepted, Bob presented a piece entitled "The Cad." It was deemed unsuitable and in the letter of rejection the editor wrote: "Who needs the narrator? He's a repulsive loser who adds nothing to the interesting story of Tommy, a devil-may-care roué who lets one act of kindness do him in. Why not turn it into the basic story of Tommy, his life and loves? That way it might well have a chance."

This was in May, 1965. Unfortunately at this stage there was nothing much to do with the piece. I rather think that by this time Bob was feeling somewhat akin to a repulsive loser himself.

EXPANDING LITERARY HORIZONS

Bob had been engaged in once again rewriting a piece that had given him an enormous amount of trouble. This was about New York and had begun with the title of "Nothing Works," then became "Nothing and Nobody Works," and ended up "Nothing Works and Nobody Cares." It was finally accepted by *Playboy* after Bob's death and published in December, 1965.

In some personal data for "Playbill" to accompany the piece in *Playboy*, shortly before his death Bob wrote: "Aging author, exhausted by London-New York-Italy living, now home in Palamos, Spain, where no phones ring because of the new dial system. Aging author got two sets of proofs to read on new book, and two other new books to commit from hunter. Aging author also got new studio built on top of house – he needs studio like the well-known hole-in-the-head – but aging author has lady friends who give him presents."

Bob then explained that different girlfriends had given him such things as wooden wall carvings from Mombasa, colobus monkey rugs, original drawings by Felix Topolski depicting the Uhuru ceremonies in Kenya, a collection of rare African masks and figurines, plus a few nude pictures of the girlfriend herself, all of which were the reason for building the new studio. There was nowhere else to keep these possessions.

Bob continued by complaining that apart from the high cost of construction, he would now have to import a painter to teach him to paint. He then added: "Having gone entire hog, I had to run into Nikolai Tregor in Capri, and he conned me into having a head sculpture to add to the other clutter. Nikki has done everybody from Eisenhower to Franco to Peron to Sinatra. He gave me the professional rate, but I'm still afraid the check will bounce. In fairness to Nikki, he said I had interesting frontal bones.

"No author's life is easy, and when you combine it with sculpture and painting, this is ridiculous. If anybody knows anybody who wants to rent a studio from a non-painting author who lives in a place where the rains in Spain fell mainly on his roof, do not write: *cable*."

Although Bob was kidding in his blurb for "Playbill," he knew that at this stage he should not have been making an already big house even bigger. Bob's association with the magazine actually ended on an updraft, as prior to his death his agent negotiated use of three excerpts from the recently completed novel, *The Honey Badger*, for a total of $15,000. These were called "Sheila," about an English girlfriend during the war; "Barbara," explaining what happens emotionally to a girl after seeing a prize fight; and thirdly, a piece called "Afternoon in Andalusia," an outline of what can happen to the same girl when she endeavors to overact when in front of admiring males."

Periodic acceptance problems notwithstanding, there can be no doubt that over the years Robert Ruark was a highly successful magazine writer. For the most part he was able to sell whatever he cared to produce. Bob maintained that there was a knack to writing an acceptable magazine article. On one occasion he summed up the whole business in a letter to his New York assistant, who was apparently a journalism student. Bob drew a diagram, which if followed provided the key to successfully writing for magazines.

Dear Ralph,

I usually charge for this, but it is the sure way to sell a magazine piece, provided the topic is right, the timing is right, and all that kind of shit.

Very soon *The Saturday Evening Post* will be running three pieces on New Guinea, which I have written in the classic commercial fashion. Study them. Some things, personal and with my name, for mags like *Esky* [*Esquire*], the late *Colliers*, will let you slant a piece or first person the lead, but the diagram I am enclosing has been responsible for nearly a thousand – paid for – magazine pieces. The only difference is that, if it's primarily a pix piece, you allow your art sometimes to sub for the anecdote.

Here how she works, Doc.

You open an anecdote most illustrative of the mood of your story. Frinstance [sic], I once wrote a piece about Clark Griffith who caught a wildcat by the tail when he was a kid. Straight narrative for about three pg's (paragrafs) [sic] described the scene of the little boy and the cast.

Then I shift to the present and start: Clark C. Griffith, at 83, still has a wildcat by the tail.

Then I proceed to justify, in one tight paragraph, why the reader should read the piece. Let's use me, now.

Today, at 42, Robert C. has two houses in Spain, a Rolls Royce, a nagging wife, less money in the bank than people think, three voracious dogs, a couple of ungrateful parents, a drunken bum named Brooks, and the clap. He parlayed all of these goodies out of shoestrings and second-hand merry widows, and he don't care if his wife hates him and the dogs bite him, because he's got a Moroccan whore stashed in every filling station between Palamos and the North Pole.

That's your statement of interest on the reader's part, in the subject.

We then come to phase Three, which would tell about my most recent successes, books, movies, columns and a good description of what I look like, what I drink, and how success affects me and what bearing it has on my family life. Have I changed, or am I still the same shit I was as a copyboy? Here is where you put in about 1,000 magazine pieces, 90 million columns, umpteen books, and an estimate of moneys made.

That brings us up to the present and future, and you say if the bum ever finishes writing that next book, he's due to make a billion, because he is the kind of guy who has confidence in himself.

Then you spice it with anecdote: "When RCR sat down to make his first notes on his project novel, Poor N. M., he headed his notebook: 'Poor No More, a novel worth a million dollars, but will settle for half.'"

This is called the nose-picker, to let the reader relax before he starts on narrative again. And remember, every time you make any flamboyant or startling or unusual statement, as the writer, YOU MUST BACK IT UP WITH WANTING AN ANECDOTE TO PROVE YOU AIN'T SHOOTING THE SHIT. THINK OF ANECDOTES AS THE RAISINS? QUINCES? CITRON AND CHERRIES IN THE SOLID BRANDY-FILLED DOUGH OF A FRUIT CAKE.

After a couple of nose-pickers, shift. This is where you get into the body of the story – the straight narrative but always illustrated anecdotally (Pugnacious, fired a general the same year he flung Lucky Luciano out of Cuba. This dates back to when he was a sports writer and took a punch at Buck Newsom). Married a gal and fights her to the last drunken comma.

Glamorous. Lives all over everywhere. War record: Solid stiff with the British in Australia, to where he still returns hoping to recapture lost youth – which also makes him a dreamer.

Rugged: Kicked his two best friends out of Spanish house for trying to screw the cook. Quote: "I got plenty of friends but where do you find a cook like Cristina?"

Lead into friends who ain't trying to screw the cook. Ruark numbers among his intimates such a varied group as Baruch, Molotov, Hitler, Lena Horne, Art Godfrey, Louie Armstrong, Broadway Rose, Polly Adler, and his house is a constant circus of bums who drink his whisky.

Stop. Pause for nose-picker.

When writing his last book, Ruark refused to screw Eleanor Holm because he had his cock caught in the space bar and his interest was purely literary.

The day the movies bought book for nine billion Ruark was drunk with his nigger rumba friends in Havana and had cirrhosis of the legs which he acquired while quail shooting with Bernie Baruch. DROP THEM NAMES.

Back to the plow. HOW DOES THIS GREAT MAN WORK SO HARD AND STILL MANAGE TO SHOOT BIG GAME, DRINK WHISKY, CHASE BROADS, STAY MARRIED, PAY BILLS, PRODUCE COPY [while] TRAVELING ALL TIME? And anecdotes.

When Ruark wrote his piece on the Queen's tour of the Pacific, he received the assignment while trout fishing in New Zealand, did the research in NZ and Aussie, and wrote the finished product in Gondia, in the Central Province of India, in between tigers, on the front porch of a dak bungalow and sent it in by cleft stick. Punch: It was in print in all 14 [*Readers*] *Digests*' translations 21 days from assignment." And by God, it was, too.

Now we come to: HOW DOES GINNY PUT UP WITH THIS PRICK?

Answer: BECAUSE OF THIS PRICK'S PRICK, AND MONEY.

Then: DOES ANYBODY REALLY LIKE THIS BUM? WELL, HE'S KIND TO ANIMALS, GENEROUS TO A FAULT AND REALLY RATHER SWEET, OR VICIOUS VERSA.

Anecdote: NOSE-PICKER.

When Ruark got a commission to write a Mau Mau piece for Life, he had just finished cutting off his best friend's head, but he didn't allow it to interfere with duty. He dipped his pen in his best friend's blood, etc.

HOW DID ALL THIS NONSENSE START?

Well, he was born of poor but dishonest Puerto Rican parents in the lady's room at Club 21, and he went to school at Smith College because he liked girls. He grew up to be a wing-puller off flies, and his first job was turning the pages for a professor in a whorehouse. Had solid record cowardice warside, married a nigger, robbed bank, and became pres. board BBD and O while taking Salvarsan (*Editor's Note:* Salvarsan was a trademark name for an arsenic-based compound commonly used to treat syphilis prior to the discovery of penicillin) for the syff because he had not yet invented penicillin.

Get out ANECDOTE, second best.

Today, as Ruark reviews his life, he wishes he had been born dead, so he went out and hanged himself in the back yard of his lavish villa, leaving a note requesting that he be buried separately from his wife, and in the back seat of his Rolls Royce. All moneys were left for the whisky ration of all whorehouses named Sphynx, anywhere, and no, but no, good works would result from his massive effort.

What about Ruark in future?

HELL. THEY GOT A SPECIAL SUITE FOR THE LAST OF THE INTERPLANETARY BIG TIME SPENDERS.

And that, Buster, is the general shape of a magola, and nobody in that school can tell you more. You write plenty good, and if you'll keep this firmly in mind, and study your chart, you got it beat. Ten percent to me comes later, but think what you save on tuition.

Best, Professor Ruark.

Ruark's prolific literary production and undoubted writing ability often formed a subject for discussion. On one occasion I referred to him as a "word factory," a description that Ginny found offensive. She suggested that I avoid confronting Bobby with the description. In realty it was quite fitting. For example, we would be heavily at work on one of the many books we did together when Bob would announce he wanted a change of pace. Maybe Nervous Nelly had sent another cable from New York saying: "ALL OUT OF COLUMNS NEED ONE OVERNIGHT OTHERS SOONEST, REGARDS or DON'T SPOIL YOUR RECORD NEED COLUMN FOR MONDAY REGARDS." Bob would then cable back something to the effect of "EYE RECOVERING FROM PNEUMONIA. COLUMNS SENT TODAY."

So Bob would leave the book for a morning and write up to six columns in a straight run. On that same day he would return to the book and get eight or nine pages of fresh copy out before dinner, then end the day with a few hours of copyreading and pencil work. Then for two or three days there would be an uninterrupted session at the book, when we would discover that another *Field & Streamer* was required. This was a monthly contribution called "The Old Man and the Boy." It would run about eight or nine pages and would normally take a morning. Then it would immediately be copyread by Bob, so that by afternoon I would be typing and readying it for the mail. Meanwhile, Bob would be back on the book so as not to lose the day entirely.

A page would represent one of quarto size, double-line spaced and carrying about 300 words. On a typical day he would write a *Field & Stream* piece in the morning, making about 2,500 words, plus say about 10 book pages in the afternoon that would total another 3,000 words or so – a total for the day of something in the region of 6,000 words, which would be mainly keepable copy. Or maybe the day's work combination would have been a chunk of book in the morning and half-a-dozen columns in the afternoon, or perhaps the whole day would have been taken up with a full-length magazine article running to more than 15 pages. Whatever the work combination, the production of words would amount to about the same, despite the fact that he was writing on diverse subjects.

Then once again it would be correspondence day, and then back to the book, and then there would always be other articles for the various big magazines often concerning a recent African trip, and then back to the book, then *Field & Stream*, but time would pass and so correspondence again, and columns again, and book, and so on.

Somehow Bob was able to turn his mind from one thing to another, as if all he had to do was turn a switch. I believe to him they were all "just words," though carefully selected, and certainly the term "word factory" fitted well.

Apart from special days when he did a batch of columns, Bob would be slipping one or two in here and there as he came across something topical that interested him. More often than not this was in the English press. Many times we would be sitting on the terrace relaxing a while before lunch, when he would go back to the studio and soon the noise of his old Underwood would be clattering through the house. About 20 minutes later he would return with a completed column either knocking or praising the English. Or I would be just about to leave for the mail at midday, having touched the car keys hanging on the tiger's teeth, with the dogs already pointed towards the front gate, when Bob would call out for me to wait a bit longer. "I really should get one column in the mail," he would say.

His speed of writing never ceased to amaze me. I would sit and glance through a *Collier's* or *Esquire* with the typewriter going at full speed in the main office. Shortly he would appear with a 700-word column finished, copyread, penciled and clipped together, ready for me to take to the mail. Sometimes all of this happened within a space of less than 20 minutes.

On a full book-writing day a normal production for Bob would be 20 pages, some 6,000 words. There would be days when he would get only 14 or 15 pages, but on other days he would get as many as 25. I believe he wrote at his fastest while working on *Something of Value*, and one day he completely ran away with himself and produced 35 pages of copy, or some 10,000 words. A large section of this day's work covered Mau Mau atrocities and oath-giving ceremonies, and Bob always maintained he was helped considerably thanks to the fact that when he awakened that morning, there was an old lady hanging by the neck from a tree opposite his office window.

This old lady was left hanging for most of the morning as there was a problem of just whom was responsible, whether it was the authorities in her Palamos home or those from just over the boundary line in Calonge where we lived. Eventually it appeared that Calonge was responsible, and this poor frail soul was cut down from the tree and taken away by horse and cart, but not before Bob had gotten maximum theatrical effect out of the incident.

It turned out that the old woman had been told by her family that she would have to go to an old persons' home. Rather than face this unpleasant prospect, she returned to Ruark's garden, where she had visited often, to die in a place she liked. Bob truly appreciated her gesture.

While all of this was happening, Cristina, the cook, was cutting cabbages in the back lot with a large kitchen knife. This also added to the general Mau Mau oath-giving effect, since Bob visualized the kitchen knife as an African *panga* and the cabbages as heads.

Bob would sometimes act out a particular incident in the *Something of Value*, as in the final scene when his hero, Peter, tracked his boyhood African friend, Kimani, to a Mau Mau hideout in the forest and attacked him with a knife. For this Bob had me on the office floor with a kitchen knife poised above my head so he could get the actual hand-hold correct.

On the typewriter, Bob was incredibly fast, though in the customary newspaper reporter fashion he used only two fingers. His typewriter sounded like an infantry machine gun as he punched away at the keys, as if he were fighting. He was terribly particular about his machine. No one used it except him, and I think this would apply even now if he could enforce this rule. He said that a typewriter became part of a person and anyone else using it damaged the balance, and it took him some time to get the machine back in shape.

When his venerable Underwood finally wore out, he wrote a column, dated October 12, 1956, entitled "Wreck of Old Ninety-Seven: Sad Blow to Ruark."

I wish to shed a tear today for the passing of an old and perhaps my best, friend. Old Ninety-Seven, more formally described as No. 11-6049748 of the Underwood clan, has been put out to pasture. The old girl's had it and deserves a peaceful retirement.

I refer to a battered standard typewriter which has provided more tea and sympathy for me and the dogs than any other thing, animate or inanimate.

With very little assistance from me, she has produced six books, about 500 magazine pieces, about 3,000 columns, a couple of screen efforts, Allah knows how many letters and a fair amount of short stories. Most of this grisly grist people were kind enough to pay for, or I would be dead of malnutrition.

I forget: One lousy play that nobody bought, but Old Ninety-Seven worked just as hard on that dog as on others less doggish.

Over the last ten years, she has learned how to speak Spanish, French, North Carolina dialect and a sort of Swahali, which is pretty good going for a machine that has been battered around by only two fingers for approximately 75,000,000 words.

On occasion she can even speak English-type English, as I have had an English-type secretary in recent years, a man who was appalled at Old Ninety-Seven's constant double negatives, such as "ain't got no." Before she fell sick, Ninety-Seven could say, "Really, my dear fellow," or "Jambo, bwana," or "Buenos dias," or "Bon jour" just as neat as you please.

What really wrecked her was when she tried to learn Catalan. She struggled with it manfully, failed and turned her face to the wall.

You understand, she had been completely faithful to me. All I had to do was roll in the paper, try the "I" key for size, pat her on the flank and give her her head.

She ate very little in the way of oil, and if her ribbon didn't gall her, she'd go like a dream. She invented plots and characters and ideas, and her song was as sweet as a linnet's when she toiled.

And faithful. You wouldn't read about how faithful she was. Any time a tough-typist tampered with her, she turned stool-pigeon and betrayed him or her. I could tell in a minute if some highfalutin shorthand-typist expert had been monkeying with my gal. Her keys lost luster, her spirit sagged and everything turned out ETOINSHRDLU.

But recently her faculties faded. She began to chew at her ribbons. The space bar kicked the door off the stable. She started catching my fingers between her keys, wounding me dreadfully and she was absolutely untrustworthy when I was a bit overexuberant from too many soda pops. She used to help me home, but no more.

Then she started deliberately to kill the the thing she loved. I would write "tonight," and it would come out "tongith." She balked at every barrier. I would try to write like "serious" and it would come out "seruorius." A simple exercise like "and" or "but" arrived as "adn" or "tub."

The back-spacer started to come in with its saddle slipped, and she deliberately started to chew the stall, leaving endings off infinitives and such like. I knew she was finished when I hit the "I" key and got "you" for my pains.

So out she goes to the green fields of retirement, and in comes another filly for me to housetrain. She's pretty and shiny and will undoubtedly break to harness some day, after a taste of the whip, but she'll never replace Old Ninety-Seven as the woman I love.

He concluded the delightful column with these words: "I intend to make a shrine of Old Ninety-Seven, glass case and all, but mama has another idea. She wants to paint her pink and plant her innards with philodendrons. But then Mama plants everything with philodendrons, and before that happens, I'll take the axe and mercifully put Old Ninety-Seven away."

As a result of this column, Bob was the recipient of a brand new Gold Touch Underwood typewriter, compliments of the manufacturer. As it turned out, he soon returned to Old Ninety-Seven and remained faithful to her to the very end.

Since Robert Ruark's main method of communication was by letter rather than telephone or personal visit, we wrote large quantities of correspondence. Here again Bob's facility in producing words easily was readily noticeable. He would say, "Come on Junior, let's write a short note to Hal." I would give a silent sigh of relief, mistakenly thinking that a "short note" would take about ten minutes. Generally it would turn out that a "short note" would become a four- or five-page letter, and not just to Harold Matson, his agent. The same sort of lengthy missives would go out to half a dozen book publishers or magazine editors, or to white hunters, and then just for luck, half a dozen three-pagers to his girlfriends.

Bob had a tremendous ability to dictate fast, always in a complete straight line. Never once was I required to read back any dictation, and I don't think I ever stopped him because he was going too fast for me. We both intensely disliked letter writing, feeling it was using up valuable book-writing time, so Bob went as fast as possible in order to get the unpleasant business out of the way. Certainly, I was much happier to get the shorthand taking over quickly.

Despite his speed and continuous flow of words, generally the letters would go out exactly as spoken. Of course, there were times when he would make alterations or corrections, but he never expected me to retype any letter.

Bob's correspondence really was an education in itself. It was lively, funny, rude and forceful, depending on his mood or reason for writing. I often thought it was good enough for publication.

Chapter 12
Ruark in His Prime

Broadly speaking, Ruark typed his prose straight onto his own machine, though sometimes he would do some book work by dictation since we managed so well with this approach. However, he really preferred to see what he was writing, so he typed it himself. He would then proofread extensively and continuously on all copy, and as a rule I would be constantly typing and retyping so that Bob could see what he had written. We were, in effect, book-writing at two speeds, and in this way we progressed through the long, trying procedure with all our existing copy completely clean and finished. This meant that when the end was actually reached, there was no necessity to go back and laboriously rewrite and retype what we had done six months previously.

Certain pages might be copied as much as a dozen times or even more. Each time Bob would lay in heavily with his pencil, but the most complicated time was when we had more than 1,600 pages, as was the case with *Poor No More* and *Uhuru*. At one time I was taking four copies, and then Bob would move 40 or 50 pages from the front to the end, or to the middle or some other part of the book. This completely confused all the numbering and all the copies would of course be affected. When this process had been repeated many times over, I marveled at myself that I was able to keep track of what was happening. Bob was likewise impressed, though he couldn't stand to watch me fiddling with all the paper. He said it made him nervous. But this was the way we produced a book, and most of Bob's prose was sufficiently flexible to be moved around as he thought best.

Many people have assumed that Virginia was of great help to Bob in his writing, but this was not really the case. She did help to keep Bob on a disciplined work regimen, but she had no part in the actual writing. When they were first married and before Bob had secretaries, Ginny did some of the newspaper clipping and similar work, but certainly during all the years I knew them she contributed little to his writing.

He always maintained that a wife was quite unsuitable when it came to assisting her husband with his writing. She would invariably criticize the plot structure on the way through, before she had any clear idea of what the intended outcome would be. Bob said he didn't want to be "knocked all to hell" while he was building a story, and in any case he found that the domestic squabble of the night before often entered into the literary assessment. On the other hand, he always said that Ginny was an excellent critic with the finished product. He would certainly listen to her views, of not only his own work but of other authors. She was a good reader.

When Bob was running well on a book, it was an exciting experience. Each day would bring a new surprise. He often would have inspirations late at night after he had spent many hours of copyreading with the aid of background music. On such occasions he would be more or less awake all night. He could not quiet down the activity of his brain, so sleep would wait until the next day. Sometimes, in order not to waste too much of the next day in bed, he would leave a note in my typewriter instructing me to give him a call.

A good example was the note he left when we were near the end of *Something of Value*. "Alan," he wrote, "I was up late – so excited I couldn't sleep. JACKPOT!!!!!! Get me up no later than ten so I can tell you while it's hot!"

This particular note referred to the sudden thought Bob had regarding Elizabeth, the wife of a white farmer who had been killed by the Mau Mau. She was seriously injured and Bob had intended for her to die as well. Then he changed his mind and let her live and overcome her injuries to give birth to a child. This act of compassion on his part helped Bob enormously with his future plot construction.

Ruark must have been the fastest book-writing author who ever lived. When we were going well, we could figure on between 70 and 100 copyread pages a week. This rate of progress would allow for other work such as columns, correspondence and magazine articles, not to mention house guests and booze. A big book of well over a thousand typewritten pages could be produced in less than six months.

Despite his speed of production, it must be remembered that Bob spent a long period in the germination of his ideas. This often included extensive research from his vast library, and in the case of the books on Africa, numerous visits to the continent.

Even as one book was barely started, he would be considering the title and general plan of the next. Accordingly, when the day arrived when Bob felt it was time to get started, matters moved fast. He would set a personal deadline, which was always too soon and never kept, though no doubt this helped him face the task of starting to write on a big book. No matter how many problems we encountered along the way, as the end of a book approached, Bob always speeded up the whole writing procedure. Like a thoroughbred, he finished at a fast clip and in good style.

If one knew the signs, it was quite easy to tell when Bob was coming to the end of a novel. He became excitedly nervous, refused all social engagements, and furiously pulled out his mustache hair by hair to the point where it looked like a dried-up patch of cut wheat. This would continue until he had shipped to his agent in New York the four or five telephone directory-sized folders of clean, finished copy that constituted a book manuscript.

The actual completion of a book was often where the real trouble started. With the single exception of *Something of Value*, there were serious over-writing problems with the other big books. Wordiness was definitely one of Bob's faults. Since he found it comparatively easy to write large numbers of words, he preferred to let his book prose run its complete length uninterrupted, then trim later. The trimming and condensing procedure would then reduce the copy to say half of the original copy. Even so, the manuscripts were often too long. The worst experience was when we were required to remove a full 400 pages from the "finished" manuscript of *Uhuru*. As Bob said at the time: "Look Junior, we throw away more words than most authors put into their books in the first place."

Some months later, when writing the original draft of the autobiographical piece for *True Magazine,* Bob wrote:

"I really have very little patience with writers who do things the hard way, unless hungry necessity dictates the rocky path. I see no nobility in the fact that it took Katherine Anne Porter twenty-four years to write a single novel. All I can think is that she spent more time looking for fresh subsidy grants from new foundations than she spent writing. Truman Capote, an occasional neighbor of mine in Spain, has been four years on one small piece of reportage. Truman writes in bed, off a bread board, I presume with an old quill pen dipped in green or purple ink, and reckons that nineteen or twenty pages a month is a big deal. But Truman has occupied four different houses on the Costa Brava during this ordeal, with separate waystops in Corsica, London and Switzerland. A man with a method can write a book in less time than Truman spends in packing up his bulldog and crating his papers."

Ruark was not to know that Truman Capote's "small piece of reportage," *In Cold Blood,* was to become a top bestseller and make an estimated two million dollars for the author by the time it was published. Paperback rights brought another half-million dollars, as did film rights. That was far more than Bob ever made on a single book.

As a book author, columnist, short story and magazine writer, Robert Ruark was self-sufficient. Even though he was a master at his craft, he needed a special service that I was able to supply. That involved nothing more than listening to the anatomy of his plots at length. If Bob was able to explain himself verbally, sooner or later he would be able to sit down and write, and he usually did so in a straightforward, efficient fashion.

So our writing procedure, used mainly for books, was to sit down in my office for an hour or two. Bob would gradually get himself into gear by going through some of what he had already written, and he would make various probing suggestions as to the future sequence and route of his story. What he needed more than anything was a sympathetic listener and someone who knew what had gone before. Since I am a good listener and don't feel compelled to speak all the time, these morning pre-writing sessions were most valuable. In these discussions the ideas would be mainly Bob's, but a suitable agreement or disagreement could and did influence him. More than anything, it helped him to size up the value of different possibilities.

This consultation procedure was our standard writing method and was used for all of our book projects. It did differ somewhat in the case of *Something of Value,* Bob was so overwhelmingly full of information before we started it all he really had to do was sit at his typewriter. Certainly, he did not know the exact form his story was to take, but he had the information so tightly packed in his head that once we got started, it was rather as if a dam had burst.

The previous winter he had made a trip to Australia aboard the *Lloyd Triestino*, and during this voyage he actually wrote the first 82 pages of *Something of Value*. His working title for the book at that time was "Carrion Men." These 82 pages were then set aside for a few months while Bob once again visited the scene of the Mau Mau uprising in Kenya, and eventually he got down to the heavy work during the summer of 1954 at Palamos. The actual writing time for the book, running out at just on a thousand pages of typewritten copy and containing in the region of 300,000 words, was no more than four months.

The manuscript, which Bob took to New York towards the end of 1954, was published virtually without change. Once it had been read by Harold Matson, all sorts of good things began to happen. There was excitement from all directions – publishers, the film world and book clubs. It became a Book-of-the-Month Club selection for May, 1955, and Matson went to the movie market immediately. In fact, the deal was made practically before the publishers got their hands on the manuscript. The key studios interested in the rights were Twentieth Century Fox and Metro-Goldwyn-Mayer.

Bob was on vacation in Cuba when an excited Harold Matson tracked him down on the phone. The connection wasn't too good, but the conversation went like this:

Matson: "That you Bob? Got a drink, and a chair?"
Ruark: "Sure."
Matson: "Well Bob, you better sit down. I sold it to the pictures."
Ruark: "How much?"
Matson: "Three. MGM bought it."
Ruark: "Oh Hal – you can do better than that!"
Matson: "Not three thousand dollars you idiot! Three hundred thousand dollars and a hundred and fifty thousand dollars for the screenplay."
Ruark: "That's nice."

He then hung up in confusion before the enormity of it all struck him.

The film deal was made before the book actually appeared in print and was really done on the word of the agent. Before the deal was actually finalized, Bob had a nerve-wracking time. This was because MGM required him to obtain signed releases from a number of people in Kenya. An agonizing six months passed between the initial MGM agreement to buy the film rights for *Something of Value* and the time that the first monies were actually released for payment. MGM was concerned about the possible invasion of privacy of people in Kenya who could conceivably claim resemblance to characters in the novel.

Bob's foreword to the book didn't help matters.

"The characters in this book are entirely fictitious, but that does not mean that they leaped full-grown from an over-inventive mind. They were painfully compounded of bits and pieces of people I know in Kenya, alive and dead, young and old, black and white, males and female, and assembled as you would build a jigsaw puzzle. But no single character is patterned on a single person. There is no intent to duplicate or compromise in fiction the personality or actions of any living person."

MGM's extensive study of the situation not only established definite similarities between all the white characters in the book and actual people, but even maintained that there was some risk of complaints from the black servants, gunbearers and staff on different farms. Jomo Kenyatta was also mentioned in this report, as there would be no possibility of masking him as the leader of the Mau Mau movement about whom Bob had written many times and whose name was in the book.

Also, reading through the reports it appeared that there was even a dog named Bonzo who came under very close scrutiny, as his name was mentioned liberally throughout, and then there was a full page of copy concerning the dog's habits and activities. Bonzo would have been considered because Bob wrote a piece originally called BONZO'S BOY for *Collier's* magazine, but printed under the title of "Nairobi Incident." In this story Bob brings out the bravery of a piebald mongrel dog against the Mau Mau and his devotion to a new-found master, a hotel manager. However, so far as I know, Bonzo was not required to sign a release.

One can sympathize with the film company's caution given their experiences with lawsuits. The outcome was that Bob was required to obtain more than 20 signed releases from people in Kenya, most of whom presented no great problems as they were friends. However, one worrisome stumbling block proved to be the two English ladies who very adequately defended their homestead during a Mau Mau attack and about whom Bob had written in his article, "Your Guns Go with You," for *Life Magazine*. He had mentioned their bravery again in *Something of Value*.

These two women figured in a bloodthirsty portion of the book and, on advice of their lawyer, decided they didn't want to sign any releases for anybody. Here was Bob with a fortune almost within his grasp, and both he and Harold Matson became very nervous at the delay. Seemingly endless intercessions and demands from lawyers wore heavily on Ruark's patience, and he remarked to Matson that the problems were "definitely attributable to legal stupidity and a lot of bloody fuss about nothing."

The problem remained unresolved late in 1955, when after further inquiries about the state of matters in Nairobi, Bob received the following cable: "HAVE INTERVIEWED WOMEN. STOP. REFUSE SIGN. STOP. VERY INDIGNANT. STOP. HAVE DONE EVERYTHING POSSIBLE. STOP. THEY SAY WILL SUE FIRST OPPORTUNITY. STOP. PLEASE ADVISE. STOP"

Ruark passed this information on to Matson and with it his thoughts on the matter:

"I am not at all perturbed at the threat of suit as I know the old trouts and this would be a typical reaction. It is one thing to talk suit and another thing to instigate international litigation against vast corporations when you are two old lesbians living on a remote hill. In any case, their only possible ground for suit would be an assumption of invasion of privacy, since they did, in fact, kill the negroes and were decorated by the Queen for it and since they were not portrayed maliciously and since finally they read and approved the factual story in

Life Magazine, written three years ago, and have had the last three years to consider suit, if they did not like the facts as portrayed factually."

Eventually, after endless legal argument, the film company decided they could ignore the episode that included these two women, and the whole deal went through as originally planned. But the strain on Bob's nervous system had been excessive and certainly contributed to his first collapse in London about a month later.

There had also been considerable nervousness from Bob's British publisher (Editor's note: The publisher was Hamish Hamilton) regarding libel, and Ruark expressed his feelings on that in a letter to Matson:

"I am planning not to coddle Mr. Hamilton's legal eagles very much as there is actually no libel in the book, since my last copyreading, and I am just not disposed to spend the rest of my life wet nursing a bunch of goddamn lawyers. I can understand MGM's reasonable qualms, but you know bloody well that nobody in Kenya is going to declare himself a murderer in order to identify himself with a fictional character. There ain't no such thing as an invasion of privacy in the life of either a white hunter or self-declared and decorated murderesses such as my two old girls on the mountain."

The filming of *Something of Value* was eventually made by MGM in Kenya with Richard Brooks directing. It starred Rock Hudson, Dana Wynter, Sydney Poitier and Wendy Hiller. Bob wasn't particularly pleased with the result, and said so, pointing out that if one hadn't read the book, then it could pass as a pretty good movie. On the other hand, if you had the real book story in mind, then you began to wonder why MGM paid $450,000 for it. Bob reckoned you couldn't even tell who was the wife and who was the sister of the hero.

Some of Bob's antagonism could have been the result of a remark allegedly made by the director of the film concerning the accuracy of the book. Harold Matson passed this information on to Bob and sent along a copy of a letter to the head of Loew's Incorporated, parent company of MGM:

"In last Sunday's *New York Times* (September 16, 1956) in the section including motion picture news and comment, there was what purported to be an interview by Thomas M. Pryer with Richard Brooks, who was identified as the director of the forthcoming picture, *Something of Value*, Mr. Brooks was quoted as saying: "When we went to Kenya to shoot backgrounds, I discovered the book was inaccurate about many things."

"It is hard to believe that a responsible person could make such a public statement under the circumstances involved. Mr. Ruark is in an advantageous position to answer such an accusation. Could you find out whether Mr. Brooks was accurately quoted, and if not, whether he intends to request a correction in the *Times*; and if he was accurately quoted, would he elaborate, giving details of his criticism for submission to Mr. Ruark?"

Predictably, Bob's reaction to this was fairly violent, and he relieved some of his annoyance in a letter to Harold Matson: "I think I told you before that I have decided to stay with the column, not only for the money involved, which is pleasant, but also because it keeps me reading, it keeps me active at the typewriter and is of course, a happy sounding board for national expression of personal opinion, such as:

"The fact is that you may inform MGM that if this son-of-a-bitch Brooks doesn't cork his beak I am going to use this sounding board rather effectively against everything I can lay tongue to concerning them. I don't know who got hold of this young man, but the facts are these. He was in Kenya one month and couldn't possibly know if there were errors even if there were, and there weren't. The solid complaint that I have had from Kenya is that the book was all too horribly accurate and true, and my worst accusation was from a British fellow in Hong Kong who maintained I could not be Ruark since he was an American, and Ruark was obviously a retired army officer living in Kenya. Concerning the last outburst of Mr. Richard Brooks, I want somebody to tell him to shut up about errors because he is inviting my columnal wrath, which I don't think they really would like to have. I like Clark, but the rest of them are as bad a bunch of obstructionist bastards as I ever encountered."

This turned out to be a tempest in a teacup, which didn't amount to a great deal, and despite everything, Bob was delighted to have some special private showings of the movie in New York and various other places. He was pleased to see that Sir Winston Churchill made a brief appearance in the film. Churchill was seen on screen looking back to his tour of Africa as a young man. "Forty-nine years ago I visited Africa," he stated. In my book *My African Journey*, I wrote: 'The problems of East Africa are the problems of the world.' This was true in 1907. It is true today."

The studio had located this Churchillian comment while doing research for the film and had sought his permission to use the words in introducing the movie. He not only agreed but was filmed speaking them.

Later, in August, 1957, the movie was considered sufficiently good to be selected by the American Association of Film Producers as the country's official entry in the big international film festival held in Venice.

Then the manuscript of *Something of Value* was received by the British publisher, Hamish Hamilton, who immediately began considering the possibility of prosecution on grounds that it was obscene. He sought an opinion from a leading British barrister, Sir Hartley Shawcross. Although it took him several hundred words to get to the heart of the matter, Shawcross, while acknowledging he was "squeamish and old-fashioned," came to the conclusion that "I certainly cannot advise that this book, if published, might not be made the subject of a successful prosecution." However, his reservations clearly were not strong enough to stop publication, because it appeared in Britain under the Hamish Hamilton imprint.

Something of Value was on the bestseller lists from the start, and within a few weeks it topped the list. Still, the publishers felt the book had failed to come up to full expectations. This dissatisfaction mystified Bob, as even at that early stage sales were over 50,000, and they ended up at over 120,000 copies in the United

States. The work sold an unprecedented 140,000 hardcover copies in England and was translated into roughly a dozen foreign languages. Then the Book-of-the-Month Club distribution, which sold over 300,000 copies, would have, to some extent, detracted from bookstore sales.

In any event, towards the end of August, sales received an extra boost from the publicity attendant on Bob appearing on the cover of *Newsweek*, dressed in safari cloths, with a backdrop of a roaring lion as added effect. The magazine cover story concerning big bestsellers hinged around *Something of Value*.

While Bob was pleased with the publicity derived from the *Newsweek* cover, he was disappointed and annoyed at the actual story. He had spent five days accommodating and working with *Newsweek* correspondent Bill Blair, but when it came to the actual write-up, very little of his interview was used. With this in mind and given the fact his publishers claimed to have assisted in the creation of the story as printed, Bob wrote an angry letter to the publishing house's editor-in-chief:

"Concerning the *Newsweek* story, I am going to be less appreciative of your aid and assistance there than you would imagine. It was a good story about books. As far as I was concerned I was merely the Foreword and the Postscript to an essay. They might just as well have run the copy of any book on the cover instead of my rugged kisser. He (Bill Blair) wrote an excellent piece I thought and I was more or less heartbroken by the fact that it was thrown away to make room for the prefabricated version the New York office did. Scope or non-scope, people still like to read people. I ain't carping, but amongst the other things that I would choose to handle more or less on my own in the future is my own publicity, as I have had considerable experience in this field."

Bob was really hoping for some prize recognition for *Something of Value*. He felt it warranted something, and though he didn't think a Nobel Prize was a possibility, he thought maybe there was a chance for a Pulitzer. At the time he said to me: "If we win it, chum, you can have the $500 prize money." We didn't win it, of course.

Lack of prize recognition notwithstanding, Bob certainly wasn't suffering financially. By the end of 1955 he had an impressive list of earnings. On top of royalty income from bookstore sales, his share of the Book-of-the-Month Club sales came to $50,000. The paperback rights were sold to Pocket Books for what was, at that time, a record amount of $106,000. This was shared between Bob and the publisher of the hard cover. Added to all of this was the movie sale to MGM for $450,000. The total amount came close to half a million dollars.

With the successful completion and publication of *Something of Value*, I had been introduced to book-writing under most favorable conditions, especially in view of the impressive financial results. The whole project had been a great experience for me, and I was particularly pleased when Bob included me among the various acknowledgements. He wrote: "Some attention might also gratefully be directed to Alan M. Ritchie, a good friend who helped me heavily in the preparation of this book." In my autographed copy of the book he added: "This is for Alan, my partner in crime, toil and tears – without whose loss of one stone in weight we never would have got the damn thing done. Sincere thanks from the co-author – Bob."

Ruark had spent a lot of time in Kenya and was there during the Mau Mau emergency, so he had considerable firsthand information that was used in *Something of Value*. This included many grisly details of Mau Mau activities during their loathsome oath-giving ceremonies. Although the finished book contained a great amount of bloody detail, Bob had in fact reduced this aspect considerably from the first draft, which was unpublishable. In addition to believing he had a good storyline, Bob felt the overall picture he drew was fair to both black and white.

The diverse reactions of reviewers never ceased to amaze and amuse both Bob and me. The critics said just about everything possible from good to bad to indifferent. *Something of Value* was referred to as "Nothing of Value," "Something of Doubtful Value," "Something of No Value" and as "a work of real value." One reviewer even styled it "a guidebook, but not a novel." To that reviewer, Bob remarked: "It would indeed have been a most unusual tour visiting the oath-giving ceremonies and the cattle chopping with a bunch of tourists!"

"Brutal," "gruesome," "heartless" and "disappointing" were used liberally, and phrases such as "gripping but revolting," "a real soaking in gore" and "carries the stench of the abattoir," were commonplace. Then there was the reviewer who said *Something of Value* is the most loathsome novel I have read in nearly twenty-five years of reviewing."

Although the book had already had a stormy passage, there was still more to come. It sat on the bestseller lists right through the summer of 1955, took top place around the end of June, and held steadily in the top four or five until the end of the year. Everything was just fine until an unfortunate incident caused a violent upset between Bob and his publisher. This came about because an abridged version, sandwiched between *Auntie Mame* and *The Scotswoman*, appeared in *Books Abridged*.

Bob was spitting fire when he received a copy of the abridged book and realized what had been done. He immediately cabled the publisher:

"INSULTING LETTER FOLLOWS BUT YOU'RE SERIOUSLY ADVISED NOT WELCOME IN MY HOUSE AFTER CHEAP DEAL ON BOOKS ABRIDGED. STOP. YOU RECEIVED LETTER AUGUST FIFTH OF WHICH I HAVE CARBON. MY SERIOUS OBJECTION EXCERPTING OR CONDENSATION OF BOOK AND STRONGLY DENYING RIGHTS TO ABRIDGE WITHOUT CONSULTING ME AND MATSON. STOP. CONSIDER ADVISABLE WITHDRAW FROM SALE BOOKS ABRIDGED PENDING CONVERSATION WITH MATSON AND LAWYERS AS REGARDS THIS DIRTIEST POOL EVER MET. STOP. IN SEVENTEEN YEARS EXPERIENCE IN THIS FIELD YOU HAVE AT LEAST FAILED TO SATISFY ONE AUTHOR. – RUARK"

The last line was a profound understatement, but it came from a blurb on the book's dust jacket claiming they had never had a dissatisfied author in 17 years of experience.

Various letters passed back and forth after this incident. The head of Doubleday pointed out that legally Doubleday had the right to make the sale of the condensed version, but that they certainly would not have done so if it had been realized how Bob might react. Actually, there was ample evidence to guess what the reaction would be, as through the previous winter Matson and Bob had been violently opposed to any condensation, any shortening, or any cutting whatsoever. They were so strong on this point that they even considered turning down the Book-of-the-Month Club deal if the Club insisted on trimming the story. At the same time no consideration was given to a *Reader's Digest* condensation.

Apart from this, Bob had never been keen on excerpting of any kind. The "insulting letter" he referred to in his cable never actually materialized. By the time he wrote, he was more in a mood to clarify what had happened. He wrote a mild letter to the editor at Doubleday.

"I have always been very fond of you personally, and that added to my stupid anger since what I felt was a cheap and stupid stab came from a friend. No matter what the arguments in favor of these abridgements are, I still think it is stupid to take the play away from a number two book, by offering bits and pieces of it in pre-digested form. A sick book, yes. A dubious book, yes. But not a book that has been running one, two, three for six months at $5 a chunk, and which has had the Book-of-the-Month selection, a Pocket Books record sale, a record movie sale, and a weekly news magazine profile, in addition to the vast amounts of huge reviews.

"I was sore for another reason. The book withstood the dreariest book summer, complicated by heat and hurricanes, and fought stoutly with fluff, *Auntie Mame* and *Bonjour Tristesse*, at half the price. It showed a sharp upturn after the *Newsweek* profile, which is unbeatable publicity for any book, and it seemed to me that the time for word-of-mouth to take over was at hand, with a good stout four months of book reading and Christmas buying to operate in our favor. It seemed to me that an additional 10,000 copies with this in mind, was a most picayunish venture to coddle into longer sales, since, as you know, it is very difficult to sell books if there are none or just a few in the bookshops.

"The way I was feeling at the time hardly seemed a propitious attitude for a host to take to a house guest (Editor's note: Before the brouhaha he had invited the Doubleday editor to visit him at Palamos), which I am afraid I made all too bluntly clear. The Irish temper has abated somewhat, which is why I put off the writing of this letter, but I still think the whole business was shabby, stupid and unethical, as well as being careless."

In writing to Matson, his literary agent, Bob admitted that "perhaps my anger was the cherry on top of a general sundae of discontent. However, if you run into anybody from Doubleday, you might quote me bitterly as saying that if I had known they needed the money I would have been pleased to have sent them $1,250, representing their share of the latest *coup d'etat*."

Of course, everybody was unhappy that this unpleasant occurrence had taken place, and I suppose there were rights and wrongs on both sides, but Bob considered it quite inexcusable to knock down your own product when it was doing so well. Also, he was frightened that maybe an infringement had been established of his record paperback contract with Pocket Books, a deal that wasn't worth spoiling for the small payment for the abridged version.

While Bob had already been considering the possibility of changing publishers, there is no doubt that this particular incident was instrumental in precipitating change. He wrote to Matson in no uncertain terms:

"I want out! Something very sour has been going on there for a long time. I don't know what it is, but I don't want it."

Ruark had commenced with Doubleday & Company in 1948 with his first book, *Grenadine Etching*, and they had also published *I Didn't Know It Was Loaded, One for the Road, Grenadine's Spawn* and *Horn of the Hunter*. They were also scheduled to get the book that followed *Something of Value*, which would be entitled *Poor No More*.

The 1959 publication of *Poor No More* saw a switch to Henry Holt and Company as publisher. They were particularly acceptable to Bob since they were the publishers of *Field & Stream* magazine, which he had enjoyed working with. In all Bob would do three books with Henry Holt, with the others being collections of "The Old Man and the Boy" articles. These appeared as *The Old Man and the Boy* and *The Old Man's Boy Grows Older*. Both books were highly acclaimed and became a special purchase for fathers to give their sons. Holt ran an excellent sales campaign with direct publicity to over 650,000 subscribers to *Field & Stream*, and the final sales were quite gratifying.

Many people had always maintained that "The Old Man and the Boy" pieces were some of Bob's finest writing. He enjoyed writing them, but toward the end of his association with *Field & Stream*, he found it increasingly difficult to produce a suitable piece. In a way this was understandable, since Bob kept these reminiscences going with an article a month for over ten years, from 1951 to 1961.

Bob was particularly pleased with the handling of *The Old Man and the Boy*, and he especially liked the line drawings by Walter Dower. He made a special trip to North Carolina in his Rolls Royce, taking the artist with him, with that in mind. He got exactly what he wanted on the cover – an enormous, spread-eagled oak across the dust jacket's spine.

Bob continued to be quite pleased with the regular sales reports for *The Old Man and the Boy*, until one day a new editor at Henry Holt advised him that they had sold some excerpts from the book to the Reading for Men Book Club, one of Doubleday's many operations. Once again Bob exploded in exasperated anger. This time, there was even more amazement, since he had been convinced this excerpting problem could not possibly appear again.

He immediately wrote the offending editor:

I ain't pleased about you selling *The Old Man and the Boy* to *Reading for Men* without informing either Harold Matson or me of your intent. The lousy $500 for your pocket and mine does not justify condensation. This was one of the two reasons I quit Doubleday and if it happens again on any subsequent, I will quit Holt too. My idea is that a book should sell as a book and not as a predigested excerpt."

The fact that this came so soon after the excerpting of *Something of Value* caused added annoyance, and for the excerpts from this new book to have been sold to a subsidiary of Doubleday, the very publisher from whom Bob had so recently fled, added insult to injury.

Once again everybody was sorry that it had happened. The excuse this time was that *The Old Man and the Boy* didn't fall into the same category as a novel. In answer to a letter of explanation and apology from his editor (written with a suggestion of nervousness, since the contract for *Poor No More* had not yet been signed), Ruark replied somewhat tersely:

"Received yours June 27th and don't want you to get your ass in too much of an uproar. I am in the final stress and strain of finishing a book, and I am afraid I might be a little shorter in temper than ordinarily. But I still think I got a good point which should be maintained in the future. No condensation or outside peddlings of our stuff should be done without consulting either Hal or me. I cite you one example FYI that Doubleday was fully prepared to sell Pocket Book rights for $3,600 when Matson got wind of it and we would have wound up with $106,000. That was just $50,000 more in my pocket than normally would have been accrued if Hal hadn't heard something and jumped into the breech."

When Bob received his first copy of *The Old Man's Boy Grows Older* he was initially very pleased. He liked the presentation and the African scene on the dust jacket with zebras, Mount Kenya in the background and a large acacia tree spreading from the front to the back of the book. He had just begun saying how pleased he was when he came to the dust jacket blurb:"But the Old Man is still there. He is there in anecdotal memories awakened by the sight of a tiger in Africa."

It seemed inevitable that with every book something was bound to happen that thoroughly annoyed Bob, and when he discovered the mention of the tiger he immediately dictated a blistering letter to his publisher:

"I think it is a very handsome book overall and can only complain that whatever genius prepared your dust jacket blurb happened to locate tigers in Africa, which is not only unlikely but impossible, as there ain't no tigers in Africa!

"A tiny little stupid mistake like this does detract from the overall value of the book, if only as a reflection on the author's right to deal with his subject. In short I would trust no outdoor writer whose claim to fame was the fact that he had anything at all to do with tigers in Africa, any more than I would consider blond Eskimos as natural in Florida."

Both of the *Old Man and the Boy* books had interesting dedications, the first giving a good indication as to the origin of most of the material – that the Old Man was really a number of people.

"This book is for the memory of my grandfathers, Captain Edward Hall Adkins and Hanson Kelly Ruark; for my father, Robert Chester Ruark, Sr.; and for all the honorary uncles, black and white, who took me to raise."

The dedication to the second volume was also of considerable interest: "This book is for two grown-up boys, who once shared an idea in a rowboat. I do not recall that we caught any fish, but the idea was a beaut."

The underlying explanation here is that he got the idea for the book during a conversation with his publisher while the two of them were fishing about ten years previously. In fact, as a further indication of his appreciation, Bob wrote to his publisher:

"Enclosed also is the dedication of this book which will be immediately obvious to you. I did precisely not mention us by name for a variety of reasons, the main one of which was that I didn't think it is good public relations to go around dedicating books to your publisher. I do, however, want you to know that there is a heartfelt gratitude in this dedication, which is why I include myself as the other small boy."

Bob always showed an enormous amount of loyalty to *Field & Stream*, and he took great pride in contributing to the magazine. He always remembered that when he threw in the towel on his newspaper column as he prepared to leave New York in 1953, his only certain source of income was $15,000 for the "Old Man and the Boy" series. Bob never forgot the people who had helped him in the past. So much was this the case that later on, when negations were taking place between Harold Matson and Holt for Bob's first book contract, his loyalty to *Field & Stream* threatened to get in the way of the deal.

Harold Matson wrote to him in this regard:

"I have been keeping in mind your pitch to me about the place in your life that has been F & S's. But I'm not giving them anything for free. Or for sentimental reasons. We're simply dealing with each other on a frank and friendly basis. I know what F & S has meant to you, and me, but as the fly-wheel on this engine, I also know what RR has meant to F & S, and leave us not belittle ourselves. The royalty scale will be realistic: It will give them elbow room in which to produce a suitably handsome book and will contribute to the general inducement to promote and distribute it."

CHAPTER 13
NEW PROBLEMS & POOR NO MORE

For many years Bob had been eager to get into film-making in some form. He was keen to try his hand at writing a screenplay, and he felt there was an enormous earning potential that should be easier than what he was doing. He had already gained a little experience when he made his *Africa Adventure* safari film in 1952 and provided the commentary for it. The narrative was written in a single day.

This was done in Barcelona during the time it took for the movie director to take a ride to Palamos to see Bob's home. By the time he returned late the same day, Bob had the commentary knocked into shape. A day or two later he narrated what he had written, and it was judged quite satisfactory. *Africa Adventure* had been sold to RKO-Pathe for $15,000, which Bob felt to be a quite reasonable return.

Later in 1955 Bob met with veteran screenplay writer Sy Bartlett, who wished to collaborate with him on an oil story. Bartlett had a good deal of research already prepared, and Bob was particularly keen to work with this veteran professional who had some 35 major releases to his credit. It was to be a 50-50 deal and about the only special requirement Bob made was that Harold Matson handle the entire deal.

The saga was later named "The Well at Ras Daga." It had all the ingredients for success – love, hate, drama, action and the eternal triangle. The screenplay's primary focus was the association of two close friends who had worked together on well-drilling projects for 17 years. A tough hard American geologist who had a reputation as ladies man was the driving force behind the partnership. His comrade, an Englishman, was a driller by profession. A solid, staid man who was somewhat older than his American counterpart, he seemed interested in nothing but the oil well business. At least that was the case until he produced an attractive Italian girl, who later described herself as a "public girl," as his wife.

This project began while *Something of Value* was selling well. At the time it seemed a fine idea to cash in on the enormous publicity this book had given Bob, not to mention MGM's forthcoming movie. Also, because of Sy Bartlett's close association with Gregory Peck, it appeared that a good deal could be made when the screenplay was ready.

Things didn't turn out quite this way. The authors experienced considerable difficulty and delay in selling the screenplay, which hung around for some four years. It looked as if this venture in writing film originals would not even find a buyer. For starters, the expectations were too big and some studios were frightened off because of the asking price. This had been set at $200,000, which was actually a compromise, since Bartlett had wanted to start even higher.

Although Bob was thoroughly annoyed as time passed, he consoled himself with the following thoughts in a letter to his agent:"I do not mind at all investing six weeks of my valuable time in learning a new medium and I think that you will agree that the experience I gain from working with an old pro like Sy is worth more to me in terms of the future than if I spent the time writing magazine pieces for *Reader's Digest* and *The Saturday Evening Post*. I have already learned an inordinate amount about screen dramatization which I would have had to acquire through painful trial and effort without the guidance of an old hand."

Finally, at the eleventh hour, there seemed to be a deal. Then there was a further delay because the contract did not include control of television rights, and Matson, thinking like an agent, wrote: "I couldn't face the possibility of this yarn being the basis of a TV series or serial with no royalty for you."

Though the deal was a bit touch-and-go for a while, this point was agreed upon. "The Well at Ras Daga" was purchased by Robert Mitchum, in conjunction with United Artist Corporation, for $100,000. However, it was never made into a movie and presumably is still on the shelf. The purchase price, when carved down the middle with Sy Bartlett, less the agent's ten percent commission, fell well short of Bob's original expectations. Yet he realized we had been lucky to sell it at all.

It seemed inevitable that when we were deep into a big book, *Something of Value* would be held up as an example of quality and speed of production. Sometimes we almost wished we hadn't written it, and no other book was ever written in a straight line. From the publication of *Something of Value* onward, we never had such a satisfying writing experience. All the subsequent books encountered serious stumbling blocks. For example, the next one, *Poor No More*, encountered problems because I developed yellow jaundice.

Bob would write in my copy: "This is for poor Senor Ritchie without whose jaundice this book would have been in print one year earlier. In any case, thanks chum – and happy new house. Bob."

We were well into the book and were progressing normally when I contracted yellow jaundice. Immediately after receiving the hard word from the Palamos doctor, I telephoned Bob, who was in Barcelona at the time, to inform him of the calamity. The note of anguish in his voice was quite discernible: "Alan, are you quite sure? This is an absolute disaster." After a pause, he continued: "Christ, then you had better pack up and come to Barcelona and stay in the apartment as the medical treatment will be better, and we don't want the whole household infected, and my liver couldn't stand a jaundice attack."

Actually I was back in Palamos within a month, but this break in continuity upset Bob's storyline, despite the fact he had the best possible stenographic replacement. I was not available for long discussions of future plot intentions so he could get matters clear in his mind. It was at this juncture he got off on a completely wrong tack, to the point that when he finished the manuscript and presented it to his agent in New York, it was rejected with a caustic comment.

"It seems to me," Matson wrote, "you may have written an elaborate treatment of a book you may have had in mind to write some day."

Then Ginny came in with criticism of her own. "Your hero is a windy bore," she said. Bob then realized that something had really gone wrong. Later he would comment: "It was like getting kicked in the stomach by a particularly well-coordinated mule, but I was actually relieved. I had felt a little peculiar about the book and didn't know why. I actually felt great relief when I heaved 400,000 clean words into the fireplace and set out to rewrite the whole opus awful. I found the hair-shirt bearable, the masochism comforting, and the work went well. When I had the next 400,000 words, and my boy took a slow read and said, 'Now that's more like it.' I felt as if I'd just been knighted."

When Bob recovered from the original shock of Matson's devastating criticism, and he was someone in whom he believed and to whom he listened, he went to Fort Lauderdale, Florida with the idea of attempting to pull the whole thing to pieces. He then came rushing back to Palamos where he could sit and ear bash his captive slave. We ripped it to pieces and put it back together again, and the whole procedure cost us about a year's delay in publication.

Bob's first finished manuscript of more than 1,500 pages had large chunks of descriptive prose, with the hero, Craig Price, talking interminably to his various girlfriends about what he had done and intended to do. Then there was at least a 50-page section of dialogue while Craig was in bed with one of these girls.

This was a very hard time for Bob, and me, as it was difficult to see any end to our toil. Each time we sat down we discovered some new incident in the book that needed rewriting. In a letter to his agent, Bob expressed our feelings as follows: "All I can say is that every time I see a lousy review from now on I wish the cocksucker who wrote it could be translated into me and Mr. Ritchie at the moment."

Matson, a close friend as well as a fine literary agent, wrote back in an effort to offer encouragement:

"I hope you have the stomach and the nerves for the kind of work required. I'm sure there comes a point when a writer has had it, and can do no more, and I hope you're a long way on this side of that point because of the great difference there'll be between the novel with Book II on stage and the present version. Actually, I'm ready to bet a bottom dollar the potential novel is the one you intended to write in the first place but didn't because of external (or maybe internal, too) pressure which made you impatient. It's all there, like an elaborate treatment of a novel to write."

During this period of transition a problem developed with our British publisher, Hamish Hamilton. He had been sent the first version and was under the mistaken impression that what he had in hand was the final draft. Accordingly, Hamilton went ahead and had the printer typeset this long-winded version, not realizing that Bob was reworking the book, changing its chronology and introducing new characters.

At some stage in these proceedings, when Bob happened to be in New York visiting with Matson, the British publisher sent a cable plaintively inquiring: "What shall we do with all this type? Ruark and Matson cabled back, succinctly, "Melt it."

Ruark then wrote a lengthy letter to Hamish Hamilton trying to explain the situation, saying he was "dreadfully sorry" for the delay and the problems with the printer. He also included mention of an ominous development. "For your information, as a friend, I had another one of my small but discomforting blackouts and have only just got my strength back." He concluded with a promise to get the manuscript completed as quickly as possible, but also noting: "I will not turn this thing loose until I feel and Hal feels that it is the best book I can write on this particular subject."

During the final rearranging of *Poor No More*, we had lunch with a certain well-known visitor, the daughter of a famous British cabinet minister. We all thought she was a very charming lady, though indeed, we were to change our opinions drastically.

At this time, all 'round my office were piles and piles of loosely numbered pages of *Poor No More* that had been ruthlessly changed into a new order with suitable connecting prose, but without pagination numbers. I was making four copies of everything, so in all there was more than 6,000 pages, plus those from which I had been copying. This would have been quite all right, providing we had been left alone to tidy up the apparent confusion. But then, several days after our lunch with the young lady, we were required to go to her rescue at one of the nearby fishing villages where she had commenced a marathon drinking session.

Arriving at the place where she was renting a room, we were greeted by a scene straight out of the classic *Lost Weekend*. It was something to behold: The artist's easel and paint-splattered canvas, dirty clothing, discarded canvases and empty wine bottles strewn everywhere along with the rancid smell of stale cheese and cigarette smoke. Then there was the leering, spittle-covered face of the drink-dazed artist and her dank, matted and unwashed hair.

Taking in this pretty scene, we started to gather up the woman's belongings. Bob told me to guard her while he went off to pay the bill, but she managed to escape out the back of the building. Soon I was chasing her through the narrow, medieval backstreets of the old fishing town. When I finally caught up with her, she was balanced precariously on a high wall from which, it seemed, she intended to jump into the sea.

With considerable difficulty I brought her back to the Rolls and we dumped her into the back seat. Bob kindly gave me the job of trying to subdue her wild antics.

On the drive back to Palamos, the woman kept trying to open her door and jump out or she would use her legs to ram the driver's seat forward, to the point where Bob was jerked toward the steering wheel. Each time she attempted this it produced some colorful language from Bob. I was kept fully occupied hauling her back into the speeding car or defending myself as best I could whenever she tried to squash me against the door, apparently to show how strong she was. I soon discovered that in her semi-crazed condition she was very strong indeed. She then spent some time ripping apart a number of magazines in the car, and this was when my mind flashed to our loose pages in the house.

Just as Bob pulled into the garage the madam was gone in a flash, rushing into the house where she first went into the office and then raced out through an open door to the front terrace and then down to the beach. Shortly our drunken nuisance came in off the beach where she had been swimming fully dressed, which should have sobered her up. The opposite seemed to be the case.

It was then that the real problem started, as she insisted on reading the manuscript of the new book, maintaining that she could be of considerable help. Unfortunately, we were unable to lock the office as we had never bothered to lock a door in the entire house and so there were no keys available. The woman was more slippery than an eel as she made for my office where some pages had already been disturbed by the rush of air through the open doors, and Bob and myself endeavored to stop her from getting anywhere near the piles of copy.

The crazed woman was persistent and refused to leave the studio and return to the living room. It was then Bob and I decided at the same moment to remove her by real force.

The sudden attack on her person temporarily resulted in complete chaos as we all fell in amongst the record player and Bob's vast collection of records. We each grabbed a leg and pulled with all our might, because at this stage we were desperate. Here was two years' work in jeopardy because of the drunken capers of a schizophrenic.

Despite being dragged out of the office upside down, she returned 'round the back way and we were required to repeat the ejection procedure. This time as Bob pulled and I pushed, I freely made use of my knee on the gracious lady's rear.

She seemed to have a secret supply of liquor as she didn't let up and in fact, seemed to become even more drunk. Finally, after reaching a point of complete exasperation, Bob delivered two quick punches to the girl, knocking her across the front living room. The first, he explained, was for therapy, and the second for real.

Soon we made arrangements for her to be removed from the premises by suitably qualified medical officials, and we all sighed with relief and fatigue as this drama had continued through the night. It was five in the morning before she was taken to the asylum in Barcelona where she remained until collected by her doctor from England.

This remarkable incident threw Bob completely out of gear. For about a week he was in a highly nervous state, just from knowing what might have happened had the deranged girl managed to get her hands on our copy.

The day finally arrived when Bob felt he could do no more to improve the manuscript, and the new version went off to his agent. The revision was accepted and of course Bob was greatly relieved to get *Poor No More* off his back. Later, having completed the final proofreading, he sent a cable to Harold Matson reading: "YOU MAY NOW GET DRUNK."

He then explained: "This doesn't apply to you, as sobriety in our case spells money. However, the author who wrapped it up yesterday, got pissed last night and put a small dent in his cherished Rolls Royce, whereupon the author's wife drove him home. The author must have been drunk, because he has driven with his wife sober and this is not an experience to be relished. In all seriousness I think we have got a bloody good book, which needs very little work. Evidently the copyreading that Alan and I did was quasi-perfect because we have had no trouble with the proofs at all."

Bob's New York publisher received the new version with delight and immediately cabled Bob: "TAIL DEEP IN PROOFS. SALUTE WORLD'S GREATEST WRITER. YOU RUARK WILL BE AS PROUD OF HOLT AS HOLT IS OF RUARK. STOP. WILL FISH FROM A ROWBOAT THIS AFTERNOON ALONE BUT NOT ALONE."

When Bob shared this cable with Harold Matson, he noted: "He has either turned fag or he is completely happy with the work."

So, after many problems, *Poor No More* was finally published. On reflection though, with the benefit of hindsight provided by the book's subsequent history and considering what the loss of a year represented to Bob economically and frustration-wise, I wonder whether it would not have been better to have published the book as first written. That would have avoided delay with other projects. The book would have been knocked to hell by the critics, but then it was knocked to hell even in its new form. Maybe we would have sold fewer books, but surely the difference would have represented less than the value of a year's delay. The real point though, and this is where the true professional in Bob was evident, was that he did not wish to release for publication a book that he felt represented anything less than his finest effort.

Poor No More was a sprawling monster about the rise and fall of a mill owner. It involved big business and sex in roughly equal quantities. Craig Price was the tycoon. He began with a North Carolina upbringing in poverty and operated under advice tendered by his grandfather: "Don't go through your life with a hookworm philosophy – just settin' and lettin' it pass. Grab it and use it and kick the stuff right out of it, and don't never, ever, let it run you."

That made sense to Craig as he struggled to escape poverty and hunger while aiming for the top. His stepping stones were various women. He started out by marrying the mill owner's daughter, partly because he had to since she was expecting his child, and partly because she was the mill owner's daughter. It took Craig less than two years to gain control of the mill, and with the credit rating thus gained, he moved into the big time.

Craig's methods were ugly and ruthless. Within a few years he had amassed a staggering fortune. He owned everything from hotels to motels, airlines to oil wells, banks to soft drink factories. He made the covers of *Time* and other national magazines as a boy wonder, but while he was successful on the surface, underneath he had nothing.

Craig Price had a driving compulsion to stay on top, to be "poor no more," though he didn't really know what he was trying to accomplish. In a moment of honest confession, he summarized matters to one of his girlfriends: "I horsetraded and gambled, mostly with a rigged deck. I bought this and sold that and borrowed from this to buy that. I bought some companies and milked them and threw them away. I met some attractive women and repeated the process. I drained them dry and threw them away"

This included his college roommate's mother, his secretary, a beautiful socialite and many others, among them his wife and even his mother-in-law. He bred an alcoholic daughter, accidentally shot a devoted Negro boy, quarreled with and was exposed then double-crossed by his best friend, eventually drove his wife to suicide, and finally, when the Securities Exchange Commission and Federal Bureau of Investigation moved in for a routine check, his vast paper empire began to crumble. There was a contempt of Congress charge, a tax evasion charge, a stock fraud action and he was permanently disallowed from trading.

From the debris, in a rather round-about way, Craig ended up with a million dollars in a Swiss bank He then evaluated his position: "A man with a million dollars waiting for him in Switzerland wasn't poor, and wasn't going to be a burden to anybody from the past. He didn't need nothing from nobody." His final thoughts were: "How very rich he'd be, if he owned anything except the million dollars waiting for him in Switzerland."

Bob always had a hand in designing the dust jackets for his books. In the case of *Poor No More,* he knew from the start what it was going to be. Despite the million-dollar twist at the end, the story was one of self-destruction, with Craig Price burning the candle at both ends. Accordingly, the symbol of a burning candle, lit at both ends, was used on the front and spine of the cover. Since *Poor No More* was to an appreciable degree autobiographical, Bob felt the burning candle applied to his own life.

Having finally finished *Poor No More* during the summer of 1959, Bob was feeling noble and quite pleased with himself. In this buoyant mood he wrote a column, ostensibly about other writers but in truth an autobiographical piece, entitled "You Needn't Be a Bum to Write Good Prose." It is worth quoting at length, because it offers considerable insight on how Bob viewed his approach to writing.

I would like today to do a piece about writers, for I have read a whimpering homily to F. Scott Fitzgerald, and I weary of the legend. Since I was also able to weary of Eugene O'Neill and Thomas Wolfe, not to mention Boris Pasternak, you cannot accuse me of playing favorites.

There is something wrong with the writing trade if you got to die, generally drunk, dope-addicted or just plain nuts, to be a legend. It does not seem quite fair to such terribly well-adjusted people as John Steinbeck, for example, who can drink a good glass like the rest of us, but who continues to love Miss Elaine and to pay his bills while writing prose.

Perhaps I am not worthy of carrying F. Scott Fitzgerald's bad checks, and I certainly will never make as much literary mileage out of my family as O'Neill or Wolfe, but I can tell you one thing. I just finished a book which involved four years of writing and which will be published on Oct. 26, and that book took a minimum of five million words out of my nervous system in order to get a clean

400,000, or about five long novels. Under one cover.

This does not preclude the columns which are necessary to my financial health, or the magazine pieces, or the correspondence, or the daily paper-reading, or trips to various foreign places such as Australia, London, and Upper Kaabong, in Uganda. This does not preclude the business of tax returns, long written communications with editors, fights with publishers, or getting loaded when the time seems likely.

But my point is that my three dogs are in excellent health, my wife is not nuts, I do not hate my mother, my mother-in-law is one of my best friends, I am not addicted to dope, I do not accept the bounty of women, and I have seldom been known to get sick in public or go around identifying myself to strangers as a famous author, a charming little habit Mr. Fitzgerald developed. When he was not climbing up walls, or being force-fed, or practicing to be the subject for autobiographies by women who kept him in his failing years, which started pretty early for a grown man.

The good Lord knows writing is not easy, because it is the most lonesome job in the world, and does not considerably enhance a good disposition. Even the dogs know when the Boss is having deadline trouble or must perforce do a massive rewrite job, and they stay clear. This also applies to the poor lady who has lived in a welter of carbon paper and newspaper clippings with me for twenty-one years.

But a great many of the pros manage a fairly orderly life, even if it entails divorces, and the point is that they don't whimper enough about crazy wives and their own booziness or bad seed in their sons or domineering mothers to make themselves a proper subject for biography. I think that possibly Paul Gallico is the best all-around pro in all the writing fields I ever met, and Paul looks better at 63 than I do at 44. And before somebody hollers, 'that ain't hard,' I'll say it myself.

Just because a guy writes or paints for a living gives him no license to be a bum, a drunk, a whiner, or a public charge. And I have always thought, frankly, that Mr. Fitzgerald was a much better actor than he ever was a writer, and that the lonely, boring posturing of Thomas Wolfe was just a collection of words. Neither Fitzgerald nor Wolfe had any more plot sense than Mamselle, my stupid poodle, and you can eat just so much mood before you start to clamor for the meat. And the meat is plot and the construction of same.

What am I so mad about? I'll tell you. Just finished this massive volume, my bills are paid, I still got the same wife, and I shaved this morning. And nobody, ever, is going to find me so violently disgusting or outright odd that any obituary longer than a stick of type will be written. That is the penalty a writer pays for neatness, hard work, no libel suits, and hitting a deadline smack on the nose. Selah.

Most critics dealt harshly with *Poor No More*, and it was consistently objected to as a vulgar, hard, profane, unsavory and an unnecessary novel. Described as a kind of Mau Mau in a grey flannel suit, it was said to be far too long. One reviewer sarcastically headlined his piece with

"Words, Words, Words!" The suggestion was made many times that it needed an editor's sharp and able copy pencil and also "that it could most certainly do without three hundred pages, two of the continents, a dozen characters and all the filth."

Apart from length, the quality was heavily criticized with such statements as "Written in the language of the gutter, crude Ruark novel is poorest fiction" and "The title *Poor No More* contains only one word, the first one, which appropriately describes this novel." That review added that it was "grossly overwritten and blatantly vulgar," then added that any worthy intentions have been "smothered to an agonizing death by the heavy, heavy hand of Ruark."

Even when a favorable remark was made, it was qualified: "The dialogue and description of Negro fish fry-revival meeting, a day's fishing, and his first love at a fraternity dance are all Wolfe-ish in character, and quite as good, but Ruark and his hero are far too preoccupied with sex and all its functions to let *Poor No More* rise above just what it is: another long and commercial bedroom story."

Fortunately, a few reviewers came to Bob's rescue with encouraging words. "It is not great literature," one wrote, "but it contains all the ingredients that make for popularity." Another commented: "Ruark may not be the 'great modern writer of today,' but if *Poor No More* is any indication, to this reviewer, he'll fill the spot until somebody else comes along."

Despite the critics, the book itself got off to a good start. The publishers reported a first printing of 100,000 copies, and there were subsequent print runs as well. There was no Book-of-the-Month Club selection, but there was a good pocket book contract with Fawcett Publications for $87,500 against 50 percent of the eventual profits. In soft cover form there was an initial printing of 450,000 at 75 cents a copy.

There was no immediate film sale, and in fact there was very little interest taken in this direction. Bob was extremely disappointed when Harold Matson indicated that the picture buyers were showing strong resistance to *Poor No More*. "For instance," he wrote, "Bill Holden is quoted by the top man at Paramount as saying Craig Price is too unsympathetic a character for him to play."

As ever, Bob had a ready reply: "Concerning the resistance of such people as Bill Holden, I am afraid we are in a miserable situation where that most dispensable commodity, the ham actor, is now in the driver's seat, and the good old studio buying days are over. It is a pity because there never was a ham who did not see himself through a cloud of greasepaint and his latest favorable press cuttings. It has occurred to me that the objection to the character of Craig Price as unsympathetic doesn't hold water. As a matter of ducking the issue, I am particularly thinking of the female reaction to an attractive heel. In the writing our Mr. Price was neither black nor white but aroused a sort of self-hating tenderness of feeling in all the women I know who have read this thing."

Harold Matson had put a price tag of $600,000 on the film rights, though Bob didn't consider this a deterrent to its sale. Instead, he felt it was the time and the current television scandals, and in a letter to his agent he also pointed out: "We wrote a book about a guy who was essentially a bastard, business and moral wise, and for the last month American immorality has been in for heavy self-inspection, and momentarily we are enjoying a tremendous guilt complex."

Poor No More was considered from time to time, but it never sold as a picture. For a while Bob did manage to stir up some interest by presenting the idea that the book might be best-suited for a leading female star, as opposed to males. He was hoping that maybe Ava Gardner would tackle the task, as she had shown some interest.

CHAPTER 14
AFRICA AGAIN

Having finally gotten *Poor No More* out of his hair, Bob needed a good rest and said he was not going to think about the next book for a very long while. His next book-length effort was to be a sequel to *Something of Value,* and he initially intended to let about a year pass before commencing heavy work. This promised respite from big novel writing didn't materialize. A good, well-informed friend from Nairobi visited shortly after this decision and easily convinced Bob that he had to start more or less at once, as the noise of possible independence was growing louder in East Africa. So without any real break from the last book, Bob got down to work on the next. This decision proved a wise one, as it enabled him to complete the novel before actual independence happened.

After considerable thought concerning the new book's plot construction, Bob decided to consult with Harold Matson before actually starting to write. In a letter explaining the situation and asking that Matson come to Spain for a quick visit, Bob wrote:

"What has happened, briefly, is this – one of those miraculous things has happened in three days in which my brain caught fire and I have been able to plot, characterize and graph the episodic development of a 300,000 word novel. There are almost no loose ends of a minor nature, and none whatsoever of a major nature.

"I will not attempt to go into the sum and substance of this book by mail beyond saying that by operating at a crash rate of speed, we will be able to synthesize in a novel the current heat and implied threat of Africa while it is still continuously in the headlines. When I say time is of the essence here I think I am sitting on a million dollars plus.

"There is much to be talked over with you before I embark on this project. In the same sense that we have talked things over after the *fait accompli*. The difference being this time is that I have at my finger tips the complete skeletal structure of the book, as well as most of the flesh, innards, and brain. All it needs is assembly and I assemble best at white heat.

"I must call to your attention now that this enthusiasm is not due to alcoholic exuberance, a sin of which I have been guilty in the past, but comes from four months work and thinking in which not so much as a sip of wine or beer has passed these ruby lips."

This novel, *Uhuru,* actually began with a different title, "Burnt Offering." Bob felt this title would be appropriate for a story about the development of Kenya after the Mau Mau emergency until just before independence in 1962, a period of about a decade. He was convinced that a "burnt offering" would be about all that would be left of the country. The title changed one day when Bob, engrossed in copyreading, leapt up from his desk shouting "Uhuru! Uhuru!" He had heard mobs of Africans shouting the word, which meant freedom or independence in Swahili. This was the obvious title for a book which had as its main theme the impending independence of Kenya.

The writing of *Uhuru* didn't prove any simpler than its predecessors, so far as delays were concerned, but during work on the novel, Bob showed his real caliber as a true pro. We had been getting along exceptionally well, and were approximately halfway through with the whole thing more or less planned. Up to this stage *Uhuru* was definitely a sequel to *Something of Value*. We had picked up where SOV finished, with the black baby being carried down the hill by Peter McKenzie, with the prospects of a better life to come. We had also continued with all the original names and characters.

Bob was producing 15 to 20 pages a day, we were up-to-date with the columns with a good backlog already in New York, and there were no magazine articles pending. We were in good health, and all of his correspondence was caught up when Bob came to me one morning, white and shaking.

In a forlorn voice he asked: "Alan, what about the *Something of Value* sequel rights of MGM?" He feared that maybe MGM would have some claim on a continuation of the story.

We immediately wrote a frantic letter, sent a cable and telephoned Harold Matson. Sure enough, in the small print it had been agreed that the first refusal would go to MGM for $75,000. This amount was completely unacceptable to Bob, because we had hopes of a much higher payment for film-making rights, and we were aiming the whole thing at a film sale.

Frantic correspondence between Ruark and Matson ensued, with the agent admitting, "Somehow I allowed myself to be lulled into an unvigilant attitude."

The solution was to redirect the novel, though it meant an appalling amount of extra work. When the decision was made, Bob took one despairing look at me, and then at the mountains of copy. Then without a word he walked out of the house with what rightly could have been suicidal intentions. He took a 20-minute walk on the beach and came back with the announcement: "Come on Junior. We've rewritten whole books before, so let's get with it."

Bob then took his two Miltowns and we started to remodel by discussion, to replot and to rename all the existing characters . . . Peter McKenzie became Brian Dermott, Henry McKenzie became Aunt Charlotte Stuart, Elizabeth McKenzie disappeared, and Don and Peggy Bruce more or less replaced the farming activities of the original Newton homestead, and became a representative Kenyan family. Holly McKenzie was replaced by Valerie Dermott, and so on, but we kept most of our black people as these had been newly created in any case. And so began six months' hard work.

We used some of the existing copy, but I wondered if it was really worthwhile, as apart from all the alterations in plot construction, I had the job of changing Peter for Brian, which was the most tedious task I have ever attempted. This procedure became known as "depetering." There was also the problem that Bob would continue to write Peter instead of Brian, and despite all the copyreading and editing, Peter once actually got through into the first edition of the book.

As part of the general rewriting plan, Bob decided that it was necessary for him to take a quick trip to Kenya. He had decided to use an incident that had just taken place. A white man had been hanged for killing a black man. According to Bob, that constituted a remarkable change of attitude in the country, and he wished to learn something of the background to this incident.

As it so happened, on the aircraft heading for Nairobi, Bob was seated next to a gentleman with whom he struck up a conversation. Bob explained why he was making the trip, and by remarkable good luck this gentleman was the very person who could help him. He was the unfortunate white man's defense attorney! This was but the beginning of a series of lucky breaks on this visit. Another came when Bob turned up information he said could be used not only in *Uhuru* but for his future African novels.

As we progressed in our rewriting task, we came to the conclusion that the necessity rewrite had been a blessing in disguise. Bob maintained that a better book was the end result. Along these lines he wrote in a later letter to his agent:

"Alan and I both agree that the business of writing a sequel sometimes is detrimental to effort, since you are constantly plagued by the old book and beset by the problem of how much or how little you can rely on what you have already written about specific characters. I have felt at times that *SOV* was looking over my shoulder, and that I was eventually going to run into a critical sneer that Ruark was trying to flog a dead horse . . . ."

As far as a movie sale was concerned though, we might just as well have left it as a continuation of *Something of Value* and taken our chance concerning sequel rights with MGM. Despite many attempts at interesting film buyers in *Uhuru*, it was never sold. It was a good story and a lot of people seemed to think so, but as time went by those in a position to buy probably became unhappy about promoting a story concerning a conflict between black and white. This was quite frustrating for Bob since he felt the storyline of *Uhuru* was fair to both white and black and that it was representative of Africa at that time.

The nearest we got to a film sale was a long, drawn-out procedure of promises from an interested producer. An independent company, Freedom Inc., was formed, which was followed by a long delay caused by a professional screenplay writer who did the script. Bob ultimately rejected it in disgust, and then there was a further delay while Bob wrote an acceptable screenplay himself.

In an attempt to sell the film, we made an extensive reconnaissance trip in Mozambique, Portuguese East Africa. It would not have been possible to film anything in Kenya, where, thanks to *Uhuru*, Bob was prohibited. On the other hand, he was highly thought of by the Portuguese, as he always wrote the truth about their country and had made many good friends among them.

The reconnaissance trip to Mozambique was made in the summer of 1963 with the intention of filming the following year. This schedule was ruined because of delays connected with the script. When Bob first saw it at the end of 1963, he exploded with anger, amazement and disappointment as he now knew that it would be impossible to make the film the following year. He rejected the suggestion of a possible second draft from the screenwriter out of hand and wrote firmly to Harold Matson:

"I absolutely refuse to waste any more time being associated with a screenwriter who shows little knowledge of what the book is about. Apart from technique, which is completely ass-backwards, I find him appallingly bad in character delineation, and even worse as a dialogue man. This is not temperament, or the usual author's over-estimation of his own property. It is just that I find the complete thing from concept to dialogue utterly ridiculous and appallingly corny, as well as badly constructed and totally misleading as to country, story and character. We have wasted the best part of a year for the mountain to labor, and it has not even brought forth a mouse. I can only assume the whole thing is meant to be an elaborate practical joke."

That a screenplay writer could have gone so far away from the original story was beyond our understanding, and in Bob's harsh criticism he picked out phrases such as "Not on your Nelly," "23 Skiddo" and "Oh you kid," which were part of the screenplay writer's curious recollection of timely British slang. In a further letter to his agent Bob wrote:

"I could pull this apart line by line, scene by scene, but won't trouble. The whole thing is a crock of shit, and I can only assume that he must have been constipated for a year before that action finally occurred." He then added a series of sarcastic remarks, among them scathing commentary linking the screenplay to popular comic characters. "We would have no problem in casting the Africans if we hue to this script and I suggest Amos and Andy, and all is not lost if there is anybody left of the original Keystone Kops, plus Buster Keaton and Stepin Fetchit. This would make an admirable comedy in its current form."

Bob then took a red pencil and went through the script entering critical remarks, which were classic in their sardonic humor. This was then returned to Harold Matson, who admitted in a letter that he had been waiting for a blast from Palamos. Bob was surprised that this screenplay had actually reached the mimeographed stage and immediately sent a cable to the effect that it was not to be shown to anybody.

Still, the damage had been done and the time lost, and as Bob was still keen to go ahead and make a movie from *Uhuru*, he agreed to write the screenplay himself. This he put together in about one month. While he had the technical help of a professional production and location manager, this was a good example of his adaptability, as screenplay writing was not his medium. Bob's script, though long in dialogue, was generally acceptable, and it appeared there was still a possibility of carrying out our film-making plans. In the meantime we were engaged in finishing off the next big book, so the film project was vaguely scheduled for 1966 in Mozambique. Sadly, Bob was not to see the results of his work. He died before anything materialized and the whole matter was dropped. The film of *Uhuru* was never made.

In 1961, when the manuscript for *Uhuru* was well advanced, and when Henry Holt and Company assumed they would be the publishers (although nothing had been signed), Harold Matson began negotiating an overall deal for Bob. "My secret weapon," he wrote, "is a plan to sell you down the river to Holt in what might be called an employer-independent contractor relationship." The plan was based on the employer becoming the owner of that which they employed Bob to write, including all rights, with a certain guarantee of X number of dollars per year for work that Holt would commission to be done. This could be a book, articles or whatever. The underlying object was to qualify the money Bob received as earned income subject to exemption under Section 911 of the tax code, always assuming that the individual's residence abroad was bona fide and that he had no residence in the United States.

In the ensuing negotiations, Holt proved unwilling to agree to the figures Matson had in mind. They were apparently first frightened away when the sum of $250,000 was mentioned for the tie-up deal, and at this stage it was suggested that Matson had better find another publisher. This didn't prove very difficult, and McGraw-Hill Book Company was available and willing to step in with a contract, which was to include *Uhuru*.

There was some unpleasantness, with the outcome being that Ruark once again changed publishers. Since Holt also owned *Field & Stream* magazine, the "Old Man and the Boy" articles got dragged into the squabble. While Bob was quite willing to continue carrying through with the contractual agreement for these monthly articles, the head of Holt made it quite clear that this was not desirable. Therefore, very reluctantly, Bob stopped writing his "Old Man and the Boy" pieces. Provision was not even made for a farewell column. This was quite remarkable after so many years of continuous monthly pieces, and a good indication of the degree of bad feeling that had occurred.

The real bone of contention, of course, was that Henry Holt had lost *Uhuru*, and they claimed that there had been a firm understanding they were to publish it. That was more an assumption than anything else, as nothing had been signed. They also insisted they should be reimbursed for their time and assistance in editing the manuscript. But as Harold Matson pointed out, the book was not committed and it had been made clear that any activity in the interim would be at Holt's own risk.

Bob was saddened to sever the relationship with Holt in such an unpleasant manner after such a long, happy association. As Bob wrote in a goodbye letter: "It is with deep regret and considerable personal pain that I sever my long and happy relationship with Holt and *Field & Stream*. But business in this case was business, and as I told you I have been with Matson a long time and trust and follow him implicitly."

The deal worked out with McGraw-Hill was interesting and covered the production of four novels for an overall guarantee of $300,000, plus an immediate loan of $50,000. The agreement was to pay a base salary of $37,500 per year for eight years, from 1962 to 1969. There were extra clauses allowing for a profit-sharing bonus, and of course the whole thing was contingent upon delivery on schedule and acceptance of the works submitted. Rejection by the publishers of any one novel could result in cancellation of the remainder of the contract. So there it was, and Bob felt a good degree of security for the future and was quite happy with his new publisher.

We were on safari in Kenya while the negotiations were taking place, and while there we received a number of messages concerning the necessity to cut the length of *Uhuru*. Apart from the fact that there was some repetition and irrelevant material, the requirement to cut revolved around the potential paperback contract.

At this time we stood at 1,600 mimeographed pages, having already cut out over 200 pages (about 60,000 words), and the remainder was calculated at nearly 500,000 words. This was just too long for a paperback. A book of this length would require two-volume packing and would cost too much. Length was also influencing hard cover negotiations. Such a lengthy novel would have to be priced at $6.95, which at that time was thought to be above and beyond the book buyer's capacity to pay, and even then the publisher would have to go to press with more than 100,000 copies on a first print run to make the project potentially profitable.

It was suggested from all directions that we reduce the book by 25 to 35 percent by carving out another 150,000 words. Also, a possible Book-of-the-Month Club selection would have been unlikely, so we resigned ourselves to doing some drastic cutting.

Bob went to work, carefully removing a line here and a line there. Finally he reduced the book to an acceptable size, which then made it possible for Harold Matson to go ahead and tie up the paperback contract. Bidding started at $106,000, which was the price paid for *Something of Value*, and jumped progressively from $130,000 to $150,000, then in steps to $178,000. Eventually there came the happy day Bob received a cable from his agent: "Magic number one hundred eighty-five – Fawcett." The bidding had been mainly between Pocket Books and Fawcett, and the final price of $185,000 was the second highest ever (topped only by *Peyton Place*).

When it was all finally settled Bob was extremely pleased. He was not alone in his pleasure, as the publisher of the hard cover would get half of the $185,000 and thereby come close to covering costs for the first printing. Additional money earned from the *Uhuru* as a Book-of-the-Month Club selection, was split with the publisher. The book also enjoyed a good reception in foreign markets, especially in England.

Bob graciously showed his appreciation for the part I played in the book's success by stating in the Foreword: "And, as ever, a special nod to Alan Ritchie, who performed so much of the heavy work of actual physical production of this monster without undue whimpering over the endless, killing hours of toil." In my personal copy Bob wrote: "For Alan – without whom I would not be able to work a 140 hr week – as ever, all thanks to the co-author. Bob."

Despite all the rewriting, cutting and carving up of *Uhuru*, the end product was a good one. It was mainly the story of a white colonial in Kenya, Brian Dermott, and his gradual disintegration in the face of tensions and horror of the past and what was taking place at the time. Bob created Dermott as a representative white extremist, who along with other hardcore settlers was prepared to resist the expected black domination.

How to deal with impending independence was the main thrust of the story, with the distribution of agricultural land being the real source of antagonism between black and white. The story was based on Bob's vast knowledge of African politics, his numerous safaris, his first-hand experiences in Kenya with the local people, and his knowledge of the farming community. Much of the action occurred on a large family farm owned by Aunt Charlotte Stuart.

Bob created considerable drama out of the actual hanging of a white man for the murder of a Negro, and he delved deeply into the African pre-independence political scene. He named actual politicians and created fictitious African characters to represent the extremist African, the rabble rouser and the moderate African.

The black extremist and potential prime minister, Matthew Kamau, became a symbol of hate in the eyes of Brian Dermott. That hate culminated in a senseless and illogical reprisal for the murder of his American fiancée. She was murdered by some thugs who came to the family farm to kidnap, for oath-giving purposes, an orphan Negro boy who had been reared by Aunt Charlotte and who was a survivor from Brian's Mau Mau activities some seven years previously.

In his confused thinking, Brian Dermott considered Matthew Kamau symbolically responsible for all his misfortune and unhappiness. He killed him in broad daylight in front of Nairobi's main hotel, then sits down at the corner café to wait for the police. In the ensuing trial, Stephen Ndegwa, a moderate African, represents Brian as defense counsel, destroying his political career in the process but leaving a feeling of hope for the future.

Claiming it was a true story, Bob made a point in the dust jacket blurb: "The characters may be technically fictional, but there is nothing in *Uhuru* that has not happened, is not happening, or will not happen in the near future."

Many critics objected to this statement, maintaining that the book should not be confused with fact and that it presented a completely inaccurate impression of the true situation in East Africa.

One dissenting critic wrote: "He comes now to the Book-of-the-Month Club with this childish horror. The book could be dismissed as an African boiler, but there is an irksome worry under the bubbles: 'You must wonder: Does he not know more than this? You must conclude: If he does not, he is a fool, but if he is a fool the wheezings of his brain disturb millions. Otherwise one would not bother with this 555-page junk of nonsense.'"

Thinking along similar lines, a member of the Legislative Council in Kenya attacked Bob in general and the book in particular. "These distorted, imaginative and almost incandescent writings," he claimed, "are doing tremendous harm to this country." This was reported in the *Daily Nation* under a front page headline "Ruark Gets a Lashing in Legco."

At the time this didn't worry Bob much. He also paid little attention to claims of inaccuracy, as he knew that he had studied the subject extensively. He also felt that a fair balance had been struck between white and black and was annoyed at reviewers who inferred he was racially biased, with remarks such as: "*Uhuru* reads like one long adolescent tirade against the black man in Africa."

There were many good reviews with suggestions that *Uhuru* was "subtler than *Something of Value*," and Bob knew that the book would make the best-seller lists when it was described as a "frightening novel" and a story "filled with murder, lust, action, tragedy, humor, pathos, and the usual Ruark propaganda."

The British publisher, Hamish Hamilton, ran into a problem when the 10,000 copies that had been sent to South Africa were seized by customs authorities since the book was banned in that country. This appeared to be because of a reference to a Belgian whore being associated with a black man. It was initially suggested to Bob that this relationship could be removed from the book. After some study Bob decided it was just not possible. Her existence was too completely tied in with the story. However, after about a year of negotiating, South Africa admitted the novel into the country.

Immediately upon publication, Hamish Hamilton also sent 1,000 copies to Nairobi and they sold in a single day. Since this was just prior to another visit to Kenya by Bob, Ginny and others implored him to cancel the trip. The Kenyan reviews of the book had been a bit ominous, and it was felt he could be in real danger. But since Bob was returning to accompany some good friends on safari, he would not listen to advice from anyone. Although nothing happened, he was extremely lucky.

At this time Kenya was not many months away from complete independence, or Uhuru, and the takeover period was already well advanced. Since Bob had always written at length concerning the black leaders of the country, generally in an uncomplimentary fashion, it could only be expected that as they gained more power, Bob's presence would be less and less desirable. With 1,000 copies of *Uhuru* circulating in Nairobi, and given the fact Bob had made direct reference to a number of the emerging leaders (in particular to James Gichuru, the Minister of Finance), he was the focus of considerable unfavorable attention. The predictable outcome was that a writ for libel was issued against Bob when he was still in Nairobi. Although this really should have been a civil charge, it rather strangely became a criminal offense, which included a warrant for his arrest.

That Bob would have risked returning to Nairobi now seems quite remarkable. Apart from the direct references in the book, he had also made disparaging references to most of the other leading black politicians, including Jomo Kenyatta, the future prime minister, in his newspaper columns.

During this time and before Bob's return to Palamos, the various new services and his agent in New York made frantic attempts to get in touch with him. UPI had received a report that a warrant issued in Kenya included the stipulation that $28,000 would have to be posted in order to bail him out of jail. They were assuming that he had been detained in Kenya, but fortunately Bob had been forewarned and stayed one jump ahead of the authorities attempting to serve the writ. Hurriedly he left his hotel by the back entrance and went to an Indian cinema to hide for a few hours until aircraft departure time. He managed to get away without being noticed, thanks to some of his many reliable friends in Kenya. Had the document been correctly served, it presumably would have included arrest. This in turn would have meant payment of the bond, and he almost certainly would have lost his money, irrespective of the legal merits of the case.

Bob was probably technically wrong in referring to James Gichuru as a Mau Mau leader, and certainly he would have had great difficulty in proving anything. While a vast number of active Mau Mau members were detained in compounds during the Kenya emergency, very few were actually charged. Any reference to someone being a member of the Mau Mau was taboo, since this was still an illegal society according to the laws of Kenya. Of course, that conveniently overlooked the fact that many former members were being called freedom fighters and acknowledged as heroes.

On the front page of the July 20, 1962 edition of the Kenya newspaper the *Daily Nation*, under the headline "Ruark Skips Out – Ahead of Bailiff" it was reported as follows:"Best-selling novelist Robert Ruark has left Kenya, his "second home," for good – just one jump ahead of a court bailiff who was looking for him to arrest him on a warrant issued by a Kenya Supreme Court judge.

"The warrant was issued in connection with a libel action brought by Kanu MLC James Gichuru, Kenya's Minister for Finance. I understand its purpose was to force Mr. Ruark to furnish security of £10,000 to ensure his appearance in court at the time of the hearing of the case, since Mr. Ruark normally resides in America – beyond the court's jurisdiction.

"The alleged libel appears on page 77 of Mr. Ruark's latest novel, *Uhuru*, in which Mr. Gichuru is falsely referred to as "the recently released Mau Mau leader."

"The Court Bailiffs went to the New Stanley Hotel, Nairobi, yesterday to arrest Mr. Ruark – but he had already left Kenya. They were told by the hotel receptionist: "You have had it, gentlemen, Mr. Ruark left the country on Sunday."

Further coverage in the Nairobi press the following day quoted Gichuru as saying:"This is not a case of an independent African government trying to harass a foreign journalist. It is an ordinary case of civil libel. Mr. Ruark apparently set himself out to the American Press as an authority on East Africa and its leaders. I hope Mr. Ruark will have the courage and courtesy to come back to Kenya to answer the allegations of libel against him and substantiate his charges against me."

Of course, Bob wasn't about to return to Kenya. He knew full well that with the new government, any bond he was required to post would vanish. It appeared for a time that while he had escaped the immediate problems of a lawsuit in Kenya, there remained the possibility that a warrant could be taken out against him and his British publisher in the United Kingdom.

Although the affair lingered on for a while, I think that so far as Bob was concerned the whole business soon ceased to have any importance. The case eventually fizzled out completely, but when the new government took over Bob was declared a prohibited immigrant of Kenya.

Thereafter, while Bob would often boast that he held the distinguished honor of being the first prohibited immigrant, he was deeply saddened about being banned from the country. Kenya was a country he loved, not only from the safari wildlife point of view, but also because of the great friendships he had developed with many Kenyans. He was also deeply grateful to the country for the vast amount of copy he had extracted from his visits to this part of Africa. Apart from his books, he had written dozens and dozens of magazine articles and hundreds of newspaper columns about Africa. He was, without doubt, an important authority on East Africa.

Even more than a year after Bob had been declared a prohibited immigrant, his general acceptance as an authoritative voice on Kenya was emphasized when American newspapers regularly referred to East Africa as "Ruark Country." This was especially the case in connection with reports on the East African Safari International Automobile Rally, which followed a route through Kenya, Uganda and Tanganyika.

On all subsequent trips to Africa, Bob made a point of not over-flying any part of Kenya or traveling on any flight that might feasibly be diverted to Nairobi in event of an emergency. He just wanted to be on the safe side.

CHAPTER 15
THE LAST BOOKS

Robert Ruark's final novel, *The Honey Badger,* was in effect a hard knock at the American woman, and the chief character, Alec Barr, was about as close as Bob would ever get to an autobiography. There were, of course, a few twists. It was a story of an American author and his involvement with numerous women, and the honey badger, a ferocious African animal, symbolized American women. The honey badger always attacks the groin of its prey instead of the jugular, and the novel suggested American women robbed males of their masculinity.

So, with this pleasant thought in mind, Bob and I got down to work on another big book. Although this time no major writing problems were encountered, thanks to continuous interruptions it took a long time to get started.

According to the terms of our contract with McGraw-Hill, the original deadline date was December, 1962. This was later extended to June, 1963, which was not a particularly long period considering that the cutting of *Uhuru* was not finished until the end of 1961. Still, under normal circumstances it would have been sufficient time.

Unfortunately, circumstances were not normal. The year 1962 found Bob in almost continuous motion between the United States, Europe, India and Africa. The year began with yet another trip to Kenya to make a documentary film with NBC, followed by a return to New York to do the dialogue, then back to Europe and on to India. In India he was bitten on the arm by a leopard and then had to flee the country to get proper medical attention and also because of non-payment of shikar fees. He was subsequently hospitalized in Nairobi with a serious infection, later went to Mozambique, then returned to Spain and thence on to New York via London. Then there were second trips to Mozambique and Nairobi, with the latter one seeing the hurried departure to Europe to avoid the libel suit. Once back in Palamos, Bob became embroiled in domestic battles as his marriage fell apart. He fled these for a spell in London before once again visiting the United States, where he fell off a horse and ended up in a Washington hospital with a broken hip.

In all fairness, no one could honestly say it was unreasonable of Bob not to have written another big book during this period. Yet his frenetic travel schedule was not the major cause of delay; rather, it was the domestic squabble that had commenced around the middle of 1962 and ended in divorce in February, 1963.

All of this left us well behind on our writing schedule. We finally got going properly in April, 1963, but progress was slow and it was not until early 1965 that Bob was satisfied with the manuscript.

During this two-year period there was the usual amount of activity. Bob had taken his normal safari trips, plus trips to New York and London, North Africa and Italy. There had also been the usual number of other things going on – numerous magazine articles and the column, along with the writing of the film script for *Uhuru*. Based on his past performances, all of this should have been normal procedure for Bob, but he had slowed down to a considerable degree and was finding more reasons for not writing.

Although Bob was behind in his writing schedule, he believed he had a good book, and in correspondence with his editor he showed considerable enthusiasm for the project:

"I can hardly wait to get back to Spain to finish HB. The book can't miss because during my first three days in camp three honey badgers invaded the fowl pens, and were brought to justice. I have the skins and I think it is a good idea if a first edition is bound in the local product for the editor-in-chief."

As the book progressed we felt the formation of *The Honey Badger* was being kept in tight shape. We tried desperately to cut as we went, always having in mind our past agonies with overly long books. The final manuscript was cut back from 1200 pages of finished copy to 900 pages.

The writing procedure on *The Honey Badger* was similar to our previous big books, except that I was not involved in discussions of the evolving plot in the same way I had been on previous books. While it was being written, Bob had a never-ending stream of female visitors, and he discussed the finer details of plot formation with them. This was in some ways logical, since it was really a sort of built-in-interchangeable-female-research-production-line. Bob gave a suitable acknowledgement in his dedications: "This book is for all the nice girls who, wittingly or otherwise, supplied the vital statistics without which there would be no book."

In *The Honey Badger*, Bob probably paid too much attention to the view of these numerous girlfriends and not enough to himself. The important thing in discussing a book in general or a particular storyline with Bob was to help him develop his own ideas rather than forcing new ones on him. In any event, Bob may have sensed from the outset that I was not keen on the book's subject. I was unhappy about some of the crudeness, and I noticed a strange, unpleasant twist in his thinking. I felt there was no need for Bob to turn to this type of book. For unsavory writing, in places it approached *The Carpetbaggers* [by Harold Robbins] and *The Naked and the Dead* [by Norman Mailer]. So much was this the case that when the first half of the manuscript was dispatched to New York, some problems were encountered with U. S. Customs officials. They read some of the copy and reported the "foul language" therein made it inadmissible into the country. Eventually, under legal pressure the manuscript was released.

Closely coupled with the slow delivery of *The Honey Badger* was a gradual deterioration in Bob's financial position. He was behind in his contractual obligations to McGraw-Hill and as a result came under considerable pressure

A Love Affair with Africa

NORTH CAROLINA SOUTHERN HISTORICAL COLLECTION, UNC – CHAPEL HILL

Holding his signature cigarette, Robert Ruark strikes a handsome pose in his Bwana garb. He would log at least ten African hunts between 1951 and 1965. Circa 1960.

BOTH NORTH CAROLINA SOUTHERN HISTORICAL COLLECTION, UNC – CHAPEL HILL

Ginny bagged these sand grouse and francolin on the couple's 1953 safari, which was made into a film, *Africa Adventure*. Top: Ruark and a tom leopard he killed on the same safari.

ALL NORTH CAROLINA SOUTHERN HISTORICAL COLLECTION, UNC – CHAPEL HILL

Above left: Ruark watches laborers clear away brush for their camp in 1961, his last hunt in Kenya. Right: Ruark with Armand Denis, a renowned photographer and the author of *On Safari*. Top: Ruark with a kudu bull taken on his Mozambique safari in 1965. With him are professional hunters Wally Johnson (center) and his son, Walt Johnson Jr., who was a close friend of Ruark.

Obviously staged, this photograph was used to help promote *Africa Adventure*. It features Ruark, along with professional hunters Harry Selby (left) and John Sutton. Filmed in Kenya and Uganda in 1953, the movie showed Ruark hunting a variety of

animals, including such dangerous game as rhino, leopard and elephant. In one dramatic sequence Ruark and Selby teamed up to drop a charging bull elephant at 50 feet. Unfortunately, the photographers failed to document the encounter.

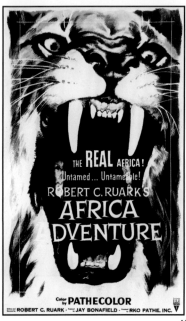

ALL NORTH CAROLINA SOUTHERN HISTORICAL COLLECTION, UNC – CHAPEL HILL

Africa Adventure is a full-color film that first played in theaters in 1954. Produced by Ruark, the limited-budget movie was amazingly successful. Top: The film included footage of Ruark shooting a charging rhino and then examining its horns.

NORTH CAROLINA SOUTHERN HISTORICAL COLLECTION, UNC – CHAPEL HILL

uark proudly displays the ivory from his first elephant, which he killed on New Year's Day, 1953, while on safari with Harry Selby in Kenya. The tusks weighed 109 and 110 pounds.

Ruark's arsenal on this 1958 safari with Harry Selby included a variety of rifles and shotguns. Fourth from the right is Selby's .416 Rigby, which would become one of

NORTH CAROLINA SOUTHERN HISTORICAL COLLECTION, UNC – CHAPEL HILL

the most celebrated big game rifles in the annals of Africa sport hunting. Selby carried it throughout his long and successful hunting career.

Ruark killed this huge bull elephant while hunting in northern Kenya in 1953. The tusks weighed 109 and 110 pounds. With Ruark are professional hunters

Harry Selby (center) and Andrew Holmberg. This was the elephant that charged the hunters during the filming of *African Adventure*.

BOTH NORTH CAROLINA SOUTHERN HISTORICAL COLLECTION, UNC – CHAPEL HILL

Harry Selby guided Ruark on his first safari, in Tanganyika (now Tanzania) in the summer of 1951. Ruark quickly took a liking to Selby's safari hat, which adorns the PH in the top photo, then Ruark in the lower picture where the two men pose with the author's trophy waterbuck.

NORTH CAROLINA SOUTHERN HISTORICAL COLLECTION, UNC – CHAPEL HILL

While on safari, Ruark would settle behind his typewriter and pound out articles for the country's leading magazines, including *Reader's Digest*, *Collier's*, *Esquire* and *Saturday Evening Post*. Top: Harold Matson, Ruark's longtime literary agent, joined his celebrated author on a 1958 safari in Kenya.

Ruark extends his thanks to the shy Samburu girl who led him to his last elephant, an ancient, half-blind bull with almost perfectly symmetrical tusks that topped a hundred pounds each. The rugged Matthews mountain range in the background

NORTH CAROLINA SOUTHERN HISTORICAL COLLECTION, UNC – CHAPEL HILL

meanders through the Northern Frontier district near Illaut Wells in Kenya. Ruark would go on to write a moving article about his hunt, which appeared in a 1961 issue of the *Saturday Evening Post*.

NORTH CAROLINA SOUTHERN HISTORICAL COLLECTION, UNC – CHAPEL HILL

Wearing Harry Selby's safari hat, Ruark struck a manly pose with his first-ever lion, taken in Tanganyika in 1951. Bob took a second, much better, lion later on the safari.

from New York. In a letter explaining a few home truths about money and Bob's publisher, Harold Matson wrote:

"The question hangs on the single possibility that you won't deliver the new novel on time or deliver it at all. In either case they would be stuck. At the moment McGraw-Hill has $156,000 advanced to you on *The Honey Badger*, and by the time you have delivered *The Long View* [Ruark's planned novel as a sequel to *Something of Value* and *Uhuru*] they will have advanced you $90,000. They are holding $77,000 in *Uhuru* earnings. So roughly speaking, *The Honey Badger* and the new book together or separately will have to earn $180,000 before McGraw-Hill gets even with you."

Then towards the end of June, 1965, came a further worried letter from his agent:

"The bare fact is that on the record of your late delivery of *The Honey Badger*, it is not considered likely that you can do a major novel in five months, which is the time you have cut yourself down to for "Long View." Add to this a marriage and a honeymoon [Ruark was planning to re-marry] and who is going to believe that you can meet a December first delivery date. Perhaps you think you can, but everybody else wants to see it to believe it. I don't have to cite chapter and verse about the writing bind you are in – or I should say the non-writing bind. You know it by the day, by the hour."

In the last letter he would write to his agent, on June 26, 1965 Bob replied to this pointed missive from Harold Matson with obvious vexation and in a fashion that revealed his state of mind:

"There seems to be a tendency to harp on my late delivery of *The Honey Badger*, which irks me a little bit, seeing that there is never any reference to managerial interruptions, changes of whim and the fact that I had a few things on my plate last year such as trips to Mozambique. Also, I remember that they seemed to be delighted to run seven months late on *Uhuru* on cutting alone. I would like you to impress on these gentlemen that I am not doing a major novel in five months. I have been working on this for a bloody year already and for your information I shall be very surprised if it takes me more than three months once I turn on the faucet and let it flow out. Reading research alone on this book has comprised the best part of a year of my spare time, and I have been germinating the thing since before I wrote *Uhuru*."

Bob's confidence in his ability to complete the next big book in three months was really pathetic. At this time he was in no condition, mentally or physically, to carry out such a feat. Nonetheless, he was fully aware of just how important this next book was. The prospect of getting started haunted him.

When *The Honey Badger* was finished, proofs were sent to Bob in Palamos, where he struggled painfully with the proofreading and with the editors' questions. It is difficult to see how a good job could have been done, since Bob was in poor condition. At the time I wondered how he managed to more or less go through the reams of paper involved. Shortly after his final proofreading, Bob wrote to the publishers with a suggestion for publicity:

All in all I think we have a good book here and I am more and more convinced that with the right publicity and advertising, plus the *Playboy* exposure, that we have got a winner. I have one suggestion on exploitation which you probably have already thought out yourself. Having founded a columnar career by enraging women, if your campaign is slanted along the lines of 'you aren't going to like it, but take a critical look at yourself in terms of what your man thinks of you.' We will enrage enough females and enslave enough males as a result of the distaff anger to get this off the ground with a big bang.

Then, among the final few letters Bob wrote, was a further one to his editor complaining about a suggested dust jacket blurb for the book:

Herewith have read jacket flap copy for *The Honey Badger*. I will let you know what I think. I think it's the worst piece of crap that I have read since some blurb boy attempted to make a writer out of Mickey Spillane. I'll buy the lead paragraph, the rest of it is sheer <u>dreck</u>.

I would be embarrassed enough to flee back to the arms of Holt or Doubleday if this thing appeared on the dust jacket of a book which bears my name. I don't know who wrote this mess, but I suggest he take up some other line of work. I quote you, "Mother's warnings" and "Ladies, remember they're women." I quote you the entire paragraph ear-marked "Jesus" and where "Divine bitch" came from, I don't like to think because I'm having enough stomach trouble at the moment.

If my prose is "Lean, masculine and muscular as his hero," I would suggest we would delete things like "Spins the yarn," "Life, loves and career" and forget "The book stores cannot keep in stock."

I am writing a supporting blurb of my own which might be designed to take us momentarily out of the twenty-five cent paperback category in some of the seedier airports of Georgia or Alabama. My copy enclosed with this copy. All I can say is, repeat, "Jesus Christ!"

Where is the cover proof you promised? All best, if a bit nauseated.

There was an immediate response to this rude letter from Bob's editor:

"Yours of June 20th received. Come off it, friend. The jacket copy was sent to you for your reaction. Obviously it has not been printed and obviously it, or anything like it, will not appear on the dust jacket 'of a book which bears your name' if you don't like it. I see no reason for the fireworks nor for the allusion to 'fleeing back to the arms of Holt or Doubleday.' If, after all of our work together, a bad piece of copy not printed but submitted to you for your perusal is going to cause a rift, then our relationship isn't worth the powder to blow it up.

"We are redoing it, using your ideas as the base. Cheer up Bob, things could be a hell of a lot worse."

His editor friend could not have been more to the point. "Things could be a hell of a lot worse." Three days after writing this letter, Robert Ruark was dead, the honey badgers having completed their work.

The Honey Badger was published shortly after Bob's death and was presented handsomely in a black and yellow dust jacket. The words, The Honey Badger, appeared in small print at the top and then over nearly the whole length of the dust jacket, front and back, was printed Robert Ruark. I think

Bob would have liked this as he always said the author's name was more important than the title, and he thought it was a good idea to sell the author rather than the book title. Nevertheless, Bob still wouldn't have been particularly pleased with the dust jacket blurb, as it was stated that he had been born in Wilmington, Delaware instead of Wilmington, North Carolina.

The Honey Badger didn't break any records but sold sufficiently well to stay on the bestseller lists for a few weeks. There was a book club sale to the Dollar Book Club for $20,000, and the pocket book contract went to Fawcett Publications. *Playboy* magazine had agreed to take three excerpts, which were printed just prior to the book's publication, and they fetched $15,000. Foreign publication rights were quite good and in particular there was a $25,000 advance for the German-language edition.

Most of the structural part of *The Honey Badger* was definitely autobiographical, and large areas of the story were based on his own life. This included some of Robert Ruark's life in New York, his wartime experiences, his work as a writer, his agent, his secretary, some of his women and some of the Ruarks' mutual friends. Of course, all these characters were changed and twisted into a good degree of anonymity. Bob's travel and safaris were part of his story, as were his wife and their divorce. Perhaps even his stated intention of one day returning to his first wife was autobiographical.

Apart from the financial implications of Ruark's death, the tragedy here really was that he finished his writing career on a rather crude, blatantly sex-oriented book instead of a dignified African novel, which he intended to start at the time of his death. This was to be a pioneering story covering from about 1900 to 1952, the period before *Something of Value*. It would have been a wonderful contribution to his African writings. This story was to have been woven around the *Uhuru* family, Aunt Charlotte Stuart and Uncle Mac, who had trekked inland from Mombasa to the Kingangop in the White Highlands of Kenya and who wrested from the jungle the most practical, beautiful farm ever to exist. They had built a most elegant farmhouse, and at the same time they were loved and respected by the African workers, who had in fact been brought into the area.

Bob's intention was to continue writing on Africa and to pick up the Stuart family in the aftermath of independence as the new black government forced them to vacate their farm. We had begun gathering information for this part of the story, and apart from our collection of newspapers from Nairobi, we were being advised by various friends of the progress of *uhuru* in Kenya. We were informed that this particular farm, after it had been vacated by the settlers, had been replanted entirely with cabbages. The wind-breaking trees were chopped down, and the farmhouse and buildings were filled to the brim with African families. Bob could have gone a long way, story-wise, on this information alone.

The intention was, in effect, to write two books at once, all the while keeping in mind that in previous works we had overwritten heavily, even to the extent of more than 300,000 words on a "finished" manuscript. Instead of overwriting to such an extent then literally throwing away months of hard toil, Bob was really going to try and confine himself to a straighter, more concise storyline from the outset. Out of our normal finished length of about 1,500 typewritten pages, with a little extra we would have two big books.

Sometimes when we discussed this plan, it sounded feasible, but in practice I wonder if it would have been workable. Bob was naturally long-winded in his books, and it was only after arduous copyreading, cutting and rewriting that we had been able to arrive at a finished product. Of course, all of this is supposition, and we will never know whether or not we could have saved ourselves the agonizing cutting and discarding of good material.

The completion of these two projected novels would have made a wonderful African quartet by Ruark – the first to be named *A Long View from a Tall Hill*, then the second and third, *Something of Value* and *Uhuru*, and the fourth, *Act of God*.

After Ruark's death, consideration was given to producing more books from the large collection of columns and magazine articles he had written. From the point of view of anthologies, the selection was unlimited. In 1966 a collection of Bob's hunting writing, edited by Stuart Rose, appeared under the title of *Use Enough Gun*. The following year *Women*, edited by Joan Fulton, was published. [Editor's note: Two further anthologies, Michael McIntosh's *Robert Ruark's Africa*, 1991 and my *The Lost Classics of Robert Ruark*, 1995 have been published.]

By and large Bob received satisfactory reviews for all of his books, at least from the publications that mattered, such as the *Chicago Tribune*, *New York Times Book Review* and *Washington Star*. On the other hand, he consistently got knocked by *Time Magazine*. This annoyed him, and on one occasion Bob tried to find out who was responsible. Jack McLarn of *The Observer* (Charlotte, N. C.) was a reviewer for whom Bob had respect.

When a writer asked him for his thoughts on reviewing of books, Bob replied: "I would say that reviews have considerable effect on book sales because they created a mood. My personal tendency is to buy a book which is either praised or not, feeling that if a guy I know and respect likes it, I will buy it. If the same guy knocks it, I want to know why." He then added this approach did not apply to Leslie Hanscom, "for whom I have neither knowledge, liking, or respect."

Bob then noted that his upcoming book, *Poor No More*, had taken four years to write, and he had serious doubts about having "some bum sit down and dismiss it when he isn't able to write a coherent letter to his mother. I can take a knock as well as the next guy if the knocker knows what he is knocking, but for some man who has never been south of Harlem to tell me about Africa annoys me."

Bob didn't mind literary criticism and realized that reviews could make a real difference. "Basically you want the book review good, bad, or indifferent. If it is worth reviewing it is generally worth reading."

Bob paid equal attention to all his writing efforts, whether they involved books, columns, magazine features, film scripts or just plain correspondence. He used to say: "If I could write it any better, I would, but I can't." The strange thing was that he could write a column in 700 words and say exactly and concisely what was necessary to make a strong point, quickly and without rewriting, yet it took him 500,000 words to write a book.

Bob seemed to think he was capable of any type of writing he cared to attempt, and he tried everything, including a musical play, which never got anywhere. Apart from film treatments and collaboration on an original screenplay, he did some doctoring of already written screenplays and finally wrote one for *Uhuru*.

Bob was not an intellectual. He invariably wrote about his own experiences, and in his books he borrowed heavily from his own life. That could possibly account for the successful, speedy writing of *Something of Value*, which was based more on fact that his other books. Similarly, the fine writing in *The Old Man and the Boy* stories probably stemmed from the fact that these were all things Ruark had experienced. All he had to do was to report them. Even though Bob did establish himself as a fine author, his background as a reporter and columnist was never forgotten.

When *Something of Value* was published, Bob considered himself to be a book author, and he felt the "C" in his name was unnecessary. Previously his byline had always been Robert C. Ruark, but as a book author he wished to be known solely as Robert Ruark.

Obviously, Bob always had a flair for writing, and this is clearly shown in a piece written for his university publication when he was 18 years of age. Entitled "Ashes to Ashes," it was part of a collection of literary experiments in creative writing. It showed not only writing ability but an almost uncanny forecast of his life to come. When the piece was written, Bob was under the tutelage of Phillips Russell, and the whole thing came under the heading "A Collection of Literary Experiments in Creative Writing." Bob also did the art, which consisted of a sketch of Professor Russell.

Ruark's contribution, given the way it presaged his career, is worth quoting at length.

Tommy's dead. He had a lot of fun before he died, though. He never got all well with his family, never would stay at home. Tommy's trouble was a deep, irrational love for strong liquor and the sea. While a love for even one of these things is extremely upsetting to a normal equilibrium, one glance at the restive, wild, intelligent blue eyes of him was enough to tell you that Thomas had an over-dose of both.

Once, in order to get Tom back from Shanghai, his father procured an appointment to Annapolis for him. Tom lasted under the Academy discipline for four months. He then blacked the respective eyes of two professors, one midshipman first-class, and a two-striper sent back to the Yard for further instruction in aeronautics, after which notable exploit he shipped as a common sailor on a tramp bound for Port Said, Egypt.

Tommy stayed abroad for a year, then came back and entered Duke. He graduated in three years, made Phi Beta Kappa, and never took one examination when not at least three-sheets-over. He graduated, I said, and, still wearing his Phi Beta Key, got a job coal-heaving on another tramp, headed, this time, for Buenos Aires. For four years, he remained at sea, working as a first mate on a

black-birder (slave-runner) in the Solomons, chief engineer of a rum-runner operating from Havana to Miami, second mate on a transatlantic liner, bos'n on an oil ship, and captain of a private yacht.

I have heard many tales of his exploits. For instance, it seems that in Port Said, one Iba Mayhruf Mohmahd and a choice gang of gutter-rats were in the act of raping a little Syrian girl, and killing and robbing her father, a venerable old shopkeeper. Tom, who would not have bowed to any empress, or have acknowledged the nod of a president, cheerfully sailed in, with bars from Kipling issuing from his mouth, and bars of crow in his hands, gleefully smiting to such good end as to total two fractured skulls and a broken neck to the marauders, and immunity to himself and the frantic shopkeeper's daughter.

It was Tom, in some unsavory *tchum-tchum* or *bapedi* joint in the *Village Negrito* in Havana, that district wherein there is little regard for right and wrong, salvaged a terror-stricken millionaire from the filthy hands of a motley bunch of half-breeds, playing upon their hard heads with two hock bottles, and still quoting his eternal Kipling. It was Tom, who, when the delivered millionaire tried to pay him for the night's joyous activities, gently but firmly subtracted said capitalist from his bulging wallet, tossing said wallet to the sadly battered horde of footpads, pushing Mr. Capitalist into a convenient gutter, and striding cheerfully (if unsteadily) into the darkness. It was Tom, who, with a woman in every port, was the unfailing champion of every female, of no matter what station in life.

There's no doubt about it, Tom had fun. But, not so long ago, he got married, married to a nice, pleasantly intelligent, moral little woman who murdered him. I saw them together the other day. He hasn't had a drink in a year, seen the ocean, or had a fight. Kipling no longer flows freely from his pleasant mouth. There is a beaten look in his eyes, a misty nostalgia, a tremor on his lips, and – oh yes, a wee infant clinging to his hand. His wings are clipped, his soul has flown. Yes, Tom's dead all right. She killed him.

Bob always took notice of what other people wrote, and he read other columnists on a regular basis. Occasionally, he would write a letter of appreciation for something they had written. He had definite ideas about most other writers and was pleased to cooperate when asked by Harvey Breit of the *New York Times Book Review* to contribute to a symposium for their 1955 Christmas issue. In answering the question "What book (or books) has been the decisive influence in your life?," Bob dictated the following:

"Before I give the business reply to yours of October 24 I should first like to thank you for your kind handling of me in the *Times*, and to tell you that I especially liked the results of the one interview we had over the phone in New York when I had the grandfather of all hangovers, and was not coming through very clearly. Most everybody I know says that you managed to capture the real me – slob, that is – and I am inclined to agree. In any case, thank you.

"I am flattered to be included in your Christmas list for 1955 and will probably have to dissimulate just a little, since the sum of the question is bound to be made up of parts. Herewith the statement:

Without undue humility, a quality in which I am strangely lacking, I would say that nearly every time I read a really good piece of writing I come down with heavy despair at ever being able to write as good as I want to. For instance, I think that Philip Wylie in *Finnley Wren* displayed the best command of the English language I have ever seen. I think that Robert Louis Taylor's *Professor Fordorski* is the funniest book on the slapstick nature I ever read. I think that Somerset Maugham is possibly the best storyteller I ever encountered despite a prose style which can only be described as a crashing bore – which Maugham himself admits.

I believe I received more satisfaction from "Big Two Hearted River" by Hemingway than from any formless short stories I ever read, and the earlier Evelyn Waugh I found completely delightful before children and the church overtook him.

I have read everything that I could get my hands on, including box tops and the wrappers on medicine bottles ever since I was a child, hence I was not suddenly smitten with any one author since I had digested Shakespeare, Charles Lamb, Walter Scott and Thomas Hardy before I was out of knickerbockers. The last impression had to be accumulated. I would say that the gorgeous simplicity of Steinbeck's collection, *The Long Valley*, had to merge with *The Sun Also Rises* and *A Farewell to Arms* in making me despair of ever being able to write simply and well. I would say that the leisure with which Mr. Maugham attacks his novels and especially his long short stories had a driving influence against undue hurry in prose construction, and certainly for wrapping it up in a neat bundle nobody ever surpassed the old hack, O. Henry or the skilled fabricator, Kipling.

I learnt a lot about texture from Thomas Wolfe whilst calling him a hopelessly bad novelist. I was never smitten unduly by the Fieldings and Lopez de Vegas, Voltaires and the rest of the furrin boys. But a lot had to rub off.

To give you as straight an answer as possible in my youth I was disturbed mostly by Kipling and Maugham, and in my early writing years, Hemingway and Steinbeck were the basic motivators. I find myself without a hero at the moment since I don't think anything of lasting worth has been written in the English language since the war.

I am sorry to have twisted and wriggled, but I have no pat answer to your question.

Of course, Robert Ruark had always read extensively, and he treasured his own books, especially a 20-volume collection of Somerset Maugham that he bought at a time when he didn't have any money. He actually went without meals to save sufficient money to buy them. Bob did a great deal of his reading at night in bed, and he would always have a half-dozen books on his night table. As he was often unable to sleep, he spent many hours reading through the night. He would also sometimes lie in bed in the morning for a couple of hours reading before he got up. When he left his bedroom in Palamos for the last time, on his bedside table there were only two books, *The Raymond Chandler Omnibus* and *The Second Chandler Omnibus*, containing a number of detective stories. Then in London, when briefly in hospital, he sent for *Wanderings of an Elephant Hunter* by Karamoja Bell as part of his preparatory reading for his next African novel.

There is no doubt that Robert Ruark had the greatest regard for his agent, Harold Matson, and he admitted that he was fortunate to commence this relationship almost at the start of his book-writing career as this proved to be of enormous help to him. Their relationship actually started in 1948 as the result of an introduction by Norman Katkov, a Scripps-Howard reporter on the staff of the *New York World Telegram*. Katkov and Bob had collaborated on a play about a newspaper in wartime completely staffed with women, and whilst the play itself didn't get anywhere, it served to bring Bob and Matson together.

Bob respected Matson's literary opinion above all others, and he was really about the only person to whom Ruark ever listened. A good example was the rewriting of *Poor No More*, which was undertaken purely on Matson's recommendation. Similarly, during the writing of all the other big books there were consultations with Matson by means of six-page letters, plus special visits by him to Palamos or special trips by Bob to New York, when he accepted guidance and made many plot changes.

Bob likewise had complete confidence in Matson's business ability, and he left all contractual negotiations entirely in his hands. Ruark repeatedly referred to him as being "the most smart, the most honest, and the most imaginative of all flesh peddlers in the business." Matson had Bob's power of attorney and access to all his banking accounts. He managed all the accounting involved in Bob's complicated, active life.

When writing to an author friend recommending Harold Matson, Bob explained:

"He is not only an editor for the client, but helps with taxes and the legal literary problems involved in contracts, and has full accounting facilities, and has a fixed address. Moreover, he will come when called, such as when I am having plot trouble here, I say 'come Harold,' and he gets on the plane and comes to Spain.

"You will find him an enchanting feller and you will soon discover that editors need Matson much worse than Matson needs the editors, so they bring him into the consultation, and you will find that he has ideas that you didn't know you had. It is said of Matson that he does not attend conferences, he just sends his eyes, and on the finalization of the big picture deal he did for *SOV*, to the statement 'but we ain't got no paper on this,' came the immediate reply, 'but Hal shoot hands, didn't he?' This is the kind of agent for you to have instead of that bloody dike you have been screwing around with."

Bob further explained that his agent more than earned the ten percent commission charged, and really didn't cost him anything, as he always got the maximum price for any literary property Bob produced. He gave as an example the incident during the *Something of Value* deal when Matson got $106,000, instead of $3,600, for the paperback rights.

At times the strain of working with Bob could be a considerable burden, as is evidenced by a letter Matson wrote shortly after spending several days in the hospital:

"Hyperventilation is my weakness, sometimes brought about by negotiation fever. The word negotiation leads me to the point of this letter. After a lot of backing and filling, and hyperventilation, we ran up the market on the paperback book rights to $106,000 with Pocket Books. This is the highest price ever paid for a paperback including *From Here to Eternity* which was the previous record breaker. What a hyperventilation guy does is exhale more carbon dioxide than he should and comes up with a state of exhaustion, which results in symptoms which are frequently misread as being from a heart condition, an ulcer, or a gall bladder. The next time I do a $106,000 deal for Ruark I shall do it in short pants."

Harold Matson had many record sales, and he did particularly well for his authors with Book-of-the-Month Club selections. On one occasion he was able to write to Bob: "It was a week ago today that we were BOMbed, first with the news that *Uhuru* was wanted for July selection and then that Herman's [Herman Wouk] *Youngblood Hawke* was wanted for June." However, Bob often remarked that it was not only the big deals Matson attended to with such alacrity, but he would put the same amount of interest into the sale of a single magazine article.

Occasionally, in order to keep the record straight, Bob would have to make a definite point concerning "the peddling of his wares." He would reply to publishers who approached him directly with a straight statement: "Harold Matson is my agent and we will sell anything I do according to Mr. Matson's advice, based on money and expediency, and nobody owns nothing of me until they have cleared with Mr. Matson."

In 1955, in order to show some of their esteem for Harold Matson, Bob and Ginny Ruark agreed to invite his young son Timothy to spend the summer with them in Palamos. For the Ruarks this was quite an invitation and in a way was an experiment. They had never been able to have children of their own and as the date of arrival approached, Bob and Ginny wondered a few times whether a mistake had been made. How would they stand up to this invasion of their privacy by a ten-year-old boy, along with a number of other boys of similar ages who would be around to keep him company. They had never been associated for any length of time with the problems of a young boy and were highly apprehensive contemplating his arrival.

But I think right from the start of the actual visit, Bob decided he need not have worried. Immediately after Timmy's transatlantic flight landed in Barcelona, he was taken to a bullfight. Afterwards, when asked what he thought of the spectacle, his reply consisted of exactly one word, "neat." Bob then knew he would have no trouble with young Timmy.

Not knowing what sort of control to put on these boys, the Ruarks placed almost no restrictions on them. The only hard and fast house rules were no swimming alone and no riding bicycles on any main thoroughfares.

Later in the summer, when the boys were well settled to life in Palamos and Bob's nerves had weathered the natural inclination of the boys, clad in pajamas, to climb out their bedroom window, crawl over the roof, and shinny down the pine trees, the day arrived when Bob realized that maybe a mistake had been made after all.

This was on the day when all the firecrackers in the village, which had been bought on a daily ration basis and saved by the boys presumably for a special show, accidently exploded altogether and appeared to be blowing down the whole house. After this excitement and when the various fires had been extinguished, Bob spoke sternly with the boys and discovered it was nobody's fault, that it was simply one of those strange things that just happen. Despite this particular infringement of the peace, one had the feeling that he was happy to have the boys around, and would have liked children of his own. He certainly was not willing to let Timothy go until the very end of the summer, and with this in mind he wrote his father:

"We will keep Timmy permanently if you wish, but otherwise you had better book him for around September 1, and in the meantime I am lending him pesetas at a ten percent mark up – trying to get some of my bait back and so far we are showing a profit on the summer."

CHAPTER 16
RUARK AS A COLUMNIST

In 1953, when Robert Ruark came to Europe and settled in Spain, the question was often asked regarding how he always managed to be on top of the news and to write timely columns from so far away. This was not a problem for Bob. He had an uncanny ability to forecast what was going to happen and thus was often writing columns ahead of a particular event. Moreover, with the aid of an assistant in New York who would clip American newspapers selectively, he was able to keep abreast of the news on a domestic level.

Bob received the European editions of the *New York Times* and the *New York Herald-Tribune*, and of course *Time* and *Newsweek*, and also there would usually be the *English Daily Express* in the house. He received a daily pouch from New York containing some selective newspaper clippings and column ideas. The pouch would also include the first page of the second section of the *New York World Telegram* and *The Sun*, thus enabling him to keep track of his own column as well as those of *World Telegram* colleagues such as Fred Othman, Inez Robb, Norton Mockridge and Henry J. Taylor.

Then there would be a weekly pouch containing the sports page of the *World Telegram* and on a regular basis a wide selection of other columnists including Walter Winchell from *The Mirror*; Jimmy Cannon, Dorothy Kilgallen, Louis Sobol and Westbrook Pegler from *The New York Journal-American*; and Leonard Lyons, Sidney Skolsky and Earl Wilson from *The New York Post*. From time to time the selection would change a little according to how Bob felt, and he would ask for columns from Red Smith, Farrell, Lippman, the Alsops, James Resden and Arthur Krock, Bob Silvester and John Crosby to be included. In this way he kept himself well covered news-wise.

The column ideas would be written by the New York assistant, which would help Bob on a dull news day. But they were really more useful when Bob was off in the bush on safari or had been traveling without time to read up at length on the most recent news.

The large, buff-colored envelopes containing all this material would arrive relentlessly, and the opening and reading became the worst chore of Bob's life. We were always ankle deep in newspaper clippings, with piles and piles scattered throughout the house, much to Ginny's annoyance, and the maids knew that no paper must ever be moved, even if it was on the floor. Many of these envelopes would never be opened when Bob found he had sufficient material without using them, but he always dug out his own published columns. As a general rule this was done when relaxing on the front terrace after the morning's work.

Regularly every few weeks there would be an agonizing outcry from Bob when he came to one of his columns amongst these newspaper cuttings. The irritation would be because of the treatment a particular column had received . . . either the way it had been cut or its position on the editorial page. Shouting at me to come back to the office, Bob would angrily make for the back room, muttering that he was going to give a blast to those idiots in New York. In the heat of annoyance Bob would usually dictate a letter to Walker Stone, the editor-in-chief of Scripps-Howard Newspapers in Washington, D. C. This letter, sent in July, 1956, is a good example:

Dear Walker

This is not a personal letter but a business one. I suppose you have been seeing something of the Chinese sports page which the *World Telegram* calls an editorial page.

It is needless to say that you can't tell the players without a program and that the ham-footed copy reading would be inferior to a kindergarten for idiots.

Over the last couple of years, especially since Dick Starnes, who hates my guts for some reason, came to the paper, there has been a definite effort to sabotage my stuff in New York. They run me or not according to whim and they cut me in some instances by fifty percent. I will agree that Lee Wood is a nitwitted son-of-a-bitch, and that Roy is a meddlesome old man, but I am Goddamn sick and tired of looking like a bum in New York.

The column contract comes up for renewal in the Spring. I happen to know where I can go with it and I also have sufficient confidence in my past reputation to know how many readers I can take from the *World Telegram* if I go across the street. I am asking you as the Editor-in-Chief of Scripps-Howard Newspapers and not as my friend Stoneface to have a sharp word in New York. The stuff is no worse and no better than it ever was, and I either want it run regularly and run as I write it, or not run at all, because I am pretty certain that the Hearst boys will guarantee that my product good or bad will be run as written.

This is not a whine from a hungry man. It is a loud beef from a boy who is being butchered by two people who don't like him. I couldn't care less if Scripps-Howard cancels out for all the papers; it is just that I don't particularly care at my age to be a victim of whim. No carbons of this letter will be sent to anybody.

Since Walker Stone was out of Washington when this arrived in his office, he had it read to him over the phone. Afterwards he instructed his office to forward Bob's letter to Jack Howard, the son of Roy Howard and at that time the president of the newspaper chain. He replied to Walker Stone as follows:

By coincidence I have complete documentation for the case – the good case – Bob Ruark makes for himself in his letter to you. He is being butchered. It is cockeyed. I resent it as an insult to me as a reader, and it is just barely possible that other readers feel the same way.

The situation seemed to me to become acute about the first of the month. As you know, I have been traveling a lot and haven't seen Bob's column here on any consistent basis. As a matter of fact, I normally read it on the wire anyway. But after they made over the Tele editorial page it looked to me as if both Bob and Fred Othman were being edited with a meat ax and a ruler.

Shortly after July 4 I started to keep a comparison of Bob's copy as run in the Tele and as it appears on the wire. Just so I wouldn't be accused, as I have been, of bias because of my friendship for Bob – which will probably perish in the crossfire of this fracas – I have had the same check made on Othman. Both support Bob's beef.

I have been waiting for the return of the editor, described otherwise by our nettlesome middle-aged man, because that is the only place to seek a remedy for this situation. Of course, I don't agree with Bob that his "stuff is no worse and no better than it ever was." I think it has been disappointing for some months. Bob can still hit the ball, but he isn't doing it as often as he used to. This isn't just my opinion, either. But, if the boys downtown feel the same way, they would be more honest with themselves, Bob, and the readers if they left columns out entirely instead of gutting them.

"I don't know what the hell is going on down there. I doubt if Dick Starnes is involved because I don't believe he handles any part of the page. I also doubt if he would let personal prejudice – and this is the first time I've been aware of any – interfere with his professional judgment. Anyway, I haven't filled my dossier on this case just for practice. I am going to find out what this is all about, and hope I can do something about it.

Except for this one thing, which is no small one, our Master Robert seems to have little to disturb him on the Costa Brava. The weather in Palamos at this time of year can hardly make starting the Rolls Royce in the morning a difficult chore.

After the dust settled a bit, Bob replied to Walker Stone with a slightly less belligerent attitude:

Thank you for your nice letter in response to my beef and for sending me Jack Howard's letter to you. I have been billed as columnist for quite a lot of years and I have either got too much dignity to be run in fragments, or the six scrapbooks full of decently written and published pieces prove me completely wrong.

I think really that the best solution in the spring is to quit working for Scripps-Howard in any form whatsoever, and if this means stopping the column completely, then all right. Fortunately I am able to do this without any threat to the beans and bread department.

I observe from Jack's letter that he has been so busy that he doesn't know what is going on in his own newspaper, which appears to me to be a real lame excuse for an executive. If I had a newspaper I would kind of make some point of knowing what's going on in it.

I can continue to preserve a personal friendship for the heads of the parent company, but my God, I am glad I've got money in Switzerland.

Also tell Jack that the crack about the Rolls Royce on the Costa Brava is cute, but didn't get bought via the letter with which he fired me and was still dumb enough to run the copy when I was off the payroll. I learned in the Masai four years ago that gratitude was not the thing you could come to expect in your old age if they would do that to you in your prime.

Apart from my usual bad temper when I consider the organization with which

I have spent around twenty-two years, we love you very much and hope to see you soon either here or there. I will be back in the States in March to do a bit of business concerning the new contract with United Features – if any.

About a month later, when it appeared that Bob's columns were being treated with considerably more respect by the *World Telegram*, there was a further letter from Walker Stone that endeavored to pour oil on troubled waters. He also said that "if, come next March, you want to call off your connections with Scripps-Howard, you do it without recriminations. Official relations can be severed without damage to personal friendships."

Suitably mollified, Ruark replied in turn indicating he was happy with the turnaround in the way his column was being handled and indicated: "I do not think that I would be overly happy across the street, and if we can keep my showcase in New York reasonably intelligent, then I hope to stay on with the Group until I quit writing columns entirely due to fatigue and riches."

Generally, when writing letters of annoyance to the people at Scripps-Howard Newspapers, Bob would send similar complaints to the president of the United Feature Syndicate. He would usually be discussing the pros and cons of staying with Scripps-Howard and regularly talked about jumping over the fence to Hearst Newspapers.

At one point he wrote: "I am not a 'single column head' man and I have no desire to be treated like a copy boy at my advanced age." On another occasion, in an exceptionally caustic letter, he stated: "You know that I have no desire to hustle my butt in a strange house with a flock of new madams, but having read my own wares in the *World Telegram* for the last year or so, it seemed to me that any self-respecting whore couldn't hold still for the kind of treatment I was getting."

Bob never had very much confidence in anyone in a position to touch his copy, and at one time with this in mind he was inspired to write a rather lengthy critical poem. It was headed "Crowell's Commandos" and was bylined Henry Wadsworth Ruark. It is essentially doggerel, but in it the editors at Crowell's are described as "bloody butchers," "vultures," "monsters culled from stews and sinkholes," and other choice names.

Probably as good an insight as any on Ruark's feelings about editors and their relationship to columnists was provided by his November, 1950 participation in a panel discussion at the University of Miami. The topic of discussion, which also included columnists Inez Robb and John Crosby, was "The Influence and Responsibility of Columnists." Each of the participants divulged some of the secrets of their trade and a question period followed. At that juncture the editor-in-chief of the *Toledo Blade* asked Bob if columnists objected to having their copy edited.

"Yes, they do object," was his immediate answer. He then cited as an example a column he wrote when the battleship *U.S.S. Missouri* ran aground at Hampton Roads, Virginia. One editor had changed Bob's line, "We ain't paying no admirals to run no battleships onto no mudbanks" to read "We are not paying admirals to run battleships onto mudbanks."

"I can spell 'are not' if I want to," Bob said petulantly, and then went on to explain that he would split an infinitive when it is otherwise awkward, then added that double negatives don't mean nothing to him."

From time to time Bob would see editing jobs on his columns he didn't like, but would let them pass. Sooner or later he would find it necessary to write more complaining letters. After an exchange of letters in the late 1950s, peace reigned between Ruark and Scripps-Howard Newspapers for a time. So much was this the case that one day he actually wrote a letter of praise to Jack Howard. Noting that Howard was always saying, "I never wrote unless I had a bitch," this time he said the editorial page of the *World Telegram* "looked like a newspaper again instead of a Chinese puzzle. It is encouraging to read copy that appears to be written in its entirety, rather than subject to the cleaver in the hands of an inept child."

Unfortunately, peace never reigned for long and in 1960, just before leaving for another safari in Kenya, Bob was again displeased. He wrote Harold Matson: "I am not, repeat not, pleased with the way that Goddamn *World Telegram* is now beginning to run me. . . . These bastards are really murdering me in my New York showcase." Despite all the efforts made to have Bob's column presented decently in New York, it just was not possible to keep him happy for any great length of time.

Although Bob periodically screamed his annoyance and threw heavy criticism at the Howard family, and even trained his old boxer, Schnorkel, to growl savagely when Roy Howard's name was mentioned, he really had a great regard and liking for them. Bob and Ginny had always been on friendly terms with the Howards, and both father and son visited the Ruarks in Spain.

Robert Ruark was rightly proud of his reporting ability and proud of his past. At heart, even after 20 years as a columnist, he was still a reporter. Accordingly, when Walker Stone made a suggestion that Bob take a big swing through Africa on a reporting trip for Scripps-Howard Newspapers, he jumped at the idea. He was thrilled to be going out on the road again, but he wanted to go out as a reporter seeking comprehensive coverage rather than as a columnist. The arrangement he made with Walker Stone was that this trip would be taken without remuneration, but with expenses. Bob would be allowed to supply his normal column material during the period, and he thought he could collect large quantities of material for books at the same time.

Stone readily accepted Bob's conditions. "You've got a deal." Heading his letter with the words "Dear Chief Swindle Sheet," he then added a fair, insightful appraisal of Bob's abilities as a reporter:

"I think you will enjoy being a reporter again. You are the best natural reporter I ever worked with. I think you have had to strain yourself at times to be a columnist, and I know you have always had to strain to write fiction. But reporting is something that is as natural with you as eating, drinking, breathing, screwing, and sleeping. Your reflexes are as responsive to something newsworthy as they are to the flutter of a covey rise. You wouldn't have had the excitement of spending as many millions, but you might have been a happier man if you had never ventured into other pursuits.

"Anyhow, I am happy you are going to undertake the African assignment. Personally I think there is just as much of a story there now as there will be one year from now. But if you wish to choose next October, that's all right with me. The right reporter can get the story on his own timing. The wrong reporter had better stay home. Africa is a wonderful continent. Much too good to belong to the Mau Mau."

This proposed reporting project in Africa promised to be interesting. Many countries had only just received or were soon to receive their independence. Bob went to Africa in December, 1959 and started the whole project off from Nairobi, immediately engaging the services of his white hunter friend, Harry Selby, to accompany him to some of the countries.

First covering Kenya, Bob began by interviewing the new governor, Sir Patrick Renison, and then spoke extensively with the farmers, the white settlers. Bob said they would be at the mercy of the black majority, and what he outlined as their plight and forecast did in fact happen to them after independence. He reported on the various political parties and the activities of the top black politicians, interviewing Tom Mboya and others. He later correctly suggested that Jomo Kenyatta could possibly be the first prime minister in Kenya. At the time that would have seemed rather unlikely, since he was still under house arrest as the symbolic chief of the Mau Mau.

All this was just a little extra to Bob's already enormous background of African knowledge. Right from the start of his reportage, Bob forecast considerable upheaval in the emerging countries and serious teething troubles. He felt there was a very small percentage of Africans who were capable of self-government. He made the point that there were so many different tribes and customs and languages that any government by the black African was bound to have enormous problems. He also predicted that while Africa was about to past completely into black hands, very soon it would pass into other hands – red.

After the Kenya report, Bob got out on the road with Harry Selby. They took off for Somalia to the north, which was due for independence in a few months. Bob didn't consider their chances to be particularly high since he was arrested five times during his stay. Ethiopia was next on the visiting list. He spent some time in Addis Ababa, where he seemed to find more Russians than Ethiopians. He had an audience with Emperor Haile Selassie and on leaving his palace, said the imperial lions roaming loose on the lawn only looked at him and yawned. Apparently Bob expected more action. He pointed out that although Ethiopians had had their independence since the time of Solomon, a matter of about 3,000 years, except for a couple of central boulevards the capital's streets were still unpaved.

Checking through Nairobi again, and having another go at Kenya's black politicians, Bob made his way to the Belgian Congo and forecast a violent outcome for future independence. Bob reported on all the emerging countries and knocked most of the black politicians pretty heavily. He then took time off from his political coverage to do a fine series on the miracles being performed by Nobel Peace Prize winner Dr. Albert Schweitzer in his mission hospital in French

Equatorial Africa. Then, on returning to the Belgian Congo, he visited a cannibal king with 500 wives, his royal highness Nymi Lukengu of Mushenge, King of the Balubas. The king made the point that he shared Ruark's dislike of politicians and didn't understand this new thing called independence.

While Ruark was preparing a report on South Africa, an assassination attempt was made on Prime Minister Hendrik Verwoerd. Bob made what was probably the only report to suggest the assassin's vanity saved the prime minister's life. The assassin, who was known to be an excellent shot, used a .22 caliber pistol to fire two shots at the prime minister's head. But Bob, thinking like a hunter, said this light pistol was not enough gun. The vanity of the assassin in shooting at a difficult target proved ineffective, whereas shots into the chest at such close range would probably have killed the prime minister.

During this assignment, Bob was in Africa for some six months and wrote over 50 feature articles. However, the whole project was just too much for him and his copy deteriorated and he missed some of his columns. Continuous travel, constant ferreting out of suitable stories, nervous tension, excessive drinking (sometimes instead of eating properly – all took their toll. He realized that the age of 45, though not being old, was a far cry from 35. A short while after his return to Nairobi, Bob completely fell apart and collapsed. He collapsed in a far worse way than he had ever done before. He was unconscious for more than a week after he ended up in the Maria Carbury Nursing Home in Nairobi. After a few weeks he recovered sufficiently to travel back to Spain. Later he wrote to Walker Stone explaining what had happened:

Dear Stoneface,

I am now making sense after having spent all last week in hospital more or less as crazy as a coot. I had what could best be described as a complete nervous and physical collapse, mostly nervous. I had three successive blackouts in a row, plus some rather gaudy hallucinations involving a beautiful ghost with a wooden leg. One whole week was entirely blank and I am told I committed some rather gaudy doings.

However, I fell among friends who stuck me into the hospital and I emerged shaken but sane. Diagnosis is that my ills were one part nervous fatigue, one part physical fatigue, and one part accumulative booze over a period of twenty years, and to this end I have been firmly on the wagon including wines, beer, whisky, and custards with brandy in them for the last week and feel fine, but my doctor, Dr. Roy Thompson, absolutely forbade me to do a stroke of work for a minimum of two weeks.

I can tell you I was a mess, as you probably gathered from that phone conversation. I skipped in from Nairobi a day or so ago and I have had a couple of days of sun and I am feeling fine again but still tire awfully easy. I am going up tomorrow to London to collect Virginia and do some chores and I will be back in the saddle to a point where you can count on publication again a week from this coming Monday. I also suspended work on the columns largely because I just couldn't think.

I am sorry to have let you down, but flesh is flesh and mine proved weak. I am off the grog because Thompson proved definitely that alcohol of any sort at this moment is a deadly poison to me and that if you keep fiddling around with these blackouts, eventually you get a brain distortion as well as a heart strain.

<u>This is important</u>. It is not possible for me to have epilepsy in any shape or form as there is no previous record of an initial epileptoid attack striking anyone after their thirty-fifth birthday. Mine is a fairly common ailment which afflicts people who have an excessive tolerance for whisky, as well as a defective liver function to where the tissues retain the alcohol and eventually it finds its way into the bloodstream to the brain.

Thompson absolutely guarantees me immunity from any further attacks so long as I don't drink for the next six months, after which he says I will be able to drink normally if I so desire. He also promises a 92 percent liver function and says that inside of three months I can pass a physical for a pilot's license.

I must say that taking on this African chore was biting off a little more than I could chew. I trust I did as well as I could and got you some fair copy. If I didn't it was not for want of hard work God knows, because I just about killed myself in the process.

Bob always seemed to have remarkable recuperative powers after any particularly tough treatment he had given himself, and he would then disarm everybody completely with the result of a medical check-up. In June, 1960, after returning from London to Palamos, he again wrote Walker Stone with an update on his health. He said he looked and felt "approximately twenty years younger," was "eating like a horse and sleeping very well," and that he didn't "seem to miss the booze at all." Yet he added a fateful afterthought, saying that it got "a little lonesome around cocktail time or when I have finished a hard day's work to go and stare at another Coca Cola or a lemonade." He then suggested to Stone that "concerning the wagon, keep right on drinking. Life is horrible enough with whisky and without it insupportable."

Robert Ruark and Walker Stone were good friends. Their friendship dated back to Bob's beginning in the newspaper world when Stone was one of the few people who helped Ruark when he was a copy boy. Their correspondence was fairly prolific and to brighten up their letters they occasionally kidded each other with Indian names, supposedly because somewhere in Walker Stone's distant past there was some suggestion of Indian origin. I think Stone understood Bob better than most, and he offered sound advice every once in a while. Bob should have paid more attention to him. A good example came in a letter in response to Bob's rapid recovery.

"The news about your health is very good and also surprising. I hope the doctor is not kidding you and that you're not kidding yourself. For you're certainly right when you say that your body has already lived 65 years. But if you can learn to pace yourself, you still may yet become a mellow old philosopher and take Papa Hemingway's place when he gets ready to cross the river into the shade.

"The big trouble work-wise is that you try to keep too many balls in the air, with column writing, book-writing, magazine writing, and reporting – any one of which is exhausting enough for any one man.

"Best wishes. Chief Good Only for Catfishing from Rocking Chair."

While Ruark got out of Africa alive, another noted reporter, Harry Taylor, wasn't as fortunate. On September 9, 1960, Walker Stone cabled Bob at Palamos indicating that Taylor had been killed by a machine gun bullet while covering affairs in the Congo. The shock of this news was doubled for Ruark, since he had hosted Taylor's mother for lunch at Palamos just a few days earlier and had kidded her that her son would probably be eaten by cannibals in the Congo.

Harry Taylor's death upset Bob considerably, as it did the entire household at Palamos. The previous year Taylor and his girlfriend had been guests of the Ruarks, and at that time Bob had made a special point of letting Stone know how highly he thought of the bright young reporter. He said he wanted to go on the record "as saying that in young Hank Taylor you have got the best piece of journalistic raw material that I have ever seen."

Despite the fact that he was still recovering from his breakdown, Bob offered to return to the Dark Continent and more or less take Harry Taylor's place. The offer was immediately refused. I think Bob wished to show that he could do a better job than before, and he had a slightly guilty conscience about the expenses connected with his six months in Africa. They had come fairly close to $30,000, and he alluded to the matter after reading a piece in *Newsweek* about the high cost of coverage in the Congo.

Stone assured him that he didn't need to fret about the expense account in Africa. "We got more than our money's worth," he wrote, and "your surcharge mostly was in having the services of Harry Selby." He noted that if Taylor had had Selby with him he would "never have been caught in that crossfire and would not now be pushing up the sod in a Charlottesville cemetery."

During his African reporting trip Bob put his finger on many controversial points, but his foresight was exceptional in the way he handled his Congolese stories. When the independence celebrations exploded into war and made the Scripps-Howard Newspapers look good, Roy Howard was the first to acknowledge his appreciation. In a July 11, 1960, letter, Howard stated: "I would like to extend my sincere congratulations and in passing restate one of the most fundamental of my journalistic beliefs, namely, that there is nothing in American journalism more important than good reporting, an art to which, over the years, you have contributed with great credit to yourself, to Scripps-Howard, and to the profession."

In addition to this private communication, the *World-Telegram* gave kudos to Ruark under the headline "Ruark Predicted Atrocities."

"The frightful panic which swept white residents of the newly independent Congo Republic this week – amid reports of rioting and rape by African troops – was accurately predicted far in advance by *World-Telegram* columnist Robert Ruark.

"Mr. Ruark's amazingly detailed forecasts began long before the end of Belgian rule in the Congo. Besides predicting the breakdown of law and order, Mr. Ruark told why this breakdown was coming. On June 13 he wrote:

" 'A faint aroma of Fidel Castro's Cuba seems to permeate the Belgian Congo today, some three weeks before independence.

" 'The volatile public already has been assured that certain *undesirable Belgians* will be kicked out, and that certain properties, now white-owned, will be given to natives. One story goes that a certain blonde hostess for Sabena Airlines already has been *sold* three times.' "

Ruark was genuinely appreciative and said he wouldn't exchange Howard's words "for a good deal including the Pulitzer Prize." He indicated he was "very happy that my Cassandra-like prognostication bore fruit and that the papers had guts enough to run my pre-independence series." He acknowledged that it "was a pretty gory forecast of things to come" and thanked Howard for his "appreciation of a job I tried to do which did not at the time fit the popular and idiotic concept of freedom for all because in Africa at least there ain't such an animal." After all of his contentious exchanges with Howard, this era of good feeling showed the man's innate warmth, and there seems little doubt he reveled in the praise.

CHAPTER 17
THE MAN WHO WAS ROBERT RUARK

There is no question that an accurate and concise description of the man who was Robert Ruark would be extremely difficult, as on analysis he was in fact most things. Bob was not a particularly complex character, but he was a tremendous one with many facets. Perhaps the following paragraph from a letter written by one of his girlfriends after his death will help a little in clarifying the difficulty in capturing the essence of Robert Ruark: "Let me hear from you Alan, and where you'll be, and if you will be in New York by chance. I have a few souvenirs committed to memory that will amuse you when you are adjusted to the bleak fact of living in a world without that big bastard we have such a special love for – Robert Chester Ruark – Don Roberto."

There would be so many, many people with "souvenirs committed to memory," and of course, each person would have their own treasured memory and their own special description of the man. Bob Ruark possibly spread himself around to the point where he seemed to know everybody no matter where he went. I traveled with him many times, in Europe and in Africa. It didn't much matter what remote airport we arrived at, which primitive African village, or what big city. Within a few minutes Bob would be greeting a long-lost acquaintance or good friend. He might be black, or he might be white, but Bob personally knew people from every possible social level – from the porter to the hotel manager, from the airline pilot to the barman in the airport building who from previous acquaintance would know exactly what to serve Bob according to the time of the day. Bob might by chance run into an Indian shikar hunter, a district commissioner from New Guinea or his Australian bookmaker from Sydney.

He had an incredible memory for the past and his tales were fascinating. Whatever the topic, he was always up to date and well informed; but most of all he was interesting. He didn't have a particularly large repertoire of jokes, being largely full of humor all the time, though if he wanted to, he could keep a small group highly and hilariously entertained to the point all present would soon have aching sides.

Bob had a loose, slangy, down-to-earth conversational manner, and he usually talked dirty. He made frequent use of four-letter words, though I don't think anyone ever really objected to this. In person as in print he was a peerless raconteur, and he made everything sound so humorous and natural that even someone who might normally object to rude language would remark agreeably, "Well, that's Bob Ruark."

Ruark didn't believe much in God in the religious sense of going to church, which he never did, but he did believe in God as the creator. When writing about safari he often wrote reverently concerning the Lord and the beauty of the African bush. He would praise nature's beauty and give God full credit for having created such peace and tranquility. At the same time he would assess himself with a detrimentally qualifying statement: "So far as formal religion goes I am a very irreligious fellow who smokes, swears, drinks whisky, ogles girls and at this very moment I am paradoxically interested in killing things."

Bob was brought up as an Episcopalian, though I never remember him mentioning this. The only actual recollection I have of him making any reference to religion was his use of a pet phrase maintaining that "the Bible was written by a bunch of bad reporters."

He often said that he hated Christmas, though I believe this was purely from the point of view that it upset his working schedule and had nothing to do with his religious perspective. Also, he had no close family gathering and in any case didn't care for any social event that involved drinking eggnog.

Despite Bob's dislike for the festivity of Christmas, at this season he would have some fine thoughts and usually wrote a New Year resolution-type column. In December, 1958 he wrote a piece ending with what I suspect were genuine thoughts: "So I have settled for one resolution, and one only – to go on living in the present, in some way that the present should not be cheated by foreboding future. And, in the process, to do as little damage to my fellow man as possible."

Bob always gave a distinct impression of great affluence. In a sense this was true, provided one ignored just how much he spent. In this connection I recall part of a conversation with Harold Matson when we were traveling together from Barcelona airport to Palamos in Bob's Rolls Royce.

Matson remarked: "Bob is not a rich man but just a writer who has made some money."

Subsequently, for some reason I repeated this to Bob, and to my surprise he didn't like it. In his own mind he was a rich man, though his agent was merely making a distinction between someone who was oil or factory or inheritance rich, as opposed to a writer who in order to make his money must never stop producing. All the while Bob was tearing himself to pieces, and in the process destroying vital working capital in the form of the author himself.

I suppose being Robert Ruark really was a way of life. Without fail all his visitors wanted to hear about his lifestyle, and everyone soon realized he was a most unusual and different person. A great many of these characteristics have been written into *Poor No More,* and later, *The Honey Badger,* but the most uninhibited self-appraisal that Robert Ruark ever did was a lengthy piece for *True Magazine,* published in September, 1963 with the title "The Man I Know Best."

There's no doubt about it, I felt myself to be one hell of a fellow. Here I was just past forty, and I had it made. I had a vastly syndicated column, and I was my own boss.

He mentioned the astounding success of *Something of Value* and said it made more money "than the combined Ruarks had ever made since we stopped painting our faces blue." Ruark mentioned his villa on Spain's Costa Brava along with a townhouse in Barcelona, that he enjoyed food prepared by an exceptional cook, had the services of an English secretary, the security of a long-term magazine contract, "a hand-shot tiger on the wall, two of the heaviest elephant tusks ever extracted forcibly from an old bull, a couple of admiring dogs, and money in the bank." Add to that the fact that "Little Rob from North Carolina" had a Rolls Royce, "a mink-trimmed jockstrap, and a closet full of fancy Italian clothes" and the picture of him becomes fleshed out in full fashion.

I will not say I was unbearable, I was just plain Saturday-night-Texas rich, and I wanted to share it with the world. Not the riches – just me and my condition of vulgar affluence, not to mention my vast accomplishment as a white hunter, lover, and big liver.

Bob then went on to talk about his poverty when in college during the Depression, explaining that he might even have been a pimp if the fees were sufficient to pay his college tuition. He admitted to his drunken escapade immediately following graduation, and then he gave a rundown of his job-hunting when nobody wanted to employ a college graduate for any wage whatsoever. Thinking back on those days and comparing them with his present affluence, Bob continued:

Now I had this Rolls, and all these gorgeous clothes, and I had been a *Newsweek* cover story, and a *Life* profile and oh, my! The premiere of the movie that MGM had made from my book, all full of Rock Hudson, Dana Wynter, Sydney Poitier and other goodies, was about to be sprung on New York.

So you know I just had to go to New York, wearing my fancy Brioni duds, and just as naturally such a stylish chap could not depend on local transportation in New York. A fine-feathered fellow such as myself had to take his brand spanking new Rolls Royce Silver Cloud, all bought and paid for, with him from Spain to New York to impress the peasants.

Naturally we had a party for about 200 people upstairs at the Twenty-One Club, attended by at least two special shows of *Something of Value* and took bows, and smirked, and drank too much with too many people, and then went off to Washington to peacock some more before the old home folks; and, finally decided to carpetbag a bit and invade the Southern briar patches whence I had hitch-hiked so many years ago. I was going to stop off and check on the old girlfriends, to see if they'd married well, and then I was going to descend on my home town, Wilmington, in a veritable fiery cloud of triumphant horses and chariots like Elijah, an earlier prophet.

I was going to give the locals a break.

Well, sir, the Rolls and I swept triumphantly into the seaboard town in which I was unable to get a job even as a copy boy on the local paper, and my triumphs rode ahead of me like a police escort.

I pressed some calls on some people, and some nice folk from my misty past decided to throw me a cocktail party. It was an excellent party, full of uncut whisky and uncut Southern accents. Dressed in something extraordinarily tasty in the way of Italian silk, I was shimmering around the garden with a julep in my hand when I heard two soft Southern female voices floating like marshmallow from behind an oleander bush. It was Miss Sarah Sue Somebody talking to Miss Dimity Ann Something Else.

"I swear," Miss Sarah Sue was saying to Miss Dimity Ann, "I swear to John. I don't believe a word of it!"

"What don't you believe a word of, sugah?" asks Miss Dimity Ann.

"Bobby, that's what I don't believe a word of. I don't care how good they say Bobby's doing; I don't care if he did have his picture on that magazine cover, right spang between Prince Philip and President Eisenhowuh, I don't care if he is a big book author and lives in Spain and all!"

"Why don't you care, sweetness?"

"Well," said Miss Sarah Sue, vehemently. "he can't be doin' as good as everybody says, or he wouldn't have come back home after all these years in that beat-up Pierce Arrow!"

Move over, Tom Wolfe, I said to myself. *It's true. You can't go home again.* Shortly thereafter I crated up the old beat-up Pierce – I mean I packed up the gleaming new Silver Cloud, and we caught the first boat back to Spain. No prophet, except possibly Elijah, achieves honor in his own home town . . . .

Along about 1940, I was as brash a coward as ever wrote sports (a subject about which I knew nothing, but it was the first job that paid more than $15 a week which anybody offered me). I was young, and stupid, and afraid that I would soon be joining the other 19 failures which a Mr. Rocky Riley, the sports editor, had sacked ahead of me in the last calendar year.

So I wrote tough. I knocked everything and everybody. I wore my hat in the office – Rocky wore his hat in the office – and I talked out of the corner of my mouth. Rocky talked out of the corner of his mouth. I wore wide-brimmed hats and an air of perpetual belligerence, which is to say I would brace the subject of a rough piece with a copy of the first city edition in my hand, on the off-chance the victim wanted to make something out of it. This took a deal of cowardly courage, for what I wanted to do, after Riley hung one of his inflammatory headlines on the story, was to slink off to another state and cover garden parties.

The man I know best might be called the most humble, grateful, arrogant, brave, cowardly, laughingly, sad, introverted extrovert I ever encountered. He is a timid swashbuckler, a former dashing newspaperman who had to force himself to interview people, a wishful devilish dog with women who is sweatingly unsure of himself on the brink of any fresh encounter with a female under the age of seventy.

He is at this writing a balding forty-seven years old, with an extra twenty years of hard living on his battered chassis. His arteries have already begun to harden, and his liver is dejected, if not downright disconsolate. He looks fat but thinks of himself as thin. Since childhood he has always embraced himself with an aura of self-importance. The man I know best conveys an impression of toughness, boldness, brashness. Inside he is a writhing mass of timidities, softnesses, and insecurities.

He is not a handsome man. His forehead is too high, his frontal bones too prominent, his nose too big and crooked. His ears are large and outflanged, and he has always, even when physically thin after illness, owned a double chin. He has practically no eyelashes, and a beard which shows greenish gray. His mustache, which he has worn since his teens, is invariably ragged and sort of multicolored. His shoulders are too wide, too square, and his neck grows oddly from them, making the best of tailoring appear to have been hurled at him in a fit of rage. No suit he wears ever appears to be pressed.

Yet the man I know best feels handsome, to such point that he is often adjudged handsome by women, who invariably hate him by reputation, like him on sight, and sometimes love him later. He prefers the society of women to the company of men. He can turn his charm on or off at whim if the audience is worth the effort. In this respect our man is pure phony, because when he is completely sincere he is apt to labor his points, and earnestness drips off him like sweat.

The man I know best talks too much, but with the partial justification that he has got a tremendous backlog of things to talk about. He gives the impression of being a phony until a check actually reveals that he has done the things he has said he's done.

The man I know best is a phony in the sense that an actor is a phony; Peter O'Toole is not really Lawrence of Arabia, but he makes you believe momentarily that he is Lawrence of Arabia. But the man I know best is a completely valid, truthful man in a sense of achievement. What he says he will do he will do within the limits of Kismet.

The man I know best conveys a first impression of falseness because his conversation is larded with unlikely names, places, and achievements. It will develop that over a period of nearly 30 years as a professional writer, his life has been intertwined with these names, places, and achievements. But this first appearance of shooting-a-line works adversely on a man who might mention Bernard Baruch, Bing Crosby, Winston Churchill, Lena Horne, Louis Armstrong, Glen McCarthy, Tom Mboya, Tallulah Bankhead, the Duke of Edinburgh, Mae West, Richard Nixon, Lilian Gish, Ava Gardner, Joe DiMaggio, Lucky Luciano, Toots Shor, J. Edgar Hoover, Carol Burnett, Dick Gregory, Ann Sheridan, Spyros Skouras, Walter Winchell, Leonard Lyons, Dinah Shore, Ernest Hemingway, John Steinbeck, Joe Louis and Joe E. Lewis, Richard Burton, John Huston, Clint Murchison, Cardinal Spellman, a wild lion named Maggie, Carmen Franco, Jimmy Stewart, and Joe Buskin in the same context with the savage tribes of New Guinea; the outback of Australia; tiger shooting in India; being mauled by a leopard; owning a castle in Spain; living out of a flat in London; having a working knowledge of two leper colonies; making the Book-of-the-Month Club with two of his last three novels; setting an all-time high for a movie sale; being kicked out of Kenya for his last novel; chasing Luciano out of the hemisphere and temporarily busting up the international drug traffic; helping Frank Sinatra lose his voice; entertaining the Duke of Windsor in his Spanish home; of using a two-million air mile plaque for a paperweight; of having spent three years in all theaters of war as a gunnery officer, press censor, and finally, outranking a Fleet Admiral of the British Navy in matters of security; of having averaged four columns a week for the past 17 years for a syndication that hovers around 180 newspapers; of having written over 600 magazine pieces for slick magazines since the end of World War II; of having helped frustrate a revolution in Venezuela; of having earned a couple of million dollars with two fingers on a typewriter; of having written 10 books, most of which were best sellers; of having sold his first original unpublished screenplay for $100,000; and having been in thick bush after dangerous animals ranging from Mau Mau gangsters to sick Cape buffalo to wounded leopards.

The man I know best is no free-loader. What I have always sought in commercial facility is the maximum of service, an easy friendship with the owner, and the right to raise hell if anything goes wrong. You can only do this by paying your own way. I have used the Twenty-One Club literally as a country store for the best part of 20 years, and have never been insulted by a proffered subsidy.

Perhaps I carry this sensitivity too far. On the publicity which I have given east Africa, over the last dozen years, in column, magazine, book and movie, you could almost call me the father of the postwar safari trade in Kenya and Tanganyika. It was popularly supposed that either I was riding free with the safari firm or that I actually had a piece of the safari business, since my best friend in Kenya ran one of the two best outfits. In point of fact, Harry Selby's and Jack Block's account books will show that I paid the top-going rates for my pleasant research, even though it is customary to deliver freebies to the outdoor writers of prestige magazines. I didn't want any bloody freebies. It would have stolen my vested interest in a country I love and robbed my trophies of dignity.

I will lend money to friends, but I never feel quite the same about them after, and when I borrow I borrow from banks, and pay interest. I also have the hard horrors of being houseguest. I love to have company in my own home, but to be at the mercy of the host's whim gives me an acute rash. Perhaps it is selfish of me, but as the late editor, John Sorrells, once said: "I stay in hotels because I like to break wind out loud."

I suspect I got to be a loner very early, because I really did not like the society of children. I don't think I was ever anything but an adult as a child. I didn't give a damn for ordinary sports – possibly because I was clumsy and slow, but mostly because I never liked to do anything with a herd.

Bob went on to say that he was always far ahead of other boys of his own age at school, and he explained a little of how he had to fight as a schoolboy to maintain his policy of being a recluse with the book, bird dog and boat philosophy. He mentioned how frightened he was at practically everything, with a continuous fear of insecurity, which followed through during the war and then later when he hunted big game in Africa. Bob then continued to explain this fear complex:

It is really a terrible thing to be chronically frightened, to such a point that you must constantly prove that you're not. One lives with the feeling that no matter what you've done, what you've got, that some day the whole world will get wise to your weakness and come to take everything away. I have been living with the idea of getting fired ever since I got my first real job, and in the back of my mind was always the thought: *Well, I can always go back to sea;* or, *I can sell the Spanish place;* or, *I can go back to reading copy.*

It is not mock humility which makes me say I never understood why people pay money to read what I write. I know they do. For years after I first came to

New York to take over the old Heywood Broun column spot, I would sneak a peek at the *World-Telegram*'s split page, to see if my picture was at the top. If the half-column cut was there, I heaved a sigh of relief, because I always half-suspected they wouldn't run the piece that day. On the few days they didn't use the piece, I was dumbly desolate and would wonder if my luck had finally run out on me.

This distrust of fortune – and I am as superstitious as any witch doctor living in a welter of ancestral ghosts – must have come from the early formative years of privation. We were deeply bitten by the Depression; the family fell apart, old traditions went out the window, the pianos were sold, and my immediate family never recovered.

College was a four-year nightmare of financial embarrassment and real frustration. I was about three years younger than anybody in my class. My folks were described, bitterly, as "bad pay," and I was in hock to everybody. I was taken into a fraternity on the cuff, a sort of poor relation, and that bothered me. I could neither dress nor spend in the same league with the good brethren, and believe me, in 1932 nobody had much money. My roommate was rich on an allowance of $10 a month, which was exactly $10 more than I had. I think that phase of my life is basically responsible for my over eagerness in check-grabbing; for an insistence on more than adequate supply of everything from clothes to whisky; for the Rolls Royce in the backyard; and for almost a psychopathic set against being given anything, even a compliment.

Conversely I don't mind criticism, nor am I unduly annoyed by bad reviews of books or insulting mail. I am basically a lazy man, but am only really happy when I'm working too hard, just to see if I can.

If you want a real nest of worms for the psychiatrists to untwist, I am as gregarious a recluse as you're ever likely to meet.

With people of my own seeking, I don't mind a mob, and in Spain we not infrequently have 25 people for lunch. But I hate to do anything with anybody in a mass movement, even something so simple as deciding who will share a cab in order to get from a restaurant to a theater. Cocktail parties drive me to real drink, after I pry myself loose from them. I wouldn't take a vacation trip with my best friends, if it involved more than two people – and I have had my last safari of more than one gun.

I revel, I literally wallow, in loneliness, which is pretty Irish of me. Give me a fire, the prospect of walls lined with books, some recordings on the machine, a sufficiency of whisky in the bar, perhaps a moon outside and nobody at all to talk to, and I could weep with sad happiness. This possibly explains an overdeveloped love of bush and sea. Space without people is my idea of the ultimate in luxury. I can sit for hours alone in a leopard blind, or ride a Somali pony for 30 miles in rocky elephant country, and be completely diverted by my own thoughts and the small sights and sounds around me. Somewhere here there is again the conscious reversion to early poverty – whether surrounded by a multitude of books or a profusion of wild animals, there crops up the idea that I'm doing it and the other people aren't.

This was followed by an outline of how Bob started as a columnist with his famous piece on women immediately after the war, and to this he mentioned some of the successful stories he had written. He pointed out that "the good stories only really happen when you are young, have strong arches, and the digestive processes of a goat with the capacity to replace sleep with booze."

From reporting and column writing, Bob then turned to some of his earlier novels, and then came mention of his more recent and successful novels:

After two trips to Africa I was hooked on Africa, and I also had a novel on my back. Writing it was taking a big chance. The column was still going well – although I had quit working formally for Scripps-Howard and was now doing the pieces only three times a week for United Feature Syndicate – and I could write for any good slick magazine in the country with a miniscule fear of rejection. I was settled and happy in Spain, with the new house, and taking on a fresh giant, in the novel shape, was really a fool's decision. I didn't know anything about novel writing, and there was the possibility I would live unhappily ever after if it fell flat on its face.

God smiled. I made no major mistake in that one, *Something of Value*, and it certainly didn't fall on its face. I got knocked for being too bloody, but that was well before the average reader dined on a steady diet of gore from the Congo. Today it's largely regarded as authoritative history.

Then I tackled another one about the home country, *Poor No More*, and made every mistake there was, doubled and redoubled. But you learn. In the last one, again set in Africa, I didn't make many mistakes. But in *Uhuru*, this time, I didn't make the mistakes on purpose. You learn even more as you go – and I had to cut 165,000 words out of *Uhuru* before I discovered that I had a stupid way of saying I was going to do something, then doing it, and then telling you that I'd done it.

I'm still at loss to say what makes a book sell, any more than I know the basics behind a fact that you can make love to a woman you may have known only 10 minutes on the one hand, and not reap so much as a smile after working on another one for 10 years. Last year, before the newspaper strike, the *New York Times* Book Section polled a flock of best sellers from 1962, under the simple question: 'What makes your book popular with the people?' And I had to confess I hadn't the faintest. But most of the good books I ever read, from Mark Twain to Hemingway in modern times and going all the way back to *Beowulf*, told me "how it was." To tell the reader how it is, or was, with a minimum of flapdoodle, has been my principal aim, and up to now it would seem that I have been abnormally lucky.

Bob also considered himself to have been lucky in having a magnificent house to work in and some good people to help him. Referring to his Mediterranean beach house as a robber's cave with everything in it harkening back to his personal past, Bob listed some of the more important trophies, and for the high decoration style gave full credit to Ginny and her interior decorating talents. Further explaining about his house, Bob continued:

The whole house is geared to keeping the writer happy, because "the money tree," as the cook calls the typewriter, needs constant pruning. The house is two complete houses – one half belonging to the guests and the other half off-limits to everybody but me and a slave named Alan Ritchie I've had chained to his typewriter for the last 10 years.

Alan, a white-haired, placid ex-sergeant of British infantry, is a rare thing. He is a secretary-major domo who actually does not want to be a writer himself. He also does not afflict me with unnecessary chores in order to impress me with his own importance, and he is the only person in the world who can read my handwriting.

Between us, over the years, we have cooked up quite an assembly line in the confection of books. I am convinced that, with the average writer, more time is spent doing useless chores in order to make excuses not to write than is ever spent in the writing. I have tried working on my own, on a big job, and it's torture.

The other great waste of a writer's time apart from conversation and drink is the necessity to cope with correspondence, go to the post office, collect the cook from the store, replenish the booze, send the cable, draw money from the bank, get the spare tire vulcanized, take the dog to the vet, meet the plane, answer the phone, make the reservations, argue with the gardener, lick the stamps – an endless round of time-eating detail.

With Sergeant Ritchie I have toppled this roadblock. I merely allow him to do all these things, while I hit the typewriter for half-a-day and punish the pencil for the other half. I can dictate enough correspondence in two hours to keep Ritchie busy for two days. If it were left to me, it would take two weeks, or more likely, I just wouldn't answer the letters.

Between us, I would say that when we are going good on a book, Ritchie and I produce about 140 hours a week of solid toil, or 10 hours a day each over a seven-day week. I have been a lusty drinker since I was 16, and I can write drunk if necessary. I have written the columns and articles with a load on more than once, from accidental necessity, but on books or any big project I work dead sober. I find that complete sobriety allows you to get up reasonably early in the morning, feeling refreshed and eager to pick up the plow again, whereas if you stone yourself into slumber it takes you half-a-day and several snorts to shrug off the morning meemies. When possible I like to pull 5,000 words out of the machine before lunch, and not hitting the pre-lunch martinis also obviates the necessity of that deadly Spanish disease, the siesta. It takes a good two hours to recover from a sodden siesta, and by that time it's the cocktail hour again and the day is shot to hell.

The snobs, the boozers, and the literary talkers rank equally among my choicest hates. I loathe the striking of off-stage attitudes in writers, to where, as in the sad late years of Hemingway, the myth obscures the man, and the writer goes away altogether. It is fatal to believe your own press clippings, especially if you are a fur-bearing author. In the case of Ernest, he finally spoke in unknown tongues and his last effort, that bullfight thing he did for *Life*, was excruciatingly embarrassing for anyone who had known the man and loved the work. It was at best a pitiful parody of the style which had made Hemingway famous.

I was a reasonably good friend and a great admirer of Ernest Hemingway, whom I never called "Papa," "Ernie," or "Hem." We corresponded occasionally, once got notably drunk in Pamplona 10 years ago, and had a lot of mutual friends. We were both embarrassed by the title 'poor man's Hemingway' that somebody once hung on me – possibly because we resembled each other physically, and certainly because my life had followed a similar pattern.

It used to bother me – at least annoy me – until one day, well taken in wine, Hemingway said: "Look, kid. Screw 'em all. You've been a better reporter, been in better wars, seen more bullfights, shot more big game, know more about Africa, lived longer in Spain, seen more of the world, and made a hell of a lot more money, and you're 20 years younger than me. You'll probably write more books, although I doubt if any will be as good as my best or as bad as my worst. Screw this second-hand Hemingway crap. We use the same alphabet. It's a different world and it's your time at bat. I had mine. Just remember one thing: Write what you know, as true as you can, and screw the critics. If they knew anything they wouldn't be critics. If you've got balls you'll always find somebody who hasn't got balls eager to cut you loose from yours."

That was about the last time I worried about being a "poor man's Hemingway," just as I quit worrying about being a "poor man's Pegler," in the early column days. There are times when I feel like a poor man's Ruark, but that's my own fault.

Bob agreed that he had learned a great many things from Hemingway and also admitted that he stole from other writers, though he regarded this as absorbing. He admitted that he had always stolen as much as he could, especially from Somerset Maugham:

The venerable Mr. Maugham, by his own written admission, is one of the worst writers in the world, with no feel for language and a positive devotion to the cliché. But Willie Maugham chose simplicity of style and structure and thereby won the title of the world's champion storyteller for the past 50 years. Maugham is a self-admitted cornball in an age of impression. He always worked on stage, and in three acts, with a neat bow at the end of the package. I stole heavily from Maugham.

For sheer cream of gentle craft, with complete mastery of sympathy, humor, storytelling ability, love and understanding of mankind – and with an oddly diverging fascination for freaks and horrors – I still replenish my quiver by reading Steinbeck. It soothes me, and gives me faith in my own ability to perform some future task, even if I have to steal a little to get me over the rough spots. John's output has latterly been ragged but on the body of it all he's the most deserving Nobel-winner we've produced.

I don't think there are any exceptionally good postwar writers. If J. D. Salinger married Carson McCullers, I would not be a member of the wedding. I don't think that being black, homosexual, or a combination of both necessarily makes a writer, nor do I think that the repeated use of four-letter words makes a war story stand up realistically. I weary of the word "shit" being used in lieu of commas. James Jones is a one-note war writer, and Norman Mailer a clown on stage as well as off. I would rather not think of Allen Drury; it makes my ears ring.

This praise and criticism of other writers was of course a preamble to assessing himself as a writer. Bob began by asking the direct question: "What about Ruark? Is he a good writer?" Bob answered by saying that he honestly didn't know and then ultimately gets around to the man he knew best:

He's a competent professional; we know that on the record. He's a good reporter – also a matter of record. He knows a lot of words, and he's been to a lot of places and seen a lot of things. He will not write about what he doesn't know, nor does he cloak himself in a lot of cheap mysticism. He is, certainly, not a literary poseur or a dilettante writer. He is not a philosopher, full of hidden intentions and three-dot indications of deeper meaning to saddle the reader with the burden of understanding. He suffers from being a white, non-homosexual Gentile who has been successful in other fields of writing apart from the novel form.

He does not write crap. He may write unpleasant truths, but the crap content is non-existent. He works hard, and he tries to gain on the craft, one book at a time. He would like to be a better writer, and he does not want to become the kind of myth which obscures the man, merely on account of the kind of life he's led. And, some day, he would like to see Ruark the man separated from Ruark the columnist and Ruark the magazine writer from Ruark the novelist in at least one review of a book. I am tired of having books evaluated in terms of whether or not the reviewer objects to the last column I wrote on Adlai Stevenson, or whether the reviewer disapproves of shooting for sport. That, I realize, is asking a great deal of book reviewers, a poozly lot at best.

I would have to say that the man I know best is not – at least not yet – a good writer. But I would also have to say that the man I know best is about as good a writer as we have around in the current flock, and a sight better, over the long pull, than a great many who think they're marvelous. We have no great writers today, but we are certainly heavy on literary lightweights with delusions of grandeur.

One thing we may say in favor of the man I know best: He works hard at his trade, in research and at the machine, and one day, with luck, he may even improve himself in his chosen profession. In the meantime he vastly enjoys its fruits, and is grateful to God and man for allowing him to practice the business of writing for a living. If things had worked otherwise, The Man I Know Best might have been a pimp, a process server, or a politician, three trades to which I attach equal nobility of aim.

The original piece contained about 15,000 words, but more than a quarter were cut for publication. It has been further reduced here with the removal of numerous anecdotes, which have been dealt with in other parts of this biography more in sequence with other events. Ruark's bold self-analysis was greatly appreciated by all his readers in *True Magazine,* and among many letters to the editor was one from a reader living in San Francisco:

"Robert Ruark's autobiography, "The Man I Know Best," gives a refreshing picture of a real man practicing the trade of writing. At a time when the literary profession is over-crowded with nuts, beatniks, and pansies, it is good to know there is one writer around with his head screwed on straight and his other parts in the right place. With the deaths of Ernest Hemingway, William Faulkner and Robert Frost, Ruark will emerge as one of America's best living writers."

There were also many letters of appreciation from Bob's friends, including a rather caustic one from an old Hawaiian friend. Headed "All Hallow's Eve," it read: "Hey old buddy – This article is the first piece of incomplete reporting I've seen you do – you never mentioned what a great lay you used to be – Aloha."

As can be clearly seen from the autobiographical piece, it is full of ego and is based on a large degree of showmanship. Indeed, Bob was a showman and he freely admitted it, often referring to himself as a ham actor. Along these lines a column he wrote about Hemingway soon after Papa's death could very well have been about himself.

"There was a lot of ham in Hemingway, as there is ham in any good writer. You cannot dramatize other people without dramatizing yourself. A writing man must of bitter necessity be acutely conscious of himself in relation to the things in the world in which he moves. But that is the simple conceit of childhood, in which the most frequent baby word is 'me.' Any author is all 'me,' or he wouldn't be an author."

While Bob's piece for *True* included many impressive statements, the most satisfying for him was his reference to his new Rolls Royce Silver Cloud. In April, 1956, Bob had sent me to London to collect the car straight from the factory, and originally it was supposed to be a birthday present for Ginny. Soon, however, Bob took it away from her and had it entered on his Spanish press carnet, in order to legalize it in Spain. Already, on returning home, I'd had to try three frontier posts before I found one that would let me in. The problem was, at least in my case, that as a Spanish resident I could not legally drive a foreign-matriculated car in Spain, though this largely depended on the customs official at the time of entry.

On arrival in Palamos, Bob was so impressed with the new car that he soon decided to take it with him on his next trip to the United States. Later, when I started to make arrangements to ship the Rolls from Barcelona to New York by American Export Lines, this intention was heavily criticized by his editor at the time as being a mistake. He suggested Bob had no need to impress his real friends. This may well have been true, but here the real point had been missed. It was more to impress Bob himself than anyone else.

Also, Bob explained that it would be good public relations for him to arrive at the 21-Club and the Stork Club in his own Rolls Royce. Then, to further convince himself that the extravagance was justified, he mentioned the number of contracts we had pending and said he wanted to be able to act from a position of strength. There was also the fact that we were researching for *Poor No More*, and Bob thought it would be helpful for him to make a swing through the South to get a fresh feeling of the area in which the book's action was to take place.

At the same time, Bob said he could visit his home town of Wilmington, as well as Southport, where his parents were living in the old family house. Then he planned to press a call on some of his old girlfriends, his University at Chapel Hill, and a few other friends in North Carolina, just to see how everybody was getting along. I rather think, however, that his main object was to show everybody just how Robert Ruark was getting along. Whereas Thomas Wolfe always wrote that you can't go home again, Robert Ruark *had* to go home again.

Ruark's return to Chapel Hill was a great success. There were many gatherings and a Saturday night party with two separate bands in his old Phi Kap fraternity house. Although the party turned into a ball and he thoroughly enjoyed himself, the next day he sat down and wrote a scathing column heavily criticizing the dress of the new sorority girls who attended the party. They were wearing sweatshirts, Bermuda shorts, long socks and tennis shoes. This appalled Bob as he would have preferred them in skirts as in the Good Old Days. Explaining that he wished to see more leg, and while agreeing that they were all basically very pretty, he said that in their present attire, "they merely look like slightly active cows, and from a rear view when they are dancing the shorts give the impression of two pigs fighting under a blanket."

Despite Bob's heavy hand at the typewriter when describing the new generation of coeds at his old university, he had a good time. In order to show appreciation for his welcome he bought a $500 ice-making machine for use in his fraternity house and then made arrangements to create a Robert Ruark Trust Fund. This trust was to make two awards each year to be known as the Phillips Russell/Oscar Coffin Creative Arts Award in the field of journalism and the Wallace Caldwell/J. P. Harland Creative Arts Award in the humanities. All four were distinguished professors at the university.

These awards were to be made on the basis of creative ability as evidenced by performance in the student's freshman and sophomore years, promise of future distinction in the field of his or her choice, academic achievement, character and intellectual curiosity. The awards were to be in the amount of $1,000 for the first year and, provided the recipient maintained a satisfactory record, to be continued a second year at the increased amount of $2,000.

Once back in Palamos after this heavy spending spree, Bob considered it necessary to write University of North Carolina officials requesting that they leave the Robert Ruark Trust Fund in abeyance for a while. He explained that his wife, agent, lawyer and business manager flatly forbade him to enter into any long-term, expensive project at this time, adding that he could argue with everybody except his wife. In his letter he mentioned that it was still his intention to begin the scholarship during his lifetime and that his residual estate would go to the University. Unfortunately, neither became effective, mainly because of will changes a few weeks before his death. All of his papers, manuscripts, photographs and letters were left to the University.

Chapter 18
PROBLEMS WITH PARENTS

A great deal of Robert Ruark's love and satisfaction in his home in Spain revolved around the fact that he couldn't quite grasp the idea that he owned such a magnificent establishment. Repeatedly in conversation he would be preoccupied with vague possibilities of being unable to maintain such a high standard of living. To some extent this stemmed from his fear of being unable to write any more, but it wasn't just this feeling. It was the straightforward fear that he truthfully didn't want to be poor no more. This was such an important topic to Bob that he wrote an entire novel around the single thought of losing or being unable to keep what he possessed, which he called, of course, *Poor No More*.

Although this is a normal, natural feeling for a great many people who have made a success of their work and reaped the benefits, in Ruark's case one has to realize that right from the start he was only satisfied to go luxury class. Everything he did was on a big scale, irrespective of whether he could really afford it or not. He was the biggest spender, always, and if you went with Robert Ruark, then you went luxury class.

A good deal of his desire for success at all costs, and to live it up in case there wasn't time later on, came from his early experiences of poverty and the mean times of the Depression. The loss of his home and the periodic unemployment of his father, coupled with an impecunious passage through college, bred insecurity. But it wasn't only these basic problems that created a combination of terrific drive and uncertainty about the future. He had other, more serious problems – his parents.

When the war ended and Bob began to get started again in civilian life, he soon realized that he had a problem with both parents. Gradually he found himself facing an ongoing financial drain because of their various activities. These included considerable drunkenness, narcotics addiction, writing bad checks and continuous medical bills. After these repeated sessions of excess, his mother would frequently end up in a sanitarium for a spell, while Bob generally just managed to keep his father out of jail by paying off outstanding debts. The resultant nervous strain over the years was considerable, and he reached the breaking point many times. It was only necessary for him to receive another letter concerning his parents' bad behavior, or a hurry-up cable to send more money, for him to be thrown into a neurotic bad temper for a number of days.

Since Bob was away frequently, Ginny would sometimes be required to answer the endless requests for assistance. In December, 1950, when replying to one of these letters in exasperation, she wrote a few home truths to her father-in-law:

I have had another call from South Carolina. Dr. Yost is justified in complaining that your continued letters and telephone calls demanding that Charlotte be released to you are upsetting Charlotte and retarding the effectiveness of her treatment. It seems to me that you would have sense enough to understand this and respect the doctor's orders.

The reason I am writing to you is that Bobbie is away on a hunting vacation – the first that he has had in two years without the worry of turning out a column. I am taking the liberty of not bothering him with your problems.

Let me point out a few facts. Charlotte has been a very sick woman and probably would have died unless Bobbie had taken over. And you would definitely have been in jail. Now by what right to you think you can demand Charlotte's release, question Bobbie's judgment, quarrel with the doctor's decision, and generally make a nuisance of yourself? I assure you that I am tired of the repeat and repeat of the same pattern of your getting yourself and Charlotte in such disgraceful shape that your son must bail you out. You have been mostly responsible for nearly driving your son insane. He was as close to insanity after your next-to-last breakup as any mental case I have ever seen. We are both sick, weary, and disgusted with opening the many, many letters beginning – "I am writing to you concerning your father's indebtedness." We have not given out your current address to any of these people in the hope that without the responsibility of Charlotte you could make a new start and possibly pay off your indebtedness.

I have this suggestion to make – until the time comes when you have paid off all your debts and have established a comfortable home for Charlotte, one that will keep her as well as the sanitarium – that you *must* shut up. Until then, try writing cheerful letters to her anticipating that time instead of disturbing her with suggesting that she is perfectly fine and being kept a prisoner – neither is true. When you have accomplished these things, then you have the right to demand.

Let me say further that Bobbie is firm on two counts: One, he will have Charlotte released when he is damned good and ready – Bobbie has the right, not you; two, he pays no more debts of yours even if this means jail – that is alright too.

So you may as well relax, accept the situation, accept Bobbie's decision, cooperate completely with the doctor, and try being a decent human being and if you can't do that you can at least stop your phone calls and demanding letters.

Over the years there is no doubt that Bob did the best he could for his parents. In an endeavor to re-establish them and to stabilize their lives, and at considerable financial difficulty at the time, he bought back the old homestead in Southport. However, for a long time his parents showed no interest in returning there. Then in 1954, without any previous contact with Bob, they suddenly moved into the house. This set off a particularly strong blast from Bob. Periodically, he would let go outbursts in the direction of his parents, but on this occasion he felt entitled to read the riot act to them.

In a controlled rage, he dictated a five-page letter to his father. These excerpts provide a good indication of his anger and frustration.

First off I want you to know that I am delighted that you and mother are moving into the house at Southport, which is why I bought it in the first place. The house is yours for as long as you both shall live . . . . Bearing fully in mind that I am glad you and mother are finally going home to Southport, I want you to read this letter not as an angry outburst from me, but as a cold progress report on my dealings with you all since I came out of the Navy and even before I went in. Enclosed is the check for which you asked Mr. Matson.

As you are doubtless aware I bought my grandfather's house expressly for the purpose of containing you and mother in your old age. At the time I was heavily beset financially in maintaining you and mother in assorted sanitariums for alcohol and drugs . . . . Whether or not you can believe it, my experiment into being a good son cost me just on $100,000, a severely damaged nervous system, and a monumental debt from which I have only just emerged. At age 26 when I entered the Navy, I was paying off one of your Morris Plan notes, and have more or less continued in the same vein since then. . . . .

I note from your letter of September 18 that you say "we are moving into your old home sometime before October first." I don't suppose that it occurred to either one of you that I might be planning to sell it, rent it, or even burn it, or live in it myself. At least you might have had the courtesy to consult me well in advance and ask my permission, since it happens to be my home bought and paid for, furnished and remodeled by me.

The first I heard of impending change was a letter from my agent, Harold Matson, saying that you had been on the telephone to ask him for money. I consider this completely indefensible . . . . You are hereby expressly forbidden to have any dealings of any nature whatsoever with Mr. Matson, who is employed by me to sell what I write, and that only.

When I bought the house and fixed it up with some hopes of retrieving what used to be a family, mother stayed about one week before Uncle Rob's table manners oppressed her to the point where she must needs borrow $2 from the drugstore in order to buy a bottle of bootleg booze and take off to be no more seen in the house which I had so lovingly and expensively prepared.

On your only visit to New York to see your son you wound up drunk and very ill in a hotel from which I extracted you in what I recall was rather a foul condition. Mother's last visit to New York was spent largely in playing hide-and-seek with the brandy bottle.

My visits to North Carolina have been largely concerned with the redemption of bad checks and the extraction of you all from whatever difficulties you were in with an eye to putting you in hospitals . . . . In terms of personal heartbreak and loss of esteem for people I loved, the price has been non-computable.

I am, of course, sympathetic with your various physical disabilities, but not with those which were aided and abetted by either whisky, narcotics, or lack of adult responsibility . . . .

Concerning the house, I bought it for your occupancy and will be the happiest man in the world if you and mother will settle down to a decent and dignified old age in the home of her father. There is nothing to prevent this, except a repetition of your old conduct. I will continue to send the same amount of money, plus the enclosed check for $150 to cover the costs of your moving. If I find when I return in November that you are either working or unable to work, I will readjust the money allowance accordingly. In the meantime, I should very much not like to hear about any checks bouncing about, since I have often and painfully pointed out that to write a check when you have no money is exactly the same crime as stealing from someone's purse or pocket.

You may count on your old age as secure within my power if any sort of cooperation is shown, but I know Southport and its assorted temptations, and I do not intend to finance either a free restaurant, a home for strays, a hangout for drunks, or a collection place for unpleasant relatives to whom I am unfortunately connected by blood . . . .

This rather long and bitter letter was not dictated by the desire to spoil any pleasure in your occupancy of mother's father's home. It was written only to refresh your memories on the various traps you have laid for yourselves over the years and to reacquaint you with realism. Realism is a thing that I have been forced to indulge in for many years, since I have only one brain and only one body, and if either brain or body is wrecked by illness, nobody eats. I must confess that there have been times when I considered chucking in the towel, changing my name, and running away . . . .

You are an old man now, Dad, and no longer permitted to indulge yourself in childishness, as I am no longer a young man and have never permitted myself to be a child. I hope you will be very happy in Southport and mine and Virginia's very best wishes go to you both for a long and pleasant old age in the house of my grandfather.

The letter didn't help much, except to act as a slight release for Bob, since the situation continued more or less the same. Possibly the biggest annoyance came from the excessive medical bills that his parents had been instructed to send to New York for payment. It appeared that his parents were both complete hypochondriacs to the point where Bob was spending thousands of dollars annually for medical fees of some sort, ambulances or night nurses, a lot of which later was proven to be an abuse. Finally, in October, 1961, Bob reached a point of desperation and decided that a change had to take place. He wrote to his father, explaining what he intended to do and why.

Dear Dad,

I am enclosing a letter which Matson is sending to the various hospitals, doctors, and nurses who have in past months been sending me on a fair way to bankruptcy.

I regret your illness, but I also regret my inability to finance a Roman holiday of doctors and nurses and hospitals, which I know from long experience is dictated by my mother's love of medical attention, unwillingness to care for you properly at home, and the rather cynical view that the doctors and nurses take of which I think there is some provincial idea of a rich son who will ask no questions but only sign checks.

I propose to put a stop to this once and for all. With what I send you and what you get from Social Security you have a net of $500 a month and a free house. This is considerably more money than most people make and is certainly adequate enough for you all to get sick on once the doctors and nurses are apprised that I am no longer willing to pick up the check. Even if I were willing I would not be able because nobody can indefinitely stand the strain of the kind of bills running into thousands of dollars which I have been receiving lately. It would take a millionaire to subsidize the way you are going.

From now on you will have to arrange your medical attention according to your budget. . . . For my own protection I am publishing the notice in the papers and have so advised the various doctors, hospitals, and nurses. I would imagine that this will reduce the desire of such people and institutions to cooperate with mother's insane preoccupation with hospitals and hysterical devotion to the medical arts.

I regret to take this tone but find it necessary. When I contracted to look after your medical attention I had no intention of becoming a happy hunting ground for the local medical profession, most of whom can't collect their bills from most people and are overjoyed to find an easy mark in me. I would like you and mother to give some thought to what would have happened to you over the last fifteen years if you had had no son in a reasonably high income bracket. Or if you had been forced to depend on David to settle your various problems, medical and otherwise. In short, what do the poor people do? Your son.

Ruark had made similar threats in the past in an endeavor to stop his parents' insatiable desire for medical treatment, but this time he was deadly serious. He went ahead and placed the following advertisement in local newspapers:

"PUBLIC NOTICE

"I, Robert C. Ruark, Jr., herewith declare that as for many years in the past, presently and for the future having made more than adequate provision for the maintenance and care of my mother and father, Robert C. Ruark, Sr., and Charlotte Adkins Ruark, that I will henceforth no longer be responsible for any bills whatsoever incurred by them. This statement is made securely in the knowledge that my provision for them on a monthly basis, paid to them directly, is more than adequate to meet any normal or abnormal requirements."

At the same time he circulated a letter to most members of the medical profession in the area. In it, he informed them that he no long intended to pay for "capricious" services. "No man," he stated, "no matter how wealthy can stand the sort of protracted drain on his income as has been evidenced in past months." He set forth explicit directions on his expectations regarding his parents' medical needs and noted that they had received a copy of the letter.

Some rude answers were received, which of course was only to be expected, but Bob felt the advertisement and circular letter to have been completely worthwhile, as one letter received from an honest medical man evidenced. "Dear Mr. Ruark, Congratulations on your stand, I agree with you wholeheartedly. Good luck in the future."

It needed only one local doctor to write in this fashion for Bob's assumptions to have been proven, and he gratefully replied, saying: "It is most gratifying for a member of the profession to understand the whys and wherefors of my action."

Certainly no son could have done more for his parents, and there is no doubt that Bob had been subjected to what happens to people who indulge in booze and irresponsibility on a long-term basis. He really should have learned lessons from this. Although he took no heed to the damage that could result from heavy boozing, I do believe that the actions of his parents encouraged a good deal of his terrific drive and desire for success. The fear of becoming like them spurred him to work hard.

The overall problem never actually corrected itself. While his parents eventually settled down to some extent, there were always plaintive letters from an Aunt Mae who held the fort as best she could in Southport. But his parents were tough, and both lived into their middle 70s despite the bad treatment they had always given themselves. His mother claimed she was so tough because of her Scottish origin and actually survived her son by about a year. She spent her final years, from December, 1963 until her death in 1966 in Dix Hill Sanitarium in Raleigh, North Carolina.

The apparent toughness of Ruark's parents in a sense hastened his own end. As he often pointed out, he believed that if they could live to an old age with their lifestyles, then he could do the same. Bob's youth is well covered in the *The Old Man and the Boy,* and from these articles it is clear that his youth was a happy one, or at least informative. Although his parents became a financial burden, he nonetheless felt gratitude to them for what obviously had been a good period in his life.

CHAPTER 19
MONEY MATTERS

Bob Ruark was always helping somebody financially and he was worried fairly regularly by a number of scroungers. Certainly, he collected a good many bums amongst his worldwide acquaintances. A lot of people took advantage of his generosity, and though Bob liked to give, he would also have appreciated the courtesy of an acknowledgement that the debt existed, instead of the usual avoidance tactics of the borrower. Bob usually found that the borrower would either disappear off the face of the earth or would come back for a further loan. Many people borrowed money from Bob, but few paid him back. What most of these people didn't know was that if they had made some small effort to repay, Bob would almost certainly have said "thanks chum, forget it."

Despite a constantly growing accumulation of bad debts, Bob continued to respond to what he thought were deserving cases. One of these was a Kenyan friend who was down on his luck at some time before the coming of independence. He was in grave danger of losing his home and business, in fact everything, because of the changing times. So Bob lent him $6,000 with the understanding that when better times came the money was to be returned. Quite soon this person appeared to become friendly with the new black administration and began to get back on his feet. However, no effort was made to repay his debt, even to the point where letters from Bob went unanswered when he wrote inquiring how his "friend" was faring. This was at a time when Bob himself was in serious need of money. The ungrateful parasite never even had the courtesy to drop a line at Bob's death, at which time he would have considered the debt conveniently terminated.

Then there was the Spanish friend who fell ill and more or less lost his income. He had eight children to feed, so Bob came to the rescue with cash and help. In this case Bob's effort was really appreciated. Another appreciative borrower was an American public relations man to whom Bob lent a thousand dollars when he needed it. When time for repayment approached, the man, while still in financial straits, was able to give some assistance information-wise. While this was not anywhere equivalent to the sum involved, Bob said his usual "thanks chum, forget it."

There were numerous friends and acquaintances who worried Bob for money at different times. He always did the best he could for most of them, possibly because he was aware that he was better able to earn money and because he fully understood what hard times could be like. Perhaps the most persistent scrounger was an Englishman with the phony title of "captain." This individual methodically managed to catch up with Bob wherever he went around the Mediterranean, though all he ever seemed to want was the fare to get somewhere else. This Bob willingly supplied.

After a lapse of many years, the "captain" appeared in Palamos with some very rich and possibly gullible foreigners, Belgians I believe, and he immediately represented himself as a great friend of Bob's. Ruark told the staff to watch the silver and thought he was in for another touch, but all our captain really wanted was to impress his friends. Bob went along with this, and while he wasn't approached for any money, somehow the man conned me into lending him sufficient funds for his Barcelona hotel bill.

Bob used to joke that the old saying "you can't take it with you" sometimes did apply, since one of his borrowers actually did take it with him. He was shot dead in a brawl concerning somebody else's wife, and at the time of his death he owed Bob $2,000.

Whether Bob could afford it or not, he loved to give presents. Most of his girlfriends did very well. There was the one who got a brand new car wrapped up with an enormous ribbon, mainly because she didn't have a car at the time. Another received an IBM electric typewriter and yet another a radiogram. He gave away attractive Spanish leather jackets and coats by the dozen, and it would have been an unlucky girlfriend who didn't receive at least two or three. Then there was the smart female visitor who managed, in a short space of time, to choose what must have been a dozen expensive swimsuits.

Bob rarely gave flowers to his girlfriends, but if he did it was done in grand style and in such quantity that usually there were insufficient receptacles available to hold them. On one occasion he sent so many flowers that even after filling the bath tub there were some left over. When the housekeeper arrived she said: "It looks like a gangster's funeral." The flowers were by way of an apology to a special lady friend from Atlanta whom he had telephoned from Spain in the middle of the night, then kept her out of bed talking for over an hour.

Bob could also exhibit finesse. In the case of his Atlanta girlfriend he gave her a gold charm bracelet with gold books attached. This started when *Something of Value* was published and continued with an additional charm as subsequent books appeared. On the inside of each book charm was a suitably endearing inscription "with love from Bob." The collection was incomplete when he died, since his last book had not yet been published. So the friend added *The Honey Badger* charm herself, but reversed the inscription to read "to Bob with love."

Bob was generous with paid trips around the world for his girlfriends, and there were those who were transported from New York to Mozambique, those who had trans-Atlantic trips to Europe, others flew to Kenya, or to North Africa and Italy. Many others received paid airline tickets in various directions, though there were also a number of girlfriends who paid their own way. Apart from his girlfriends, Bob often offered to pay for trips, either as a wedding present or purely and simply because he liked someone and wanted to see them. He was especially generous with white hunters and transported a few of them from Africa to Palamos or London, though some paid their own way to see him. Broadly speaking though, Bob was the provider, including half a dozen new suits and made-to-order shirts at his Barcelona tailor awaiting them on arrival.

Bob was incredibly generous to those who were around him on a daily basis. Immediately after he arrived home from a trip he would start to give away things, including clothes that he had bought for himself in places such as Capri, Rome or New York. I soon had a wardrobe with such famous name tags as Brioni, de Free's, Saks Fifth Avenue, Lord and Taylor, and Abercrombie and Fitch. I came in personally for a great deal of this spontaneous generosity, which included African trophies and furniture, and on one occasion more than a hundred meters of garden wall for my house. After a visit to Kenya, Bob gave me a Zeiss Ikon Contarex camera with all the lenses, explaining that this had been bought with his winnings from a successful horse-racing afternoon in Nairobi. His generosity extended to other staff in a great many ways as well, including a large television set for the gardener and an even larger one for the cook.

Bob started the gardener's son in Gerona College, and had in mind to send him to Barcelona University later if the boy warranted such treatment. When Bob died, this plan was terminated for lack of money, which was a frightful shame as the young lad was particularly bright and hardworking. After a spell, when it seemed as if the boy's education would suffer, a good lady friend of the Ruarks came forward with a plan to get some of Bob's friends to make donations and started the ball rolling with a sizable personal contribution. A sufficient number of the friends responded, and Bob's wish has been carried out. The gardener's son is now successfully finishing off his college education.

There was one occasion when Bob's generosity had an ulterior motive. This was when he first came to Spain and began regularly using the Barcelona airport. It was a tiny, friendly place, and we soon got to know all the customs officials. So when one official asked Bob to bring a Remington electric razor, unobtainable in Spain at the time, back from London, he obliged by returning with half a dozen – one for each customs official. This immediately set off a chain reaction, as on his next trip to London he was asked if he could bring another half-dozen razors for officials who had been off duty the first time.

With everyone equipped with electric razors, our passage through customs was eased considerably. Bob felt that we should never have any future difficulties with customs, though in any event we never did any serious smuggling. Not long afterwards, however, arriving at the airport and expecting his usual warm greeting, Bob was dismayed to discover that his electric razor friends had been removed and replaced with an entirely new, unfriendly customs staff. He later debated on whether to equip the new force with razors and decided against doing so, as it seemed a poor investment.

Traveling with Bob was an enlightening experience, especially upon arriving at a hotel where he was known. The staff would always be delighted to see him. Similarly, in London at the various clubs and restaurants he frequented, as he handed out five-pound notes to any of the staff who greeted him, he would say over his shoulder, "They like me here and always give me a warm welcome." I remember that leaving the New Stanley Hotel in Nairobi was rather like a stampede. All the colored staff descended on Bob and completely surrounded him as he handed out bank notes.

When Bob Ruark gave a tip, which was always generously excessive, I believe he intended to give the receiver a hand as opposed to just paying for whatever services had been rendered. I have seen some amazed faces as the size of the tip was realized, and there was one porter at the Barcelona railway station who ran after Bob pointing out that there must be a mistake – he had been given too much.

Robert Ruark made a career out of giving, out of generosity, and out of always catching the check for the restaurant or at the bar. Maybe some people took advantage of this, though Bob never really complained except to say, jokingly, "nobody never gives me nothing." When in Palamos, he would moan that while he made large sums of money, he never really saw any to spend himself. This was really because Ginny would do most of the check writing, and Bob rarely went out. Then it was only to the Hostal de la Gavina, the luxury hotel at S'Agaro, where he ran a tab.

The Gavina was really Bob's local, where he would go when in between girlfriends. He would invariably drag someone back to show them his house, and he made many good friends this way. He would go in his Rolls Royce, which on its own was sufficient for an introduction to anyone he cared to speak to, but this was especially so when other Rolls Royces were parked outside. The owners of these Rolls were particularly welcome to return with Bob, as in the case of an elegant English doctor and his wife. Thereafter Bob was delighted when they visited and he could observe "a brace," as he put it, of Rolls Royces in his carport. On the arrival of these guests, Bob's invariable remark was: "Park close to my Rolls and let the buggers breed." It was on these occasions that he really knew he didn't want to be poor no more.

CHAPTER 20
A LOVE AFFAIR WITH AFRICA CONTINUES

As can be seen quite clearly in Robert Ruark's writings, he enjoyed nothing better than to be in Africa, preferably Kenya, and out on safari. He once said: "At its worst, a safari is the greatest adventure that can happen to a man in this bemused and muddled age. At its best, a safari is a venture into magic, an experience so rare and fine as to be almost too good for the people who enjoy it."

Prior to Bob's departure on his first safari in 1951 he wrote some inquiring letters to the safari company explaining exactly what he had in mind:

"I am not a real head-hunter. On this first trip, I want only to know how brave I might be in front of a buff, even with inferior horns, and as of this writing a lion is strictly a lion. The common bobwhite quail of South Carolina scares me stiff, and you have no hero on your hands. I would like to assure Mr. Selby along certain lines: None of this will be fun unless I do it according to your rules.

"Elephants wish I not. Anything that God takes so long to build does not interest me as a corpse. I would love to see some, but Bwana Tembo and I are strictly friends from a shooting standpoint. The zebra thing is strictly a joke."

In a letter of recommendation, it had been explained that Bob was keen to shoot a stack of zebras, as he had a pet project to cover the walls of an entire room with their hides. This was apparently to whittle down the ego of John Perona, the proprietor of El Morocco, who possessed a zebra-cloth covered saloon.

Later, Bob wrote again to the safari company:

"I would love four weeks after the bigger stuff, and a week or so on the birds. I do not know much about me as a rifle shot. I do know much about me on anything that flies and would love a week with a shotgun. Before we scare the hell out of Mr. Selby, I will say that I have killed a running kangaroo from a car careering about at 45 miles per hour, with somebody's else's .303 – which is supposed to be sport in Australia – and up to now have never slain a deer, or a guide, under the mistaken idea that the one was the other. I am fetching along a .375 magnum, a .30-06, a hopped-up .22 for my old lady, who shoots pretty good, and I think a 12 gauge semi-automatic and a .410. I won't bother, as you advise, with shotgun ammunition, but would like very much to have an estimate of how much fodder for the big rifles I need."

In a letter to the United Feature Syndicate making a point concerning his intended absence while in Africa, Bob was at considerable pains to justify the trip.

"Having taken only one two-week vacation from the typewriter in the last six years, and having been overcome simultaneously by a desire to fight an elephant bare-handed, I am throwing myself on your mercy and grabbing a four-week leave from the deathless prose.

"I am not having any guest columnist write for me for a simple reason: If the guy is better than I am, I will look like a bum and if he is worse, I will still look like a bum for letting him take over the space."

Bob instead offered about 40 old pieces he had written before syndication began, then added:

"If this sounds anywhere near presumptuous forgive me, but I have got a date in Tanganyika with a lame, toothless lion with no dependents, and an awful big gun is currently resting under my pillow every night. Small boys will be small boys and I hope that all the small boys I work for have just as much fun on their vacations as I hope to have on mine – and at considerably less expense."

As Ginny was going along on this first safari, a number of people thought it would be a good opportunity for her to get a little revenge for the rough treatment Bob had given her in his writings. Thinking along these lines, one female columnist wrote:

"Marse Robert Ruark, the hottest thing in syndicate columnists this season, is now footloose on the Dark Continent, sniping at lions instead of women for a change. Mama, which is Ruark's romantic sobriquet for his long-suffering spouse, is also along, and you can't tell us girls that Mama's trigger finger doesn't sometimes itch to avenge the many cruel insults to her sex when Papa's sturdy derrière inches up within gunshot. There have been no rumors of accidents as yet, so Mama's well-known passive acceptance must yet be holding out, but we girls are still secretly hoping to hear of a minor skirmish in which Mama clubs the brash boy gently, or Numa, the Lion, nips his sassy pants. We really don't want the blabbermouth to suffer too much, because, perverse sex that we are, the more Ruark snarls at us, the more we love him, the sadist."

Ruark quickly developed a great love for African bush life, with the result that subsequently there was some reference to safari experience in all his bigger books. *Horn of the Hunter,* of course, was the best example. It was full of hair-raising anecdotes of jungle pursuits and descriptions of wild animals, and it was also an informal, breezy and sometimes hilarious account of Bob's first safari on the Dark Continent. All this was coupled with a degree of philosophy, some excellent narration and descriptions of rare beauty.

From then on Bob returned to Africa at least once a year, and sometimes twice or even three times a year, mostly to Kenya and Uganda or Tanganyika, which incorporated with Zanzibar to form Tanzania. Then, when he was unable to return to this area, Bob went many times to Mozambique, Portuguese East Africa.

Bob got a vast amount of satisfaction out of all safari life. He regarded it as a means of escape, escape from his writing chores, escape from his matrimonial problems, escape from New York, escape from everything. It gave him a chance to try and discover what he was looking for in life. I don't believe he ever really knew, but at least when out in the bush he possibly came closer to what he thought he wanted. Certainly there is a delightful feeling of a man at peace with the world in an article written for *Esquire* and published in March, 1952. Bob entitled it "The First Time I Saw God."

The story commenced with a vivid description of a torpedo attack during the war, when Bob was aboard a merchant ship carrying a cargo of explosives. He explained that as he did little business with the Lord in those days, he did not pray while waiting for the ship to blow up after being struck amidships by a torpedo. Prayer hadn't seemed necessary until ten years later when the wondrous experience of being on safari in Tanganyika made Bob overwhelmingly glad to still be alive:

I didn't make any sort of formal speech out of it. Just told Him thank you very kindly for not blowing up the ship that day in the Mediterranean and for letting me live till this day. It was a little late coming, this thank-you note, but I never meant anything more vehemently. I was very grateful to be alive, at that moment, for I was alone in the nearest thing to the Garden of Eden I ever expect to see. We had stumbled, while on safari, onto a piece of land which had largely been untrammeled by human feet and uncontaminated by human presence. The exact location remains a secret. The place was too good for man to louse up. Its keynote was perfect peace.

We marveled. Here was country as the first man saw it. We were camped on the river's edge, beneath a vast grove of acacias. It was like living in a natural cathedral, to look upward in the cool, created by the flat tops of the giant trees with the sun dappling here and there to remove the dank darkness of moist forests. It reminded you of sun rays streaming in through the stained glass of a church window.

The straw beneath the trees had been trampled flat by all the generations of elephants since the first elephant. The silence was unshattered by traffic sounds, by the squawk of radios, by the presence of people. All the noises were animal noises: The elephants bugled and crashed in the bush across the little river. The hippos grunted and the lions roared. The ordinarily elusive leopards came to within 50 yards of the camp and coughed from curiosity. The hyenas came to call and lounged around the tents like dogs. Even the baboons, usually shy, trotted through the area as if they'd been paid taxes on it.

Bob continued to marvel at the abundance of wild life and that the animals were so remarkably tame, including dozes of normally wild and elusive greater kudu. Timid eland antelope, which ordinarily almost never stopped moving, walked inquiringly close. Even the dangerous Cape buffalo were placid and unafraid and could be shooed into the bush like a herd of domestic cattle.

You felt that here was a capsuling of creation, unsoiled, unspoiled, untouched by greed or selfishness or cruelty or suspicion. We didn't want to shoot; we didn't even want to talk loud. Here you could see tangible peace; here you could see the hand of God as He possibly intended things to be. We felt unworthy of the clean, soft blue sky, of the animals and birds and trees.

It was not until we found this camp that I became aware of what had happened to me in Africa. It had been happening daily, but my perceptions had been so blunted by civilized living that I had somewhere lost an appreciation of simplicity, had dulled my sensitivity by a glut of sensation and the rush of modern existence. All of a sudden I was seeing skies and noticing mountains and appreciating animals and cataloging the flowers that dot the yellowed, grassy plains of Africa. I was tabulating bird calls and marveling over the sheer drop of the Rift and feeling good. I was conscious of the taste of food and the sharp impact of whisky on a tired man, and the wonder of dreamless sleep. I was getting up before dawn and loving it, and I was feeling kind, and acutely alive, and very conscious of sun and moon, sky and breeze.

This has to be a paradox, because my primary business in Africa was killing. I was there to shoot, and I shot lions and a leopard and buffalo and all the edible antelopes and all the good trophies I could rustle up. But I never shot needlessly and I never killed anything for the sake of seeing it die. We killed for good trophies, and we killed to feed sixteen hungry people.

Killing does not seem wrong in Africa, because the entire scheme of living is based on death. The death of one thing complements the life of another thing. The African economy is erected on violence, and so there is no guilt to shooting a zebra that the lions will have tomorrow, or a lion that will eventually be a hyena's breakfast.

Things are very simple in the African veld. You are a courageous man or you are a coward, and it takes a very short time to decide, and for everyone you know to detect it. You can learn more about people in three days on safari than you might run down in a lifetime of polite association under "civilized" circumstances. There is no room for selfishness.

A safari is as intricate as a watch. It is pared down to the essentials of good living – which is to say food, transport, cleanliness, self-protection, and relaxation, or fun. It has a heavy quotient of hard work in which everyone has a share. It is like a ship, on a long cruise, in that respect. There is a thing for every man to do, and if he fails in his duty the failure affects everybody.

Bob then made the point that really very few things were necessary for happiness and contentment, and that civilized life had over-endowed us with too many supposed necessities. For Bob, the basic requirements consisted merely of a night's sleep, a day's work and a full belly. He said that although he lived in an approximation of a palace in New York and was accustomed to light, heat and running water, he had found he was happier in a tent. He was also impressed with the cleanliness of Africa.

There is a neatness to Africa that needs no sanitation corps, no street-cleaning department, no wash-down trucks. What the hyenas and jackals don't get the buzzards get. What they don't get the marabou storks get. What else is left around the ants get. There is no garbage – no waste.

Maybe that's one of the things that hit me hard. No waste. Back home I seem surrounded by waste – waste of money, waste of time, waste of life, waste of leisure, mostly waste of effort. Away out yonder, under the cleanly laundered skies, there seems to be a scheme that works better than what we have devised here.

What I have been driving at all along is an explanation of why I want to go back to Africa, again and again and again. It is because I discovered in Africa my own true importance, which is largely nothing. Except as a very tiny wedge in the never-ending cycle that God or Mungu or somebody has figured out. In Africa you learn finally that death is as necessary to life as the other way round. You are impressed with the tininess of your own role in a grand scheme that has been going on for a very long while, and from that starting point you know true humility for the first time.

I believe today I am a humble man, because I have seen a hyena eat a lion carcass, and I have seen the buzzards eat the hyena that ate the lion, and I saw the ants eat one buzzard that ate the hyena that ate the lion. It appeared to me that Mungu had this one figured out, because if kings fall before knaves, and they both contribute to the richness of tomorrow's fertile soil, then who am I to make a big thing out of me?

It was not so much that I was a stranger to the vastnesses of Tanganyika, or that I was lost in a jungle, so much as if I had finally come home, home to a place of serenity, with a million pets to play with, without complication, with full appreciation of the momentary luxury of being alive, without pettiness, and finally, with a full knowledge of what a small ant I was in the hill of life. I belonged there all the time, I figured, and that's why I say I had to go to Africa to meet God.

For all the great satisfaction and happiness Bob derived from his safari experiences, there were a few unpleasant occurrences that resulted in a good deal of bad temper being shown and with the termination of a few friendships. During July, 1957 Bob had a dispute with one of the safari companies in Nairobi. This came about because of remarks made in a letter written by a member of this business to the president of the Shikar Safari Club in the United States. It implied that Bob had financed a new safari company and that he had grossly exaggerated his information on Kenyan wildlife, suggesting that he was misrepresenting the facts in order to boost his own company. Bob had written a piece for *Field & Stream* that said:

"There is no more beautiful spot in heaven or earth than this Eden-like pocket of Tanganyika freshly greened by the rains and the animals pouring by the millions from the reserves of Ngoro-Ngoro, the Serengeti Park, and from the Masai country in Kenya." He indicated that when the migration was in full swing, "it's easy to see a million zebra and wildebeest crossing the plains in a day."

The heavy criticism focused on his reference to "millions," and also alleged that there were other exaggerations. The author of this offending letter felt that the only reason for Bob to write what he referred to as nonsense was to plug his own company. Unfortunately, what had been intended as a private letter was read out to all the attending members who attended the Shikar Safari Club meeting in Detroit in the early part of 1957.

Bob was extremely angry about the whole business, though the suggestion that he was "trying to give his own company a boost" was the most serious accusation. In response, he wrote: "In case you people who run safaris and hotels don't understand what a writer's reputation is, I shall endeavor to explain that an allegation that I employ my various media to exploit an outside operation from which I might gain money is comparable to calling a lady a whore or an honest man a thief." He noted that he had "always paid the check" and added: "You can inform Mr. XXXXX that my forces for evil are even more potent than my forces for good, and I have the same circulation as always, and if the boys want to play dirty, in the best known poker fashion, I can not only call them, but I can raise them."

Bob's anger and annoyance were exacerbated by the fact that there had been a recent *Field & Stream* piece called "The Sportsman's Africa" [it later appeared in book form], which gave good credit to the safari company in question and in particular, praise to the professional hunter involved in this accusation.

In reference to this point, Bob wrote: "I consider it indefensible for a man who has received nothing but good at my hands to assassinate my character and reputation, and I suggest that he reread the *Field & Stream* piece and ponder over the connotation of the component parts of an ungrateful man."

Bob had done nothing but good for East Africa in general and the safari business in particular. According to his calculation, at regular advertising rates his coverage could be priced at roughly two billion dollars. Certainly, he never had a financial interest in any safari company and he always paid the full charge for his hunting trips. As he pointed out, "It would put me in an embarrassing position with my various outlets to where I should not write honestly about people in whom I was financially interested." He then added, with more than a modicum of truth: "I have enough [financial] trouble without taking on a safari firm." This constituted his final sentiments on this unpleasant incident, though his anger remained for a long while.

Chapter 21
RUARK ON SAFARI

Even before I really knew who Robert Ruark was, my first conversation with him involved a lengthy description of his intention to write a book on the Mau Mau in Kenya. He was full of this project and was also full of Africa in general. At this time he told me something of his safari experiences, and subsequently I realized that in Bob a vital feeling for the vast African continent was always present. Before long, he converted my thinking into a longing to visit Kenya and to go on safari. Bob gave me this opportunity in 1961, by which time I presume he felt I was qualified to accompany him after having been involved in all his African writing for so many years.

As we were putting the finishing touches to the second big African novel, *Uhuru*, he got up from his typewriter, came over to my office, and said: "Junior, I figure we've both earned a special bonus this year. How would you like to come on a horse and camel safari in the Northern Province of Kenya?" That was quite a question from a man like Robert Ruark, and not really knowing what a horse and camel safari was, I replied enthusiastically: "Yes Sir, I would very much like to come on a horse and camel safari."

In truth, Bob didn't know much himself about what was involved in this type of safari. This method had not been tried before. It was a new idea of the Game Department in Kenya to open up areas in the north that hadn't been hunted before. I think I had some vague idea that we would be engaged in riding camels, rather like Lawrence of Arabia, while chasing buffalo and elephant, but it was not like that at all. The camels were only used as pack animals instead of trucks, because the terrain we were to traverse was generally so rough it was unsuitable for vehicles. I discovered later that the horses were for the white hunters and the clients, which in my case was a doubtful privilege. The rest of the safari boys went on foot.

First I accompanied Bob on a safari in the Masailand of Kenya, along with other parts of the country, on a normal safari basis operating from Land Rovers. This was followed by the horse and camel safari in the northern part of the country. Accompanying us on the first part of the safari was Bob's good friend, Walker Stone, editor-in-chief of Scripps-Howard Newspapers. He was also on his first African safari and, like me, enjoyed this wonderful experience. Apart from the joys of being with Bob, who was by this time extremely well-informed on the safari business, we were fortunate to have along Harry Selby and John Sutton, whom Bob always put among the top-quality white hunters.

With two of the very best professionals to show me safari in Africa, I had a privilege I can never forget and that cannot be taken from me. Bob expressed it aptly in an "Old Man and the Boy" piece published in *Field & Stream* in September, 1961. Entitled "People Like Us Never Grow Up," it began:

This piece is being written in a bug-ridden swamp on the banks of the sluggish yellow Tana River, in northeastern Kenya, where the big elephants bugle and the baboons swear at the hunting leopards, and the lean Northern Frontier lions rumble asthmatically just outside the camp. I have been watching, with mounting delight, the reactions of a couple of boys – middle-aged, white-haired boys – an editor friend from America and a reserved Londoner who never saw a hedgehog, let alone a lion, until recently. It has become almost a ritual with me in recent years to get back to Africa every couple of years with some newcomers to the scene, to watch the wonders through new eyes.

And I have been thinking, as I watched the response of my two old friends, that I have lived through the end of an era, and it's a sad thought. The pure delight of these two men in the friendliness of the lions and the surly majesty of the buffaloes and the awesome bulk of the elephants was the delight of a child of my own generation, of my father's and my grandfather's generations. It was simple, unaffected glee, mingled with a disbelief that they were lucky enough to be in Africa at all. This could not be happening to them.

The dream to be in Africa might have begun for one when he was a British King Scout, and for the other when he was shooting rabbits on his father's farm in Oklahoma. For me, certainly, it started with the Old Man and a succession of dogs and guns and boats in Carolina. People like us never grow up, even when we graduate to elephants from a timid start on rabbits. We don't grow up chiefly because we don't want to.

Bob complained that the present-day youth generally had no perception of wildlife, and were only interested in TV, moon shots and hotrods. He said that often he had been tempted to introduce some youngsters to the fascination of safari, but having tried them on some simple hunting and fishing expeditions, decided not to take the risk. Then, after proudly discussing some of his trophies, Bob continued:

But I feel apologetic when a young son turns on me and demands a justification of my right to slay God's beautiful creatures, or some younger daughter fixes me with an eye that would make Bluebeard feel sheepish about his collection of beheaded wives. I find myself mumbling, "Well, I don't actually shoot much more – I just like to look at the animals and maybe shoot a few birds once in a while." Then the bird lovers clobber me: "And what have you got against birds?" Nothing, I just like to see them, and shoot them, and eat them. I see no difference between a fried chicken that has been butcher-killed and jointed and a breast of pheasant that has been hand-slain in the sparkling autumn woods.

I am sad for myself and for those my age and older who love the outdoors and find its discomforts pleasant, who love its birds and fish but who do not feel guilty about shooting reasonably for sport and meat and relaxation. I am sad for the hunters and the fishermen who obey game laws and attempt to practice conservation. But I am not so sad for tomorrow's generations. Perhaps they do not care if all the elephants are poached and all the rhinos slain.

I think it is a pity that super-sophistication has combined with modern pace to cheat our younger people of the sort of fun my set enjoyed as kids. I regret a kind of thinking that regards hunting as shameful, if not sinful. I do not admire a concerted attempt to sell the idea that the killing of game is a cruel sport, because no game dies a natural death, and preys as naturally upon itself as man upon man. And above all I deplore a substitution, via movies and television, of the bloody deaths of cops and gangsters and Western bad men as high adventure, notably heroic in the mind. We may have slain innocent rabbits, but we were not taught by sponsors to applaud the wholesale slaughter of people in order to peddle merchandise.

The mosquitoes here were fearful last night, and I have just plucked a tick from a tender portion of my anatomy, and for the last day no gun has fired. Also, it has been raining. But my two middle-aged chums and I are happy here on the Tana, surrounded by wild animals and a lot of simple savages who have not yet heard of the boons of modern civilization. Perhaps my friends and I, like the elephant and the rhino, are a dying breed, but it was fun while it lasted."

In this article, and also in *Horn of the Hunter*, Bob went to curious lengths to justify his hunting trips, when he explained the reasons why it was all right to hunt and shoot animals. This was no doubt because he had a feeling for them, which led him into attempts to justify the killing of wildlife for sport. Though sometimes the justification was strange, as for example he implied that if you didn't kill off lions in their prime, they would be condemned to slow and painful deaths in their old age by scavenging hyenas. At times, he almost seemed to be explaining away a guilty conscience, though I don't think he was making any excuses for himself, it was simply a compulsion for him to go hunting.

Although I wanted to go on a safari and while I knew perfectly well it involved killing, I was at no time willing to join in this part of the activity. I was born and bred in London and had never hunted an animal in my life. When Bob offered me a full license before we arrived in Nairobi – it would have included a dozen different trophies along with the Big Five – I immediately refused his generous offer. It was left that maybe I would take out a very limited license to shoot plains game. Once I realized what that was really all about, I never did have a proper license of any kind taken out for me. I only shot one Thomson's gazelle for the kitchen. At that point I knew quite definitely I did not intend to use a rifle any more. Some people can shoot an animal and the killing means nothing to them. Others can't. All I wanted to do was observe the animals and to take photographs.

I have labored to some extent my feelings towards hunting, simply because it may appear curious that a man like Robert Ruark, with his great love of sport, would have a close associate who emphatically did not want any part of killing any game animal. Actually, this helps to illustrate the understanding we shared. While Bob didn't want someone who was always going to dispute his way of thinking, it was not necessary for me to conform exactly to his wishes or to agree with what he did.

When on safari, Bob literally seemed to merge into the countryside. He became part of the safari camp, part of the surrounding jungle and bush, part of the bustle and Swahili jabber coming from the direction of the kitchen, part of the excitement of just being in Africa. To any uninformed onlooker it would have been difficult to say who were the white hunters and who was the client, as Bob fit in so well with everything that happened in the camp life of a safari. At the same time, he made me feel content to know nothing. He meshed into the scene because he had been on at least two dozen big safaris, apart from a great many shorter jaunts into the bush. It wasn't just because of previous visits that Bob fit so well. It was due to a great perception and feeling he possessed for the country. To be on safari was a fascinating experience for anyone, but with Robert Ruark, it was really something incredibly special.

My first safari concluded in the area of the Tana River, and from there we all went in different directions. Walker Stone flew back to Nairobi, accompanied by Bob, who wished to catch up a bit on civilization and also avoid the long truck drive. John Sutton also left at this stage in order to collect a new client. After we broke camp, Harry Selby and I took the heavy transport off in the direction of the Uasonera River and along towards Isiola, where we were joined by the new second white hunter, an ex-game warden.

In Isiola we made preparations for the horse and camel safari and when we were organized with new stores, set off upcountry to a primitive Samburu village called Baragoi, where we were to meet Bob, who was to arrive by air from Nairobi. After we had waited at the tiny airstrip for over three hours past his scheduled arrival time and were beginning to wonder about the delay, a small twin-engined Cessna winged in over the trees, made one straight run low across the grass as the pilot searched for pig holes, then touched down for a perfect landing.

As Bob pushed his way through an excited gathering of natives, I could see that he didn't look very pleased. It was then that he explained sadly that Ernest Hemingway had shot himself and that he had been delayed while writing a couple of pieces about him. Bob was noticeably upset and appeared to somehow show a degree of loneliness. He exhibited a feeling that – well, now there was only Robert Ruark left in the African safari, bullfighting, world traveling, wenching and drinking league.

In Bob's memorial columns concerning the death of Hemingway, he reminisced over the green hills of Africa that Papa had known so well, the Masai and the Kikuyu country, Mount Kenya, Mount Kilimanjaro and her sister, Mount Mawenzi. He entitled one of his pieces "This Safari Is for Ernest," which he concluded in poignant fashion:

"Sentimentally, I shall try to see the old Africa this last, sad time for my old friend Ernest Hemingway, who first infected me with a love for this troubled, bloody continent. He would like to know that the long, low hills are still green and the gin around the campfire comforting. He would also like to know that this country, where he missed death twice by a whisker, is deeply affected by his death.

"Africa had its effect on Hemingway, and certainly Ernest Hemingway made his mark on this land."

I had a feeling that Hemingway's death affected Bob more than he would have admitted at the time, and during the remainder of the safari he was puzzling out a problem . . . the destruction of a writer . . . and why? Around the campfire quite late one evening, after everyone else had gone to bed, Bob began to talk about Hemingway. He recalled some of the writer's past and his great writing ability and, in Bob's opinion, the eventual decline of this ability. He noted how as long ago as 1955, when he had finished *Something of Value* and was in the States enjoying its terrific success, he had deliberately avoided contacting Hemingway. This was because Bob had heard he was having some trouble with his latest novel, and he didn't wish to embarrass his old friend with his presence at a difficult time.

Although Bob had a great admiration and affection for Hemingway, he continued at length to make a strong point that he, in fact, knew Africa better. He had been there more often and had traveled far more and had far more safari experience than Hemingway. In addition, he'd had the advantage of jet aircraft, something which made an enormous difference to the world traveler. Then Bob turned to his frequently expressed objections to criticism that he had copied Hemingway. He denied angrily that he had ever done so. He said that the fact they both had been to Africa and Spain was sufficient for some critics to make this accusation, but that they conveniently overlooked the fact that a great many other people had also traveled to these places.

After a lengthy silence, during which we both stared into the campfire, Bob got up to replenish his whisky glass and to kick the fire into a crackling roar with the aid of an abundant supply fresh logs, something he loved to do. Reseating himself on a large log, he then expounded on what was *really* worrying him – the possibility of a prolific writer running out of words and arriving at the stage of being unable to write.

A great many people would have wondered why a man like Hemingway wanted to shoot himself, why he couldn't have relaxed and enjoyed his past successes and perhaps written a little when he was able. But I could see very clearly that Bob knew why. I believe that it frightened him that he would one day arrive at the same point, and maybe at this moment he decided he would not allow it to happen. Authors have a habit of destroying themselves, but there are various means of self-destruction. Robert Ruark was never a potential suicide – not with a gun, that is! He used other means to destroy himself.

Later, in a column Bob wrote:

I hunted hard for three weeks in new country, and I couldn't get Hemingway out of my mind. We were friends and I greatly admired some of his work, but I did not think his work was flawless. He preyed on my mind, and one day when I shot a very old elephant, I sort of got rid of brooding about Papa. What bothered me, I think, was that both Hemingway and Negley Farson had died more or less by their own hands in the last year. Farson didn't actually kill himself – he wore himself out just living hard and free. But to me, both writers stood for something that we seem to be running short of. I am talking of manhood, pure and simple, and the uncontrived joy that man has always derived from hunting and fishing and camping and firelight and good bourbon and a reeking pipe and a sound collection of poker players, who also tell tremendous lies about past exploits which have become fact instead of fancy merely by the rubbing of frequent usage.

Up until the last year or so of Bob's life, there was always a great urgency in his writing, an impatience in his attitude towards his work, and the desire to get on with it. When he was running well, he dearly loved his work, he loved to write, and he got a great deal of satisfaction from what he wrote. He also got a lot of fun out of some of his columns, because they enabled him to let off steam in almost any direction he felt like. But I think this urgency was because of a fear that one day maybe the words wouldn't come so easy. Periodically in conversation Bob mentioned this feeling, and I believe there was a thin veil of fear present during our campfire discussions. To start with, though, I didn't understand what he was talking about. When he spoke in a doubting fashion it surprised me, because he always seemed so vital I couldn't ever see him being any other way.

We spent a few days getting properly organized, during which time I commenced to transcribe the vast amount of shorthand notes taken on the journey, and as I was working on the typewriter, Bob came to my tent and seeing the agony on my face, immediately did a quick sketch, maintaining that he had not seen such an expression of hurting ever before. This was true as I hadn't worked for many weeks and the strain was considerable. Bob continued to amuse himself by sketching most of the safari boys. He was able to achieve most excellent likenesses, which were cleverly drawn with the very jet-black native against the white paper, giving them remarkable contrast.

Preparations had been made for the next stage of our journey, and when all was ready the camel caravan moved off with an appearance of something out of the Arabian Nights. Bob looked the part, and took on the resemblance of Beau Geste with a white Arab rag headdress hanging down the back of his neck. He was a good horseman and rode well, but I soon discovered that I was not. We had a string of half-a-dozen horses and Bob immediately began naming them, "Kasavubu," "Lumumba," "Gizenga" and "Mobutu," and I quickly spoke up before mine also had the name of a Congolese politician, and tagged her "Nellie," which somehow seemed to fit.

As a result of these horse names, a vehement protest was made against Columnist Ruark by the Congo Republic's Central Government delegation to the United Nations. It was reported in the *Nairobi Daily Nation:*

"The delegation of the Congo to the United Nations is most indignant in stating that Mr. Robert C. Ruark, well known for his racist manoeuvres, has named his horse after the President of the Republic of the Congo (Leopoldville). With a twist as sarcastic as it is insulting, the author and at the same time actor, says that he climbed upon the back of his Somali pony named Kasavubu."

Bob's reaction when being confronted with this complaint was an immediate counter protest, as he put it, on behalf of the horse, and in his reply he said:

"The only reason I called the pony Kasavubu was because the tame baboon had already got a name. We had another pony called Gizenga. Neither of them could run. For years I've been calling these Congolese politicians thieves, liars, clowns, buffoons, idiots. The track record shows their complete irresponsibility in facing up to responsibility. It was impossible to name just half a horse or I would have done so."

In answer to the question whether he was the special representative in Africa of the Ku Klux Klan, Bob replied angrily: "I was a member of the National Association for the Advancement of Coloured People in the days when to admit you belonged to it was like saying now that you were a communist. I'm one of the worst enemies the Ku Klux Klan has got."

Meanwhile, our horse and camel safari continued, and there were plenty of unusual and even frightening incidents along the way. One day we were charged by a very angry female elephant, and it was only by luck and good fortune that we didn't have some serious casualties. We were out with the horses on a reconnaissance to see if there were any elephants in the area, and were loping slowly along a dry river when the horses stiffened a fraction. Just in front came a charging elephant with its trunk straight out going 50 miles-an-hour towards the three gun bearer/trackers acting as vanguard to our party. As these three dived onto the other side, the maddened elephant sheared off into the jungle, presumably in search of the rest of the herd.

This was an unnerving experience. As Bob pointed out, if we had been just 50 yards ahead we would have been in real trouble. Riding a horse on soft sand allows for absolutely no maneuverability, and I doubt that even an unmounted horse could have avoided the charging elephant with its big, flat feet designed to run over any surface. Then we got to wondering what would have been the outcome if it had been the previous day, when we had passed the same spot with a long line of slow-moving camels laden with camp gear. From then on it seemed advisable to take the horses up over rocky crags where we figured an elephant would not normally go.

Another near miss came a few days later when an aggressive rhino treed a couple of boys. They were so frightened that even when the rhino was away in the distance they still didn't want to return to the ground. Here again, if we had been confronted by this beast at close range while on horseback, the story would have been quite different.

During the next few weeks we changed locations many times with a series of fly camps, sometimes setting up without anything except mosquito nets. The whole experience was intriguing. I must admit, though, that sometimes at night in a half sleep I found that a camel's grunt sounds awfully like a lion's roar.

On one of these moves we had been going all day with the horses and had ridden or walked a good 25 miles over boulders, rocks, dry river beds and dusty game trails. The temperature was stifling and on arrival at our new camp, we were all completely dehydrated. I even felt as if I had a touch of sunstroke. While everyone else settled down to drink tepid soft drinks in order to come back to life, after a slight attempt at one Seven-Up, Bob turned to the gin bottle and proceeded to quench his thirst with half glasses of neat gin.

On these occasions Harry Selby and I became very nervous, and we couldn't really look at Bob when he was drinking. Selby had all too clearly in his mind what had happened the previous year in Nairobi and various other places. He had seen the result of Bob's excessive drinking, and the collapses and fits that followed. Although Harry was frightened that Bob was drinking so heavily there might be a repetition, it was extremely difficult for him to try and stop a client from drinking, just as difficult as it was for a secretary to admonish his employer. We were particularly worried because if Bob collapsed here, it would be many days before he could receive proper medical help.

Fortunately, nothing serious happened. The safari progressed and the campfires at the end of a hard day were a delight. We had many hours of good conversation around the fascinating light of flickering fires in the middle of nowhere. I noticed that Bob would sit staring into the log fire long after everyone else turned in, though this was normal for him as he never went to bed early.

The safari was on the whole a happy one. Bob was enjoying everything and I was still wide-eyed at everything. Still, I worried a little more each day about Bob, because he appeared to be drinking at an increasingly high rate. I think he was inclined to give the impression that because of his contentment on safari, he tended to drink far less, though I would say that from my observations this was about opposite the truth. For one thing, the fresh air and exercise made him feel fit and probably increased his tolerance for alcohol. Also, Bob was a great one for the satisfying drink, and no better place to enjoy a bottle of whisky can be found than around the campfire after a hard day in the bush.

We had been out for a number of weeks when we began to realize that we probably would not find any big elephants. It was so terribly dry they were no doubt all on the other side of the Matthews mountain range where there would be suitable green forage after the rains in that area. Still, as we searched for an elusive big elephant, we were sufficiently entertained by fascinating countryside.

It is a fantastic country – scattered aimlessly around as if God just got tired packing and threw His leftovers out the window. Its mountains are aimlessly placed, and the people, what there are of them, match the mountains. It is desert-hot, hence the camels, and as dry as the martini I wish I had but haven't.

I have seen all of Kenya, save this area before, and some of Kenya is unbelievably beautiful – soft and cool and green and vibrant with life. But I like this north country best, I think, possibly because everything and everybody in it is lean and hard and tempered to tough times as a steady diet. Everything in the north is functional. Either it is functional, ascetically honed to the bone, or it dies.

But man has not trampled this land, and nearly everything that we have done so far has comprised a "first," which is thrilling in itself. This country is exactly the same as it was since the day the great earthquakes tore the African continent apart and created the Great Rift Valley. There must be elephants here who were born before 1800, and although the object of this safari is to find and shoot some monster bull whose tremendous teeth are achy and whose ancient bones are weary of 150 years of ceaseless searching after water, I really don't care if we do or not. It is enough, in this harassed and confused world, momentarily to enjoy the simple act of wandering lonely as a cloud through a vast wasteland which was never seen even by the first white man who clapped eyes on this part of the continent.

Then finally the day came, and as it so happened with the aid of a ten-year-old Samburu-Rendille maiden, that Bob got on the trail of what promised to be a very big elephant.

Bob wrote:

We jogged the nags to a little hill and climbed up it just as the sun began to paint the stern blue mountains and the sere brown of the scorched wasteland. Selby and Metheke had the glasses, and they began to sweep the terrain. Suddenly both Africans – white Selby, black Metheke – began to coo. "Ah-ah-ah-ah-ah-AH-EEEEE!" both Africans said, in a rising scale that lilted to a falsetto. "Ah-ah-ah-ah-ah-AH-EEEEE!"

They turned, beaming, twin-like despite the disparity of race and color, soulfully in delight. They handed me the binoculars, and pointed. Something filled the binoculars and suddenly, I began to coo too. "Ah-ah-ah-ah – ah-ah-AH-EEEEE!" I crooned. Then we all slid down the hill and kicked the horses into a trot. Cap'n Ahab, crudely adapted to camels and Somali ponies, had finally raised Moby Dick.

In many columns that Bob wrote on this safari he included some reference to Hemingway, and he would have had in mind his old friend when reporting the end of the hunt for the "impossibly big and old elephant." He fittingly entitled the piece "Death in the Afternoon."

The old man was old, very, very old. He had lived too long. It is possible that he saw the 18th century change to the 19th – the 19th switch over to the 20th.

For many, many years – as long as the few permanent natives could remember – he had lived on Illaut. He came to drink every day at the water hole a few hundred yards away from the Somali dukah, or tiny tin-roofed shack.

He was long past breeding – long outcast from a herd. His memory of women and palm toddy were dim. The young bulls no longer came to him for counsel, although his accumulated wisdom was vast. He had long since run through his repertoire of jokes, and no longer found listeners for belly rumbling, nostalgic tales of the good old days before the white man came with guns – the quiet good days before iron birds made cloud-tearing noises in the blue Kenya sky as they flew toward Ethiopia.

He was deaf, possibly, and certainly his eyesight was dim. His great ears, which once clapped like thunder as he flapped at flies, or shook furiously as he screamed in anger and charged, now hung in shreds; hung limp and fluttered feebly as he waved them. Over most of his back a mossy excrescence, like barnacles on any ancient turtle or moss on rocks, grew thickly. He was pitifully thin, tremendously wrinkled.

There would have been the curious growths inside his belly that very old elephants have, and the enormous black tusks would be too heavy to carry in comfort now that so much weight had left his other end. How he had reached this age without breaking one or both tusks was a mystery. But there they were, great ivory parentheses stretching low and out and upward from his drooping lip.

He rocked and grumbled to himself, as old men will, and the litany of complaint was clearly audible on the wind as we walked close, leaving the ponies tethered to a thorn bush. He had been a traveling man in his time – he had possibly been to Ethiopia, to Uganda, even as far south as Rhodesia. He knew Tanganyika well. But now he was all alone – chained by necessity to the creaking rocking chair of age.

All the cows and calves and younger bulls – who tolerated his presence at the water hole – had gone over the mountain to the green, following the rains. But he was too old to trek with them – too feeble.

He was alone, because he could not leave certain water. And he was starving himself, because he could not graze for more than a five-mile area from that water. The forage was almost gone, because of the three-year killing drought and because he had eaten down the land to rock-hardness.

He was all alone, and soon he would die.

Unless the rains came to green his prison area, he would die, of senile decay and lack of nourishment and, most of all, of boredom.

There he stood, alone and magnificent on the slope of a sere brown rise with a harsh, cruel, blue hill behind him. There he stood, his two enormous tusks a monument to himself, and a monument to the Africa that was – the African that had changed, was changing.

"Poor old beggar," Harry Selby muttered. "Poor, poor old boy."

I am an elephant hunter, so I will not say that my eyes were misty when I shot him twice through the gallant old heart. They misted after, yes, but we had come to find a testimonial to another age and the way to keep him was to shoot him. He lurched to his knees, recovered, staggered a few yards and died in midstride. He fell with a mighty crash, splitting a tusk, and when he died, old Africa died with him.

The shooting of this grand old elephant gave way to a feeling of anticlimax, as the search had been so long, and the *coup de grace* had come on practically the last available day, because Bob had given up his high hopes and was preparing to leave the area immediately for Nairobi. Later, when weighting the tusks at an Indian dukah, there was some disappointment. Because the elephant had been so old and thin, the tusks had appeared much bigger than they really were. Still, they went just over the 100-pound mark, weighing out at 101 pounds on one side and 103 pounds on the other.

CHAPTER 22
ATTACKED BY A LEOPARD

Although Robert Ruark was regularly exposed to dangerous animals during his hunts, and though he had a great many narrow escapes, he only got hurt once. This happened on shikar in 1962 in the Madhya Pradesh region near Betul in Central India. There, a wounded leopard attacked Bob and inflicted serious injuries to his arm and shoulder.

As had been the case on a previous Indian shikar, Bob was again accompanied by Ginny. She had expressed a special wish to return to India. On his previous visit Bob had an experience that would have led one to assume he knew the dangers associated with dealing with wounded animals. At that time he had shot three tigers, though after about half an hour, one of them got up and walked away.

On the 1962 shikar, Bob had been hunting a tom leopard with a water buffalo as bait. He had waited for hours before leaving his blind and returning to the dak bungalow. It appeared that the male leopard would not come to the bait because he was more interested in a leopard bitch in the area. As it so happened, when departing the blind Bob and his party accidentally stumbled upon the female in the middle of the road.

Bob afterwards said that he shot the female out of cold spite, and he admitted he broke an old rule about never shooting at night. Still, with the aid of a torchlight, he walloped her straight down the front with a rifle that had slain a hundred leopards. The animal appeared to be dead until one of the boys threw a rock. Despite the fact that two buckshot blasts had been fired into it from point-blank range of less than ten feet, the leopard suddenly and violently came to life, flew into the air and landed on top of Bob.

Bob's first shot had been fired from a .30-06 rifle, but the cartridge case had split and it was only with great difficulty that the jammed case was removed and another one placed in the breech. Meanwhile Bob's companion, an Englishman resident in the area, was engaged in fending off the thrashing cat with the shotgun barrels rammed into her mouth. Bob was able to fire a finishing shot, somehow managing to hit the leopard and not his companion, who in the meantime had been badly hurt in the scramble. The Englishman probably saved Bob's life, though the whole incident was made more hazardous by the Indian gunbearers. At the first sign of danger, they ran away, taking the lamps with them. At the same time the moon disappeared behind a cloud.

By the time they killed the leopard, the two hunters were bleeding profusely. They tied tourniquets on each other and then started the 20-mile midnight drive back to camp. Of course the wounds were bad enough, but serious infection was likely to follow. The more maggoty a kill becomes, the better a leopard likes it, so their fangs and claws are full of every possible disease.

On this Indian shikar many things were lacking, including a proper medical kit. So even after the men reached camp, the best that Ginny could do was to feed them gin to drink and use it to sterilize their wounds. Nothing else was available. They went to sleep in a drunken condition and naturally the next morning their wounds were terribly inflamed. Fortunately, there was a Swedish Lutheran mission in the little town of Padhar about 30 miles away. This was run by a British minister who stitched them up and supplied them with penicillin and tetanus shots, which undoubtedly saved their lives. Still, Bob had a very bad arm for many weeks afterward.

This whole leopard fiasco could be directly blamed on faulty local ammunition. Afterwards, they found that the buckshot had barely penetrated the leopard's skin. Not surprisingly, Bob was quite displeased with the way this shikar had been run, and not only because of the incident with the leopard. Before it happened, he had been out hunting at night and was frantically told to fire at something the Indian shikar hunter had pointed out. Bob didn't do it as he couldn't see anything to shoot. After a little investigation, it was discovered that there was a dead leopard planted for him to shoot at. This was an insult to his intelligence as a hunter, and he was furious.

Owing to a general disagreement with the Indian shikar owner, it was necessary for Bob and Ginny to leave in a hurry. A heated argument about how much money Bob owed under the circumstances of a badly arranged, badly run shikar led to their hasty departure. According to Ginny, there was more noise from the railway marshaling yard of shunting trains than from wild animals, and it also appeared that the shikar manager was off attending to other business instead of looking to the requirements of his clients.

So they made their way to a distant railway station with the intention of getting out of India as quickly as possible. They decided to carry out their original plan and make for Kenya, where proper medical attention would be available. Bob's leopard wounds were developing into a very serious infection and, as he said afterwards, "the liquor laws were more flexible."

To relieve his general annoyance at the shikar, Ruark began to unleash his wrath against all of India. He wrote a number of political pieces criticizing the country and the fact she continued to beg from the U.S. even while having more gold tucked away secretly than any country in the world. These pieces were dictated from his hospital bed in Nairobi. He figured that his series on gold hoarding cost India in the region of a quarter-billion dollars in aid from the United States, as at the time there was a bill being debated in the Senate that was defeated.

Bob advised all tourists to avoid India because of the country's ludicrous prohibition laws, excessively suspicious customs, and a booking system for trains that required constant and considerable bribery to get anywhere at all. He didn't like the unusually slow system of state banking, and among other things noted that there was a tendency for Hindus to give short weight and supply shoddy goods. When vexed, Bob could be quite ruthless in his criticism, but on the other side of the coin he wrote a column praising the work of the mission where he had been treated for his leopard wounds. He requested financial help to build a new hospital at the mission, and this got some response from donors. A complimentary reference was also made concerning the American Consular Service in Bombay, which had helped him get out of the country.

All the unfortunate occurrences on this Indian trip notwithstanding, he subsequently got a great deal of mileage out of the leopard attack. He not only wrote numerous pieces about animals that fight back, but often, when showing his war wounds, he would also include his leopard scars. This always seemed to finish any discussion as to who had seen the most action.

CHAPTER 23
NEW VISTAS IN AFRICA

In 1962 Bob began using Mozambique instead of Kenya because of his prohibited immigrant problem. He liked the area and made so many visits that a camp was named after him. Camp Ruark was on the banks of the Save River, about a hundred miles south of Beira. It was a paradise of peace with comfortable thatched-roof huts and campfire circle, an abundance of varied game close by, and a full melody of jungle sounds coupled with the sight of numerous log-like, lazy crocodiles sprawling on the opposite bank of the river.

Camp Ruark was one of a number of fixed camps run by Mozambique Safarilandia, which controlled a very large hunting concession in the area. Bob made good use of Camp Ruark and was back again the following year when I was fortunate enough to accompany him. Although this trip to Mozambique was ostensibly made in order to perform reconnaissance for the possible film production of *Uhuru*, I rather think the real object was simply to go on another safari.

While I was delighted to be on safari once again, I found I still had my old problem of not wishing to harm the animals. Many people would have had the impression that I was a most unsuitable person to go on a hunting safari. This was of course true in a sense, though I did not realize from the start that in order to enjoy safari I had to forget my feeling for animals and really regard the day's shooting as the difference between going to the butcher in the market as opposed to shooting your own meat. Then, as Bob pointed out in his various writings and descriptions of African life, wild animals invariably ended their life far more tragically at the hands of another animal or, worse still, caught in a wire snare of a poacher's trap. Bob would explain that trophy hunters killed far less game and in a much cleaner way than other methods, and also it mustn't be overlooked that even the game departments would kill dozens of elephants or buffalo, for instance, in control shoots. They did this in order to clear a certain area for native habitation or perhaps to take care of a herd of elephants that had wandered onto farm land.

As our safari progressed, there were many occasions when the setting and the animals themselves were so completely beautiful that I felt they should have been left alone. One day this sentiment involuntarily overcame me. On returning from a day's hunting with a truckload of dead animals, we pulled off the main track to a good observation point overlooking an area where there were usually some reedbucks. A few hundred yards away, just visible through some high grass and clearly outlined in the last rays of the sun, stood a handsome reedbuck with its longish neck reaching for some foliage.

The whole panorama was so beautiful that it seemed quite wrong to spoil it, and I immediately commenced trying to capture this wonderful scene with my camera. At the same time Bob had lined up his gun sights on this reedbuck, and precisely a split second before he fired I released the shutter of my camera, which was a particularly noisy one. Bob was very angry indeed, and it was quite obvious once again that photography and hunting definitely do not go together. However, my indiscretion didn't affect Bob's shot, and the reedbuck fell very dead, thus adding another trophy to the day's collection.

On this particular safari it was the custom to go on what was known as the "pig run" each afternoon. The warthogs were so numerous that Bob would invariably clobber a good one every day. The "pig run" would start by cruising slowly in the Toyota jeep until a pig was sighted. Then it was a matter of hanging on for dear life as the vehicle bounced and leapt from pig hole to anthill to pig hole while being handled with unbelievable skill by an old elephant hunter named Wally Johnson. This was a nerve-wracking experience for me until we caught up with the unfortunate pig. It would generally stand still long enough for Bob to line up his rifle on the pillow rest across the engine cowling of the jeep, and the pig would fall over dead. This was not always the case, however, and each pig caused a different set of problems.

There was, for example, the one Bob wounded, which raced over to hole up behind some bushes. Bob got down from the vehicle, then ventured around the corner just as the pig prepared to charge. He raised his rifle to fire and at the same time his trousers fell down around his ankles. In the general confusion it appeared as if he didn't know what to do first, hitch up his trousers or fire another shot. Naturally, the tendency was for everyone to laugh, which we all did, including Bob afterwards. But the outcome could have been another story if he hadn't hit the pig properly, as they can be extremely dangerous if given the opportunity to attack. In this instance Bob would have been at a distinct disadvantage.

On these crazy careening chases in the Toyota, once a pig had been sighted, things became hazardous for occupants of the vehicle as well as the pig. Racing at full speed around trees and bushes, the driver would occasionally hit a hole. Then the vehicle would either practically turn a somersault or would end up pitched at an impossible angle – sometimes up to 50 or 60 degrees. We would then be entertained as the white hunter, with the help of the boys, would extract the vehicle by the use of ingeniously arranged wooden poles and a system of leverage.

On three of these occasions Bob was violently thrown out of the vehicle. For some strange reason he didn't seem to think it necessary to hold on all the time. Of course, he would reprimand Wally Johnson with savory language, maintaining that he had done it on purpose. Obviously, this wasn't so, but only the pig family getting a little of their own back. Each time we got stuck in this fashion, the pig we were trailing would escape.

On a dull day or when conversation flagged a little at a meal, it was only necessary for Wally Johnson to say "wanna go pig hunting this afternoon, Bob? Or maybe you would prefer some time off to do some columns." Bob wouldn't necessarily answer, but both men would leer at each other with looks of great expectation in their eyes. Apparently it was some strange, hidden compulsion, a sort of pig fever, that would seize them. On other occasions it would only be necessary to mention "pigs!" and everyone's face would brighten as if, after all, they now knew why they were on safari.

One day while cruising in the Toyota on a "pig run," Bob and the white hunter spotted what appeared to be a big warthog. It looked to be a female, which are usually quite easy to tell as the tusks curve 'round in a half circle rather than a less pronounced curve in the case of the male. So off we went, slowly at first until the pig took fright, and then hell-for-leather as soon as it saw us and took evasive action, slipping from bush to bush to elude his pursuers. After a while we noticed that the female was being trailed by four little piglets, but the chase continued. They led us over lots of rough ground and through brushy shrub country, over rocks and boulders and 'round trees. For a time it appeared they would get away, at which point I was sighing with relief. But a short time later they were spotted again, and I could see it was only a matter of time before Bob got off a shot.

In anguish, I plaintively said to everyone: "What about the little piglets?"

Bob replied in a scoldingly cold tone, "To hell with the little piglets. They can look after their bloody selves!"

To me this showed a cruel streak in his character that upset me for the rest of the day, though I kept my feelings private.

The day came when the safari was declared an unequivocal success. On this day I remained in camp and thus was present when Bob, Wally Johnson and the boys returned triumphantly from their most successful pig assault. They were completely drunk with a combination of delirious success and alcohol. Both had unforgettable expressions on their faces, looking as if they had done something nobody else had ever accomplished. They had an assorted collection of animals, but there was one that must have been the most remarkable warthog ever created. Its tusks were completely curved and practically made an entire circle. It was an old female and to the two spellbound pig hunters, I am sure it represented the most beautiful warthog that ever existed. In fact, it was an incredibly ugly creature. It was Bob's intention to make a full head mount, and either to hang it in one of our bathrooms opposite the water closet, perhaps to take one's mind off one's problems, or to give it a prominent place in the new studio we were building so Bob could get down to oil painting. There the beautiful ugliness of this beast would have given him some strange inspiration. This, alas, was not to be.

Bob was a good shot most of the time, and he took the whole hunting and shooting procedure quite seriously. While in Kenya he was always very careful to abide by the rule of not shooting from or near the vehicle. However, as he got older and more experienced, his ideas of correct shooting etiquette changed considerably. In Mozambique he did most of his shooting while sitting in the front of the Toyota truck with a cushion as a hand rest. Although some hunting circles would doubtless condemn this as poor sportsmanship, there is no doubt the practice increased the accuracy of Bob's shooting and reduced the likelihood of wounding animals. Actually, this method was probably started because of the fact that when Bob first went to Mozambique, his arm was in a sling as a result of the leopard attack in India a few months previously. He needed a rest as much for his arm as for his rifle.

From time to time Bob did some remarkable shooting. Sometimes he had the rather gruesome habit of indicating which eye, left or right, he would shoot a zebra at distances up to 400 or 500 yards. He accomplished this with his favorite rifle, a Holland & Holland .244 magnum with a Bausch & Lomb Balvar 2-1/2 x 8 power wide-open scope.

Possibly the most unusual shot I ever saw Bob make was in Mozambique while bird shooting. He took a quick potshot at a guinea fowl perched out on a limb of a high tree. As we waited for the bird to fall we were surprised that it remained on the bough some 40 feet off the ground. Bob's shot had been so clean it hadn't moved, and eventually the bird had to be prodded down with a long pole.

Along with the dangerous encounters with leopards and warthogs, and some near misses with elephants and rhinos, Bob had other close calls. There was the tiger that got up and left after having been dead for half an hour. During that time Bob and the shikar hunter had waited in a tree platform for the boys to come with a ladder so they could get down and inspect the trophy. Fortunately, the boys took double their normal time to react to the shot, and just before they arrived the tiger got up and left. Bob then began to think about what would have happened if there had been no delay, as at the time of the tiger's departure he would probably have been holding its head with someone taking photographs.

Bob had a great attraction for hunting the big black Cape buffalo. The fear he had for this beast became an abiding fascination until he actually courted buffalo as a hair shirt to his conscience. It seemed he wanted to see how many possible ways there were to be killed by one. As a result of this obsession, Bob had many exciting experiences. There was the time, for example, when the only possibility of survival was to shoot the lead bull of a stampeding herd and then crouch against him so the remainder of the herd veered to the side when seeing the fallen animal's bulk.

There is no doubt that Bob took some enormous risks with buffalo. Once, when accompanied by Harry Selby, a large herd began moving rapidly toward their rather skimpy cover. It seemed they would be enveloped by buffalo. The animals were nervous and a wild charge appeared imminent. Since there was no point in running away from them, Harry Selby decided to charge the buffalo before they completely made up their minds. This they did, with Bob shouting and waving his hat furiously. The buffalo stopped in their tracks with amazement and then changed their direction.

Then there was the safari when Bob even got into trouble with a zebra. It had apparently fallen dead, but as Bob and the boys approached the animal, it suddenly got up and charged the vehicle. It narrowly missed Bob as he jumped to one side, but it landed on top of Selby, pinning him against the steering wheel. Bob shot the zebra a second time, and then he and the boys became slightly hysterical with laughter as the white hunter, though unharmed, was unable to move until the zebra was pulled from him.

These colorful experiences and many others made good material for magazine articles, but mostly they helped Bob with his front-of-the-book articles for *Field & Stream,* which was his main outlet for hunting stories. There were many articles about African wildlife. Bob generally dealt separately with individual animals and chose intriguing titles, such as a piece entitled "My Friend Fisi," which was about hyenas, and an informative piece on crocodiles called "The Vulgar Assassin." Bob wrote about tigers, about lions and leopards, and then as his first elephant and rhino hadn't proved particularly difficult, he wrote two pieces under the title "Collected but Not Earned." Later, when writing about buffalo, this title was reversed to "Earned and Collected." Another buffalo piece was truthfully called "Suicide Made Easy."

Gradually Bob became an accepted authority on African safari and big game hunting, and in August, 1956 he did a full-coverage piece on every possible aspect of safari. "The Sportsman's Africa" was a 24-page spread including color art. It was subsequently used in a hunting book put out by the editors of *Field & Stream* under the title *The Sportsman's World.*

Robert Ruark went on his last safari in August, 1964. He was at Camp Ruark in Mozambique when he received a hurry-up request to write a detailed outline of safari in Africa. This was the "Far-Out Safari" piece for *Playboy.* It included an overview of what Bob had done in the past:

> I have shot three elephants of over a hundred pounds per tusk, killed a couple of lions and attended the deaths of a dozen others. I lost count on leopards – maybe 20 – and have no idea about buffalos; maybe a hundred. The small game – zebra, impala, Thomson's gazelle, Grant's gazelle, wildebeest, gerenuk, oryx, duiker – in general, camp meat, must run into a thousand. I have shot three tigers, been severely mauled by a leopard, shot gaur and water buffalo, cheetah cat and chital deer, wild dogs and hyenas and guinea fowl and sand grouse and bustard and francolin, and I have had cerebral malaria, infectious mononucleosis and have been poisoned by tsetse flies and maddened by mosquitoes. I have walked a thousand miles. Jeeped a hundred thousand, and have rung up another hundred thousand in light planes on homemade airstrips in deep bush. I have slept in tents, as well as rondawels [sic] and native huts, and have also slept on the ground in the pouring rain. I have eaten elephant, snake and fried grubworms. I have drunk native beer, palm wine and a tasty mixture of blood, milk, cow urine and wood ash.

On this last safari to Mozambique Bob was accompanied by Eva Monley, who had been a safari companion on many previous occasions. For the first two weeks they were joined by newspaper Editor-in-Chief Walker Stone and Ben Wright, publisher of *Field & Stream.* Although the actual safari probably came up to normal hunting standards and

I expect everyone enjoyed themselves in a normal fashion, it was unfortunate, inasmuch as this was to be Bob's last safari, that certain problems occurred in dealings with the safari company.

The problem started when the bill for the safari was placed on the breakfast table on the second morning after their arrival. The usual deposits had been paid in advance, and Bob felt that this was incorrect and insulting to his two hunting friends. From this point a quarrel developed into a heavy argument, which gradually came to include many other things. In a letter at least as long as a full-length magazine article, Bob tore everything to pieces. He complained about the high cost of whisky and the fact that unemployed white hunters around camp were always available to drink it. He noted that the whisky supply ran out completely on one occasion. He also complained that there were never any flashlights or lamps in camp, and there "ought to be shotgun shells for the shotguns, and bullets for the rifles."

I think that this particular quarrel could have been avoided if the people concerned had understood Robert Ruark better and had been aware of a part of his character that was becoming more and more prevalent as the years passed. That is, his tendency to get real mad and real mean for apparently little reason. Then too, it should not have been overlooked that Bob would not be forced into doing anything at all he considered unfair or incorrect. He would go to almost any length with untactful and possibly insulting prose, irrespective of any considerations of previous friendship, in order to make his point. This he did all too clearly when he wrote in his letter of complaint: "We are neither freeloaders nor cut-rate bargain seekers; we are just people who want to pay for what we get, and stop acting like an Armenian rug peddler."

Bob pointed out that he had produced many good clients for the safari company and that he had written numerous articles and columns giving the company and their white hunters considerable good publicity. To him, it purely seemed to be a question of "not dunning sterling clients on the second day of safari."

This whole unpleasant business was conducted almost entirely by correspondence during and immediately after the safari, and it concluded when a member of the safari company wrote Ruark:

"Having had the time to think over everything carefully and also reading your letter, I've come to the conclusion that you were ninety percent to blame for all the commotion caused, while you are 90 percent right in the way you have chosen to settle your bill which, I understand the office has accepted as a full settlement. I still consider you my friend. I still consider you a first-rate tramp, friend of your friends, and a good guy to hunt with. And let's forget about all this fuss."

Chapter 24
PERSONAL INSIGHTS

Robert Ruark had always been an ardent gun-lover, and after a few years of safaris he had an ever-increasing arsenal of shotguns and rifles. He was quite unable to pass a second-hand gun shop. He purchased old elephant guns used by W.D.M. "Karamoja" Bell, author of *The Wanderings of an Elephant Hunter*. When in England he could not resist visiting his friends at Westley Richards in London's West End and ordering yet another custom-built shotgun or rifle.

Some of his desire for collecting expensive guns would no doubt have derived from the shortage of fine guns when he was a boy. There was, to be sure, an abundance of old shotguns. Long before Ruark shot grouse on a Scottish moor, he got in the habit of taking two double-barreled shotguns into duck and goose blinds. Bob often recounted how he shot two rusty old 12-bore shotguns from a blind in a cornfield as a great flock of geese came in off the water to raid the corn. "I downed two coming in with one gun, and then with the second gun clobbered two more as they went away. All of a sudden the air was full of falling geese." He always insisted that this experience packed more emotional wallop than the three large tigers he shot in India.

It was difficult to know exactly how many guns Bob possessed at any one time, since he was always giving them away or lending them to white hunters or friends. However, on one count in 1962 he had an impressive collection that was listed for his *Playboy* gun piece called "The Gentleman's Hunting Arsenal." At that time Bob had in his gun rack a .30-06 Remington, Bell's old .275 Mauser-action Rigby, the .244 Holland & Holland Magnum, a Jeffery double, a 20-gauge Lewis shotgun, a 12-gauge Webley & Scott double, the ancient Ithaca 12, a .416 Rigby, a .375 Winchester Magnum, a .243 Winchester Magnum, and a Czech Brno .22 long rifle. Then at the time there was a brace of Spanish doubles given to a Texas friend, a matched pair of English 12s in Spain, a Marlin .30-30 left in Japan, another .375 lent to a friend on safari, a .318 in the hands of the Kenya police, and a .330 magnum in a gun shop for rebluing.

Around the house in Palamos was an old Churchill double that hadn't been used in years. One day Bob hurriedly yanked it out of its case and rushed into the front garden, rapidly unpackaging some new Spanish shotgun shells I had purchased in Barcelona. He had finally decided to shoot a large, noisy magpie that had been annoying him with its non-stop, raucous squawking. I waited in the office for the sound of a shot, but instead Bob returned angrily complaining that the Spanish shells would not go in the Churchill, even though they were marked as being the same gauge as the gun. So the magpie survived.

Apparently excusing himself for always buying guns, Bob finished off his *Playboy* article with:

"There is very little in the way of luxury a man may buy for himself, unless he fancies yachts, foppish jewelry, a redundancy of automobiles, or a stable of lady friends. A battery of good weapons has a decided advantage over both women and yachts; the initial payment is less, they don't need so much constant care, don't fall out of fashion so fast, and have a definitely more dependable trade-in value. This I keep telling myself every time I succumb to another fancy piece of weaponry and hate myself in the morning. But the way I see it, a man can't have too many guns. For a gun nut too much is never a sufficiency, and if it's status symbols you seek, I'd look silly as hell in a mink coat."

Except for hunting, Robert Ruark had no desire to participate personally in any other sports, even though he had started his reporting career as a sportswriter. He said he couldn't see much point in following a golf ball for miles and that tennis was too strenuous. He didn't swim much and he thought motor racing was ridiculous. He disliked baseball and football even before he started writing about them. Also, he had the strongest objection to winter sports and fervently maintained that skiing was much more dangerous than hunting big game.

Bob considered skiing so dangerous that he forbade me to go during the writing of a book or during the approach period before we got started, as he was frightened I would surely break something. Apparently he had tried skiing on only one occasion. He started from the top of a slope and after having gone 20 yards without falling over, decided that was quite enough. Bob removed the skis and thereafter proclaimed himself an unbeaten champion who had never fallen while skiing.

One thing Bob did like was bullfighting, though it was not really a sport but a tragic spectacle. He went whenever possible. He understood quite well the intricate art of the bullfighter and was sufficiently well known at the ring to have a bull dedicated to him from time to time. To begin with, he would automatically book a seat for me, and for a while I used it. But I never enjoyed the performances. The whole concept of bullfighting is against my nature, so eventually I asked Bob not to include me in any more bullfighting parties.

Bob had been to all the big bullfight fiestas in Spain, and occasionally he wrote bullfight pieces, though he didn't really claim to be any sort of authority on the subject. He had attended bullfights with Ernest Hemingway in Pamplona, and a column headed "Papa Goes to the Fights" was included in a book edited by his friend, Rex Smith. Called *Biography of the Bulls*, it contained a drawing by Bob of the famous bullfighter, Manolete.

Robert Ruark had a great obsession about things being practical in their use and service to his needs, thought I don't think he was particularly practical in doing things himself. If something didn't work or was awkward to use, or if it got in the way, then he really didn't need it and said so. Added to his definite views on practicality, Bob had a fairly active temper that he displayed periodically, especially if he encountered what he considered to be stupidity. But there was usually a good laugh after any particular incident, and Bob was the first to laugh.

Bob could not stand a barking dog, especially when we were trying to work, and there was one living across the road close by that barked continuously, as he was generally tethered. Carmen and I had many times spoken politely to the owners, asking if they "would please keep their dog quiet as the senor was an *escritor* and wished to work," but the barking continued. Finally one day Bob was so annoyed that he rushed out into the adjacent garden and in a mixture of languages, mostly Swahili, roared at the dog's owner. After this particular outburst, the dog stopped barking and there was no doubt that the owner got the message. On this occasion, Bob really had lost his temper.

Bob's temper came out in various ways and would depend on the pressure of work and his general disposition at the time, but one of the more common occurrences was when he would grab the fire poker and bend it in two in order to make a point. Afterwards he seemed to feel better. This Bob would generally do when having his nightly arguments and discussions with Ginny. The next morning he would request that I have the poker straightened as it was another matter to try to straighten an already bent poker with bare hands. The iron workshop across the road must have wondered what we were doing as at one time it became a nightly occurrence. At the time of Bob's death the poker was hanging on the wall, bent in two. It stayed in that condition until a year later when his girlfriend [*Editor's Note*: Presumably Marilyn Kaytor] came to stay on her honeymoon and immediately had it straightened. This of course indicated a complete lack of knowledge and feeling for its significance. The staff and I had left it untouched.

Bob had no mechanical ability whatsoever, even to the point of changing a typewriter ribbon, which I always did for him. He had a great impulse to rid himself of anything he couldn't work properly, and there was the time when hunting in Kenya that he threw away a telescopic gun sight because it had become inaccurate. He unscrewed it from the gun and threw it into the bush to rust in the long yellow grass.

Bob always seemed to have problems with the slide projector, which was a nuisance since he enjoyed showing visitors slides I had taken of his African safaris. I would generally set up the machine and arrange the slide trays. They would be ready for Bob to start that evening, but the show nearly always terminated when he got his fingers tangled up in the mechanism and jammed everything with a slide bent in the middle he couldn't extract. This would be left for me to unravel when I came in the next morning.

Then there was a tape recorder that Bob tried to use for recording editorial discussions, but this proved to be a failure as he seemed to have difficulty in pressing the right button. More often than not he would wipe out whatever was on the tape rather than recording anything new. An attempt was made to dictate correspondence into the machine, but this did didn't work very well either, as usually the letters were only half recorded. Mechanical things baffled Bob, though there was one machine he swore by – an electric toothbrush that he was able to work without any problem at all.

With the exception of a typewriter, Bob was usually unable to work anything successfully that had a moving part to it. When it came to sharpening a pencil, for example, there would be a few choice expressions in the process as the lead broke off, but the strongest language would come when Bob wound the curtain into the sharpener.

Bob also had difficulty with wrist watches. None would work correctly on his wrist, presumably because of excessive electricity generated by his nervous system. He tried at least a dozen expensive watches, all unsuccessfully. Then one day he discovered that a Rolex Oyster Perpetual went perfectly on him, and he was so pleased that he wore this watch continuously for years without removing it for anything, whether showering, swimming or sleeping.

Anything to do with cameras made Bob very nervous, as did all photographers when they started fiddling with their stops and light meters. He disliked cameras so much that even when all the photographic equipment was stolen on his first safari, Bob actually seemed relieved. There had been a Cine, a Leica, an Ikoflex, and a Rolleiflex, all full of exposed film. Yet his reaction was vintage Ruark: "Ah, the hell with it. I'm glad they're gone, and there's no use spoiling lunch. This camera business is a damned nuisance. Let's all have another drink in celebration of no more damned nonsense with f-7s and apertures and the rest of that rot."

Although Bob liked to have music playing more or less all the time, he didn't seem to respect the delicate machinery of record players, nor was he careful with records. When a record got stuck, Bob would hurl a shoe, thus making everything jump, including the record play arm, and the music would continue. On one occasion, as a result of a direct hit, it was necessary to change the needle, and for Bob that was impossible. His problems with all things mechanical weren't the result of overbearing or impossible nervous tension. It was really more of a joke, because Bob knew and I knew that he just could not fix anything that needed fixing.

In a column written in July 1957, Bob discussed some of the things that wouldn't work for him:

As possibly the only man who ever shot a radio with a .45 pistol in Northern Kenya because the news was unpleasant, I claim to be one of the oldest living enemies of machines now practicing that enmity. I reckon I have kicked more tables and chairs for armed assault on my person than anybody I know. And the other day I even kicked a parking meter for not accepting my nickel.

At this moment, in my house, there are three record players, all busted. There are two fancy radios which have never worked. The stove is set in lefthanded and draws wrong. The fireplaces – kind of machines – smoke. The car's got a knock nobody can locate.

For twenty odd years I have played a typewriter for my bread and beans, and I still can't change a ribbon without severely wounding myself. The only time I ever washed a dish I dropped it, and the only time I ever helped Mama in a kitchen emergency I was out of play for weeks with a hand that got burned nearly all the way off.

PERSONAL INSIGHTS

I own more scars for trying to separate ice from trays, from trying to open card tables and sort out the angularity of deck chairs than anybody. If I try to change a needle on a phonograph arm I (1) bust the arm and (2) get electrocuted.

Other people open bottles with ease, but it seems to me that every bottle I ever tackled was permanently sealed to keep me from evils of drink. Short of biting off the neck I have to holler for Mama or the cook. A can opener and a can is a bigger threat than the atom bomb.

Some people can open suitcases. Not me. The lock jams, but this is of no importance, as I've already lost the key. I find that jumping up and down sometimes helps . . . .

Bob had very little appreciation of a car motor, and even though he loved his Rolls Royce he didn't treat it with any more respect than any other automobile. From somewhere he had gotten the idea that the engine had to be warmed up before he drove off. To him, that didn't mean letting the engine idle for a short while until it stopped sputtering; instead, it meant a long period when he sat with his foot hard on the gas pedal with the engine roaring and the whole car shaking. From the house it seemed as if he was revving up an aircraft prior to take-off, and nothing I could say would stop this take-off procedure with his Rolls.

Bob was a notoriously bad driver. On the road he continuously cursed at other drivers, all the while proclaiming what a good driver he was. I remember overhearing an English girlfriend whisper in his ear: "I suppose all Americans are good drivers," she said, whereupon Bob replied: "Yes, we are. We have to be in order to stay alive."

Although Bob never had an accident, there were always mysterious marks on the car. In actual fact he went too fast when demonstrating the powerful kick-down accelerator on the Rolls, and he often passed when he definitely should not have done so. Or he would go too slow. There was the time when he went very slowly for miles and miles where the roads were narrow. Nobody could pass him or they protested with their claxons. I can only assume that because of the Rolls Royce, everyone must have thought it was funeral. On pulling into our garage Bob announced how well and safely he had driven, but sitting at his side, I had never been more embarrassed for him and myself.

This regular display of bad driving was more noticeable during his final few years. It is possible that Bob realized that he was not so reliable, and more and more he began to use our temporary chauffeur, Enrique, who was a taxi driver in Palamos and who was always delighted to drive the Rolls Royce.

Alternatively Bob would use a hired car service from the Ritz Hotel in Barcelona, where the number one driver was named Jesus. There was the time when Bob cabled from London for me to send Enrique to meet him on arrival at the airport in Barcelona, but on this particular day Enrique was unavailable, so I made arrangements for Jesus to collect Bob. In order to be sure Bob would be looking for the right driver I advised him of the change by cable. I couldn't resist the opportunity to be facetious, so my message read: "HALLELUJAH – JESUS WILL MEET YOU – ALLAH."

So far as normal living was concerned, Bob always maintained that he had the most practical bar ever invented, mainly because it produced ice at once. For the gin and whisky to be handy, and ice available in its correct place, was in Bob's view the first requirement for normal living. He didn't want to have to wait 20 minutes while the host shouted for Juan or Maria to fetch the ice, only to find they had run out of whisky or gin and there was only half a bottle sweet sherry. This he considered to be bad management and insisted that a bar should be stocked with the basic requirements at all times.

Practical and easy access to one's house was another important concept in Bob's idea of sensible living, and that is why he jumped at the property in Palamos when I first showed it to him. It is on flat ground a few minutes from the village of Palamos and right next to the beach without any road in front.

Bob once had a most unpleasant experience in getting back home from someone else's house. He went to dinner with some friends who lived out back of Palamos, and even though he had been given exact instructions on how to get there, he lost his way almost immediately and had to return to the telephone for further instructions.

Bob had taken the Rolls Royce, which probably didn't improve his disposition when he realized the state of the tracks he had to travel. But when he started back in the dark, he got completely lost and afterwards explained to me of his great fear of being stranded all night. He was so appalled and annoyed by that prospect that he just kept driving wherever he could drive. This included ploughed fields, rocky river beds and narrow passages covered with overhanging trees. He eventually arrived back home for the night, relieved though notably shaken.

The next morning I was dismayed at the appearance of the car. There was at least a foot of earth and stones packed up on the front bumper, the wings were dented, and the whole car was badly scratched and scraped on the sides and even on top. A complete new paint job was necessary that cost over a thousand dollars in London. As Bob ruefully joked afterwards, all of this had been for a poor dinner and drinks without any ice.

Bob Ruark had no sense of direction whatsoever, never mind the fact that he had traveled so many thousands of miles, and somewhere in the house was a two-million-mile plaque with his name presented to him by United Air Lines in 1956. When we lived in Barcelona, Bob went to the airport hundreds of times, either to travel himself or to collect friends, but if he went on his own he would invariably get lost and sometimes would end up on the road to Sitges, a town ten miles past the Barcelona airport. He would get out on the Madrid road and then try to cut across instead of going the correct and more direct way through the town.

Bob even used to lose himself coming back from the center of town and wouldn't know where he was until he arrived practically at the top of a fairly high hill and landmark called Tibidabo. I sometimes wondered why he never got lost in Africa, but he seemed to know his way around jungle country far better. On one occasion he drove straight out from the middle of Paris, which is a difficult city, in the right direction and without asking. He afterwards said that this was possible because of the city's similarity to the African jungle.

On this particular trip from Paris, Bob proved himself to be a nervous traveler and was not happy until he had arrived at his final destination. We were traveling in the Rolls and left the center of Paris about midday and drove until arriving in Palamos at two the next morning, a distance of about 1,200 kilometers. There was no particular reason to arrive quickly, and we were both very tired. Towards the end of the journey, when Bob could see that I was wilting, he took my turn at the wheel as he had remarkable stamina, though he had kept himself going with sips of whisky.

Then there was the time in 1955 when Bob arrived in Paris from Amsterdam and wanted to continue straight on to Barcelona. He was unable to do so because of heavy tourist traffic, and after hanging about for a couple of days, he took the first available flight out in sheer desperation. It happened to be going to Lisbon, and since there was no immediate flight out of Lisbon for Barcelona, he hailed a taxi and told the driver to take him to Madrid. The taxi charge was $150, and then Bob had a further delay of three days before getting a direct flight to Barcelona. He reckoned that including taxis and hotels the trip had cost him about $1,200 and had taken a week instead of the two hours required for a normal direct flight.

Bob was often an impulsive traveler and many times he packed up and left for London or Rome, just for the change. There was the time when he was so keen to go somewhere that he actually arrived in Rome for a convention exactly one month too soon. In his enthusiasm to get out of the house, Bob had misread the cabled instructions. This was the only time that I ever knew Bob to think of going to a convention, as he greatly disliked them.

When traveling with company, Bob was definitely very nervous, and he could never travel happily with Ginny. It seemed that if he had anyone with him, the responsibility of the extra baggage weighed heavily on his nerves, and if the opportunity was presented, he was liable to cause an awkward situation. There was the time when we traveled together to Mozambique and at the start of our journey were passing through the customs barrier at the Barcelona airport. Bob couldn't contain himself when I was being questioned by a police official concerning my resident's permit, which I did not have with me as it was being renewed. The matter was being arranged peacefully when Bob suddenly shouted at the official:

"For the love of God, let him pass; we are not bandits!" This outburst embarrassed the customs official and for a while it appeared he was not going to let me pass, which would have wrecked our entire travel schedule to Africa.

Then, on arrival in Nice, Bob checked the baggage for the rest of the trip while I attended to the dispatch of some cables. Somehow during the tagging of the baggage by an obviously confused airlines clerk, our bags were marked Johannesburg instead of Salisbury, with the result that Bob's largest bag went on to Johannesburg. I was luckier and didn't lose any of mine, though on arrival in Salisbury I noticed with some surprise that one bag was actually tagged Johannesburg on one end and Salisbury on the other!

One thing Bob could never lose or mislay was his over-the-shoulder bag, which I believe was his own invention and had been made by an Arab in Tangier. It consisted of a soft leather hold-all type bag and measured about 18 inches deep, about 9 inches wide and about 15 inches across, with a long leather strap that allowed it to hang at hip level. The bag was ideal for Bob's requirements as there was space for his passport and documents, his notebooks, pencils and paper, his current working manuscripts and newspaper clippings for column work, one or two books, current issues of *Time* and *Newsweek,* a carton of Chesterfield cigarettes, and a bottle of White Horse whisky. Also, Bob always carried a razor and a change of underclothing so that he was equipped for traveling delays or being separated from his suitcase. This bag would never leave him, no matter how many bags he was looking after for other people.

In 1948, when Bob was on a trip through South America, an engine of a chartered plane conked out over the Brazilian jungle and a forced landing was necessary. This deposited Bob and his party in the wilderness for two days. But with his over-the-shoulder bag, Bob was prepared. When asked whether he shared its treasures with his companions, he indignantly answered: "I did nothing of the sort. Let them carry their own bags. Everyone was miserable. But I was shaved. I had a highball when I wanted it. I lay under a tree and read, and I used the time to knock out five columns. It was one of the pleasantest two days I've ever spent."

Each year Bob seemed compelled to travel even more and more. It appeared that he just could not slow down, a point he made clear in a column covering a six-month rundown of travel activity in 1962. It was headed "A Dog-Tired Rover":

As I was tottering into town the other day, bearing a variety of foreign bugs, airplane ankles – the swelled kind – and a stale aroma, it occurred to me to curse the rootlessness of the male, borne to full fruit by the jet plane.

The female, I do believe, is largely content with the semi-permanent nest if an occasional escape from the chicks is afforded – so long, of course, as the cockbird hovers in the vicinity. But I cannot believe the male was originally intended to be planted. He was a drifter, nomad, in the beginning, and his sketchy hut could always be dismantled – by the women, of course – or his camelhair tent struck when the far hills beckoned.

You can, however, carry this to a ridiculous degree . . . .

I have been sick in more strange hotels than Ernie Pyle ever was, because he traveled mostly by car. I have covered more strange real estate than Cortez, Columbus, Magellan, Vasco de Gama, Pizarro and Balboa.

There is a flat in London which I have not lived in more than three weeks in eighteen months, and a house in Spain where the dogs have forgotten me. I have been dirty oftener than clean, unshaven oftener than shaven, mostly with what appears to be a knife and fork.

The old feet are flat from pounding airport terminals, and there's permanent shoulder sag from portable typewriters and one-ton shoulder bags.

I curse the day they invented the jet aircraft, and I cry a triple pox upon the invention of the air-travel credit card. Man, the rover, the nomad – the bum – has

PERSONAL INSIGHTS

finally found the perfect answer to his built-in unwillingness to stay home, and he needs a small excuse to exercise his fiddle foot.

It is possible I will pause for station identification, but just you watch: About the time the laundry's clean, old Dad will be off and winging.

After his globe-trotting travels, Bob was always glad to return to his home in Palamos, and this prompted him to write many "homecoming" pieces. This wasn't just to make an easy column, but showed a genuine feeling of thankfulness that he had arrived back in the place he loved. Yet, as soon as he was comfortably settled, he was impatient to go again.

Although Bob made a joke of his continuous motion, it is difficult to understand why he didn't spend more time in his home, as he had a great facility for enjoying home life. If he wasn't writing, then he was perfectly happy reading and listening to his favorite records. Bob would put on six or seven and would continuously play the same ones, only making a slight variation by turning them over periodically. A group of half a dozen might consist of Ella Fitzgerald, Louis Armstrong, Nat "King" Cole, Lena Horne, Keely Smith, Tony Bennett and Bing Crosby. Or maybe his selection would be Jeri Southern, Frank Sinatra, Benny Goodman, Peggy Lee, Jackie Gleason and Paul Weston, to name just a few. Included in his selections would nearly always be something by Joe Bushkin, Bob's favorite piano playing friend.

Bob liked his mixed drinks and enjoyed nothing more than to have crackling log fires in both ends of the house. He was really a firebug at heart, and whenever he could there would be fires, even in the summer late at night. Once the fires were roaring, Bob could not resist throwing on another log. On one occasion in the front living room he had such a big fire that it burnt right through the wall into the room behind and nearly set light to a drunken guest. Fortunately, the smoke from the smoldering bed was noticed before the guest suffocated.

When the Ruarks were in residence in Palamos they would entertain spasmodically with the emphasis more on the midday luncheon rather than dinner. The larger luncheon parties would include about 20 people, and the menu would invariably alternate between Southern fried chicken and home-grown sweet corn, or an extensive Indian curry that the Spanish guests loved. But for the evening Bob would not want anything very complicated. Although he would normally encourage people to visit for a drink, he would cease to be the gracious host if he felt he was being taken advantage of, which happened occasionally.

Once in a while Bob was annoyed by intruders, especially in the tourist season, and there was the time when on stepping out of his studio office and looking over the back garden, he spotted a stranger browsing around as if it was his own place. Bob shouted at him, "I presume you are enjoying yourself," whereupon the tourist intruder gaily announced in guttural English, "Ja, zank you very much, here I am, you have very pretty garden."

"Well, that's nice." Bob replied, "Now get off my land bloody quickly, or I'll throw you off." The stranger, probably from Hamburg, went away muttering that "I vos only looking and you must be a very rude man."

In actual fact, Bob was very polite as a rule, but since the house had been designed to guarantee privacy insofar as was possible, it annoyed him when people ignored the garden wall. It was good sport in the summer to go out and chase tourists off the property, where sometimes they would even park their cars. But as often as not, Bob would find them to be nice people and fetch them in for a drink and sometimes for lunch as well.

Robert Ruark was basically a very ordered person, in his work schedules, his intentions to do one particular thing, or his plans for a safari, even though it might be two years hence. He always kept his promises and always showed up. Generally, even before one particular project had been completed he was planning the next. This certainly applied to book-writing. He was always looking beyond the next book, still unwritten, and considering the title and setting for the one to follow.

In his dress too, Bob was orderly, neat and correctly turned out. He could carry off unusual attire if he wished to do so. Often he would go to dinner at the nearby luxury hotel dressed as a complete Texan, replete with a ten-gallon Stetson, and once he even managed to get me dressed up in a similar outfit. Or he might go to the Liceo Opera House in Barcelona wearing a bright red dinner jacket. While he was noticed, he fit in just fine.

For a poor boy, Bob had come a long way. He would have his tailor travel the 60 miles from Barcelona to Palamos for suit fittings. From practically no clothes at all in his youth, Bob's wardrobe was impressive to say the least. Apart from a great many more suits and shoes than he could possibly wear, there was a dazzling collection of colored corduroy slacks purchased on various visits to Capri. There would have been 30 pairs at least, ranging from bright Chinese red to butterfly yellow through shades of green, mauve, orange, blue, brown, pink and, in fact, every imaginable color. Despite this display of flashy colors, no one would have ever dared suggest that there was any fairyfied motive.

Strangely enough, though Bob owned a vast array of stylish clothing, more often than not he would be found wearing an African *kikoi*, consisting solely of one piece of material. These are very comfortable and are worn wrapped around the waist. Bob had become accustomed to them in East Africa. The *kikoi* is extremely colorful and would generally have a Swahili saying or a political slogan around the edge and would be decorated with designs of elephants or lions, or umbrellas, or even Coca-Cola bottles.

Amongst this large, varied wardrobe, Bob did, of course, have a collection of safari clothing. It was generally in new condition with the single exception of a battered safari hat he had become very attached to. It was bent and dirty looking and had been on all of his safaris, from the beginning. It certainly looked it. One day Carmen, his efficient maid, came across this unkempt safari hat. Since she always kept his clothes impeccable, she decided it needed to be washed. Later, when Carmen produced a new-looking hat, clean and shining and stiff-brimmed, she knew immediately by the expression on her master's face and his loud, agonized groan that she had made a mistake.

CHAPTER 25
DEMON RUM & HEALTH PROBLEMS

During all the years I knew Robert Ruark, his health was quite variable. One way or another he had just about every type of illness. He was either in remarkably good health and bubbling over, or he was complaining of a mysterious bug or some obscure virus that was attacking him, usually having been caught at the last place he had visited. He either had pleurisy, pneumonia, grippe, sinus, hives, ptomaine poisoning, a troublesome wisdom tooth, bad stomach bloat or worms from eating zebra meat. Or mononucleosis, which he explained was a complaint caused by atomic fallout, from which some of his white hunter friends were also suffering. But in Bob's case, it was probably his liver acting up because of too much whisky. Then there was the common cold that made his head feel as if it were "stuffed with concrete" and made him "look for footprints on the ceiling."

In between his various ailments Bob was an acute gout sufferer. Although this gave him a great deal of pain and discomfort, in a way he seemed to be quite pleased with himself, as he always maintained that only highly intelligent people suffered from the gout. He suggested it was the result of excessive cerebration and creative ability, thus producing an oversupply of uric acid in the blood. Bob was a sufficiently active gout sufferer to write, at the age of 35, a column on "The Glory of Gout!" based on his own experience.

On a visit to the United States in 1955, during the *Something of Value* film negotiations, Bob had to have surgery. He went to Houston for two fairly extensive operations on his legs to remove varicose veins. Later, in a general report to friends, he wrote: "The surgery has been successful and I am in excellent health and spirit – apart from a strained shoulder, a suppurating ulcer on one leg from the last operation, small legal fights with two Catalan criminals, hoof and mouth disease and a new attack of sinus trouble."

Bob and Ginny both suffered continuously from sinus trouble and in July, 1955, when in London, they had a series of tests taken by a Harley Street specialist. He reported: "I found Mrs. Ruark has a dull right antrum opaque to X-rays, and antral puncture and wash out yielded a little clearish mucus. I found Mr. Ruark's sinuses were normal, and I think his symptoms are due to a grossly deviated nasal septum following several blows to the nose." He then, in no-nonsense fashion, got to the heart of the matter. "I believe considerable alcohol consumption together with over 60 cigarettes a day is affecting both these patients' nasal condition adversely . . . [and] I would strongly recommend stopping smoking and drinking to see how much bearing this has on the condition before considering any drastic treatment."

Then there was the time in 1957 when Bob was ill the whole way back from East Africa. This was before the jets were in service, and the journey was a slow one from Nairobi via Entebbe, Khartoum, Addis Ababa, Cairo, Rome, Nice and Barcelona. For most of the journey Bob was practically a stretcher case.

On arrival in Barcelona and before customs had been dealt with, Ginny sent an urgent message for me to arrange for a doctor to be waiting at the house, as she thought Bob was seriously ill. This was against Bob's wishes but Ginny insisted, and when I saw the bad state he was in, I also thought he should see a doctor.

After a complete examination the doctor had no idea what was wrong. Bob continued to suffer from incredibly high temperatures, 104 was quite common, and there were appalling sweating sessions when he would completely soak up a bed. Sometimes it was necessary to change the bedding four times a night.

The Barcelona doctor made a number of visits and came to the conclusion that a worm had built a cyst on Bob's liver and that surgery was necessary. He recommended an operation as soon as the high temperatures stopped. This frightened Ginny and myself, as a liver operation would most likely have finished Bob off completely.

Frantically searching around for a second opinion, we were introduced to a first-class general practitioner who visited on a consultation basis. This new doctor immediately diagnosed the symptoms as malaria, and discovering that no blood test had been taken, he ordered this to be done. We were told that the malarial germs are about the easiest to discern from a blood test, and of course this doctor was right. Bob had a type of malaria called cerebral malaria.

He prescribed a drug capable of curing malaria with no possibilities of recurrence, but it was unavailable in Spain at that time. However, with the help of the Barcelona consular service and the American ambassador in Madrid, arrangements were made for the Mediterranean Sixth Fleet to call in at Barcelona with the required drug. Within a very short time Bob had recovered.

Soon after this illness, we were working well in Palamos when Bob decided he had a toothache. He complained for a day or two, then asked me to book him a flight to London and to cable for an appointment there with a dentist he had used before. Ginny decided she would go along for the ride, and so everything was arranged that they would both go to London.

I drove them from Palamos to the Barcelona airport, a distance of about 75 miles over narrow, badly potholed roads. I said goodbye to Bob and Ginny and they boarded the aircraft for London. The plane trundled out onto the runway, then after a longish wait while revving up in preparation for take-off, returned to the airport apron and all passengers disembarked. Apparently an inquisitive passenger had touched one of the emergency escape windows. It had sprung loose and there would be some delay in fixing it.

Bob told me afterwards that he wasn't worried about whether I would be waiting or not, as he knew it was my custom to see the aircraft airborne before leaving. When he arrived in the waiting room, Bob had already given instructions for his luggage to be off-loaded. He explained to me that his toothache had stopped and that he wished to return to Palamos immediately and get back to work.

Periodically, Bob had medical checkups in different parts of the world. Invariably he was given the usual medical advice concerning alcohol and cigarettes. This advice he studiously ignored. Then too, he wasn't very consistent with his medical attention. At times he would settle for visits from a local medico. Though extremely friendly, he was known as "*el puerco*" or "the dirty doctor," who kept a mangy mongrel in his surgery. However, we were told he had been very successful sewing up wounded soldiers during the Spanish Civil War. At other times Bob would insist on what he considered to be better treatment in London, despite the fact that Barcelona, a city of two and a half million, had just as good medical services as anywhere in the world.

Very often Bob included some reference to health in his abundant correspondence, especially to his agent. There was always some reference to not drinking, which was often untrue. I think these were put in as some form of auto-suggestion, with the idea that perhaps this would help Bob to kid himself that he wasn't drinking.

Robert Ruark was a man of good physique, who weighed in the region of 200 pounds, was just on six feet tall, and had a broad build. He would normally appear to be perfectly fit, unless he was recovering from some complaint caused by general stress and strain. However, one of the causes of his final decline in health, without doubt, would have been his self-administered B-12 injections. He would collect large supplies of these on his visits to New York and would come back with 50-unit packs of sterile disposable glass syringes, and 24-unit packs of Rubramin PC. 10 cc multiple dose list 5194 Squibb vitamin B-12 injections. I figured the B-12 was prescribed to build up his liver because he always abused it, and because of his connections he was able to obtain a large supply.

Bob liberally used these injections on himself, and any time a girlfriend wanted to be jabbed, he would willingly administer the injection. He always convinced them that it would liven them up and make them feel better. In themselves, these B-12 injections might have been all right, but this was a false economy in Bob's case. They encouraged him to pretend that he was perfectly healthy and able to drink at his normal pace, when in fact, finally, a serious hemorrhage was only a few days away.

There is no doubt whatsoever that all his life Robert Ruark drank heavily, and the remarkable thing was that he never showed it and never had a really serious hangover. At times Bob would appear shaking the morning, but he seemed to recover after one or two bloody Marys, or Cuba libres, or rum punches, or screwdrivers, or whatever. Although you might not have known that he drank at all, it was this remarkable tolerance for alcohol that finally killed him. Everybody who knew him wondered at some point how he could stand the pace, and this thought was expressed to me soon after Bob's death by an old Washington friend who remembered Bob from his early reporting days. "Hell Alan," he said, "I knew Bob Ruark 25 years back, and he was on a plan of self-destruction even then!"

Bob was never a secret drinker. He was a social fun drinker, or he drank just because he liked to drink. He always maintained that he was not an alcoholic, as alcoholics drank and didn't do their work, whereas Bob always did his work and practically never missed a deadline. He literally loved drink and drinking, and admitted it freely. On one occasion when being interviewed, Bob began by describing the glass he was holding: "I love the drinking glass, don't you? Such clean, artistic lines. Easy to hold, too. Such a friend. Never talks behind your back."

"I take it you are a drinking man," the interviewer replied.

Bob put down his glass and replied aggressively: "I would fight any man who described me otherwise."

His admiration for alcohol can be read many times over in his books. Bob always managed to describe so well the act of getting a drink or having the drink in the right place. In *Horn of the Hunter*, for example, he wrote:

"It is funny about booze. I have been drinking it constantly since my first tentative sample of North Carolina corn liquor when I was fifteen. I love liquor. It has been a good and constant friend for over twenty years."

Despite his many references in the book to Dr. Ruark's nutritious, delicious, bone-building gin, one of the many Ruarkisms that profile writers pounced on was a bland statement he made about martinis:

"The martini is a drink unfit for consumption by any but professional sword swallowers. I have known more weepers, fighters, fallers, screamers, mumblers, and stumblers among the martini alumni than among all other branches of the tipple tree. You cannot talk long to a martini hound – not unless you get down on the floor with him."

Bob often mentioned drinking in his columns. Whenever the occasion arose he would attack any suggestion of prohibition. "There are two things on earth that no amount of regimentation can control," he wrote in November, 1958. "One is the well-known way of a man with a maid. The other is the grim determination of a man who wants to drink his fill. Castles may tumble, cabinets may fall, but old Single-Purpose Charlie will get his load."

Before Robert Ruark did anything at all, it was first a question of getting a drink. It was his automatic reaction, and at the same time he would offer to fetch one for anyone else present. Bob's drinks were always large and he had an extremely heavy hand. I soon decided that I would fix my own Cuba libres after he fixed me one. I am sure there was more rum than coke in his measure.

When Bob was working he would always have a glass alongside his machine, and he would generally progress from bloody Marys through Cuba libres after breakfast, to dry martinis halfway through the morning, changing maybe to pink gins on the terrace after he had done his morning stint of work. Then when I returned from the village with the mail and newspapers around 1:00 p.m., there would be more pink gins as we discussed any new developments. We would then sit down to a late lunch.

Lunch would include wine and then afterwards not necessarily a brandy for Bob, but more likely a whisky on the rocks after the coffee. He would take the whisky back to the office, though this drink would be more for company than anything else. Often it would not be consumed. Bob would probably have a siesta of about an hour on the office couch. He would then go to work, first serving himself a fresh whisky that would be followed by a varying number before dinner, depending on how the work went.

Some days would be different and Bob's hours would be quite irregular as a result of working late or of a sleepless night. There would be days when he wouldn't surface until twelve or one. On those days there would probably be a five o'clock lunch and the dinner would likely be forgotten altogether. But his drinks would be about the same. This was a bad plan for Bob as even under normal conditions he did not eat well.

Bob didn't want to be without a drink for even a short while. When he made short trips in the Rolls from Palamos to see friends in the next village, he would always take a tankard of something with him. He placed it on the floor at his side. In the first Studebaker Champion we owned, he had a special wire holder fixed in the floor between the driver and the passenger. It was designed to hold two glasses or two beer bottles.

Eventually this excessive alcohol intake caught up with Bob in the form of sudden collapses. Over a period of a number of years he had a total of about a dozen in various parts of the world. The first occurred in London in 1955 when he was inspecting a new Rolls Royce prior to ordering his Silver Cloud. He collapsed in the automobile showroom and hit his head on an English oak desk. Bob woke up in St. George's Hospital speaking Spanish, and he later wrote a rather amusing piece praising the English and their hospital system, though he found it a little strange that a patient was required to bring his own egg for breakfast. As he pointed out, this wasn't practical when one arrived the way he had.

Despite warnings from various specialists to go easy on the booze in the aftermath of this collapse, Bob Ruark wasn't about to ease up. So there were more collapses – some in Africa, one in Alaska, some in the United States, and I caught him falling off the stairway in the house at Palamos. Bob had been posing for photographs all around the house, and we were finishing with a shot at the top of the living room stairway, which was to include his lion trophy in the background. He was standing four steps up holding a tankard filled with rum and coke when I noticed it was spilling. I instantly leapt towards the stairs and just managed to catch him as he pitched forward. Ginny, who had been watching from the side, was also there immediately, and together we lowered Bob to the floor.

In the scramble that followed, Ginny suffered some badly bitten fingers since lacking anything else at the time, she had tried to force her fingers between Bob's gnashing teeth to stop him from damaging his tongue. Once she was able to partially open his mouth, she screamed in agony and quickly removed her hand. With the help of the gardener we lifted Bob to the sofa and within about fifteen minutes he regained consciousness. Later, Bob said he was quite all right, and the next day when we all went to Barcelona, he insisted on driving the Rolls, I suppose just to prove to himself that he could. The car ride was most unpleasant as I felt there could very well be another collapse at any moment.

These frequent collapses should have been warnings, but Bob ignored them. Various doctors told him this type of collapse was caused by an imbalance of liquid (alcohol), coupled with nervous stress and strain. Physical hardship, such as excessive travel, made matters worse. When this happened, his liver malfunctioned and alcohol more or less went straight through into the blood stream and directly to the brain. Bob explained all this freely and on many occasions, adding that he had been told it was more than likely that each collapse could destroy some brain cells, and that eventually matters would come to a point where serious damage would have been done.

At one time Bob blamed Ginny for these collapses, saying that she encouraged them by making him nervous. This was patently unfair since he only had one while in her presence. Altogether there were plenty of obvious signs that alcohol was directly or indirectly responsible for his blackouts, yet Bob didn't stop drinking. I think it was left that there were a combination of reasons, and since there were no collapses for a long time, we assumed he was all right again.

But then, after a particularly heavy drinking session on a 1960 trip to Africa, Bob had a series of collapses and went completely to pieces. He was in Nairobi, where a doctor convinced him that if he continued to drink, he would be lucky if it killed him. Of greater likelihood, the doctor explained, was that Bob would suffer some degree of insanity or become paralyzed. There is an episode in his book, *Uhuru*, based on his own experience. The coverage, which is graphic and disturbing, was based entirely on Bob's own research into what had actually happened to him. He probably over-emphasized some things in order to make a strong point in his story, but certainly it is quite evident that he knew the full risks involved if he continued to drink.

In the aftermath of the 1960 blackout, Bob vowed to go on the wagon. "This new Ruark," he wrote to Harold Matson, "is on the wagon for keeps." He indicated that he felt fine after just a week without drink, and that "my good friend Booze is no longer a buddy." The threat of insanity frightened Bob, and he did go on a six months' water wagon. The Nairobi physician, Dr. Roy Thompson, had managed to do something that nobody had ever done before – to stop Robert Ruark's drinking.

About the fourth month of a completely honest water wagon, I was having lunch with Bob at the old Parellada Restaurant in Barcelona. On reaching the dessert course, we both decided to settle for that remarkable Spanish institution, the flan. It so happened that this one was laced with cognac, and on leaving the restaurant Bob appeared a little lightheaded and suggested it could have been the flan. At the time it seemed an incredible transition that Robert Ruark could get a slight buzz from an innocent custard dessert.

During this dry period Bob would write and tell everyone about his predicament, and a letter to his parents really indicated that he was at grips with the problem:

"Dear Mother and Dad – I suppose you reckon I am dead, which is not quite true, but I was gone an awful long time in Africa and have been very ill. I am only now just getting caught up from a tremendously serious illness which hit me in Africa and which, among other things, means that I will never be able to drink anything at all again, which I naturally find unpleasant as a prospect.

"Mostly it was a combination of African bugs, twenty-five years of combat fatigue, overwork with liver complications and Christ knows what all. I am all right now and have gained my weight back and will probably be all right as long as I stay away from any form of alcohol. Oddly enough I don't find it very difficult. I have nothing new to report except that life goes along and the work gets done, and the more I make the less I seem to keep."

Shortly after this spell of good intentions and good behavior, we commenced to plan the next safari for the summer months of 1961. I was still worried about Bob and his drinking, and when it came to giving instructions to the safari company for the usual large quantities of booze, with the emphasis on whisky, gin and wine, I realized that this was not going to be a Sunday School outing.

So far as Bob's consumption of booze was concerned, the safari proved to be anything but a Sunday School outing. Afterwards, when the doctor in Nairobi learned about Bob's flagrant defiance of all medical advice and that he had broken all the fine promises he had made, he wrote a further note of advice to him:

"While I understand your mental attitude towards your trip here and appreciated your effort to recapture your past experience in the 'good old days' in Kenya, I must say I was scared stiff by the results. I hope you have now at last realized that the 'quacks' were absolutely right when all and sundry advised you that alcohol is now a downright poison as far as you are concerned. There is, I assure, NO SAFETY LIMIT at all. I hope you will remember that a bottle of paraldehyde awaits you here if need be!!! Seriously, Bob, I hope you won't find it too difficult to revert absolutely to life on the wagon – which is very, very necessary for you."

During his six-month period when he stayed dry, Bob received many letters from well-wishers offering advice and encouragement. In response to one of them, he assured the correspondent that he was "not an alcoholic in its general sense and that he "might be pleased to know that I haven't needed any adjusting to sobriety, nor has my life changed for better or worse since I drove up the Coca-Cola shares. I just think it is a God damn shame that a man who can afford booze at my time of life ain't allowed to spend his money on it." He then added a postscript: "If the doctors ever give me the green light with a reasonable amount of assurance, I intend to mix a quart of martinis, drink the lot and not give anybody none."

As late as July, 1961, when Bob was still more or less claiming to be on the wagon, he wrote a column complaining that his general consumption of booze had declined. But gradually Bob started again, first on wine, then progressing to hard spirits, explaining all the time that the medical checkups in London and New York had shown that his liver count was nearly one hundred percent. Bob would have known this wasn't true, but I think eventually he convinced himself by repetition. So his drinking was soon well underway again and it was impossible to stop him. Perhaps to some extent his older and better friends helped reduce his intake a little, but on the other hand, younger and more recent acquaintances did not help at all.

In any event, Bob was mostly scarred by self-inflicted wounds acquired in the super society in which he lived. He loved people and always wanted to have company, preferably females. Whereas his visitors generally arrived in fresh condition, Bob would have just delivered the last girlfriend onto the previous departing aircraft. He would then start off again at a high pace, and in the end this ran him into the ground. In play with the opposite sex, Robert Ruark was like a long-distance runner competing against a relay team with an unlimited number of runners.

This excessive activity was not always possible while he was still married, at least not in his own home, so for long periods when we were working on a book he became fitter. But when he removed the brake of marriage, the procedure of destruction quickened. This was nobody's fault except Bob himself, because in the final count a man does what he wants to do. Bob was an extremely strong-willed person, and even if one tried to advise and help him, if he wasn't inclined to agree, then he would more than likely tell you to "fuck off."

Robert Ruark drank far more when he was away from home, and in certain cities he would appear to commence a plan of complete destruction. Rome was particularly bad, though New York and London or wherever probably were about the same so far as alcoholic intake was concerned. His trouble really was that he knew so many people, and there was only one Robert Ruark.

I don't remember a single trip when Bob didn't return in a complete state of shock, whether it was from New York or Africa, and generally a week or so would pass before he managed to get his feet on the ground and commence work. Not all of his degenerated condition could be attributed to high living, but there would invariably be a severe nervous reaction and the necessity to calm down after a tiring trip.

It seemed that for Robert Ruark there was no answer to the problem of alcohol, despite his own efforts to reduce his consumption. Owing to all the circumstances in his life, the unhappy truth was that there really was no solution. This is made more than clear in a pathetic letter to Harold Matson written in July, 1962, when Ruark returned to Palamos after yet another trip:

"I found in Mozambique and for the short time in Kenya that the booze was beginning to smack me hard again, and that last two weeks in New York damn near killed me. It was just one more whisky lunch in a series of interminable conferences.

"Actually, every time I go on the wagon I wonder why I fell off the last time, because I am sleeping well and eating well and feeling wonderful again, but, as you say, there ain't no wagon in Manhattan, and I have to stay half stiff to stand the bloody place."

After Bob's trips, his letters would always refer to the rough time he'd had, and here is one of the shortest notes he wrote to anyone, and I think it was probably the last letter written to Ginny before his death. "Dear Baby. Back home in one piece after the usual shattering New York experience. Please let me know what the doctor said. I will write you in detail later but right now I am up to my ass in escrows. Much love."

Ginny was always worried about Bob's health, since she knew he didn't look after himself at all. But the main worry was the drinking, and they both knew that they would be much fitter without so much whisky. Bob admitted that his sinus problems were really caused by whisky and cigarettes, but he figured the discomfort caused was worth it. Broadly speaking, I think a proportion of Bob's complaints, while not being imaginary, were to some extent exaggerated or at least self-created. All that was really necessary would have been taking reasonable care and getting suitable rest.

After the Ruarks were divorced, they met periodically when Bob was in New York, and on the last occasion, less than three months before he died, Ginny implored him to get a medical checkup. She could see that he was ill and drinking heavily. Ginny was recovering from a lung operation, and Bob and everyone was concerned about her. Yet as an old Australian friend who was also in New York at the time said: "Don't worry about Ginny, it's Bob who won't last, and if he gets out of New York alive I'll be surprised."

Despite everyone's efforts to stop Bob's drinking, he never really stopped for very long. His attitude seemed to be: "Do I want to live as the person I am and know, or do I want to live for the rest of my life with a stranger?" If it was a question to be decided by himself, he said he preferred a short, active life to a long, dull one.

Part of this losing battle with alcohol had been recorded as far back as 1951 when Louis Sobol wrote in a column:

"Paragrapher Robert Ruark drinks a farewell double scotch at 21 and announces sadly that it is the last drink he will ever have for the rest of his life – on doctor's orders." Then in a later column by Earl Wilson, he stated "Bob Ruark's friends are again worrying about his liver." Bob often referred to the advances of medical science and figured that when he really needed some replacements, such as a new liver, that a transplant would be possible.

I really think that Robert Ruark had always been well aware of his alcoholic problem, yet despite all his promises, he was never able to come to grips with it. In fact, I don't really think he wanted to come to grips. This was evident on many occasions, and in this respect it is significant that when in New York the year before he died, he pointedly declined an invitation to attend a play that to some extent was a blueprint of his own life.

The play was about the Welsh poet, Dylan Thomas, and had been taken from the book by his wife, *Left Over Life to Kill*. The theme was the life of Thomas, his genius, his success, and finally the destruction of his life by alcohol. The play ends with the poet's return to the bottle with full knowledge that this time it will kill him – a kind of suicide by alcohol.

Bob said emphatically that he did not wish to see the play, as he knew the story and was annoyed that the suggestion to attend should have been made at all. He said, pointedly, "Don't you think that for me it is too close for comfort?"

Even on his deathbed in London, Bob was still making promises to the effect that he would not drink any more once he got well. At this stage, sadly, it was much too late to be making promises about the future.

Chapter 26
PLAYBOY BOB

As a part of Bob's general and alcoholic decline, and particularly when he was in London, he took to gambling in numerous clubs. The activity was most unusual for him as he had never bothered much with gambling on a regular basis. The object certainly didn't appear to be to win money, as he was a bad gambler and seemed to go more with the object of losing than anything else. He would figure to lose about a thousand pounds a night, was irrational and erratic, and would completely ignore any friendly advice to go a little slower. He preferred to play blackjack and would often run three games at once. He would usually be quite drunk.

Bob was popular in the clubs and the club owners would often say: "We don't wish to take Bob's money." While they may have meant it, they took it just the same. On the occasion when Bob received a $2,500 legacy from an Uncle Fletcher, he went out the same evening, lost the lot, and then passed it off as a joke. "Uncle wouldn't have minded," he said, "and anyway, it was only spending money," which was his attitude toward all money.

This last gambling spree came at a particularly bad time. Bob was short of money in all directions. He hadn't worked properly for a long time and was having to make transfers from a dwindling Swiss bank account. He would have been the first to agree that he had his share of the good things in life, that life owed him nothing and he had savored it in full, and certainly he dipped deeply into the joys of the female sex. It is really only necessary to read his books, especially *Poor No More* and *The Honey Badger*, to know that Bob had done his research properly and with a great deal of enthusiasm.

The truth of the matter was that Bob was a compulsive womanizer. He propositioned practically every girl he spoke to and maintained that if he could make them laugh he could get them into bed. Bob was generally scheming and planning to acquire some new paramour, and he would go to great, involved lengths to get his wish.

Among Bob's many conquests was the woman who suddenly developed toothache while her husband unsuspectingly went to a bullfight. This project involved a 30-minute taxi ride to Palamos for the wife. Since a bullfight only lasts about an hour and a half, there was the possibility that the husband would return before she could get back to their hotel in order to pretend she was still suffering from toothache.

Then there was the time when Bob flew from Barcelona to Nice, a halfway meeting point for a girlfriend from Rome. At the same time I drove the Rolls Royce to Nice. The intention was for Bob and his girlfriend to tour southern

France and then return to Barcelona by road, but this plan turned into a complete failure. At the time Ginny was due to return from the States, though her arrival date was uncertain. So from the start of the trip Bob was nervous, and the closer he got to Spain the more nervous he became. He feared he might find Ginny already in Barcelona. Bob was in such a state at the end of the trip that he drove directly to the airport and packed the girlfriend off on the first departing aircraft without staying a single night in Barcelona.

I didn't really understand why Bob got so nervous on this occasion, as even when Ginny was present it didn't necessarily make a difference in his womanizing. She always had to be vigilant when there were other women around. She would sometimes complain that she had to be watchful even with her own friends when it came to Bob's wandering eye.

Bob wasn't always successful with women. On one occasion a well-known, strikingly beautiful friend turned up for the first time without the handicap of her husband. As bad luck would have it, Bob already had a woman present. He cursed his luck for a long while afterwards, since this particular conquest had been a goal of his for years.

Bob was always on the lookout and found that airports were good for collecting new girlfriends. Often he would have his traveling companion singled out even before boarding the airport bus. There was the time at the Barcelona airport when we were having our usual final discussion prior to Bob's departure for New York. We were seated in the lounge when we both glanced up just in time to see a shapely female rear disappearing through the customs barrier. Immediately cutting off the conversation and jumping to his feet, Bob said: "Alan, that's mine. Goodbye. See you next month." He rushed off, leaving a number of important questions unanswered. He later reported to me that he had been successful in his quest.

Occasionally Bob got his lines crossed, like when three girls turned up at the same time in Mombasa. I don't recall how he got out of that one, though I doubt it presented any great problem for him. Usually at his cocktail parties there were three or four women who would be making a special claim on his affections even as they hissed at each other. Bob was like a magnet, and wherever he was, he would create problems for himself. This excerpt from a letter written in New York is a case in point.

"Speaking of female logic your beautiful friend Beth arrived in New York to watch Gretel lose the cup and was prepared to stay with me forever with or without matrimony. As I find it difficult to maintain a steady schedule of a minimum of four space shots a day and still get one well done, I was forced to disagree with her. Nymphomaniacs are fun but I am past my first youth so I fled to Fort Lauderdale where the action is less brisk. There was also the complication that Miss Debbie has some sort of claim on my charm and walking between raindrops in New York was rather trying on my already ravished nervous system."

This was actually a postscript to a letter addressed to a Kenyan friend and written at the time of the impending divorce. It inadvertently fell in Ginny's hands. She was absolutely furious with indignation and said she intended to use the letter as evidence of Bob's infidelity.

Life around Robert Ruark was always lively and humorous, though one particular visit to London brought real excess. In the space of one week there were seven girls through the apartment, though I believe there were two repetitions. One of these girls stayed well into the next morning and got mixed up with the cleaning woman. Our wonderful cockney charlady had commenced her cleaning duties in the office only to find a completely naked girl on the floor. She considered it her duty to report the fact to the Master, as she wished to get on with her dusting. Knocking on Ruark's door, she was heard to say: "Good morning Mr. Ruark, excuse me please, but there is a strange naked girl on the office floor. What shall I do?"

There was a short pause, and then a brief, muffled answer came from the bedroom: "Kerist – feed her!"

A few days later Bob had to get up early and left a girlfriend behind in bed, still asleep. On his return in the afternoon he found a short note on the pillow containing one word – "Really!"

Bob was funny with his girlfriends. Although he went to great lengths to transport them around the world, he explained to me many times that he didn't want so many "broads around the house." He thought it better that way because no particular woman would get any special ideas.

To Bob, a woman was just another woman. He loved them all, though he didn't want any particular one all the time and said so frequently. So he had frequent changes, and if they couldn't come to him, then he would go to them, though he would not always disclose the real object of a given trip. Sometimes he would give the strangest reasons. For example, he once made a trip from Spain to Paris, ostensibly for the sole reason of making a telephone call to New York. He said the connection from Paris was better than from Barcelona.

On one occasion, to my considerable distress, Bob seduced a pretty young cousin of mine. That was the only time we ever had cross words. During a discussion and in answer to Bob's question as to where my cousin should reside on a return visit to Palamos, I pointed out that she was different from his other girlfriends and should not sleep in the "bridal chamber." Bob's immediate reply was: "In that case, you have just lost a cousin and I have acquired a new girlfriend." But I knew Bob, and so didn't make any more of the incident. I knew it wouldn't have made any difference if I had produced a pretty mother.

Bob had considerable charm if he bothered to turn it on. Then too, girls' heads were easily turned with the high-powered pressure of a good-looking rich and famous author who had so much fun and vitality to share and who could speak interestingly about so many foreign adventures and successful projects.

Apart from Robert Ruark's attractive personality, he had something else going in his favor which, once discovered, his girlfriends were quite reluctant to relinquish. When boasting about his prowess as a lover, he would talk excitedly and explain that he was aided and abetted by a more than adequate sexual organ, which was made even more effective because of a large bump near the end as the result of a rather clumsy circumcision. This additional asset put women completely in his power. As an added inducement, they didn't have to worry about becoming pregnant as Bob was sterile.

Bob was extremely attentive to all his women friends. Although he referred to them as honey badgers in his book by that title, he made each one feel that she was the only one who mattered. He employed a number of effective gimmicks, such as usually lighting two cigarettes himself, then handing one over. Sometimes by the look in their eyes it was easy to see that this single act endeared him to them as their personal property. They would then get an extra feeling of possessiveness when Bob would repeatedly elect to dine at home. Many of his visitors were unduly influenced, thinking this was some special and cozy treatment for them alone. They had no way of knowing that he almost never wished to go out for dinner.

Nearly all of Bob's female visitors had the possibility of marriage in their heads. Certainly, some of them were led along these lines, mostly out of kindness at the time so as not to upset them. Also, they would all, at some time and in some form, have been in love with him.

Something the continuous stream of honey badgers didn't realize was that in Spain there are two distinct types of women as well as a distinct difference between respectability and non-respectability. Maybe in Anglo-Saxon countries a woman who becomes a temporary mistress would not be heavily criticized, but here in Spain, especially in so small a village as Palamos, she loses all respect from the ordinary Spaniard. While the village people appeared to accept these women because they were friends of Senor Ruark, they were mostly sniggered at behind their backs.

This was something Bob never seemed to understand, and he would even take his female companions into one particular bar in Barcelona where the women normally present were purely business girls. Bob always insisted, however, that these bar girls were all doctors' receptionists or secretaries. Presumably that is what they told him. Bob would not normally bother with professional women, but he did have some interesting encounters with one in Barcelona. She was not only very attractive, but also had the name of Inmaculada Concepción (Immaculate Conception). To Bob, this put the whole procedure in a different light.

Although Bob Ruark had friends all over the world and many people liked him tremendously, he wouldn't normally admit to having a best friend. If anyone claimed that title, he had been known to suggest "then we had better start to knock off the friendship department." Bob would not be knowingly possessed in any way whatsoever, and remembering this well during a discussion concerning Somerset Maugham's adoption plans for his secretary, I made it quite clear to him that I didn't wish to be adopted by him.

Of course Bob made enemies, and in actual fact some very violent ones. This was mainly through his writing. I do believe, however, that even those who did not agree with his views and who had been angered by what he wrote would at least have admired him for his outspoken opinion. Some of the people who disliked Bob only knew him slightly, and the basis of their dislike seemed to be purely envy of his talents and successes. There was really only one person who had legitimate grievances against Bob. That was Ginny, and she never ceased to love him.

All those who knew Bob well were very fond of him and to most people he was a unique character, one who was described in varied ways. Some saw him as flamboyant and resplendent, some as a whirlwind, and some as a delight. Author John Phillips envisioned him as wearing a Japanese kimono with a dry martini in one hand and a Lugar pistol in the other while walking down the beach shooting crabs.

Chapter 27
'I KNOW HE'S A BASTARD'

There had been domestic crises between the Ruarks in the past when there were overtones of separation or divorce. At one time when they lived in New York, Bob actually left Ginny for six months and then returned to try again. On this occasion there had been another woman in the picture. The joke around New York was that Ginny agreed to give Bob a divorce, but said he would have to marry the other woman as a condition of the divorce. This was sufficient to bring him scurrying back to Mama.

Then on Bob's arrival in Spain in 1953, and before Ginny was there, he gave his new local friends a highly critical description of her. When she did arrive, a number of people were wondering just what sort of demon she was. They were surprised to discover she was charming, normal and a human being. Bob spoke of divorce at this juncture as well, but if he was really serious, it is difficult to understand how he could undertake the big project of buying property and completely renovating a home if he really meant to terminate the most important part of his life – his marriage. It is also noteworthy that when purchased, the property was put in joint ownership.

Among the many times Bob contemplated changing his marital status, there was the occasion after the couple had been in Spain a few years when he expressed every intention of divorcing Ginny in order to remarry. When matters reached the critical stage, however, he did not have the courage to tell Ginny. Instead, he set to work on a new book.

Many people felt it was only a matter of time until the Ruarks' marriage would break up, though since it had continued for so many years, one felt it might be an institution that could weather all storms. Nevertheless, the beginning of the end came when Bob brought another woman to the Costa Brava, or so Ginny thought. If she has to, a wife can suffer "other women" at close quarters, but not "another woman." That was the case with Ginny.

Because of Bob's many trips and frequent absences from home, I spent a vast amount of time with Ginny. So when Bob left during the summer of 1962 with the announced intention of more or less leaving for good, or at least until his matrimonial status was straightened out, he left me, as he put it, "in charge of the problem." At that time Ginny really did need someone to look after her. She had worked herself into a highly emotional, neurotic state as a result of what had been, in all respects, a most difficult summer.

To start with, our big poodle, Mamselle had died of cancer after an operation. This upset Ginny a great deal. Then too, she had health problems, suffering on and off from amoebic dysentery and chronic sinusitis. Then, to keep things lively, she had been accusing Bob of a great many things. Among her accusations was that he had "imported" his Kenyan mistress and planted her in my house for the summer. The visit was expressly for the purpose of helping the woman with a book she was writing, and to be sure, Bob was always willing to help other authors.

This type of assistance annoyed Ginny a great deal, even more so when the author turned out to be an authoress. Ginny had warned Bob quite clearly when she learned of the plan, more or less giving him an ultimatum to the effect that there would be big trouble if he persisted. Bob did persist, but there was no way he could convince Ginny that the visit was purely an innocent friendship, even though the woman came with her family.

That summer Bob had intended to start his next big book, The Honey Badger, but the mistress accusation became an obsession with Ginny to the point it was almost impossible for him to work. Accordingly, he took off for London in great confusion. This was really the beginning of the end of their marriage and quite soon Bob's divorce talk became more definite. Within a month Bob left for the United States with the stated intention of staying away until his nervous system had been repaired.

For several months afterward Ginny was in a very bad way. We went to London where she was treated for her nervous condition and also for alcoholism. This was basically a complete waste of time and money, since she continued to drink and continued to be nervous. Of course, Ginny really had only one problem – Bob. She realized that maybe this time she really was going to lose him. This sent her almost out of her mind, and it seemed impossible to stop her drinking. I did the best I could for her, but I got tired of hauling her out of her soup, or off the floor, crying and wailing all the while and not making even a single attempt to pull herself together.

I wanted her to stop drinking, begin to look good again, and then let Bob see a changed woman, or at least some of the girl he used to know. I felt that this could be the only possible path to reconciliation, but there was nothing I could do. I tried to decrease her alcohol intake by various methods, even to the point of watering down all the bottles on the bar. The most effective method was to insist on pouring Ginny's drinks myself. For instance, in the case of whisky, to place the ice in first, then the water, which she always took, and then last of all the whisky. She would take a sip, notice that the whisky seemed to be all right and fail to observe that the drink's color was decidedly anemic.

In so many, many ways Ginny was truly a wonderful person. She could be very kind, generous and a lot of fun. She had a good sense of humor and most people liked her immensely. But Bob sometimes had other opinions and said that she had a knack of not being able to let a thing go. He felt she would always drag up some unhappy event from the past just when things were going along happily and peacefully. She was never able to ignore what she knew or suspected he had been up to on a trip. Accordingly, when Bob returned, there would invariably be tension as if he had been a naughty boy (usually he had, though there would be no immediate proof of this).

During one of their many drunken discussions, which hovered between quarrels and matrimonial drinking, Ginny threw at him an incident that had happened in Australia ten years earlier. She accused him of sleeping with a certain girl (ironically, Bob swore to me that this was one of the few he hadn't slept with). This was the first time Bob bent the fire poker, and afterwards he would boast that he subsequently made a special trip to Australia just to seduce the woman in question.

Ginny learned of Bob's activities from several sources, but I wasn't one of them. I never once passed on information concerning Bob's extracurricular escapades, which was only common sense in my case. If I had, I would have been fired in a hurry. My silence made Ginny angry on many occasions. She realized there was no point in asking me for information, though she knew very well that I had it. In frustration, she consumed more whisky than she should have. Here, Bob was cruel. He knew Ginny loved him, and of course the more she drank, the less he liked her. Yet it was his fault that she drank more.

Periodically Ginny would make an attempt to decrease her intake of alcohol, usually during one of Bob's absences. The idea was to set a good example when he returned. She never, ever made a completely dry run, but a week or two before his expected return she would try. About the closest she ever came to not drinking was when she would commence the "bottle of champagne a day treatment" as a step to becoming completely dry.

Unfortunately, any progress she made in fighting the drinking problem would be forgotten once Bob returned. It was extremely difficult for her not to drink along with Bob. Then once she started drinking, she would begin to wonder what exactly he had been up to during his most recent trip. Soon emotional annoyance would set in and the endless cycle of arguments would resume.

When these domestic arguments were in full swing, Ginny would appear in my office after breakfast and cautiously say to me: "Has he said anything this morning? Last night Bobby was going to divorce me." Then she would toddle off in the direction of the bar.

Although many arguments occurred, to my knowledge Bob and Ginny only once came to actual blows. This was in Barcelona, when for the express purpose of punching Ginny in the eye, Bob removed her glasses and afterwards replaced them. The next morning she had a blackened eye and was wearing dark glasses. She explained to the maids that she had fallen down the single step leading into the powder room.

This incident was the climax of an argument about other women and the result of a frustrated outburst in which Ginny suggested Bob must have turned queer. Apparently at the time, as far as their personal relations were concerned, there was no way of knowing that this was not the case.

Ginny didn't contain her criticism of Bob to just the two of them. She often informed her girlfriends that, judging by his present performance at home, that Bob must be impotent. Yet she would usually terminate any criticism of Bob by saying: "Sure, I know he is a bastard – but I love him."

Their arguments covered matters other than sex and infidelity. For example, when Bob once explained to Ginny that he wanted to paint and become known "as a Costa Brava Picasso," he seemed to expect some encouragement from her. Instead, she replied "that will be the day, Beauregard." At this point the artistic discussion came to an abrupt conclusion as Bob grabbed the poker and bent it in half. Another time the poker needed straightening was in the aftermath of a financial squabble when Ginny accused Bob of having "pissed away all the *Something of Value* money on booze, safari and taxidermy."

I am not at all sure whether Robert Ruark was ever actually in love at any time in his life. I just don't believe he had that facility in his makeup. He simply would not be possessed completely by any one person. Although he had been known to state his love for Ginny, it was often with reservations. I do believe that she was the best possible wife he could have found. She lasted 24 years; I doubt very much if any other woman could have lasted 24 weeks. Nearly all women in their various ways loved him, and that was the trouble. Bob had too many female options, but he couldn't live with any of them very long. Yet he needed their company just about all the time.

One woman, however good in all respects, was just not sufficient, for a number of reasons. Bob needed an audience, and he needed it on a daily basis. Even though an admiring wife could try quite hard to meet this need, Bob had to go on a wider plan. This wasn't necessarily sexual. As a complete extrovert, he needed continual outside contact for himself and for his writing, a requirement that did not lend itself to a harmonious marriage.

There were times when Bob and Ginny were happy together, and their marriage could have and should have been a complete success. They had a great deal in common – a high degree of intelligence and conversational ability, vibrant senses of humor, a mutual love of books and reading, a wanderlust travel desire, and a shared lack of interest in any active sport for themselves as they both preferred to sit down and drink as a pastime.

The thing they didn't share in common was that Bob had a great love of hunting, while Ginny didn't really care for it. She was a city girl at heart, and I think Bob finally decided against taking her on any more African trips after one particular safari when she did nothing but play gin rummy with another disinterested woman. Ginny told me that a lot of the time spent on safari was boring and quite uncomfortable. But I don't think this was a particularly important difference. Safari activity was really part of Bob's business, and surely it is not a requirement of a happy marriage for the wife to understand or to like all aspects of her husband's business. Yet Bob never really understood Ginny's disinterest in safari.

Shortly before the divorce, and after a period when they hadn't been getting along well, Bob decided to make another trip to India, to be followed immediately by a safari in East Africa. The main object of the Indian portion of the trip, apart from Bob's own desire to return to the subcontinent, was to take Ginny along in order, as he put it, to keep "the old girl happy." Despite Bob's good intentions, the whole thing ended in absolute and complete disaster. Everything from accidents to general discomfort to bad health went wrong.

The trouble started on arrival at the shikar camp. Owing to poor organization by the Indians, Bob's rifles and typewriter had been held up by customs officials. His liquor and cigarette supply had been temporarily lost, and he had to start off by drinking Indian gin. Then there was Bob's accident with the leopard, his general displeasure at the way the shikar had been run, and the hurried exodus from India. By the time they arrived in Nairobi, Bob was not the only casualty. Ginny had developed a serious attack of amoebic dysentery, and Bob's grand idea had foundered completely.

They returned home separately. Ginny arrived first and suffered for many months with her complaint. It was certainly worsened and kept going because she insisted on drinking hard spirits, never mind the fact that she had been told that alcohol was the worst thing for her complaint.

Apart from Ginny's disenchantment with hunting trips, the casual onlooker might have thought the Ruarks got along fine, with considerable friendliness and good humor between them. Despite outward signs of compatibility, things were often not right. Bob sometimes insisted that Ginny drove him away on trips by her imaginary accusations and righteous attitude. In truth, I discovered over the years that Bob's desire to depart was not necessarily in order to escape wifely control. He often left just for the sake of leaving or because he had been stationary for a few weeks.

Whenever Bob returned from a trip, he would vow that he had no intention of traveling again, saying that all he wanted to do was settle down to a quiet life with the dogs and get on with his writing. The chances were, of course, that he wouldn't stay put for long. Interestingly, while Bob said Ginny drove him away, she was also responsible for keeping him at home when there was a book in production, when it was difficult for Bob to find a suitable excuse for leaving.

If Ginny was not present at such times, Bob would work for a time, then be off again to London, Madrid or Paris. Or on one occasion he went to Angola via Lisbon on a wild goose chase to report on the hijacked Portuguese ship, the *Santa Maria*. This was a trip he really didn't need. We were in the middle of *Uhuru* and well behind schedule. Of course, Bob didn't need any excuse to travel, and there were times when he seemed to keep himself in perpetual motion. About the only thing that would keep him fixed for a good spell was a hard deadline for a book or, on many occasions, the presence of his wife.

Because of Bob's seemingly endless trips, each time things came to a boiling point in his marriage, there would be a period of separation that left the status quo intact but dangling in uncertainty. This avoided forcing the issue and divorcing. Or, instead of a trip, Bob would pitch himself headlong into a new book. He could not or would not face the problems of any serious change in his life. He usually referred to such possibilities as "too much of a troop movement, with the necessity of dividing the dogs and the silver."

Whatever his matrimonial shortcomings, nobody could fault Bob as a provider. He never put any control on Ginny's spending and all bank accounts were joint ones. Nor was there any control on travel, and some years Ginny traveled as much as he did. Bob was always most generous, and this was particularly the case when it came to purchase of furs. Once in Nairobi he purchased Ginny a striking full-length coat made from carefully selected dark leopard skins. This priceless coat was later stolen while the Ruarks were at a cocktail party in London, but it was covered by insurance.

Later, Bob managed, with considerable difficulty, to buy Ginny a second leopard coat. Then the first stolen coat was recovered by Scotland Yard, and he found himself with two leopard coats and the necessity of refunding the insurance money.

Bob often said jokingly, but with meaning, that just about everything and everyone cost him money. In truth, though his operation was a fairly big one, he made it a great deal bigger. It wasn't just the Palamos property and the apartments in Barcelona and later in London. It was that both Bob and Ginny would often be somewhere else staying in expensive hotel suites. For long periods they would be at the Savoy in London or at the Elysée in New York, or maybe Bob would be off on safari. The end result was that at any one time there were three or four separate financial expenditures on living alone.

The Ruarks had nearly always lived separately for long periods, and one begins to wonder why it was necessary to go to all the bother and expense of a divorce. Bob explained to me that he didn't want to feel guilty every time he did something he knew he shouldn't do. He figured a divorce would give him the freedom he wanted.

When Bob left Palamos after the dreadful summer of 1962, he first went to London for a short spell, then returned home briefly before setting off for the U.S. After a week or so and having spoken with various friends, he wrote a casual, friendly letter to Ginny, apparently trying to sum up every aspect of their domestic problems. He addressed Ginny's emotional problems and alcoholism in detail, and then turned to the financial aspects of a divorce. He stressed "an equable division of what is jointly owned, plus a guaranteed share of actual earnings."

While he said little regarding his own shortcomings, Bob did go to the heart of the entire matter, at least from his perspective, when he wrote: "I do not want a divorce, and I DO NOT WANT TO MARRY ANYBODY. I think you will agree that I am lousy husband material." He urged Ginny to take better care of herself and not worry about him, and then concluded, "I love you, strange as it may sound."

I kept Bob advised of Ginny and her state of health and wrote many letters in an effort to influence him in thinking clearly and carefully about the finality of divorce. The basis of my message was that Bob and Ginny should think of the future when they would be a little older and not so active, and when thoughts of the past would become more important. I pointed out that they had enjoyed so many good experiences together and suggested they think in terms of all the people they had known mutually. Surely their great number of good friends should add up to satisfaction together, not separately.

I dwelt heavily on what would happen to the house in Palamos. They both loved it and it meant so much to them in terms of hard work and accomplishment. I told them that if they divorced, the property would almost certainly fall into disuse. Later I was to be proven right in this respect, and the divorce led to what amounted to the destruction of their wonderful home. Unfortunately, all of my efforts were of no avail.

Bob freely admitted to me that he had been at fault in staying married for 24 years and then suddenly insisting on a termination. He realized that he should have taken the step when they were much younger, when he first began to realize that things were not going to work out. He agreed he was poor marriage material. Although he had been on the verge of divorce a number of times, one thing seems quite certain. If he hadn't landed in the Doctor's Hospital in Washington in October, 1962, after breaking his hip from a horse fall, there would not have been a divorce.

He had been off with his friend Walker Stone, spending a few days on his Virginia property during the final pre-divorce runaway period, when according to Bob:

"I mounted the oldest, slowest plug on the place, and ten minutes later wound up with a broken pelvis. This horse was never known to go faster than a slow walk before, but he suddenly went mad and pitched me into the daisies. I lit on my right hip and put a nice crack in it."

Apparently a bee stung the horse's rear and it took off like a rocket. In a moment of quick decision as to what was the least dangerous thing to do, try and stay on the horse's back or get off as it proceeded down a steep bank, Bob decided to throw himself onto the ground.

During the time Bob lay in hospital, wrapped in a plaster cast with nothing much else to do but think, he gradually got himself properly acclimatized to the idea of divorce. In fact, having once made up his mind, it seemed he was unable to change it. I do believe, however, that at various stages of the divorce procedure he was not quite sure why he was divorcing Virginia.

Bob admitted many times that he loved Ginny, sometimes adding "in my fashion," an expression that didn't please her much. She seemed to think their marriage was a sort of institution that wouldn't change. She always maintained that she loved Bob, and I am quite sure this love was genuine. She was mostly faithful . . . but unhappy for long periods.

Ginny told me that there were spells when she and Bob had been very happy together, but the trouble usually started when Bob began to be Robert Ruark in his natural way of spreading himself around. This part of him you couldn't change, nor would anyone have wanted to do so. That's the way he was, but from a wifely point of view, it was extraordinarily difficult. She told me once that Bob had been unfaithful to her right from the start, but that she had learned to settle for a lesser part of him in order to stay married to the man she loved.

Ginny definitely did not want the divorce and only agreed with the attitude, "Well, if Buster wants it, then what's the good of resisting." She didn't want to upset his book-writing plans, and Bob had said he couldn't write any more because of her. This of course, was a figment of Bob's imagination, though in time it became an obsession. With that in mind, Ginny could see no point in trying to fight the divorce. Here she was wrong, and certainly Bob was wrong. He wasn't divorcing her for anyone else. He was just taking off in order to get out of the house, though possibly from the perspective of pride, this was more damaging to Ginny than if Bob had been leaving her for another woman.

During the fall and winter months of 1962 Bob and Ginny exchanged a series of bitter letters filled with recriminations, and there was no hint from Bob of a change of heart. As the letters between them became increasingly accusatory and hostile, it seemed fairly certain Bob really was going to divorce Ginny. Towards the end of the year, Ginny left Barcelona, where she had been staying, for New York. From then on I received a number of pathetically sad and demoralized letters from her. She realized there was nothing she could do to stop a divorce she didn't want.

(*Editor's Note:* At this point in his manuscript, Ritchie included many of the Ruarks' letters in their entirety. Following are a few excerpts from Bob's letters that readers might find interesting:)

"The prime bad joke of American history is the husband's fear of the 'little woman'; the right of the litte woman to 'give the husband hell'; the popular habit of calling the wife the 'ball and chain'; the bad gags about who wears the pants in the family – and finally, a husband who is always guilty until proved innocent. And, in the proof of innocence, the resentment of the innocence lingers, along with all the memories of real and/or fancied injustices, until they weld into a great ball of resentment – a resentment that pops up in every argument about anything, and winds up with 'you're another,' and 'remember what you did.' "

* * * *

"I am a rover, I am a loner and I am selfish. Perhaps MacKenzie was right when he said: 'Get rid of him; writers will kill you,' so very many years ago."

* * * *

"I am sorry that fate separated us so much at first. Perhaps if there had been no sportswriting, no war, and then no column, I might have conformed more. If there had been no Africa, no Spain, no novels – I don't know."

From the start of this final domestic squabble, there really never was much possibility of the outcome being any different, but there was always some hope until the *fait accompli*. This came on January 18, 1963, and I first learned of the divorce in a cable from Ginny: "NO CHANCE RECONCILIATION. ROBERTO FAIRLY PLEASANT SO FAR BUT ADAMANT. STOP DIVORCED TOMORROW. SAD AND SORRY. ALERT MAIDS. LOVE – GINNY."

Then Ginny provided me details in a letter written later the same day:

The agreement is roughly this. I give up the house, and that is the part that kills me, and there is no way I could ever have it again unless Bobby wills it to me. I'm so damn sentimental about it and I have put so much into it that this was the stumbling block. However I have the use of it for three (or four) more years during July and August. Roberto assures me that I will always have the use of it

on a friendly basis but what it doesn't say on paper is never certain. Bobby has the right to use it this summer because he is going to have to do that book.

In return he gave me $100,000 which is just about what it would cost if I moved bag and baggage back to N. Y.

I have alimony of one-fourth of his gross income, which sounds like a lot but I have to pay taxes on it and have no deductions, so if I get $35,000 a year for instance I am only left with $18,000 to spend. I cannot keep the London flat beyond this year unless I get terribly smart and rent it or figure out some deductions. Actually Bobby wants the London flat too so if I have to move out I have agreed to try and get it for him (It is in my name, remember?) There are some furniture agreements as to who gets what. I gave up the Southport house, cars, etc., and that is about it.

My lawyer seems to feel that I have quite a good deal, but I don't quite agree with him. However there is one thing for certain, I'm going to have to change my way of living to a vastly down-graded standard.

For his part, Bob also wrote a letter to me confirming that he was in fact divorced.

It looks very much as if most of the divorce business has been completed, including property settlements, alimony, and all of the rest of the dirty details. It has not been nearly so sad as I expected and Virginia is so much improved over her condition when I left that I think that the kindest thing I might have done was exactly what I did. She will be more than amply provided for and we will be broke for quite some time to come. I intend of course, to maintain the full staff and the status will remain almost exactly the same except for the absence of Virginia. I HAVE NO INTENTION OF REMARRIAGE! Assure the cook.

The whole proceedings – the proper settlement and divorce proceedings – have been most amicable and we have both been blessed with good lawyers. There has been no publicity, no scandal, no mud slinging on either side, for which God be praised. The whole proceedings may sound sad to you, but not nearly so sad as what we had and I for one feel better than for years. My hip has healed beautifully, sobriety has afflicted me, and we are in for a long, dry winter and spring.

We have a good new novel called *The Honey Badger*, not about Africa, with which everyone here is terribly excited. As you can imagine, I can't wait to get back home and go to work, to see that old '97 and her opposite number are in good working order. I can impress on you one more thing – due to certain banking peculiarities it is necessary that we have a publishable first draft of *The Honey Badger* before June 1, which means be careful driving, don't go skiing, and I positively forbid you to catch another hepatitis.

So there it was – finished – against Ginny's wishes, though presumably what Bob wanted. Divorce in Juarez, Mexican style, January 18, 1963, after what Bob termed as a "friendly affair" and Ginny as an "unavoidable tragedy and emotional error." Twenty-four years of marriage was at an end. Robert Ruark had finally gotten his freedom, but this freedom didn't work out the way he thought it would. He found he did not have the rudder and control to which he had been accustomed. No doubt the lack of control pleased him, and at first it seemed as if he had a greater peace of mind. As time went by, though, he did less work and drank more. At the same time his liver decided to give up the fight.

While his girlfriends didn't really become any more numerous, they probably became more lethal in his freer, unshackled capacity. Then, too, I think that as he continued to go his own way more than ever, he possibly felt even more guilt than he had before the divorce. He realized he had made Ginny terribly unhappy and found that a 24-year marriage was hard to get out of the system. Certainly, Bob immediately began to be extra kind to Ginny, with such offers as a paid trip to Australia. He appeared to be genuinely sorry he had divorced, but the bitterness remained. The Ruarks kept in touch periodically after their divorce, but Ginny usually managed to make Bob very angry. He concluded one of his letters by asking: "Why don't you quit being a bitch?"

Ginny no doubt felt that she was being shortchanged in the divorce agreement, and she really got upset when she heard about Bob's intention to build a large house on a property he was buying in Virginia. It was about 150 acres of farming meadowland in Rappahannock County alongside a property owned by his friend Walker Stone. Apart from the house-building project, the intention was to make a suitable lake and then to stock quail and ducks to make a shooting preserve.

Bob had other plans for his property; he intended to import some African plains game such as impala, Thomson's gazelles, nyalas and maybe some waterbuck. None of this came to pass and the house construction was never carried out as it was soon realized that there was insufficient money. Nevertheless, learning of this intended project, plus knowing that Bob was about to go on another expensive safari, was just too much for Ginny's peace of mind.

After Bob's death I endeavored to straighten out some of the differences Ginny had created following the divorce, as I realized they were mostly caused through drink and emotional stress. We became friends again, which was the way it should have been, as old friends are the most important. Really this patch-up came about because I said: "Look here, Ginny, it's all my fault, I'm sorry, let's forget it." My experience has been that some women (Editor's note: Ginny appeared to be one of them, in Ritchie's view) don't ever give way, despite their own unhappiness, whether they are right, wrong, unhappy, disenchanted, confused, or whatever. They will never say "Sorry, it was my fault." So in order to put a thing right, it is far better to say sorry to them and forget it. Then maybe they are able to start again as if nothing had happened.

These are only details, and the overall picture of Ginny in retrospect is one of liking, rather than disliking. Despite herself, she was widely loved, and she did have a great and interesting character. Ginny gave out an awful lot to those who knew her. In a nutshell, Ginny was fabulously wonderful in all respects, yet incredibly difficult and impossible on some occasions. She made life interesting, if nothing else.

In her defense, the divorce was a cruel thing for Ginny, and under all the circumstances I saw it as illogical. I couldn't really believe it had actually happened, and when I started to assess the reasons, perhaps the most important one has been largely overlooked; namely, that Robert Ruark changed considerably during the last few years of his life.

In varying degrees, most people who knew Bob well noticed that he had changed. He became somewhat remote and even close friends felt that they had to some extent lost him. This change from the vital, active person he had always been was noted in an obituary column written by Norton Mockridge, a fellow *New York Telegram* columnist, under the title "Requiem for a Long-Lost Friend."

When Bob Ruark died the other day, I didn't know exactly how I felt. I've thought about it since, and I still don't know exactly how I feel.

You see, I met Robert Chester Ruark right after the war when he came up from Washington to the *World-Telegram* and was making like about a hundred bucks a week and was a little staggered by the big city and really didn't know which end was up.

He used to sit with me at the bar in the Barclay Café, a waterfront restaurant near the *World-Telegram*, and the owner, Arthur Kotick, would serve us Johnny Walker Black and water, and Lt. Ruark, late of the U.S. Navy, would tell me how he was gonna take the world by the tail and give it a twist like it sure never had before.

I was a rewrite man then and Ruark wrote a piece in which he called me the best he'd ever known, and I mention this only because it helps establish our relationship. Ruark used to show me his column, fresh from the typewriter, and ask me to "Fix 'er up." Many times as we sat in the Barclay, or other inspirational inns, we'd kick around ideas which soon erupted into columns.

There's nothing wrong with this. I do it myself. Hell, if I didn't get ideas from people much brighter than I, you wouldn't read me. Anyway, as a result of all this, Ruark and I became close friends. For quite a while he had a penthouse at 1016 Fifth Avenue and I had an apartment at 1075 Park Avenue, a few blocks away, and his wife, Ginny, and my wife used to go to Central Park and walk the Ruark dogs and the Mockridge children.

We often partied together – I was at his house the night he gave Ginny a magnificent grand piano, complete with 16 yards of red ribbon tied around it and topped with a big red bow, and Arthur Godfrey played that piano, and Billy Rose jokingly said it was a piece of junk he wouldn't have used underwater in his Aquacade, and Jan Morgan trilled in French and Carol Channing lovingly caressed the pretty piano but reminded everybody: "Diamonds are a girl's best friend!"

And Bob was at my house the night that Tallulah Bankhead and ZaSu Pitts got into a hair-pulling match because Talu was shilling for the Democrats and ZaSu, in comparison with whom the John Birchers look like leftists, took violent exception.

That was the night that Bob discovered that two of my guests, Dr. Brandt Steele and his wife, Dr. Eleanor Steele, were psychiatrists, and sat up until 6:00 a.m., telling them acidly what he thought of "skull feelers." He got so hot he divested himself of jacket, tie, shirt, shoes, and socks – but still he lost.

I was with Bob the day he decided he'd fallen in love with Faye Emerson, and I agreed with him when he said: "Mama sure ain't gonna like this." And I met Bob the day he came back from a round-the-world trip, without Mama, explaining that Ginny had stayed in Hawaii "Cause she needs time to think." And I was there the day she finally came back – but a changed Mama! Her brown hair was bleached a dazzling blond, she had shed twenty pounds or so, she was wearing harlequin glasses studded with brilliants, and she was as alluring as Harlow or Monroe. "If this is what Bob wants, this is what Bob gets," she told me.

I was with Bob on the day that the doctor told him there was no reason he knew of why Bob and Ginny couldn't have children, and Bob said: "I just dunno why. We're healthy as horses. We do everything we're told, and nothin' happens. Ain't that hell!"

And I was around when Bob got some of his first big checks from book publishers (*Grenadine Etching*, *I Didn't Know It Was Loaded*, *Something of Value*, and so on) and we celebrated together. Then, as time went on and Bob got more and more papers on his string, and wrote more books, and sold the books to the movies, and the movies poured millions into his lap, we seldom saw each other any more. He drank a lot and his liver acted up, and his ankles swelled, and his hours were at the wrong end of the clock.

"I got an image I gotta keep up," he told me when we met one night in the bar at the Algonquin. "I gotta travel, roam the world, make the safari, see the people and do the things. I gotta live it while I got it."

It was none of my business, of course, but, anyway, I told him I thought that a guy with gout and cirrhosis and other assorted ailments shouldn't drink so much and chase so hard and live it up so much, and he said, quietly: "Advice like that, I don't need."

"Look," he said, seriously. "I'm better than Papa (referring to his friend, Ernest Hemingway), and I'm gonna prove it. But I gotta move, I gotta have room. I gotta build the right image!"

Well, that was some years ago. In recent years, we didn't get together. A few months ago, I sat only two tables away from Bob in the Laurent Restaurant, a favorite haunt. We were facing each other, and he didn't see me. Mr. Romano, the owner, noticed this. He shrugged and said: "He sees nobody."

Well, I don't know. Maybe Bob caught the image he wanted, or maybe he tripped while chasing it. All I know is, I'm sorry I lost a friend. Not a few days ago. Years ago.

Chapter 28
LIFE'S COMPASS LOST

Possibly for a few years Robert Ruark had the image he wanted or the image he *thought* he wanted . . . of the active and successful writer, the world traveler and big game hunter, the big spender and successful lover. But during the last year or so, many people noticed a change. It was a change from an extremely interesting man to someone not so interesting, to someone who had lost to some extent the full zest for life, to someone who had lost his life's compass. It was a change to someone who even his old and more honest women friends reluctantly said was nowhere near the man he used to be. They said, "He became a bit of a bore and smelled of alcohol and vitamin pills." They still liked him as a friend but sexually they were not keen anymore.

About eight weeks before he died, Bob went to Madrid mainly for the purpose of seeing the Spanish Minister of Information and Tourism in order to obtain a press carnet for an American girlfriend. On this trip, according to some old friends who saw him there, he was not particularly well. They said he was hardly able to walk across the street to go to dinner, not through drunkenness, but through pure fatigue. After the girlfriend's departure from Madrid, where Bob attended a couple of cocktail parties, he was heard to say "Thank God she's gone." That remark didn't really seem logical when one bears in mind that Bob was to leave for London shortly to change his will in her favor.

On arrival in London he didn't appear to be in any better shape. When he went to lunch with an old friend who took him to the Carlton Towers, he ate nothing, didn't talk much, and just sat with a stare. His friend later said: "Bob was staring past me into the distance and was kind of dried up, in sort of a standing up mental collapse." Again he was not particularly drunk, just completely worn out. The next day he signed the changed will.

Many people noticed the decline in Robert Ruark during the final few months of his life. All of us in Palamos saw some change, but we were so used to Bob returning in a completely rundown condition that when he got back two weeks before his death, while he didn't seem very well, in comparison to the normal he didn't seem too bad. Admittedly his loss of weight was noticeable and he did have a gaunt look about him. Overall, though, it appeared to us that this was part of the normal stress and strain, and that all Bob required was a good rest period. We felt that he would then buck up again as he had always done in the past. Plus the fact that Bob himself indicated he was really all right. Also, since we knew he had recently been in New York and London, we felt he would have taken advantage of the ample opportunity for medical attention if it had been required.

Bob had been on a three-week trip to Italy, where, of course, he was accompanied. He then returned to London for a few days before leaving for Palamos with another female companion, the new secretary who was to live in the London apartment and manage things at that end. This was a further indication of his mixed, confused thinking. The last thing we needed at that time was another permanent employee, as for all the work we had done in the past we had managed quite nicely. Only occasionally, when particularly hard pressed, had we obtained some local assistance on a temporary basis. Since Bob had been working less, we certainly didn't need more assistance, quite apart from the matter of expense.

There was also the point that if Bob actually intended to go through with the marriage he had mentioned a month earlier during his previous visit to Palamos, how could he have this young "secretary," who was being mostly used as a girlfriend, living with him just a few days before the expected arrival of the supposed fiancée? It seemed as though poor Bob had reached a point of no return. Many of his actions were quite illogical. This particular girlfriend, for example, was a heavy drinker and also had a heavy hand at the bar. As she poured out drinks, she would say, "The boss says all drinks have to be big."

During this final sojourn in Palamos, Bob wasn't very happy and was drinking excessively. Owing to the circumstances in the house, I was not as close to him as I had been. There was also the added problem that lunch had reached the point where it occurred at five or later in the afternoon on a regular basis. Since I was not prepared to wait so long to eat, I was not sitting in on the midday meal as had been my custom. No work was being done, so I saw very little of Bob. This was unfortunate, because if I had seen more of him, I might have realized better what the true situation was and what was happening to him.

One day Bob explained to me that he didn't feel too good and that he had stomach bloat, so we called in the local doctor. This doctor didn't consider anything serious to be wrong, just an excessive amount of gas, and he prescribed some liver treatment. I was not present for the doctor's visits, as I had usually been in the past, so I was not fully acquainted with what transpired. Apparently the physician said he was not worried in the least.

Bob was always very definite about what he wanted to do, or not do. He didn't wish to see any doctor in Barcelona, though after a discussion one day he agreed that I should make an appointment with the Barcelona doctor he trusted. As it happened this physician was away for a few days, and when he became available, Bob said it wasn't necessary to see him. During this period a number of good, long-standing friends to whom he normally would have listened told Bob to see a reliable doctor at once. He ignored their advice. After his death I was told by one of them that Bob had commented to him, a week or so before his death, that he was finished, that he would be dying quite soon and that all his affairs were straight.

Eventually Bob went down to Barcelona for the purpose of returning his female companion to London and at the same time to meet Nison Tregor, the Polish sculptor. Tregor had completed a bronze head of Bob and was coming by ship from Naples with his work. Bob had sat for this sculpture in Capri on his recent Italian trip, and afterwards I remember Tregor telling me how intense Bob had been. There had been an ever-present urgency to finish the job, as if there might not be sufficient time.

The bust was finished, and Tregor sculpted into the head a remarkable amount of poised apprehension, an impression of dread for the future and a gaunt expectancy of something unknown. I don't know if Bob would have liked the result, but I believe Tregor captured what Bob had in mind – a feeling of impending death. This we shall never know, for Bob did not live to see the finished work. Before Tregor's boat arrived, Bob suffered a serious internal hemorrhage in the Ritz Hotel and was flown to London for surgery.

Bob had been out on the town with his new secretary prior to her departure, had dined on lobster curry the night before and had been more or less drinking his full quota. The next day he was terribly hung over when he went to meet an American friend in the Marfil Bar with the intention of dining together. When the friend saw the condition Bob was in, he insisted that Bob return immediately to the hotel. He did this, but during the night and the next day the hemorrhage increased in seriousness. When the hotel doctor saw him, Bob was told that he should have immediate surgery to stop the bleeding.

Bob's reaction was that if surgery was required then he would go to London, which he should not have been allowed to do as by this time he was in a very bad state. He was losing blood from his rectum, and then began coughing and spitting blood into his handkerchief and periodically passing out on his bed.

The American friend who had arrived to be Bob's house guest was present some of the time, and she helped Bob pack and dress for the journey to London. When Bob was ready, he made what appeared to be one last effort, lifted his favorite over-the-shoulder bag on his own, and walked out of the hotel with that "nothing can happen to me" attitude, as if he were invincible.

On a number of occasions during this drama it was suggested that Palamos be called. Bob replied that this was not to be done, saying "it would only get everybody in an uproar and it is not that serious." This, of course, was quite wrong. Someone in the hotel should have called me and I could have been down to Barcelona within two hours. Also, it is difficult to understand why the doctor in attendance allowed Bob to travel to London. His insistence on doing so should have been ignored as by this time he was really too ill to think correctly. Indeed, he was so ill that when he arrived at the airport, the British European Airways station master initially refused to allow him on the aircraft. After some discussion, he did relent and agreed to let Bob travel.

Bob's American friend had assisted him with the travel arrangements and was present at the airport. Shortly before the flight was announced, he noticed that Bob had a bottle of whisky in his bag and endeavored to stop him from taking it with him. Bob replied to her, "Oh no, I am not going to drink it. I *must* have it – it is always with me. I wouldn't feel right if I didn't have a bottle with me."

This friend later explained to me some of the drama surrounding the incident, "He was dragging and appeared to be forging ahead on a plan which he knew was lost and wrong. He knew he was very ill but it wouldn't have been Robert Ruark if he had admitted it." Then she referred to Bob's actual condition and what he thought at the time: "I could see he was very sick and I thought he was dying."

Despite the obvious seriousness of Bob's condition, he was allowed to travel unaccompanied to London. Right to the end he remained the lone traveler he had always been.

Under the circumstances, it is difficult to appreciate that such a sick man was allowed to go unaccompanied, but unfortunately for Bob, the people around him at this 11th hour did not measure up to the situation. In Palamos there was no message that Bob was seriously ill until after he had arrived in London, but I like to think that things would have been different if I had been present in Barcelona. Maybe I would have started out for the airport, if Bob had insisted, but then would have ended up at one of the excellent clinics. Then Bob would have had no other choice than to stay, as it would have been previously arranged. [Editor's note: This is almost certainly unfair on Ritchie's part. Ruark was so strong-willed he would have overridden any and all objections to a course of action other than the one *he* chose].

From the Ritz Hotel, some telephone calls had been placed to the London apartment advising of his expected arrival. Apparently it was understood on the Barcelona end that arrangements would be made for Ruark to be met at the airport by an ambulance and doctor. The ambulance could have gone alongside the aircraft, thus avoiding the struggle through customs, and then taken him straight to the hospital. None of this happened. He was met by a private hire service car and taken to his apartment in Park Lane, at Fountain House on the seventh floor.

The stress and strain of the journey and the change of pressure during the two-hour flight were too much for his already weak condition, and shortly after his arrival at the apartment, Bob commenced another serious internal hemorrhage, again bleeding from his rectum and coughing blood all over the apartment. By the time he was brought down the elevator and through London traffic to the Middlesex Hospital, it was too late. Of course blood transfusions were given, but Robert Ruark died 48 hours later on the first day of July, 1965.

Bob had died of repeated haematesmesis – bleeding from distended veins on the lower part of the gullet caused by cirrhosis of the liver. Repeated transfusions and an operation did not help. The only operation possible at this stage consisted of the insertion of a tube with a balloon on the end down his gullet. Inflation of the balloon would compress the veins in an effort to stem the loss of blood.

We shall never know whether it would also have been too late if he had stayed in Barcelona, but at least an operation by one of the many excellent surgeons in the city would have been possible. One well-known Spanish surgeon afterwards stated he was very angry he was not given a chance to save Robert Ruark. There was no advantage in going to London. Bob had not gone to see any particular specialist, but to the end Ruark insisted on doing it his way.

CHAPTER 29
LAST TRIP TO PALAMOS

On arrival in London, I learned that full arrangements had already been made for cremation. This didn't seem right to me, since at no time could I recall Bob expressing this as his wish. The only thing I could recall was that whenever the subject came up, Bob would say: "It really doesn't matter much, but plant me in the back lot underneath the pine trees alongside the dogs."

I then had a telephone conversation with Ginny, who was in New York. It was one which I shall never forget in terms of personal distress and tortured bitterness. She was too sick to travel, otherwise she would have been over to London. All I wanted to establish with her was to know her wish for Bob's burial. She did not recommend cremation and could not recollect Bob ever expressing such a desire. I knew what had to be done: The cremation plans would be canceled forthwith and Bob would be taken to Spain for burial in Palamos.

I had come to London with the knowledge that the people in Palamos had offered full facilities for burial in their village, claiming him as their "adoptive son." Since Catholics do not permit cremation, the whole burial procedure had to be changed at short notice. The change in plan was announced as widely as possible, but some people still showed up at the Golders Green crematorium. Among the floral tributes sent, there was one lone orchid with a simple message . . . "With love from Barbara." Barbara was a leading character in his last novel, *The Honey Badger,* which at that time had not been published.

Apparently the intention of the assembled girlfriends in London had been to cremate Bob and then have the ashes brought back to Palamos and sprinkled either in the back yard or out in the Palamos Bay. During one of my many phone calls to Spain to make the necessary arrangements, I mentioned this intention to the staff. They were appalled at the idea, and Bob's personal maid said she would never swim in the bay again if this were done.

On a British European Airways flight from London, we arrived in Barcelona at four in the morning along with a hundred or so tourists who were quite unaware that they had flown with a distinguished world traveler on his last journey. We had brought Robert Ruark, the roving author, back for burial in Palamos, the Spanish village with which he had fallen in love more than a dozen years before.

It was the correct thing to do, as I am sure it would have been Bob's wish. It took a period of ten days from his death to his burial. The whole village turned out either at the service in his garden next to the house, along the roadside, or at the Palamos cemetery where their beloved neighbor was put to rest.

As a clear indication of the esteem they held for their most important resident, Bob was buried in the Catholic section of the cemetery, even though it was well known that he was not Catholic. This had probably never happened before in Spain. Notwithstanding the singularly generous act of the people of Palamos, I rather think Robert Ruark would still be trying to work out exactly how he ended up in a Catholic cemetery, since he had always been high critical of the Catholics. The epitaph on Ruark's gravestone reads: "Gran Amigo de Espana – E. P. D."

Among the many people who journeyed from afar to pay their last respects to Robert Ruark was his old friend, columnist Bob Considine. He wrote two obituary pieces for the *New York Journal American,* appropriately headed "Where Ruark Planted Roots."

Palamos Spain: Bob Ruark's closed coffin of yellow pine looked smaller than the man and his works. It rested in the center of the flower-littered, high-ceilinged study where he hammered out *Something of Value, Poor No More, Uhuru, The Honey Badger,* soon to be published, and more columns and magazine pieces than even he could remember.

His mute Underwood sat by his huge desk. It was spent, too. On the desk lay the familiar clutter of a writer's tools and products, *Roget's Thesaurus,* a dog-eared dictionary, a stack of carbon copies of his last columns, letters opened and unopened.

The spoils of his safaris pressed around the coffin like creatures tremulously met at a water hole. The bier stretched across a rug made of hides of zebras his guns had felled. Like rigid acolytes, two enormous elephant tusks bowed to the head of the casket. From the white walls the glazed eyes and head and flaring horns of an impala, a Grant's, a Robert's eye, a greater kudu, lesser kudu, sable, nyala, and two fierce black buffalo regarded the somber scene.

The simple yellow box was decorated with a lei of golden gladiolas and 'mums. An engraved steel plate attached to the cover read more simply than any sentence this facile man had ever contrived: "ROBERT RUARK – Died 1st July 1965 – Aged 49 years."

Around the plate was arranged the ribbon and medallion of the Spanish government's Order of Civil Merit. Bob Ruark was a good and courageous friend of this country back in the early post-war days when it was not particularly popular for writers to show it anything but contempt.

Not one relative had come to say farewell. But this man was not unmourned. Cristina, the noble cook, sat in soundless grief in the dimmed room with Pascual the gardener, Pascual's wife and Pascualin whose education my old friend was underwriting when all his hot blood left him. There was, in addition, the grocer, the butcher, and the baker all in stiff black and genuinely touched.

By 6 o'clock in the bright evening more than a hundred were in the house or the garden that reached down to the sand and water. There were the American Consul General from Barcelona and many old friends, including Madeleine Carroll, whose house Bob and Virginia – then his wife – rented the year they fell in love with Palamos. The actress in a gay summery print embraced magazine sub-editor Marilyn Kaytor, in black, another who loved this extraordinary man. They sniffled for a trice before Miss Carroll said: "I came dressed this way because I could hear him say, 'What are you doing in that silly black dress? It doesn't become you.' "

A Spanish TV cameraman turned his lights and lens on a malevolent tiger pelt and ferocious head that sprang from the living room wall. "Hold it a moment," Marilyn said. She raced out to the garage, brought back the keys to Bob's Rolls Royce, hung them on one of the tiger's fangs and told the cameraman to carry on. "Bob always kept the keys there," she explained. "He liked to look at them hanging there from his tiger's jaw and say with a grin, 'How rich can you get?' "

At the bar where some of the mourners were drinking the dead man's whisky, Nicky Tregor, the Polish sculptor of famous peoples' heads, put down his drink and said, "Come, you have not seen my head of Bob." He took us back into the room of the coffin and turned a light on the bronze. He had caught Bob excellently: The jut of the jaw, the thick and straining neck, the perpetual need for a haircut.

There was a tear in the Pole's eye. "Bob's the fourth head I've lost in a fortnight," he sighed. "Nina Dyer commits suicide, George Litman just dies, Rubirosa hits a tree. Now Bob."

Someone murmured a word of sympathy to the bereaved headhunter and then we all moved to the garden, where the services would be held. Four sad Spaniards in black carried Bob Ruark out of the house in his yellow wooden coffin and set it down in the bright sunshine of the emerald garden.

Father José Fonosas, a young priest given to gestures, stepped forward when the mourners stopped moving about. He fished notes from his cassock, settled his glasses on his nose and launched into a religious ceremony unlike any he had ever celebrated or witnessed in Catholic Spain. His bishop had not gone into great detail. He had simply said go ahead; it would be all right.

The priest droned on in Spanish pointing now and then to the box that embraced this spent skyrocket of a man. He had never known Bob, but was trying. Bob was not one to take formal religion or its emissaries seriously. Once at our place in Jersey he watched me lead my brood home from Sunday Mass, all feeling outrageously pious, and looking at me over his newspaper as he lolled on the porch he said, "Okay, take off your deacon's suit and mix us a mess of martinis."

The beach life at the edge of Bob's garden went on uninterrupted, for the most part. But bathers and others who had noticed the little Spanish hearse and two cars into which erupting volcanoes of vivid flowers had been arranged came to the hedge and peered into the garden, straining to catch what the priest was saying.

What he was saying mainly, and he summed it up at the end in painful English, was: "Let God be mindful of his servant Robert Ruark, and grant him peace."

The U. S. Consul General to Barcelona did not know Bob, but he had done his homework. "In 12 years the roots of a tree reach ever deeper," he said in Spanish. "They cling to the earth. It is difficult for them to be pulled out without leaving a deep scar. The people who have known Bob Ruark for the past 12 years in this region will remember how much affection and recognition he showered on

Palamos. He will leave an empty space in the corner of Spain and a heaviness in the hearts of those who shared this part of his life. Here in Palamos will sleep forever one who came to this land and planted here his roots."

My friend Ruark's casket had looked too small for a fellow who had once flattened Bobo Newsom in a player vs. writer fight, and during the war had decked the resident goon aboard a Merchant Marine war transport on which he commanded a Navy gun crew. But when the four Spaniards slid it into the Spanish hearse a good foot of it protruded out the rear.

The funeral party came out of the bottom of the garden and walked behind the hearse, the flower cars, and Bob's Rolls Royce, which followed in empty elegance, save for the chauffeur, like the riderless horse of a dead leader. And so we marched slowly between ranks of people who had come up from the beach to look on, a cortege moving through a gay travel poster, and once could hear my friend say, with his fierce black and white smile, "What a way to go!"

A suggestion of the gay holiday spirit from the beach seemed to creep into Robert Ruark's wake during the short funeral procession around the property and along the Palamos seafront promenade, as a number of drunks were seen to stagger and fall out heavily from the walking lines. They had no doubt figured that this would be the final opportunity to drink on Bob and had accordingly made the most of the last invitation.

Later, some feeling of festivity was also shown when the mourners returned to the Ruark household. In some cases the black mourning clothes were replaced by bright colored slacks, and the new claimant heiress to Bob's property soon had his record player blaring out his old records at double sound. This action was considered unbearable by the remainder of those present. They felt that even Bob Ruark himself would have preferred a little peace for at least the rest of the day and the time spent in a more dignified manner.

Chapter 30
The Honey Badgers at Work

The whole story of Robert Ruark's deteriorating health is in some ways incomprehensible. Here was a highly intelligent, successful man with everything, a man of 49 years of age with everything to live for, and knowing that he was bleeding internally. Yet he didn't bother to get proper medical attention and kept his condition more or less to himself. While friends can give advice, in the final count it is the person concerned who is responsible. In all of this Bob proved to be his own worst enemy. He continued to drink and in fact knowingly committed suicide.

It really appeared as if he couldn't be bothered to face up to the schedule he had set for himself, or that had been set for him – his work projects and financial problems and marriage plans. Also, he knew that his last book was not good, and he knew that he had begun to fail as a writer, or at least as the writer he wanted to be. The impending marriage held frightening portents for his future, and he could also have been influenced by the embarrassment connected with his deteriorating body and general physique. All this, combined with the fact that just before he went to Barcelona, Bob had developed a very bad skin eruption in a very personal place. This was probably caused by the general malfunction of his liver.

Bob's deterioration had been going on for a long time, but I learned after his death that for about a year he had noticed signs of some form of internal hemorrhage. Then during a short effort at a non-drinking period, he appeared to lose some weight. He was vaguely pleased about this to start with, but when it extended to his arms he changed his opinion. Still, he didn't bother to see any doctor of value.

There were so many opportunities to have a proper medical checkup, because during this time Bob was in New York, London, Barcelona, Madrid and Rome. On his last visit to New York, about three months before he died, he told various people he intended to go to Houston for a medical checkup at the Texas Medical Center. Instead, he suddenly took off for Palamos with a girlfriend. One can only assume that Bob was frightened of learning what his problem was. Yet the aborted American checkup would assuredly have put a finger on his complaint, and without doubt he would have been told once again to stop drinking.

Robert Ruark's death was a shattering blow to every single person who knew him, and each would have grieved in their own personal way. Here in Palamos there was indeed intense grief. Apart from our love for our patron, we had lost the head of the household, the helmsman, the one person who was really necessary. To compound this misery, and to drive home its truth, construction on the unfinished studio was stopped and the building left in a derelict-looking condition.

Possibly no one suffered from Bob's death more than Ginny, who was still recovering from her lung operation. Although she had been divorced more than two years, I believe she still considered herself Bob's wife. At the time of his death she sent me the following cable: "THANK YOU FOR EVERYTHING. I HAVE NO MESSAGE EXCEPT TO SAY I SPENT MY LIFE LOVING ROBERTO. GOD BLESS – GINNY."

Later she wrote:

I have been so shattered by Bobby's death that I have not been able to think straight, or I would have written you sooner. I want to thank you for all you did after his death about the funeral arrangements. It did not come as a complete surprise because he looked so terrible when he was in New York that I was shocked. Of course, I did my usual pleading with him to go to a doctor.

Poor Ginny. In her weakened state after her operation and because of the continuation of her illness, she was vulnerable to anyone who decided to move in on her. To her considerable distress an old friend took advantage of her sad position, and towards the end of 1965 when explaining some of her troubles she wrote:

I'll be brief. I've had just about all I can take for one year. The man I was going with and was in business with has been jailed for forgery . . . on my bank account, so I'm losing money and friends at a great rate of speed. So now I have to go to court day after tomorrow.

Bobby and I had known him for twenty-five years, and I have been so distraught this week I can't think. He had been terribly nice to me after Bobby's death when I was so shattered by that and the illness that I was half insane.

To many of his old friends, the death of Robert Ruark came as no surprise. The general reaction was more of acceptance of something that had been inevitable. Among the large number of letters of condolence I received, one said: "My particular commiseration to you. Bob seemed almost suicidal in New York and London, and I'm sure he was difficult for you recently. However, we've all lost a helluva guy."

At the beginning of 1965, when Bob was feeling the strain of his financial obligations, the question of the final payment to Ginny of her lump sum money was being considered. This was $25,000 and there was also about $10,000 in London furniture money still to be paid. At this time Ginny was unwell and indications were that sooner or later she would have to undergo surgery. Bob realized the seriousness of her condition and expressed his concerns in correspondence with his agent. He suggested that Ginny should be approached in order to delay payment of these two amounts, and he offered even to pay interest if she agreed to a delay.

While Bob was concerned about Ginny's health and financial needs, there was a certain mercenary element in his thinking as to the money he owed her. He wrote to Harold Matson in February, 1965 and said "I would like to delay payments to Virginia out of a horribly practical notion that much more of my money paid into her account might very well result in a legacy to four nieces in whom I have no interest whatsoever." He clearly thought he would outlive Ginny and said: "In the frankest of terms, if the lady dies I don't want my hard-earned dough left to a bunch of Goddamned relatives, so I will trust your tact to say we are a little busted at the moment and please delay."

While Bob often stated after the divorce that he would never marry again, he did add that he might "end up by remarrying the old girl." He spoke to Ginny in an expansive way along those lines during one of their post-divorce meetings, and I think that had they both lived, this could have been a distinct possibility.

Although Bob from time to time mentioned the names of various girls as possible marriage partners, he consistently maintained that he couldn't marry because he couldn't afford another divorce. So, in the spring of 1965, when he produced a sharp, mink-clad American girl and secretly announced that they were to be married, we were all shocked. Bob told his staff that the girl would be no financial drag on him, as she was sufficiently rich not to worry. She worked herself, as a magazine editor and writer. (Editor's note: For some reason Ritchie seldom included names when it comes to Bob's girlfriends. Presumably the individual in this case was Marilyn Kaytor, since Eva Monley, the most prominent among his post-divorce loves, was a movie producer and had refused his offer of marriage at least once.)

Everything appeared to be nicely set up for the future, and then I was instructed to make inquiries about how and where would be the best place to get married. Gibraltar seemed to be the best answer for two non-Catholic Americans. But the plan had a pathetic end. While nothing was definite in any way whatsoever, the intended bride of a week hence was due to move to Spain on July 5. Instead, she just had time to fly to London from New York to see Bob briefly on his death bed.

Even allowing for all of Bob's varied plot twists and involved endings to his novels, these didn't approach the drama caused by his own death. What followed afterwards was something even Bob would have found difficult to write.

The latest in a series of blows to Ginny came with the discovery that Bob had changed his will concerning the Palamos property from her favor to that of the intended bride. This hit Ginny below the belt, because only a few weeks before Bob died, he had assured her there would no changes in his will concerning the property. He promised that the Spanish land, house and furniture all belonged to her forever. This last-minute change may have been because he thought there was a real possibility Ginny could die, and at the same time he knew that maybe he didn't have long to go either. In his confused thinking, since he didn't want his property to go to Ginny's family, he felt he had to safeguard it.

To some, it might seem that Bob's decision to change his will was ill-considered, since two days before the first anniversary of Ruark's death, his elected heiress arrived at his home in Palamos with a brand new husband, a small man with a full beard, on their honeymoon. The staff was speechless and the village horrified. The villagers repeatedly said: *"Ella se ha burlado de nosotros"* ("She has made a joke of us.").

Ruark's estate affairs quickly deteriorated into a catfight between Ginny and the girlfriend/fiancée, with in-laws, executors, lawyers, notaries and secretaries all mixed up together. This was the one performance that poor Bob did not want or expect. He truly thought he had everything straight, but just the opposite turned out to be the case. The opposite, because in this drama the two most important documents – the divorce agreement and the changed will – were in conflict.

The new will was signed in London just under eight weeks before Bob died and left the whole Palamos property to the American fiancée/girlfriend. At that time he didn't have the right to do this because of restrictive clauses in his divorce agreement. The agreement obliged Bob to make a will with provisions stipulating that if Ginny survived him and both were unmarried at the time of his death – conditions which in fact occurred – that Ginny should be entitled to one-half of Bob's entire estate.

There was then a letter-form agreement with respect to the Spanish property under which Ginny was to convey to Bob a deed giving him sole ownership. This document was to be executed on the payment of $100,000 to Ginny, to be paid in installments of $25,000, the last of which was in fact paid a few months before he died. Also in this agreement, it was stated that in the event of the sale of the Spanish property, Ginny was entitled to 50 percent of the gross proceeds over and above the $100,000. The initial $100,000 was to be retained by Bob or his estate. One further provision stipulated that if Bob died within a three-year period, which in fact happened, then subject to Ginny's first refusal, the Spanish property was to be sold by Bob's estate as expeditiously as possible and for the best available price.

Notwithstanding these agreements connected with the divorce, in Bob's final will he only left Ginny one-half of the residuary. A Surrogate Court judge ruled that the will was inconsistent with the obligation under the separation agreement to leave Ginny half of the entire estate. He ruled that the Spanish property should be included as a part of the estate, and that in effect invalidates the specific legacy of the property to Ruark's girlfriend/fiancée. This whole business has been argued for eight years now [Editor's note: The word "four" has been stricken out in the original manuscript and replaced by eight. This places Ritchie's completion of the book manuscript in 1969 or 1970].The outcome seems to have been summed up by the Surrogate Court ruling as follows: "If the will is inconsistent with the separation agreement and the letter-form agreement of Jan. 14, 1963, then the contractual obligations of the agreements must govern."

There is not much doubt that during the creation of these documents Bob lost his way. In practically every possibility the outcome was contrary to his real and spoken wish, that the Palamos property be kept in existence and eventually to go to the University of North Carolina. In Bob's last will, there was no reference whatsoever to the conditions laid down in the divorce agreement, so they were immediately contested by the fiancée/girlfriend. She claimed the complete rights of the will so far as the property was concerned. It was estimated to be worth in the region of $350,000.

While to the uninitiated it seemed incomprehensible that these documents conflicted and were open to different interpretations, particularly given the fact that the same lawyer acted for Bob on both occasions, there was also the fact that no document had been made available in Spain that would enable the Spanish land deeds to be changed from joint ownership to Bob's name. Despite all the apparent problems, the situation could have been turned to the advantage of everyone in order to save death duties, and used to save the Ruark property, though this could have been accomplished only if dealt with in the accepted manner here in Spain. It would have been purely and simply a matter of cooperation between two women. Here, unfortunately, the situation got lost in a fog of individual gain and female stupidity and illogicality as neither of the two women would make one move to see the other.

With such a complicated mess, cooperation was the only way. At the beginning, perhaps it could have been possible to deal with the matter quietly and cheaply. In the settling of any estate the one thing to do is to avoid paying unnecessary and crippling death duties if there is any feasible way to do so.

In this case one possibility along these lines, as far as the property in Spain was concerned, would have been to ignore the divorce. It was not openly admitted here, this being a Catholic country, then despite the will, it merely became a question of allowing Ginny to be the actual heiress. After all, half the property was still in her name. In this way there would have been about eight percent death duties on Robert Ruark's half and of course nothing payable on the other half.

On the other hand, if the fiancée/girlfriend was to be the legal heiress, there would be approximately 80 percent death duties payable on the entire value, since she was no relation whatsoever. Obviously there was a vast difference between these two alternatives, and the logical course was for the two women to reach a private agreement. This could have been done with minimal fuss, but in order for a plan of this type to be put into operation the two women had to meet and agree to cooperate.

Both Spanish and American lawyers who had represented Bob did little. So, despite my efforts and those of many other friends of the Ruarks, neither of the women would see the other. They elected to fight it out at a distance through various lawyers. As is usually the way in such situations, they went nowhere for a long time.

To some extent I can see Ginny's viewpoint and can understand her reluctance to see the girlfriend/fiancée. On the other hand, the other woman commenced a hate campaign against the ex-wife, with such nonsense as a confusing accusation concerning her pregnancy, claiming that Ginny Ruark had invented this story in New York. It turned out that the girlfriend had been the one to concoct the story, and she even entered his agent's office with the announcement: "I'm pregnant and Bob and I are going to get married."

Of course, Ginny knew better than anyone that Bob was unable to have children, as he was sterile. In fact this was explained, rather crudely, in *The Honey Badger*. I supposed, in a way, Bob and Ginny were a strange combination of self-destruction, and I truly believe that the divorce killed them both. They couldn't quite live together, but they also couldn't live apart. When Bob thought Ginny was dying, he began to fade, and when Bob died, Ginny just faded away herself.

Ginny's lung operation involved the removal of the lower third of the right lung. This took place just before Bob died, and for this reason she was unable to travel to Spain for the funeral. A year later Ginny succumbed to complications, presumably cancer, in the liver region. For a good spell before she died she was in a poor state, though she never lost her keen desire to read. Her pathetic request to be sent paperbacks, because they were lighter, was an indication of her decline.

Ginny died at 49, the same age as Bob, and both had their birthdays on the same day, December 29, but with one year of difference between them. As Harold Matson said after Ginny's death:" All of a sudden it seemed as if there never had been any Ruarks." That thought is all the more remarkable when you consider just how active and vibrant they both had been.

They destroyed themselves, each contributing something destructive to the other – Bob by just being Bob, and Ginny, whatever her wishes, having herself in an emotional uproar most of the time. I believe that the distress of Bob being absent, combined with his serial philandering, was an important contribution to her trouble. When the misery and distress that she suffered during the divorce period were added, I think it became more than any normal person, let alone someone as unstable as Ginny, could endure.

The existence of her unshakable love for Bob was something Ginny had to live with, and this was possibly the root of all their problems. Bob didn't need such devotion and couldn't live with such possessiveness. Ginny suffered enormously as his rejection of her great love became ever more apparent, and in this respect Bob was never really very considerate. I think she would have been willing to settle for just a few kind words, and for him to at least keep his lovers at a distance and out of her way.

Bob could be incredibly kind, but he could also be incredibly cruel and inconsiderate of another person's feelings. There was the time when he visited New York immediately after the divorce. He called Ginny and arranged to have dinner with her, which was a big enough ordeal, but the day he picked would have been their 25th wedding anniversary had they stayed married. On top of that, Bob turned up drunk and late, so there was no point in having dinner together. Instead, they argued, and Bob insisted on remaining in Ginny's apartment overnight – just one more strain for an ex-wife who still loved her former husband.

Their mutual friend, Walker Stone, paid Ginny a fine tribute in a letter he wrote to her parents following her death.

"Let us not grieve overmuch about Ginny. To do so is to be selfish – which she never was. She had a fuller life than most of us – more than a share of joy and gladness and excitement before she had more than a share of sadness and tragedy.

"Ginny was gentle and kind. She was sweet and thoughtful. More than that she had antennae tuned to the heart chords of so many that gave her such a sensitive enjoyment of living and sharing.

"I had many treasured hours of good talk with Ginny after her difficulties with Bob. I marveled at her absence of bitterness which I believe you and so many of us felt. Finally I understood. Ginny knew better than all of us how sick Bob was and how unaccountable for his actions. Instead of grieving, let us cherish Ginny's generosity of spirit and of her love of her family and her friends."

After Robert Ruark's death and with Ginny gone, there were many unorthodox happenings at Palamos. One such incident was when the rhino head disappeared. One morning I could see that something was very wrong from the look on the gardener's face as he approached across the lawn. He carried an expression of absolute incredulity as he commenced to explain: *"La cabeze del rinoceronte ha desaparecido,"* he said. "Something very strange has happened, the rhinoceros head is missing from the outhouse!"

Although everyone else thought this to be important, I didn't really care one way or the other. The loss of the rhino head, compared with what had already happened, didn't seem to represent much. Suggestions were being made as to who might have been responsible for its removal. It would have been extremely difficult to lift from the hook on the wall and rather difficult to hide. I thought it unlikely that it could have been anyone from the village. Then after a bit of thought it occurred to me who was almost certainly involved in this raid, and I was very pleased to know that at least one of Robert Ruark's trophies had gone to a good home.

Farther north along our coast, Robert Ruark had a very distinguished neighbor – a Catalan gentleman, the surrealist painter, Salvador Dali. I recalled that many years earlier Bob had advised me to expect in his absence a visit from Dali, saying he would be calling for the rhino head. Dali never came at that time, but shortly before Bob died, he indicated to me that at some suitable time this rhino trophy would be delivered by sea aboard the yacht of a Catalan friend who would then ceremoniously hand it over to our artistic neighbor at his home in Port Lligat, some 60 kilometers north of Palamos. This would have been fun, and Bob would most certainly have written a column around the whole affair.

A recent newspaper photographic report on Salvador Dali's house confirmed my suspicions. There, among many strange heads, Robert Ruark's rhino trophy appeared in a specially prepared rhino room. I am pleased to record this incident, as there is no doubt that Bob would have approved of the timing of the acquisition, apparently carried out while we were all engaged in the burial service, instead of as a formal request for the promised trophy.

Other occurrences were far less acceptable. The sacking of Robert Ruark's house, though not really qualifying as a Zorba the Greek operation, at least came fairly close symbolically. Apart from the immediate round of a good many things, a few months before Bob's death, Virginia Ruark came with a large truck and removed a good proportion of the furniture, just about all the antiques, and a few other things. This she was definitely entitled to do as there was a clause in her divorce agreement with a list of furniture that she could remove at any time. She had just not wanted to do this while Bob was alive. Still, this first furniture removal was a serious shock to Bob's staff, and we all stood numbly around, not really believing it was happening. We knew that Bob would not have been pleased.

The second serious attack on Robert Ruark's possessions came later, when the honey badgers went to work with a will. The fiancée/girlfriend removed all the valuable skins, leopards, colobus monkey rugs, etc. that she could lay her hands on, plus the full tiger mount over the fireplace in the living room. It was then that we really knew that Robert Ruark's home and boyhood dream were doomed [see Introduction]. We were all quite sure this tiger should not have been taken; Bob would never have condoned its removal by *anyone*. The tiger was taken to New York, and later the fiancée/girlfriend explained that it had been removed so that the tourists could not steal it!

There were problems for everyone when Bob died, and quite apart from all the financial issues, I often found myself in the middle of a female tug-of-war for the acquisition of Bob's possessions. Despite the fact that I never really took sides, I was accused first of all by Ginny of having removed certain things, which in fact the girlfriend/fiancée had hidden or removed herself. Then later I was accused by the girlfriend/fiancée of having stolen certain furniture and other things that Ginny had taken as her right under the divorce agreement and in the presence of a notary public.

There were other articles such as a pair of binoculars which I had handed to Ginny when she asked for them. They had been a gift from a close mutual friend of the Ruarks and were inscribed with their names. I was first accused by the girlfriend/fiancée of keeping them myself and then of not having the right to give Ginny her own binoculars. I even had to fight to keep my own Zeiss Ikon camera that Bob had given to me. It was claimed that it was the house camera, and I actually lost a slide projector that got packed up in the night after I had loaned it on good faith to these people so they could see some of my African slides.

There were many packing-up sessions at night when the servants were too frightened to venture into the back part of the house. A big blow-up came when they discovered that the visitors had packed up all the table linen, which Ginny had promised to them once she cleared with the executors. The linen had been collected by Ginny over the years and generally selected with the help of the servants.

Acceptance by the staff of the new status quo probably would never have been possible in any case, but the adjustment might have come easier if it had been dealt with differently. We all suffered terribly with the presence of these strangers, especially with the bearded husband sitting in Bob's place at the head of the table wearing his watch and his clothes. This was quietly stopped after a few days. Bob's maid ceased to place table settings at the ends of the table so no one could sit in his place.

Eventually the girlfriend/fiancée quarreled with everybody, though to start with we were all very willing to help her. But after her first visit the staff was in a state of shock for a long while. We all remembered how she repeated Bob's words when first arriving in the house: "Bob said I can stay if Alan and the staff are in agreement." All we got for our trouble at this stage were large telephone bills left unpaid.

At the time of her "honeymoon" visitation, the staff and I had very little actual authority. We had never been given any proper instructions by the New York executors, so we reluctantly allowed the visitors to carry away their selection of the Ruarks' possessions. Of course, legally nobody should have been allowed to stay in the house or remove anything, but since this girlfriend paid some of the house expense at that time (later more than doubly refunded to her), she no doubt felt she had some right. Certainly these people knew they were doing wrong, as even the aged parents with their weak hearts were humping heavy packages and cases out to their car instead of asking the gardener or the maid to assist them, which would have been the normal procedure.

Once I fully realized what had happened and what was happening to the Ruarks' home, I finally decided to remove my own personal possessions before they, too, got packed up and sent away. As well as my office, the house had been my home for 12 years. I wanted the carved wooden desk at which I had worked on Bob's books. It had been made specifically for me and designed by Ginny and myself. I expected the desk to be given graciously. Yet when I asked the supposed new owner of the property, I was told "no." I took it anyway, along with my battered typewriter plus a few trophies that had been given to me or promised by Bob.

After a while the whole procedure became rather like a comic opera. At different times I received instructions from Ginny to stop the girlfriend/fiancée from entering the house, and then I would receive instructions from the girlfriend/fiancée to stop Ginny from entering. Among the many kind words that came my way, I was called a "meddler and a conniver." First one woman then the other issued orders that I was not allowed to enter the house myself.

These instructions weren't very logical since I was acting in the capacity of administrator, and I was required to supply my own money to pay house bills. This was necessary to avoid the property being embargoed and a forced auction sale being held.

The regular payment of estate expenses in Spain was a continuous headache ever since Ruark's death. Maybe this is because of the lack of available funds, or because of the disagreement between the pretenders to ownership, or maybe because of the lack of interest in something that is four thousand miles away. All the staff had in mind was to avoid disgrace to his name caused through non-payment of ordinary domestic expenses. Matters even reached the point where his maid, Carmen, was required to step into the breech and pay a recent electricity bill!

Although Robert Ruark never shortchanged anyone in his entire life, in the settling of some of the estate affairs in Palamos, a number of his Spanish creditors were forced by the executors to accept a 15 percent reduction. These creditors included such people as the butcher, the plumber, electrician, local garage, carpenter and builder, and the shop on main street where Bob bought leather and suede coats for his girlfriends. This non-payment of debts would not have pleased Bob and naturally has left a bad feeling in the village.

All efforts to cover up a deteriorating situation were in vain. All we were trying to do was preserve his memory, and we were unable to stop the gradual decline of a property for seven years [Editor's note: As was the case earlier, the number four has been replaced, though this time by "seven" rather than "eight."]

Dampness, broken shutters and rusting iron is today's picture, and things are not helped by the forlorn- and derelict-looking part of the house where Bob had planned to have his studio for painting. Nor does the presence of the shrouded Rolls Royce languishing in the garage help. It is impounded by customs and without any legal registration as well as being tied up in the general stagnation of probate.

The memory is kept alive a little by Cristina, the Ruarks' Catalan cook. She goes daily to place fresh flowers in the large studio office at the base of Bob's sculptured head by Tregor. She says she feels some sort of compulsion to return to the spot a number of times daily. Once a week she also goes to the grave in Palamos with flowers.

This dedication to the memory of Robert Ruark would also be the driving force behind the work done by Pascual, the Andalusian gardener. He has continued to keep the garden as it always was, though hardly anyone ever sees it. He has continued to work a good ten hours a day, six days a week, even though he has to wait up to nine months for his salary. In fact, he recently had to sue through the Spanish labor syndicate to be paid.

With the Ruark property lying in a state of limbo, in a way a full circle has been struck. The maid and her husband and young daughter, Cristina Virginia, live in the main guest quarters. This, I know, Robert Ruark would have liked.

Ginny once referred to Bob's last will and testament as "a Chinese will," and on the occasion of her one visit to Palamos after his death, she said: "Alan, if I wanted to, I could break this will easily, but I won't do it." Ginny then went on to explain that it wouldn't be difficult to prove that Bob was not in a suitable state of mind when he made the final change. The evidence of a few old friends who had been in contact with him at the time, plus medical reports, would have been sufficient to break the will.

I felt Ginny was correct in her reluctance to expose Bob's physical state in his final months, but she was quite wrong not to have struck when she could. What should have been the guiding line was Bob's true wish for his property. He wanted it eventually to go to the University of North Carolina. Had Ginny lived, presumably she would have seen this carried out.

Many times Bob told me that he did not want the property to go to nothing. He wanted it kept in existence. His idea was that it was to be made available for his friends to visit, to stay awhile and read his books, his newspaper column scrapbooks and magazine articles, to admire his trophies, and to talk about Robert Ruark while using his bar. This plan was to be under my stewardship, since I knew who would qualify, but Bob's most important wish was that it would also be available for use by journalism students from the University of North Carolina or as a European sabbatical base for faculty, or for any individual interested in the accomplishments of Robert Ruark. At some future date it was to become the property of the University.

All this was set up in some form of trust in his will, with suitable requirements for the maintenance of the property and other expenses, for the employment of his staff, and for final disposal to the University. However, as a result of the Surrogate Court decision, the lion's share of the property shares went to Ginny's heirs, irrespective of whatever wishes Bob appeared to have and without any hope of acquisition by Bob's university.

After Bob's death it soon became apparent that the whole business was going to be tangled up with legal battles for many years to come. At this writing over seven years [Editor's note: Once again the number four has been replaced by "seven"] later and despite court orders, it looks very much as though the whole property could be swallowed up in a maze of death duties and legal costs.

Prior to their divorce, Bob and Ginny always had wills that complemented each other, with suitable clauses in the event of simultaneous death. In these wills, I figured as the beneficiary of the Palamos property. This was to show appreciation of my efforts in its creation and also because they knew I understood clearly what their wishes were. Also, the staff had been included as pecuniary beneficiaries. In Bob's last will the Spanish staff were bequeathed $10,000 each, with $50,000 for me, though so far none of this has amounted to anything. Bob died in debt owing in the region of $200,000. This indebtedness has subsequently been removed with the sale of new books, royalties and the like. Whatever happens, the knowledge that Bob wished to show his appreciation to us is comforting.

In the last will there were other bequests. In all, five women were named, some being left as much as $25,000. As an indication of Bob's esteem for Harold Matson, his agent was bequeathed his Rolls Royce. This was indeed a compliment, since it was Bob's most prized possession.

The cash value of Ruark's beloved home is one thing, but to his good friends and to his staff, there was another, less easily defined value. This involved the creation, from nothing, of a place to live, which its creator loved deeply. In Bob's eyes it was a sort of pirate's hideout, and what happened in this hideout, the thousands upon thousands of words pulled from one man's brain and the shocking backache after hours at the typewriter – all were part of its story. So was the frustration of rejected magazine articles, of books that had to be rewritten, of the master's return after miles of uncomfortable travel in search of material, of the hilarious lunches and the gracious dinners and the lively cocktail parties, of the importance of the dog family, of the laughter the night before and the lively late breakfasts on the terrace with Bob and guests staggering out with true or exaggerated hangovers, of the smiling maid attending to her bed-making chores, of the good looking cook being congratulated so often by Bob's appreciated guests, of the devoted gardener, and of the friendly village people who were always so pleased to see Don Roberto drive his Rolls Royce. These and many other ordinary things in the everyday life of the household of Robert Ruark represent the real value of Bob's home and his realization of a boyhood dream.

Quite apart from what happened after Bob's death, there was of course the financial situation which put the continuation of his property and this dream home and workplace in doubt.

Despite his previous high earnings, Bob had been living far beyond his means for a good while. He was spending normally and getting advances, but he wasn't working well. He owed a whole book for which he had more or less received payment. This was not like Bob, a fact of which he was fully aware. He had never really had any heavy advances in the past and had always been up to date with the supply of copy against receipt of payment.

His divorce placed him in this strained financial position, abetted by a simultaneous slowing down because of age and health. At this time Bob would have known what Ernest Hemingway meant when he said: "There is only one requirement to being a successful writer if you have the talent – stay healthy."

Equally applicable to Bob's situation was another comment from Hemingway: "One thing you have to remember is that the economics of people having bust ups is almost fatal. You not only lose the children no matter what you are promised, but you go straight into economic slavery, and what's left, unless you hit jackpots, is never enough to satisfy anybody else."

Bob didn't have any children, but he certainly had reached a state of economic slavery, though had he stayed healthy, there is no doubt this would have been straightened out.

CHAPTER 31
THE END OF A GRAND RUN

Robert Ruark had been known to say that he didn't want to live for more than 50 years. He thought that would be just about enough, and towards the end it appeared that perhaps this is what he had in mind. Certainly, many things had gone badly for him, and maybe he realized that slowly catching up with him was that dreadful fear about which he had occasionally spoken – the inability to write.

There had been a lengthy period when Bob hadn't actually produced any new words, other than his columns. Finishing off *The Honey Badger* had been painfully slow, and though he had completed a film script for *Uhuru*, it was really a rehash of old words and an old plot, not to mention that this picture project seemed to have foundered again. He had long since finished with his *Field & Stream* pieces, was having a number of magazine rejections, and there were many requests for re-writes. Finally, a few months before he died, Bob officially finished with his column. He had kept it going with difficulty for a long while, but this break was a milestone in his life.

At the end of April, 1965, Bob wrote his "signing off" column after more than 20 years as a syndicated columnist. In it, he admitted he was weary after a lifetime of deadlines.

This is a sad column. I am saying goodbye to an old friend. The old friend is United Feature Syndicate, which has handled me lovingly for twenty years. Between five a week and later three a week I reckon I averaged out at about four thousand columns in twenty years, and that is a mess of type. It would amount to two million, eight hundred thousand words, not counting rewrite and pencil-carving, plus envelope-addressing, cables and the rest.

I'm not quitting the big syndicate field because I'm mad at anybody. Quite frankly, after thirty years in the newspaper business, I suddenly realize that I am nearly fifty and am weary of deadlines. Counting college classes, afternoon newspapers, the Navy and syndication, I have been on a deadline since I was fifteen, and that was thirty-five years ago.

My feet hurt. My fingers hurt. My brain is still sharp, I trust, but I am less and less willing to punish it on a daily schedule. News used to be fairly simple. You bust a three-star general, wreck a dope ring, interrupt a hoodlum summit conference, deport Lucky Luciano, do a series on leprosy, retrack the G.I. trail in World War Two, write some funnies about men, women, children and cats up trees, and it was pretty easy.

For example, I once wrote sixteen – make no mistake about the sixteen – columns on Gen. John (Courthouse) Lee in one day at the machine. That was on a

creaky portable in a seedy hotel in Rome. And I still had strength enough to get drunk at Bricktop's later. That was the old Ruark. The current Ruark writes slower. And drinks less.

There was a time when I would go anywhere, eat airline food, use gin as a substitute for sleep, fight against the Mau Mau, chase elephants on horseback, slug athletes, enjoy being jailed, and wrestle with leopards, all for love of the newspaper business.

I still love the newspaper business but I intend to stay in it in a different manner. I am going back to where I started, and in much the same manner. I started on the *Washington Daily News*, a Scripps-Howard newspaper, and I am, in a sense, going back to being a copy boy in the Daily News Building in Washington, D. C.

When I was a copy boy the editor of the Scripps-Howard Newspaper Alliance literally gave me the coat off his back to cover a story, because I was coatless and tieless at the time of need. I covered the story – it was a $100-a-plate Jackson Day Dinner and I promise I ate one hundred dollars worth, because I was hungry. The editor ran my story and gave me a $10 bonus.

So in a way, I am going back to work for the same editor, who is now editor-in-chief. I am going to be a kind of copy boy emeritus, except that I now have a coat of my own.

I will cover stories, and I will pursue the original course which got me syndicated. Anything that makes me glad, sad, or mad I will write. But I am not (repeat not) going to try to keep up with the situation in Viet Nam or try to remake the world with two fingers.

Walter Duranty once wrote a book titled, *I Write as I Please*. That is what I propose to do for SHNA on a scattergun basis. If I find a piece worth five columns, five columns shall I write. There may be a week when I am pursuing a lush brown maiden in Tahiti and then I shall not (repeat not) write.

I figured when I started this syndication job that I might be good for five, at the most, ten years. I lasted twenty. The deadlines were pasted in my head.

I shall still afflict the Scripps-Howard editors with my deathless prose, in between lush brown maidens and palm toddy, but on a highly irregular schedule.

Until the next dispatch floats back in a bottle, my deepest thanks to you all for being so kind and tolerant of a typewriter which seems determined not to write this last, sad piece.

Bob was pleased about the new arrangement with Scripps-Howard, as he felt it would help keep him on his toes and abreast of the daily news. Yet he almost immediately found difficulty in producing and offered to miss a month's salary as he had not written anything. His offer was refused on the basis that he was to write when he felt like it and not on a deadline basis.

Here in Palamos, as always we had seen him come and go, and while the trips had seemed very frequent during the last year, they were probably no more than normal. We did notice that he was running more than usual, as if trying to catch some elusive prize, the identity of which even Bob could not have known. He had been living in a nebulous paradise that would never materialize, searching and running all his life.

He had nearly always been uprooted from any form of satisfying family life, and for many years he had even been detached from his own country. This was really in more ways than just physical absence. Bob had no family and no children to give him a reason for carrying on a difficult fight. He likewise had no religion and was really living without hope at this time. He had terminated his column, which in fact was the easiest of all writing for him, but he knew his mind had lost the agility needed for this kind of work. He had lost his spirit and his mind was already a little clumsy. He had reached the "talking about book-writing" rather than the "writing of books" stage.

Bob couldn't quite get going on his new Africa book, and every time we should have gotten down to this work, he would either go off on a trip himself or send me off on a skiing trip or any trip I cared to take. Each time he explained that he wasn't quite ready to get down to work. All this was in reality an escape plan to put off the writing, which was not like Robert Ruark. Usually, he had jumped impatiently into new book projects. He may have cursed heavily on the way through but he got the job done with a will.

Here was the deterioration and the end product of a worn-out writer. Robert Ruark had arrived at the end of his run, after a full life to which at least another 50 years should be added if you measured things in terms of living and accomplishment. In a great many ways he had been a rogue with the women and the liquor and his general plan of living. He had been hard and tough, even cruel, in his relationship with many people. His reporting and column writing had frequently been ruthless. But Bob had also been kind and considerate so many times. He had been industrious and hardworking, fun-loving, humorous and generous to a fault, and he had always been quick to give a handout to a person less fortunate than himself when he thought it was warranted. He had been widely respected, loved by many and a good friend of his friends. He had given millions of people throughout the world many good hours of reading pleasure. So I would say, at the end, that on balance the scales were well loaded in Robert Ruark's favor.

EPILOGUE

By GEORGE SAFFOS

It was a colossal accident that I met Robert Ruark. If not for the fact that we were from the same home town of Wilmington, North Carolina, that his parents were frequent customers at my family's restaurant, that *Star News* was located on the corner of the same block as our restaurant, and had he not come in for a late lunch, I might never have met him. Sometimes fate plays strange tricks.

When Ruark came up to pay for his meal, I didn't have the slightest idea who he was, and in truth I didn't care. However, the next customer to approach the cash register asked me if I knew who he was. I replied, "Sorry, but I've never seen him before."

He answered, "That's Robert Ruark, the famous columnist."

I remained unimpressed, since there were newspapermen in and out of the restaurant all day long, and I said something to that effect.

"Yes," the customer pointed out, "but this one makes $50,000 a year." That grabbed my attention because I was making perhaps a tenth that amount. Fifty thousand dollars in the late 1940s was a lot of money.

Well, I thought, if he can make that much money, I guess I need to start reading him and see what he's all about.

The next day I read my first Ruark column. It hooked me immediately and I joined the ranks of 15 million people who eagerly anticipated the appearance of his material every morning. To me, as a young man in my 20s, his work was interesting, amusing and informative.

At that time Ruark's articles ran in about 150 daily newspapers and he was truly the "rock star" of writing. Moreover, he seemed to relish living the life of a celebrity. Years later, during the week I spent visiting Bob in Palamos, I got to know him better.

That splendid sojourn in Spain came about as the outgrowth of Bob's triumphant return, at the peak of his career in 1957, to his native North Carolina. It began with a stop in Chapel Hill, where he had attended the University, before driving on to Wilmington. Fortified by success and a new Rolls Royce, Bob was a genuine rags-to-riches millionaire. When I learned he was in town, I made it a point to try and meet him. The next day his mother came into our restaurant and I asked if she could arrange it. "Miss Lottie," I said, "there is nobody in the world I would rather meet than your son."

She replied, "Give me the phone." After less than a minute of conversation with Bob, she told me to be at the motel the following day at 2:00 p.m.

EPILOGUE

The next day I approached his room, duly impressed by the somewhat incongruous sight of his Rolls Royce parked in front of the door. I knocked and Ruark responded, appearing to be intoxicated. He invited me in and we proceeded to imbibe cocktails for the next few hours. I had never talked with or listened to such an interesting man. By evening we had become friends.

As I was about to leave, I noticed that Bob seemed sober while I was unquestionably wasted. I was also intoxicated by the fact that I had been able to spend so much time with this man who had become my idol. After a decade of reading his books and daily newspaper columns, I was a dedicated fan. Yet I found this intelligent man to be down-to-earth and completely lacking in pretentiousness. Within minutes I felt like I had known him for years. His glib tongue, sense of humor and depth of knowledge fascinated me. He had the ability to charm the birds out of the trees and was a splendid storyteller. Our four hours together passed like four minutes.

As I left I told Bob of my plans to visit Greece during the summer of 1958 and, without realizing it might be presumptuous of me, invited him to come along. I told him he would be able to gather enough material to last a lifetime. With that, he looked at me and invited me to visit him in Spain on my way to Greece. Furthermore, he said that if he could get away, he would accompany me.

In June 1958, my wife Sophia and I boarded the ocean liner *Frederica* in New York en route to Greece. Our itinerary called for a stop in Gibraltar, and that is where we disembarked for a 12-hour train ride to Barcelona. This was not a trip one would make voluntarily. It was hot and dusty, and the train offered no water or soft drinks, much less air conditioning, and there was no dining car.

After a night in Barcelona, we got up with plans to take a walk around the city. Barcelona is one of Europe's most beautiful cities though it rarely gets the attention it deserves. Prior to setting out on our walk I had called Bob's home, but found he was not there. I was told he would call me when he returned. Back at our hotel, a very excited concierge approached us and said Ruark had been waiting for us for an hour and a half. I really felt badly that he had waited so long.

We walked into a lovely garden, which was surrounded by a vine-covered wall. There sat Ruark, reading a newspaper with his cup of coffee and the usual cigarette. After exchanging pleasantries, he told us there was a great bullfight scheduled late that afternoon and that he would pick us up at 5:00 p.m.

That evening, after the bullfight, we dined with the Ruarks in their Barcelona home. We found Virginia to be a lovely, hospitable lady, and she and my wife immediately became fast friends. Ginny Ruark was a statuesque, attractive, intelligent and well-rounded lady who was a stabilizing influence for her energetic, eccentric husband.

Bob once said to me: "Look at Virginia. She's an alcoholic."

When he described her in this manner, I wanted to respond: "If Ginny is an alcoholic, what are you?" But being a guest in his home, I kept my thoughts to

EPILOGUE

myself. If he didn't realize he was worse off than his wife, it wasn't my place to tell him. I did not see Virginia intoxicated or "out of the way" during my visit, but later in life she did have to seek treatment for alcoholism.

After dinner that first evening, Bob said he would return to pick us up at 9:00 the next morning as he planned to take us to Palamos to see his "castle." We were unprepared for this level of hospitality and absolutely delighted it was being extended to us so freely. How many famous individuals would, after just two casual meetings, treat someone in such fashion?

By car the fishing village of Palamos is about an hour and a half away from Barcelona. When we reached the top of the hill overlooking this quaint, almost hidden little village, Bob stopped the Rolls and took his first drink before motoring on into town. The thought occurred to me that Palamos must have reminded him of his boyhood days in sleepy Southport, North Carolina, the locale which served as a catalyst for his timeless "Old Man and the Boy" tales.

The Ruarks' villa was an exquisite, Spanish-styled home with a Mediterranean tiled roof. It was picture perfect in every way – situated on the oceanfront and graced by a lush lawn leading down to the sea. When the Ruarks bought the home, they had it taken down almost to the bare walls. Virginia, an accomplished interior decorator, had been in charge of the project.

Each room featured a trophy mount adorning the walls. The animal heads looked ominously down on every visitor, and the furnishings included leopard and zebra bedspreads. Ginny had done a marvelous job of blending and softening the harshness of Africa with other décor. The end result was the height of elegance. The home reflected Ginny's grace and fine taste along with Bob's love for the hunt. I would be remiss if I failed to mention that Ginny did not allow some of the ugliest trophy heads to be displayed in the house. These "boys" were relegated to the garage.

Sophia and I were assigned the upstairs guest apartment, which afforded the Ruarks their privacy downstairs. The stairway to the second floor was framed by a pair of massive elephant tusks. To the right of the bottom step stood a foreboding lion, which stared at anyone who dared to pass.

On our first morning in Palamos, as I was enjoying the sun-drenched patio, Ruark rushed around the corner of the house calling for Virginia. "Ginny, Ginny, come see the bush. It has its first flower." Somehow this seemed sharply at odds with the brash, macho man who was himself a regular subject of news coverage.

The week flew by, with the girls doing their thing and Bob and I the same. We swam in the afternoon and lit big fires in the fireplace at night. One day on the way to the beach from the front of the house, I saw the gardener cutting the lawn, which was about the size of a football field, with a reel-type push mower. I commented: "Bob, for a hundred dollars you can go ahead and get this guy a power mower."

He stopped, looked at me and said: "Are you crazy? He thinks this lawn mower is one of the most advanced machines around. Do you want me to spoil him?"

EPILOGUE

Bob and Ginny never had children. His dogs, a French poodle called Miss Mamselle and a male boxer named Schnorkel, were his children. He loved them dearly. The poodle would swim with us every day, and Bob said: "You know the poodle is a water dog. In New York, she would try to get into the john, and when she got here and saw the Mediterranean, she thought it was the biggest john in the world."

Bob was full of surprises and endlessly entertaining. Many of his thoughts have had a profound effect on me. For instance, he was fond of commenting, "A house is not a house without a library." He also once remarked that when the money started coming in, "Everything I saw I wanted, everything I chased I caught, everything I caught I enjoyed – but my life was a matter of giving, too, because everything I got, I gave something of myself first to get it." Another profound statement he offered was, "When you change a man's way of life, you need to have something better to replace it or else leave it alone."

Most of our conversations were in the room with the massive fireplace, and over it was an Indian tiger that covered the space from the ceiling all the way down to the hearth. The key to the Rolls Royce hung on the tiger's teeth. Bob would look up at the tiger, smile and say, "How rich can you get?" His wealth and success seemed an endless source of astonishment to him.

We also discussed the label that had been attached to him: "Poor Man's Hemingway." In 1958 that didn't seem to bother him because he was doing everything possible to be like Hemingway; he admired his style of writing and his style of living. Bob's aim, however, was to be better than Hemingway. He told me he wanted to write a third book on Africa, joining *Something of Value* and *Uhuru*, so could have a trilogy of African novels. He reckoned that he had about ten more books to write.

Bob said that there were really two Robert Ruarks – Ruark the man and Ruark the myth – and that he recognized the realities of his life were considerably different from his public persona. Despite being remarkably introspective in this regard, he ignored the severity of his addiction to alcohol like a smoker who believes he won't ever get cancer. Hemingway drank and drank hard until he was 60, which gave Ruark a false hope of more productive years to come. He basically ignored all the warnings from his doctors.

At the time of my visit, Bob told me he had a quarter of a million dollars in a Swiss bank. In today's terms that would be the equivalent of well over a million dollars. His money came in by the buckets full but went out by the barrels full. He had no real concept of budgeting and, like the movie idol who thinks all he has to do is star in another movie, Bob figured the money would keep pouring in so long as he continued writing articles and books.

He could be prodigally extravagant. For example, the royalties earned by the British editions of his books could only be spent in the British Isles. So whenever he went to England he invariably purchased expensive items such as coffee, cigarettes, tweed coats, alcohol and of course the Rolls Royce, his most prized possession. Ginny aided and abetted Bob with her extravagances. She always dressed in the finest designer fashions along with mink coats, jewelry, perfumes and other costly items.

There were plenty of rumors bandied about that Bob was not taking care of his

EPILOGUE

parents. We discussed that subject at length and Bob insisted that the rumors were patently untrue. He spent over $100,000 on his parents as he attempted to deal with their excessive drinking, use of dope and pills, and the hypochondria that found them in hospitals all too often. Finally, Bob told me, he just had to draw the line and put an end to it.

When Bob died, he was flat-out broke. He really had no concept of money, and generous to a fault, he simply could not show restraint. As he admitted to me, on numerous occasions his agent Harold Matson would call him and say: "Bob, you've got to stop. There's no money in the kitty."

Bob obviously loved Palamos and took great pride in showing us around the village. He even pointed out the actual marble stairway where Ava Gardner was filmed in *The Barefoot Contessa*. On this and other tours with him, whenever we stopped Bob would jump out of the Rolls, run around to the passenger side and open the door for Sophia – always the well-mannered Southern gentleman.

Detractors and critics have accused Bob of being brash, arrogant, self-indulgent and a braggart. Unquestionably, he could be all of these things, but on a personal basis I found him to be kind, gentle, hospitable and a fine, honest gentleman. That was the true measure of the man, which only a few ever got close enough to discover. I fancy myself as a fairly astute observer of the human character, and I studied Bob and tried my best to understand him. Certainly, he had no ulterior motive for trying to impress me. He was at the peak of his career when we spent time together. He had just finished *The Old Man and the Boy*, and there's no denying he was full of himself as well as full of an incredible zest for life. Still, the portrait of the man so often presented was a stranger to the real Robert Ruark.

As that idyllic week came to an end and Sophia and I packed for our return to Barcelona, we discussed what we could do in terms of offering some token of our appreciation to the Ruarks. To our dismay, we had nothing to offer, and the shops in Palamos certainly held nothing that seemed appropriate. Then, as Sophia arranged a suitcase, I noticed the roll of Charmin toilet tissue we had brought with us. Inspiration struck me and I said: "Don't put that in the bag. We are going to make a present of it." My lovely wife expressed some doubts about my sanity, but in reply I just asked her: "See if you can find a ribbon to go around it."

I had been saving the Charmin for our upcoming trip to Greece. As anyone who traveled in Europe during this era will vividly recall, one could sand a house with what passed for toilet paper at the time. It was simply atrocious.

Just as we finished wrapping this unorthodox gift, Bob and Ginny walked into the room. I picked up the Charmin and said: "Bob, there's only one thing missing in this palatial home and I've got it." Then I humbly offered our precious gift. Ginny and Bob looked into the bag containing the Charmin and seemed momentarily puzzled, but then it dawned on them. They walked over to me and Ginny kissed me on one cheek and Bob on the other. You would have thought I had brought them a gift straight from Tiffany's showcase, and I'll bet that years later they shared a good laugh with friends as they described the gift.

EPILOGUE

After lunch the next day, as we loaded up the Rolls Royce for Alan Ritchie to drive us back to Barcelona, I walked up to Bob and told him there was no way I could ever express my thanks for the memorable experience he and Ginny had given us.

He said: "Why don't you just say it was N-I-C-E?" I replied that I didn't know such a little word could hold so much meaning.

Ruark kept everything nice and simple. As we left, I saw a forlorn look cross Bob's face and intuitively realized that I would be one of the last vestiges of his North Carolina roots he would ever see. Although he had put up a brave front, he had been devastated by some aspects of his reception during what he expected to be a triumphant return home. We discussed the matter at length, and I assured him there were thousands of admirers like me in Wilmington and Southport who would be delighted for him to retire in the area.

Bob seemed to make as many enemies as he made friends. For example, he talked to me about his articles attacking Frank Sinatra and Lucky Luciano, and said that after they appeared, he began receiving phone calls telling him he might find a lot of cement around his shoelaces. I guess that was a pretty uncomfortable way to live, but Bob didn't mind attacking anyone he thought needed to be attacked.

On the other hand, he was by no means a muckraker. I related a story to Bob about the strange antics of a young man who had been on our ship from New York.

Ruark listened attentively while I recounted my tale. "You know," he said, "I like that story. Why don't we write it out?" In about 15 minutes the piece was done and he had his column for the next day. I watched him punch out the draft with two fingers. He could type as fast as any secretary, and this was yet another of his many talents that amazed me.

When he finished he looked up and said: "You know, partner, you've earned your keep." That pleased me immensely.

Poor No More was in Bob's typewriter at the time of our visit. One day he read a particular paragraph to me and began laughing as hard as he could. It was as if he had read it for the first time. He kept on laughing and you would never have thought he was the writer. Most of his novels were based on real-life experiences, but to some degree they perpetuate the myth of Robert Ruark as a worldly, brash macho man.

In the eight days I spent with him that was not the man I witnessed. He was gentle, thoughtful, respectful, kind, generous and well-mannered. Perhaps we liked each other because we were from the same home town. At any rate, we got along quite well and talked about intimate things, including some I'll probably take to my grave. While I was not sworn to secrecy, I did and still do respect his privacy.

I would be lying if I did not acknowledge that as a young man I was awed and influenced by his abilities, his quick wit and obvious desire that his writing ring true. Yet he was down-to-earth, and liked nothing better than to sit in the middle of the floor, cigarette and drink in hand, sharing stories with his friends.

EPILOGUE

On one occasion Bob drew my attention to a palette and asked me to pick a color for a book cover. In my naiveté I didn't know what colors were that important in selling books, and I was a bit hesitant to make a choice. I finally chose yellow, even though it is not really one of my favorite colors. Sometime later I noticed that both the dust jacket and binding of the American edition of *The Honey Badger* was a mix of yellow and black.

When we were in Spain, Bob gave me one of the first copies of *The Old Man and the Boy*, which had arrived fresh off the press. He autographed it for me and it continues to be been one of my prized possessions. Robert Ruark, incidentally, signed few copies of any of his books and they are almost never offered on the out-of-print market.

When I visited Bob's office, which was an extremely large room, I found him seated at an enormous, semi-circular desk measuring possibly 12 by 15 feet. An impressive mount of a Cape buffalo on the wall and Alan Ritchie's desk completed the office.

Ritchie had the reserved countenance of an Englishman. He disappeared after working hours, rarely participating in any social activities when Bob had guests, but he was always cordial, reserved and unassuming when we were around. When no guests were present, the two could not have been closer.

Alan Ritchie was Bob's trusted secretary and confidant for 12 years. Because of this closeness and compatibility, Ritchie was able to climb into Bob's mind. Had that not been the case, this book would never have been possible.

When I left Robert Ruark in 1958, he was wealthy and at the top of his game. Yet for Bob, insecurity always seemed to be lurking just around the corner. He realized that success was a fragile, ephemeral and sometimes fleeting thing.

Bob imitated most everything that Hemingway did. He had no qualms about copying Hemingway's style of writing and was not shy about admitting that he would copy any writer whom he admired if it would enhance his own writing. While Bob respected or even revered Hemingway, he unquestionably knew more about Africa than Papa.

Bob Considine wrote an article about Hemingway's Cuban villa, which Hemingway's wife, Mary, gave to Fidel Castro after her husband's death. Castro made it into a museum, leaving it exactly the way it was the last night Hemingway was there. In his bedroom, lying on the pillow, is Ruark's *Poor No More*. Bob Ruark never knew about this, but if he had, his likely remark would have been, "See, even Hemingway reads Ruark."

According to one of Bob's peers, when Ruark was good, he was the best. When he was bad, he was still better than most of the rest. The man was truly brilliant, and his ability to remember and retain material, regardless of how inebriated he might be, was unbelievable. As an investigative reporter, no one could touch him. Ruark once said that a writer is just a ham actor with the ability to put things on paper; he also said that a writer is an exhibitionist.

For my part, in writing this little recollection, I have acquired an even higher respect for the challenges writers face. For Bob, words generally flowed effortlessly, but he felt that even his talents did not make book-writing easier. Columns, on the other hand, came with great ease. He liked short sentences and getting straight to the point. This was the newspaperman in him.

While I could tell he still respected Hemingway, he was beginning to find fault with him. Bob said Hemingway always wrote in the first person, but the fact of the matter was that Ruark frequently found a way to insert himself into his columns as well. Following Hemingway's death and with alcohol taking its toll, Ruark came to feel he was better than his idol and that he personally deserved to be recognized as the best living American writer. He also took liberties, once Hemingway was gone, regarding how well he had known him. Bob may have met him at Pamplona during the running of the bulls, but there is only a single letter from Mary Hemingway that suggests that they were to meet. Ruark claims Hemingway once told him he was the better of the two writers. This is difficult to believe considering Hemingway's ego. Why would the king suggest that a prince was superior?

As my wife and I were leaving Palamos, Bob crouched down behind the iron fence as if he were in a jail cell. I joined him behind the fence and we posed for a picture as if both of us were incarcerated. He said, "You're going on to Barcelona, Madrid and Greece, and I'm to be left alone to finish my book (*Poor No More*) so I can continue to live in style." He then asked me if I had ever driven a Rolls and when I replied that I had only seen them in the movies, he suggested: "Why don't you drive the Rolls back to Barcelona?"

I did, humbled by the fact that he offered me use of his most prized possession – more evidence of his generosity.

Several years later, in July, 1965, I was driving through the mountains of North Carolina, listening to music on the radio, when I heard the news flash: "Robert Ruark, famous author, dead at 49."

It was a sad day for me. I felt as if I had lost a dear friend whom I would never forget or be able to replace.

As I was completing this little memoir of my days with Robert Ruark, my son, Tony, asked me to join him for breakfast on Father's Day, 2006. He gave me the most wonderful gift. As we waited for breakfast to arrive, he said, "Dad, you would not believe the dream I had last night. I dreamt Robert Ruark came into my office and as we were talking, you suddenly appeared at the door. You were so elated and surprised to see him there. I got up and left the two of you alone in the room, laughing, carrying on and having a wonderful reunion. This went on for the longest time."

I got very excited when Tony shared his dream with me. It would be so wonderful to have another opportunity to visit with Robert Ruark. As it is, I was singularly privileged to have stayed at his home, to discover what a delightful, talented human being he really was. The image of a candle burning at both ends, which adorns the dust jacket of *Poor No More*, is perfect for this man who accomplished so much in so little time, and whose literary legacy is still treasured by readers around the world.